T0314309

HUMAN RIGHTS AFTER CORPORATE PERSONHOOD

Human Rights after Corporate Personhood

An Uneasy Merger?

EDITED BY JODY GREENE AND
SHARIF YOUSSEF

UNIVERSITY OF TORONTO PRESS
Toronto Buffalo London

© University of Toronto Press 2020
Toronto Buffalo London
utorontopress.com

ISBN 978-1-4875-0696-4 (cloth)   ISBN 978-1-4875-3529-2 (EPUB)
                                  ISBN 978-1-4875-3528-5 (PDF)

Library and Archives Canada Cataloguing in Publication

Title: Human rights after corporate personhood: an uneasy merger? /
   edited by Jody Greene and Sharif Youssef.
Names: Greene, Jody, editor. | Youssef, Sharif, 1974– editor.
Description: Includes bibliographical references and index.
Identifiers: Canadiana (print) 20200284711 | Canadiana (ebook) 2020028486X |
   ISBN 9781487506964 (hardcover) | ISBN 9781487535292 (EPUB) |
   ISBN 9781487535285 (PDF)
Subjects: LCSH: Juristic persons. | LCSH: Corporation law – Social aspects. |
   LCSH: Civil rights of corporations.
Classification: LCC K650 .H86 2020 | DDC 346.01/3 – dc23

University of Toronto Press acknowledges the financial assistance to its
publishing program of the Canada Council for the Arts and the Ontario Arts
Council, an agency of the Government of Ontario.

Canada Council   Conseil des Arts
for the Arts   du Canada

ONTARIO ARTS COUNCIL
CONSEIL DES ARTS DE L'ONTARIO
an Ontario government agency
un organisme du gouvernement de l'Ontario

Funded by the   Financé par le
Government   gouvernement
of Canada   du Canada

Canada

Contents

Acknowledgments

Financial support for the publication of this volume was provided by the UC Santa Cruz Division of Academic Affairs, the Social Sciences and Humanities Research Council of Canada, and the University of Toronto Faculty of Law. The seed of this project was planted in Ian Lee's seminar, "Corporations, Individuals, and the State." It flourished under the advice and mentorship of Simon Stern, Mohammed Fadel, Angela Fernandez, Lisa Austin, Peter Benson, and Patrick Macklem. A year of conversations with Lawrence Douglas and Adam Sitze of the Department of Law, Jurisprudence, and Social Thought at Amherst College enriched our understanding of the corporation's relationships to sovereignty and liberalism. Jerome Christensen provided fruitful research leads at an early stage of the project. Arushi Massey provided invaluable research assistance. We are grateful for Greig Henderson's and Daniel Quinlan's sage editorial advice, to the press's two anonymous reviewers, and for the hard work of the University of Toronto Press's manuscript editor. Finally, debate and rigorous conversation with our contributors made this a worthwhile endeavour.

HUMAN RIGHTS AFTER CORPORATE PERSONHOOD

Introduction: Corporate Persons, Revisited

JODY GREENE AND SHARIF YOUSSEF

Amid the array of economic and political issues around which the 2012 US presidential election turned, one seemingly polarized the candidates more starkly – and concisely – than any other. When Republican candidate Mitt Romney faced off at a rally in August 2011 with a vocal opponent of corporate tax cuts, he made his views on the topic immediately and patronizingly clear: "corporations are people, my friend."[1] Almost a year later, as the election cycle neared its close, incumbent president and Democratic nominee Barack Obama was still scoring points and whipping up support at a rally in Iowa by contradicting what he saw as his opponent's nonsensical view: "I don't care how many times you try to explain it," Obama told the crowd, "corporations aren't people. People are people."[2] It's easy to forget, in the alternately numbing and searing aftermath of 2016, the decisive role played by candidate Obama's stinging refusal to make common sense of corporate personhood in his victory over Romney. One need only think of the selection of Neil Gorsuch to fill the first Supreme Court vacancy of the Trump administration to see how decisively the tables have turned on corporate personhood, as well as how central the issue remains in contemporary politics. Gorsuch, in his role on the Tenth Circuit Court of Appeals, contributed directly to the expansion of corporate personhood in the *Hobby Lobby* decision of 2014: "Specifically, the Tenth Circuit ruled that privately held, for-profit secular corporations are 'persons' under the meaning of

---

1 "'Corporations are people,' Romney tells Iowa hecklers angry over his tax policy," *New York Times*, 11 August 2011, https://www.nytimes.com/2011/08/12/us/politics/12romney.html, accessed 2 October 2018.
2 "Obama: 'Corporations aren't people,'" *Washington Post*, 5 May 2012, https://www.washingtonpost.com/posttv/politics/obama-corporations-arent-people/2012/05/05/gIQAlX4y3T_video.html, accessed 2 October 2018.

the Religious Freedom Restoration Act (RFRA), and could qualify for religious exemptions from the Affordable Care Act's mandate to provide reproductive health services."[3] From Gorsuch's confirmation to the massive corporate tax cut written into law in the Tax Cuts and Jobs Act of 2017, it is easy to conclude that corporations are not just persons but the most privileged citizens of the Trumpian nation.

Litigation around the rights questions that arise out of the United States' corporate personhood doctrine has been spilling over into other jurisdictions. In Canada, for example, various business organizations continue to test the Court's willingness to expand the range of rights available to incorporated entities. In 2015's *Loyola High School v. Quebec (Attorney General)*,[4] a Jesuit high school in Quebec sought relief from the province's mandatory core curriculum, which required a course that "teaches about the beliefs and ethics of different world religions from a neutral and objective perspective ... in order to inculcate in students openness to human rights, diversity, and respect for others."[5] The Supreme Court of Canada opted not to decide the case on the grounds of the high school's religious freedom. Typically, religious rights claims can be made by individuals on behalf of groups, and famously, in *R. v. Big M. Drug Mart* (1985),[6] a drugstore chain was able to challenge the constitutionality of a provincially mandated day off on behalf of its employees and customers. But *Loyola High School* skirted dangerously close to granting an organization standing to bring a religious freedom claim in its own right. In the end, the court evaded the American example: " I do not believe it is necessary ... to decide whether corporations enjoy religious freedom in their own right under s. 2 (a) of the Charter or s. 3 of the Charter of human rights and freedoms ... in order to dispose of this appeal."[7]

When we began to put together an anthology grappling with the problem of human rights after corporate personhood, and with the judicial and political anxieties to which that intersection gives rise, we decided that we would not participate in the outrage culture arising from the legal decisions in *Citizens United v. Federal Election Commission* (2010) and *Burwell v. Hobby Lobby* (2014). Instead, we would revisit the assumptions underlying the most recent attributions to corporations of legal personality

---

3 Campaign Legal Center, "Supreme Court nominee Neil Gorsuch: Judge's record raises questions about the future of democracy law" (blog), http://www.campaign-legal.org/sites/default/files/Gorsuch%20Backgrounder_0.pdf.

4 *Loyola High School v. Quebec (Attorney General)*, 12 CarswellQue (SCC 2015).

5 Ibid. at para. 1.

6 *R. v. Big M Drug Mart Ltd.*, CarswellAlta (SCC 1985).

7 *Loyola High School v. Quebec (Attorney General)*, 12 CarswellQue at para. 33.

(a phenomenon, it should be noted, with at least a four-hundred-year history) and the ever-expanding set of rights arising from these latest attributions. Rather than presuming that corporate personhood is *exclusively* a political and economic tactic to increase (late) capitalist profit margins and advance (neo)liberal ends – although it can certainly be both – we wanted to at least consider whether and in what circumstances delinking personhood from the autonomous human individual could be turned to support aims of justice or liberation. Given that corporations seem to have triumphed in almost every legal and political battle of the recent era, the question may be not how we can reserve personhood to human persons, but rather how we can appropriate the privileges currently granted to corporations to advance the well-being of human and non-human entities whose interests fall outside those of profit-hungry corporations.

Our notion of an "uneasy merger" of rights discourse with corporate power, then, tracks in at least two directions: on the one hand, we review the long history of the encroachment by corporations on realms of rights many believe ought to be reserved for human persons; on the other, we visit recent cases in which the definition of a corporate entity has been appropriated for aims that might be viewed as anything but congenial – hostile, even – by the likes of Romney, Trump, and recent US Supreme Court appointments Neil Gorsuch and Brett Kavanaugh.

The most widespread politicized response to the rights of corporations, the one so bluntly articulated by then candidate Obama in 2012, generally entails a sense of outrage that an artificial person could utilize all the rights of a natural person. As many of the chapters in this volume demonstrate, however, a theorist of personhood would insist that the corporation helps us see that standing as a person in law is already an abstraction and does not enjoy the kind of sanctity that it is accorded in the recent popular furore over corporate personhood. One assumption of the outrage response is that corporate rights are being used to diminish civil and human rights, if only through being granted priority when the rights of corporations and persons are pitted against each other. Former Clinton labour secretary Robert Reich sees the danger in terms of a slippery slope: "The perfidious notion that corporations are people can lead to even more bizarre results. If corporations are people and they are headquartered in the United States, then presumably corporations are citizens. That means they have a right to vote as well."[8] Polemic aside, Reich fully understands

---

8 Robert Reich, "Why BP isn't a criminal," http://robertreich.org/post/35848994755, accessed 1 January 2017.

that this is not how corporate personhood rights work (although we would be naive to think that corporations are not using their considerable political and economic clout to participate decisively in political decision-making of all kinds. Put otherwise, *they already do have a right to vote*, just not in a manner that gets them an "I voted" sticker to wear on their lapel). Corporations are granted rights selectively, and the *Citizens United* decision did not affirm any new rights for corporations; it simply used an established right to expression to overturn what, to the majority of the Court, seemed to be an arbitrary limit to corporate election expenditure limits. Reich is a well-known critic of the role of corporate donations and lobbies in degrading democracy, and his objection to corporate personhood rights is consistent with his objection to the corrosive effects of corporate election spending on the American political process.[9]

Other critics of corporate personhood locate its harm more precisely in the way that, in the United States, the "Roberts Court is marching on the rights of real people, steadily extending to corporations our civil and political rights, even as it chips away at the civil rights of women and minorities."[10] Joseph Slaughter is here referring to the way in which the Court rules to diminish the application of the Voting Rights Act (1965) at the same time as it hands down decisions that reaffirm the personhood rights of corporations. While the first set of critics take issue with corporations being granted the rights of abstract persons, the second object to the ways in which corporate personhood materially damages the rights of actual human persons. We sympathize with both these positions, yet we want to step back from them to suggest that we are outraged for the wrong reasons and unable, because of our "commonsense" sanctification of personhood, to predict or even to adequately describe the full range of corporate personhood's potential or actual effects within the current era, let alone how we might creatively and even subversively respond. One danger of this outrage is that it too readily accepts a zero-sum antagonism between the corporation's accounting of its rights and the commonly accepted rights – liberal rights, citizenship rights, international human rights – that attach to humans. That is, it fails to account for how artificial and natural personhood constitute each other juridically and discursively in ways that could be creatively leveraged for as yet unanticipated ends, particularly as those

---

9 For example, see his simultaneously timely and prescient *Supercapitalism: The Transformation of Business, Democracy, and Everyday Life* (New York: Alfred A. Knopf, 2007).

10 Joseph Slaughter, "We're in the middle of a corporate civil rights movement," *TPM*, 7 April 2015, http://talkingpointsmemo.com/cafe/corporate-civil-rights-movement.

ends relate to the extension of personhood to non-human animals and to non-capitalist corporate entities such as biospheres and other *living* things. This volume as a whole is intended to launch such an accounting, a task to which this introduction contributes by offering a brief review of the intricate and infuriatingly slippery categories that frame the project as a whole – the corporation, the person, human rights – followed by a snapshot history of four hundred years of thinking about corporate rights and responsibilities from Hobbes to *Hobby Lobby*. Many of these topics are treated in detail and with far greater nuance in the chapters that follow, but for the non-specialist reader in particular, the introduction should serve to lay out, in the broadest terms, the theoretical issues at stake in debates about natural and artificial persons and their standing, duties, and benefits in law.

Impersonal Persons, Corporate and Otherwise

What is a corporation? The term invokes taxonomies interchangeably and arbitrarily. The normative question, for starters, should be "who is," rather than what is, "the corporation?" A provisional answer might then be, the corporation is an artificial person. By some accounts the tension between a natural person and an artificial person is imbedded in the very nature of corporations as separate legal personalities that exist apart from natural persons, as codified in the case of *Salomon v. Salomon & Company* (1897). The contemporary cri de cœur from human rights activists upset by brutal, unchecked corporate power echoes the frustration of Aaron Salomon's debenture holders, who were bankrupted by a legal fiction that raised a veil between a human individual engaged in (failed) business transactions and the legal understanding that those human transactions were the actions of a separate, rights-bearing corporation. The case, that is, offers a kind of prehistory of the outrage expressed in recent years that ruthless natural persons use the limited liability of the corporation as a means to swindle others. Some try to taxonomize corporations into categories such as, for example, publicly traded corporations with thousands of shareholders, multinational corporations composed of a parent and its subsidiary corporations, not-for-profit corporations that lack shareholders altogether, or permutations such as the recently infamous "closely held corporation" mentioned in *Hobby Lobby* with its limited number of shareholders (often family members) and infrequent trading. However, in *Citizens United*, as Stefan Padfield points out in his contribution to this anthology, Justice Stevens rejected the need for the Supreme Court to offer either a definition or a taxonomy of the corporation. The majority in *Hobby*

Lobby attempted to limit the scope of their decision to the closely held corporation while "offering no definition of the term and [while] not acknowledg[ing] that there is no singular definition under corporate law."[11]

Elizabeth Pollman similarly observes that courts draw lines between corporations formalistically without developing a meaningful scheme of classification between different organizational forms: "the Court's characterization of corporations as associations has not properly evolved to account for the wide spectrum of organizations labeled 'corporations.' This has become increasingly problematic as the Court has moved from early case law concerning the property and contract rights of corporations to the realm of corporate speech, political spending, and exercise of religion."[12] Because judge-made distinctions are offered without definition and normative justification, "the Court's derivative and instrumental rationales for granting rights to corporations do not support broad rulings as to all corporations and all rights."[13] Without offering either a political theory of the corporation or a legal definition, capricious references to different organizational forms impoverish theoretical discourses about the corporation that offer substantive normative accounts of their forms and purpose, and they do so while simultaneously propagating wild and unchecked mutations of the corporation in a case law that lacks cohesiveness. This theoretical lack also evinces a wilful blindness to the practical implications for the socio-political world that corporations inhabit as well as a carelessness in regard to the need for predictability in business practices.

Yet corporations are not the only kind of persons that remain ill-defined under the law. An even cursory interrogation of the category of personhood more generally belies any notion that "natural" and juridical personhood are creatures of parallel universes. Rather than casting individual, embodied human personhood as natural, universal, or primary, the contributors to this volume remind us that personhood is from the outset a deeply impersonal form, difficult to define and virtually impossible to accurately historicize and taxonomize. Typically, this form is traced back to the Roman law of persons (*ius personarum*). Connal Parsley and Ed Mussawir assert that the "anthropological embedding

---

11   Elizabeth Pollman, "Line Drawing in Corporate Rights Determinations," *DePaul Law Review* 56, no. 2 (Winter 2016): 601.

12   Elizabeth Pollman and Margaret M. Blair, "The Derivative Nature of Corporate Constitutional Rights," *William and Mary Law Review* 56, no. 5 (2015): 1677.

13   Pollman, "Line Drawing in Corporate Rights Determinations," 602.

of the juridical person ought not to be anachronistically attributed to the Roman 'law of persons' in which its craft originated. Rather ... the well-known Christian metaphysicalization of the judicial person as a moral entity not only adds to but transforms and displaces that law as a juristic enterprise."[14] There are several origin stories for legal personhood. Mussawir and Parsley's follows a similar trajectory to that of the nineteenth-century philologist Friedrich Adolf Trendelenburg, who used Etruscan and Latin etymologies of the word *persona* and linked its origin as a legal term back to its theatrical usage as the assumption of a role. In his story, as the Roman judiciary developed and relations between constituents became more complex, courts assigned legal "roles" to individuals in the courtroom scene. Trendelenberg's archaeology of personhood pits its legal meaning against its eventual culmination as a moral concept in Kant's work. This Christian metaphysicalization naturalizes personhood as a project, that is, as the individual's attempt to achieve or accomplish the "task" of becoming a person. It is this moral striving for personhood that in the minds of many makes a person worthy of human rights, in much the same way that in Hegel's schema "the imperative of right [which is] 'Be a person and respect others as persons'" sets one on the road to ownership and the rights, duties, and standing in law that flow from it.[15] Alexandre Kojève glosses this as follows: "the specifically human being creates himself from the animal *Homo sapiens*."[16] This is not to say that Hegel could never envision an artificial inhuman juridical personhood. Indeed, he acknowledges that in civil society we may opt to expand personhood, and he includes the corporation among those options. Yet from a Hegelian perspective, the corporation must still find a way to reconcile the selfish impulses that drive its profit-driven operations with the human being's moral striving – its "respect" for other persons – if it is to qualify for personhood. We will return to this problem of the Hegelian corporation and its relationship to human rights (and duties) in the final section of this introduction, but before doing so, it's worthwhile to pause over the very notion of "human rights," the sacrosanct category against which overreaching and unnatural corporate rights are most often detrimentally contrasted.

---

14 Edward Mussawir and Connal Parsley, "The Law of Persons Today: At the Margins of Jurisprudence," *Law and Humanities* 11, no. 1 (2017): 45.
15 G.W.F. Hegel, *Hegel's Philosophy of Right*, trans. T.M. Knox (New York: Oxford University Press, 1967), ¶37.
16 Alexandre Kojève, *Outline of a Phenomenology of Right*, ed. Bryan-Paul Frost, trans. Robert Howse (Lanham: Rowman and Littlefield, 2007), 209.

Human Rights and/as Corporate Rights

The contributions in this collection collectively trouble the apparent self-evidence of the category of "human rights," and it might be more accurate to say that this anthology addresses the problem of personhood in general – including corporate personhood – and its implications for rights. Yet we continue to use the term "human rights" because it marks a distinction that, while theoretically questionable, remains symbolically potent. Instead of the various political entitlements codified in or derived from international human rights law and the Universal Declaration of Human Rights, or anti-discrimination law that operates under the name of human rights in the human rights codes of various nations and provinces, our contributors examine the relationship of corporate personhood to rights that we typically naturalize as attributable exclusively to human persons on the basis of dignity.[17] But unlike natural law theorists, who rely on personhood as a precondition for dignity, the contributors to this volume critically analyse human rights as the product of changing figurations of both personhood and humanness, rather than simply relying upon those rights as norms or features of the human self.

Legal positivists, by contrast, argue that international human rights have a political function, which is to structure an international legal order: "They represent reasons that social, political, and legal actors rely on international arenas to advocate interfering in the internal affairs of a State and to provide assistance to States to promote their protection."[18] That legal order makes states the subjects of non-binding international law, thus generating norms that have pragmatic effects on diplomacy and the internal affairs of nations while enshrining the principle of sovereignty. *Some* international law takes the form of binding treaty obligations. In circumstances where a treaty obligation is enshrined in national legislation there can be mechanisms for enforcing some of that law through national courts. For the most part, however, the realm of international human rights is one of norms and moral obligations rather than one of legally binding legislation.

In this volume, to clarify the relationship of corporations to human rights taken generally, we pursue a line of thinking in regard to human rights that begins with Hannah Arendt's work on stateless peoples and continues through Roberto Esposito's recent scholarship on

---

17   James Griffin, *On Human Rights* (Oxford: Oxford University Press, 2010).
18   Patrick Macklem, *The Sovereignty of Human Rights* (Oxford: Oxford University Press, 2016), 18.

personhood. Arendt identified a tension within human rights: their conferral depends upon our legal status and national membership. Stateless persons and those victimized by genocidal projects are, ordinarily, not accorded those rights. These groups of displaced or dispossessed persons have been reduced to pure humanity, or, as Esposito glosses it, to their biology. Esposito links the human in human rights to the way in which nineteenth-century thinkers reconceptualized personhood. He argues that "the concept of 'person' was intended to fill in the chasm opened up between the pole of human being and citizen that had existed since the Declaration of 1789. If we compare this text to the Universal Declaration of Human Rights of 1948, the difference is plain to see: the new semantic epicenter, shifting away from the revolutionary emphasis on citizenship, is the unconditional demand for the dignity and worth of the human person."[19] In the regime of human rights, the natural, biological person exercises rights, but the ground for those legal rights is the assertion of a pre-existing, even primordial "dignity" in human biology that precipitates a universal duty to consider all human beings as worthy of "humane" treatment and as moral subjects. To put this another way, the primary difference between natural law theorists and legal positivists revolves around this question: do human rights emerge by virtue of our *nature* as humans (either moral or biological), or are they simply assigned to us by virtue of our *being* human?

However, these two theories of personhood share one striking similarity that will prove problematic in the arena of human rights: each continues to embed in our language a Kantian metaphysics that treats human rights as individual, liberal rights. Yet the international legal order that formulates and assigns human rights is essentially a law of peoples. John Rawls chooses to view "[human rights] as belonging to an associationist social form ... which sees persons as members of groups – associations, corporations, and estates. As such members, persons have rights and liberties enabling them to meet their duties and obligations and to engage in a decent system of social cooperation. What have come to be called human rights are recognized as necessary conditions of any system of social cooperation."[20] Although, according to Rawls, there *should* only be human rights that apply to individuals, it is not always the case that individuals assert human rights claims or that they are asserted on behalf of individuals. Human rights claims can be raised on behalf of groups, communities, classes, minorities,

---

19 Roberto Esposito, *The Third Person* (Cambridge: Polity Press, 2012), 70.
20 John Rawls, *The Law of Peoples: With "The Idea of Public Reason Revisited"* (Cambridge, MA: Harvard University Press, 1999), 68.

indigenous peoples, and collectivities of many kinds. This is evident in human rights around food, water, labour law, social rights, and indigenous rights and in the assertion of a right to self-determination by the formerly colonized. Unlike individualist liberal rights, human rights are asserted vertically through, or diagonally in the name of, categories of peoples or groups, who strive to obtain full or quasi-legal status by virtue of the category to which they belong. Human rights, that is, are more often than not asserted on behalf of a collective.

To what extent does the corporation resemble or constitute such a collective? Corporate personhood jurisprudence and corporate legal theory posit the corporation as a form of association or assembly whose artificial personhood opens out onto a naturalized group of stakeholder humans, a people, whom the association is meant to serve or represent. A perverse but inevitable effect of this apparatus is that when institutions are accorded dignity, or when those who inhabit roles in those institutions are accorded *de facto* dignity, at the same time as human political subjects find themselves deprived of such dignity, the clash between the picture and the practice of human rights inevitably leads to disillusionment with the very notion of individual rights. In many of the objections to rulings like *Citizens United*, the category of legal personhood extended on behalf of the corporation elides the human in human rights, naturalizes the corporation, and then supplants individual humans with the business organization – the profit-earning ficto-collectivity – as the bearer of rights. Corporations themselves may harbour such a fantasy. As Joshua Barkan argues in his contribution to this volume, a world that continues to grant all manner of legal persons human rights is one in which the fantasy of a transnational corporation that can act as a stateless person may materialize.

One takeaway from this is that we ought to be guarded in the use of our legal grammar, careful to distinguish personhood rights from human rights. Another lesson is that the language of rights (and duties), when extended to non-human entities, can be used to discipline them, to promote guardianship over vulnerable entities, and even to promote the development and flourishing of human capabilities. However, the very same extension of personhood can be used, in a neoliberal vein, to allocate distributions and manage opportunities for human capital on the basis of racial, gendered, and ethnic classifications. The decision to grant corporations rights brings to light the extent to which the capacity to bear rights is always constructed – and constructed, at least in part, through the creation of categories of entities excluded from rights. Colin Dayan, for instance, has argued that, in thinking about the rights of persons, we must attend more thoroughly to the history of negative personhood, which has included (and continues to include) "slaves, animals, criminals, and detainees who are disabled by law. Legal thought relied on a set of fictions that rendered the meaning of persons shifting and tentative: whether in creating slaves as persons in law and criminals as dead in law, or in the perpetual re-creation of the rightless entity."[21] Put simply, creating legal persons – whether corporate or individual – also requires deciding which entities will be defined by their non- or negative personhood.

Parsley and Mussawir assert that "today the law of persons also exists in relation to another of its modern products: a *naturalized* conception of the person."[22] Modifying arguments advanced by Michel Foucault and Roberto Esposito, they claim that this naturalization masks the operation of jurisprudence as "a craft, art or technique" – a legal technology, one might say – that creates persons and corporations rather than merely representing them. Although many have sought to unmask the operations of law that craft and naturalize some persons, and not others, in order to map what the law negates, most recent commentators assert a relation between positive and negative persons, one that is nevertheless singular and that affects populations differentially. Indeed, the persistent complicity between the attribution of personhood and that of non-personhood remains opaque to the champions of rights-bearing personhood on all sides of the political debate over the status of corporations as persons. Personhood, that is, whether artificial and corporate or natural and sacred to the individual, is never not political; it invariably operates through a process of exclusion, differentiation, and hierarchization that distributes rights and responsibilities in inequitable and – to borrow Hegel's idiom – deeply "disrespectful" ways.

From Hobbes to *Hobby Lobby*: A Microhistory of Corporate Rights and Responsibilities

In *Corporate Sovereignty*, Barkan shows that the pervasive progressive argument against corporate economic power's extension into the political realm misunderstands the four-hundred-year history of the corporation as both an economic and a political entity. Starting in the early modern period, states granted charters to create private trading companies as a means to outsource the costs of imperial wealth extraction. Barkan remarks that in "seventeenth-century England, the Crown

21   Colin Dayan, *The Law Is a White Dog: How Legal Rituals Make and Unmake Persons* (Princeton: Princeton University Press, 2011), xii.
22   Mussawir and Parsley, "The Law of Persons Today," 45.

removed itself from the direct management of much daily life, using corporations to manage hospitals, schools, philanthropy, and imperial trade in a specifically decentralized and liberal mode of government."[23] The corporation was "simultaneously an autonomous disciplinary apparatus and an object of regulation by the state."[24] Its disciplinary functions were justified by the concept of *oikonomea*, which understood the corporation by analogy with "the noble household," whose duty to manage subjects virtuously (or, in today's idiom, corporate social responsibility) was at odds with its profit-seeking imperative. J.G.A. Pocock describes this patriarchal management of the rights of others in this way: "The landed man, successor to the master of the classical *oikos*, was permitted the leisure and autonomy to consider what was to others' good as well as his own."[25] Aristotle's *oikos* constituted a patriarchally governed household life at odds with the marketplace. But many modern corporations exhibit a closely held corporate form that, in *Hobby Lobby*, was allowed to resemble an extension of a family's religious life.

In contrast to Hobbes, whom several of our contributors cite, Hegel dismissed the notion that corporate charters could conflict with the sovereignty of the State. Hobbes feared the corporation because he understood civil society as primordial, coming into being at that historically unlocatable moment when man first submitted to the law. He feared as well that the corporation would generate a competing law, and, indeed, in a world where corporate charters were granted to extend the sovereign's rule extraterritorially and where municipal parish corporations created a parallel ecclesiastical State, Hobbes's concerns about corporate sovereignty were warranted. Hegel, on the other hand, understood the State as "rooting" the family and the corporation in order to generate civil society; thus, for him, the family and the State were partners in governance and helped generate civil society. He relied upon an alternative genealogy of the corporation according to which corporate regulatory discipline did not extend solely to the association's members.

Hegel's understanding of the corporation did not refer to the charter corporation as much as to parishes and guilds – formal and voluntary organizations with administrative control over subjects – whose function was to mediate the relationship between the selfish impulses of

---

23 Joshua Barkan, *Corporate Sovereignty* (Minneapolis: University of Minnesota Press, 2013), 29.

24 Ibid., 28.

25 J.G.A. Pocock, *The Machiavellian Moment: Florentine Political Thought and the Atlantic Republican Tradition*, rev. ed. (Princeton: Princeton University Press, 2003), 464.

individuals and the general welfare for which the State was responsible. In his critique of welfarism, Hegel pointed to this alternative genealogy, referring to poor laws that replaced the guilds as sources of relief for the poor:

> In the example of England we may study these phenomena on a large scale and also in particular the results of poor-rates, immense foundations, unlimited private beneficence, and above all the abolition of the Guild Corporations. In Britain, particularly in Scotland, the most direct measure against poverty and especially against the loss of shame and self-respect – the subjective bases of society – as well as against laziness and extravagance, &c., the begetters of the rabble, has turned out to be to leave the poor to their fate and instruct them to beg in the streets.[26]

His claim was that welfarism, not corporatism, had created a permanent "rabble," that is, an underclass that had been disincentivized from participating in society. Part of this difference in views between Hobbes and Hegel relates to the separate times in which they lived. Hegel was writing in reaction to the discontinuation of the parish corporation's regulatory duties by the welfare state. Hobbes was writing at a time when the State was much less bureaucratically developed, and thus the crisis for him lay in the proliferation of competing forms of authority. Hobbes may have embraced welfarism as the mark of a stronger, more internally consistent sovereign State. His view would be surprisingly consistent with what he might have dubbed the "outrage culture" that springs up around corporate personhood jurisprudence. This culture embraces the welfare state as a preserve of rights that should not be misappropriated for the purposes of corporate welfare from a benevolent central sovereign authority attending to the needs of vulnerable (if alienated) human subjects.

In his recent past, however, Hegel had witnessed what he contended was a more efficient and morally uplifting world of public–private partnerships. As our contributor Scott MacKenzie observes in his earlier work, vagrancy laws in Britain made parish corporations "the primary administrative unit of poverty management and their restriction of movement (both geographical and social) for the laboring classes."[27] For Hegel, without the parish, without the guild, without the workhouse, a rabble mentality had developed where persons felt themselves

---

26 Hegel, *Hegel's Philosophy of Right*, n. ¶245.
27 Scott R. MacKenzie, *Be It Ever So Humble: Poverty, Fiction, and the Invention of the Middle-Class Home* (Charlottesville: University of Virginia Press, 2013), 41.

to be apart from the system of cooperation, alienated, instead of engaging as free and equal citizens participating under fair rules. The welfare view had blurred their perspective on corporate, civil life and impeded their moral striving toward freedom.

Today's neoliberal austerity policies resonate hauntingly with Hegel's views about late medieval business organizations. Indeed, *Hobby Lobby*'s recasting of the corporation as patriarchal *oikos* is consistent with nineteenth-century accounts of the role these corporate antecedents played in civil society, which was to shape preferences and affections[28] and in so doing protect employees from the caprices of the market: "[the corporation's] right is to come on the scene like a second family for its members, while civil society can only be an indeterminate sort of family because it comprises everyone and so is farther removed from individuals and their special exigencies."[29] The purpose of the Hegelian corporation was not to shape preferences in the direction of unfreedom, yet the idiom of the noble household has been used by companies that seek to resist collective bargaining, and Vince Pecora hears in this view of the corporation as noble household a nostalgic fiduciary duty that recalls a slavery-era plantation life in which "one's laborers could number into the hundreds, but any of those hundreds could also be one's children."[30] We also hear echoes of the *oikos* in the neoliberal idiom of the developing nation and in calls for (voluntary) corporate social responsibility as a means to enhance the capabilities of workers in developed nations.

Not all rights attach to individuals on the basis of their individual juridical status; sometimes they are contingent on group membership and presuppose underlying models of social cooperation. Morton Horwitz points to the credence given by turn-of-the-century Anglo-American lawyers, who sought to understand corporate personhood by turning to a spate of German, French, English, and American philosophical work on "corporate personality," a body of work also referred to as "group personality" or "moral personality."[31] In their efforts to retrospectively provide a theoretical justification for the incidental attribution of personhood to corporations in the 1886 ruling on *Santa Clara*

---

28 See Lisa Herzog, "Two Ways of 'Taming' the Market: Why Hegel Needs the Police and the Corporations," in *Hegel and Capitalism*, ed. Andrew Buchwalter (Albany: SUNY Press, 2015), 416–55.

29 Hegel, *Hegel's Philosophy of Right*, n. ¶252.

30 Vincent P. Pecora, *Households of the Soul* (Baltimore: Johns Hopkins University Press, 1997), 18.

31 See Morton J. Horwitz, "Santa Clara Revisited: The Development of Corporate Theory," *West Virginia Law Review* 88, no. 86 (1985): 173.

co. v. Southern Pacific Railroad Supreme Court, these jurists and philosophers required an analysis of juridical personhood that lent itself to an account of artificial collective persons, rather than taking for granted an exclusively individual person under the law. Such artificial persons, like so-called natural persons, could be the subjects of rights, but by extension they could also be rendered subject to liability in a manner that seemed promising in its mitigation of an exclusively rights-bearing model of corporate personhood. A recent issue of *Law and Literature* devoted to the notion of the "body" of the person has pressed forward in this promising direction: "the formal legal notion of personhood needs to be informed by an analysis of our changing cultural ideas of the general notion of the person."[32]

In his 1916 essay "The Personality of Associations,"[33] political theorist Harold Laski rejected what many now refer to as the real-entity theory of the corporation in a bid to remind us of the trouble with naturalizing individual personhood. Talking about the corporation as if it were a real person in order to discipline it with criminal law was, to Laski, a denial of reality. After all, disciplining corporations under the criminal law as if they were natural persons required a finding of *mens rea* for crimes, that is, subjective intent. Corporate persons were safeguarded from conventional criminal liability by the very attribution of personhood meant to discipline them. The theory of the corporation that made it the subject of disciplinary power forced awkward and inconclusive attacks on individual agents, and it obfuscated the real ways in which a corporation's capacity to express an intention (and feel consequences) could be distinct from that of its members. Laski called for a theory of corporate personality that did not treat it as a concession of the state bound by its charter, since corporations had long acted outside the constraints of their original charters with no legal repercussions. Neither concession theory nor real-entity theories of corporate personalities reflected the full scope of corporate behaviour or ultimately proved effective in rendering corporations accountable for their wrongdoing.

Over the remainder of the twentieth century, corporate law and legal theory would respond to the central incoherence of the corporate person, which manifested a will that was, by definition, out of control. Most influentially, Michael C. Jensen and William H. Meckling asserted in 1979 that corporations had no owners. Rather, corporations were a

---

32 Yasco Horsman and Frans-Willem Korsten, "Introduction: Legal Bodies: Corpus/Persona/Communitas," *Law and Literature* 28, no. 3 (2016): 279.

33 Harold Laski, "The Personality of Associations," *Harvard Law Review* 29, no. 4 (1916): 404.

"nexus of contracts" where "the conflicting objectives of the individual participants are brought into equilibrium."[34] Models of the corporation matter partly, then, because they provide ways to clarify and categorize the role of persons within and around business organizations – managing the population of the household, so to speak – while also allowing us to see the unstable history of naturalized notions of the person more generally. In each model, liability for corporate actions, the relations of individuals to corporations and corporations to the state, and, ultimately, the way we understand the rights of the corporate person, are transformed. Only by beginning to understand the features of the corporation highlighted by each of these models – and the limitations of the models themselves – can we begin to imagine new ways of understanding corporate personhood that might render the phenomenon available to strategic or subversive reappropriation in the name of human – but also of post-, para- and even anti-human – rights.

The Volume Ahead

Part I, "Noble Households, Ignoble Subjects," develops the political theory of the corporation by examining the implications of theorizing the corporation as the simultaneous extension and subject of sovereignty. In chapter 1, "The Corporation's Neoliberal Soul?," Matthew Titolo theorizes a neoliberal *oikonomia* that seeks to link the family, the self, and the firm. Titolo moves away from access to resources and rights to consider how corporate personhood participates in subject-formation. He warns that under neoliberal ideology, corporate personhood doctrine is part of an interlocking set of legal and economic doctrines designed to colonize the subjective lives of human individuals so that we become risk-assessing beings who cultivate entrepreneurial habits in line with corporate interests. This figuration of the person proposes a very narrow understanding of rights as always already in the service of corporate interests.

In chapter 2, "Cosmopolitanism, Sovereignty, and the Problem of Corporate Personhood," Joshua Barkan considers the transnational corporation's claims to cosmopolitan right and to cosmopolitan care. He thinks about the corporation in reference to the refugee, a similarly stateless entity. If the corporation's claims to cosmopolitan right are indeed legitimate, what does that imply for the basis of cosmopolitan

---

34 Michael C. Jensen and William H. Meckling, "Theory of the Firm: Managerial Behavior, Agency Costs, and Ownership Structure," SSRN Scholarly Paper (Rochester: Social Science Research Network, 1 July 1976, https://papers.ssrn.com/abstract=94043.

right? In chapter 3, "Watched Over by Assemblages of Providential Grace," Angela Mitropoulos writes about how, under neoliberal theory, the Aristotelian principle of *oikonomia* casts the corporation as a risk-distributing legal instrument that fancies itself a "noble household." Mitropoulos examines the *Burwell v. Hobby Lobby* decision as well as the Trump Corporation and finds corporate reasoning, with its patriarchal origins, shot through with providential dispensationalism. Mitropoulos sees the *Hobby Lobby* decision as not merely extending to the corporation the right to exercise religious freedom, but also authorizing the closely held corporation to manage the exercise of the religious freedom of its employees. Moreover, it does so in a patriarchal fashion that deprives women of access to rights and resources in favour of prenatal entities. After all, what is a fetus but a potential man? In this way, corporate personhood doctrine in the United States has "narrowed protections to prenatal and post-incorporated entities."

In Part II, "The Social Theory of the Corporation," the contributions of David Golumbia, Frank Pasquale, and Richard Hardack seek to demonstrate that corporate personhood *is* a social theory that generates social effects. In chapter 4, "From Public Sphere to Personalized Feed: Corporate Constitutional Rights and the Challenge to Popular Sovereignty," Golumbia and Pasquale use M.T. Anderson's young adult novel, *Feed*, to meditate on the ethical implications of the imminent public sphere that the novel depicts, one in which private corporations exercise public functions under the protection of expressive rights. Whereas Titolo maps out the ways in which corporate personhood doctrine helps shape individual subjectivity, in chapter 5, "Exceptionally Gifted: Corporate Exceptionalism and the Expropriation of Human Rights," Hardack shifts the focus to the social figuration of the corporation as a responsible and deserving instrument of public welfare in contrast to traditional human subjects of welfarism, with the corporation assuming the attributes of the undeserving poor. In Hardack's account, corporate personhood doctrine abets political theories of the corporation that place it in relation to the state as a subject, and thus as a legal instrument for expropriating resources from the public sphere to commercial entities. This political theory takes for granted that corporations are superior rights candidates to natural persons.

In Part III, "Discipline and Guardianship," Stefan Padfield and Angela Fernandez engage in the kind of creative reappropriation of corporate personhood doctrine that we have suggested recent case law may make possible. Both contributors examine the limits of current law in order to suggest tactical avenues for change. In chapter 6, "Killing Corporations to Save Humans: How Corporate Personhood, Human Rights, and the Corporate Death Penalty Intersect," Padfield examines the theoretical accounts of the corporation used in legal decision-making to spell out the implications of various models of corporate personhood, and to devise a means of using the theory of the corporation to allow it to be disciplined rather than granted the *de facto* immunity and advantage about which critics such as Reich and Slaughter raise the alarm. In chapter 7, "Already Artificial: Legal Personality and Animal Rights," Fernandez discusses the 2016 documentary *Rattling the Cage*, which follows the history of animal rights activist Stephen Wise and efforts by his Nonhuman Rights Project to create precedent for animal legal personhood. As Fernandez points out, this is a limited legal personhood that would establish guardianship and standing for animals in order to create further means of legal sanction for those who would abuse their "property," rather than an attempt to grant animals the full benefit of rights generally accorded to either human or corporate persons under the law. Nonetheless, we see in these pieces the beginnings of some of the opportunities that may exist to steer neoliberal expansions of corporate personhood in unforeseen, oppositional directions.

In Part IV, "Corporate Personification," the literary historians Scott MacKenzie and Peter Jaros extend the implications of "incorporation" back in time, and in doing so give us a revised account of the sheer pervasiveness of the corporation's cultural reach. MacKenzie, in chapter 8, "The Livestock That Therefore We Are: Two Episodes from the Prehistory of Corporate Personhood," writes about the rhetorical nature of corporate expression. His focus is on the late eighteenth century, when Edmund Burke rejected the Declaration of the Rights of Man on behalf of the British people, whom he figured as a herd of silent cattle. MacKenzie shows that James Hogg understood the implications of the figure of corporate personhood imposed on the British people, and furthermore understood that the silent uniformity of the cattle had direct bearing on the relationship of the British to rights. In contrast, MacKenzie glosses Hogg's use of a flock of bleating sheep to figure the corporate differently – at odds with its leadership, uneasy with solidarity, and, because internally more conflictual, more deserving of rights. In chapter 9, "Immortal and Intangible? Corporate Metaphysics in Jacksonian America," Jaros further develops the argument that representational figurations of the corporation have historically mattered in constructions that challenge the ways that theoretical accounts of the corporation have been used to narrow the rights attributed to human citizen-subjects.

We end historically because it is easy to casually speak of rights in the abstract and to either generalize theoretically about corporate entities or to casually dismiss their importance for human and other persons. There are wide variations in categories of rights and in corporate forms. We know from the *Hobby Lobby* decision that a closely held corporation accesses rights differently from large, publicly owned corporations. Should it matter to constitutional law experts that a business organization is a partnership or a cooperative? How should the Bill of Rights apply, if at all, to corporations joined to global production networks? Can governments utilize corporations as rights distributors and enforcers, and does doing so transform how we think of property and sovereignty? This volume is a first step in untangling the confusing – the potentially transformative as well as devastatingly inhumane – impersonalities of corporations, persons, and rights.

PART ONE

Noble Households, Ignoble Subjects

Once upon a time, law schools offered courses on the law of agency, which dealt with juridical personhood – that is, the relations between and among persons and things. Casebooks contained the definitive cases on "lunatics," divorced women, boats, and other entities whose juridical personhood intersected with contract, property, or tort law. With the expansion of corporate law as a field of study and practice, agency as a field went by the wayside. Yet juridical personhood remained one principle focus of twentieth-century theories of the social sciences. The French sociologist Marcel Mauss broke down the distinction between person and thing that liberal legality purports to take as fundamental and in doing so made the agency question of personhood the key to a century of scholarship around subject-formation. In "The Concept of the Person," Mauss treats this porous movement from thing to person as predating so-called civil society, understanding personhood through the study of tribal affiliation and the workings of kinship relations. In his research on the naming of newborns in the *pueblo* of Zuni, Mauss took for granted that, insofar as personhood is contingent on aspects of a tribe's totem, Zuni personhood is a social concept. Each clan possessed only a finite number of surnames. Every surname, or totem, prescribed to its holder specific roles and rituals within the clan. Clan members could only inherit surnames,and this established generational continuity and stability within the group. Mauss acknowledges that while clan members had individual identities, their collective purpose remained to ensure that the clan flourished by filling a set slate of open "offices" with new clan members. By accepting reincarnated clan surnames and their accompanying roles, members guaranteed the perpetuation of the clan through social reproduction and assumed a personhood that can only be construed as non-autonomous and supra-individual – that is, "corporate."

In these clans, one's social role, which includes one's rights, duties, liabilities, and powers, was relational. Only one person could hold a particular office at a time. The attributes (powers) of the totem came with those offices. Through the features of its kinship arrangement, a totem worked as a social theory of the person and of that person's rights and powers within the collective. As Marilyn Strathern points out, moreover, what was true for the clan must also be understood as true of legal personality as a whole in modern Western liberal democracies: "The socialized, internally controlled Western person must emerge as a microcosm of the domesticating process by which natural resources are put to cultural use. Hence the person is a homologue of society thought of as a set of rules or conventions."[1] In our introduction, we broached the subject of the *oikos* (the noble household), a convention by which corporations have long managed populations under their control (quasi-feudal, colonial, industrial, settler, plantation, and so on) as subjects in whom they have made a proprietorial investment. This concept, adopted by neoliberal theorists, shares an unsettling resemblance to notions of corporate social responsibility and to development policies.

High courts in Canada, South Africa, Germany, and the United States have adopted a language of corporate social responsibility, that is, the language of the corporation as a rights-distributing noble household. The idiom takes the form of legal language positing a stakeholder or clan model of the corporation. In *Peoples Department Stores Inc. (Trustee of) v. Wise* (2004), the Supreme Court of Canada ruled that "[a]t all times, directors and officers owe their fiduciary obligation to the corporation. The interests of the corporation are not to be confused with the interests of the creditors or those of any other stakeholders."[2] The Supreme Court has elevated the corporation to the role of a transcendent entity that owes a duty to all stakeholders, not simply to owners, and it reiterated this holding in 2008.[3] Conceivably, this duty is owed to neighbourhoods in which facilities are located, lakes their factories overlook, their vendors, and so forth. According to our contributors, one can begin to comprehend recent corporate personhood case law in the United States through this lens.

Our first contributor, Matthew Titolo, in his excavation of the corporation's role in neoliberal ideology, points out that "markets and commerce still civilize people, but they don't do so alone. They will

---

1 Marilyn Strathern, *The Gender of the Gift: Problems with Women and Problems with Society in Melanesia* (Berkeley: University of California Press, 1988), 135.
2 *Peoples Department Stores Inc. (Trustee of) v. Wise* [2004]. SCC Case (Lexum), para. 43.
3 *BCE Inc. v. 1976 Debenture holders* [2008] 3 S.C.R. 560, 2008.

require an active corporate state, which will work to transform us into neoliberal subjects." In Titolo's view, neoliberalism is the return of the repressed clan *contra* the common understanding of neoliberalism. Typically, neoliberalism is read as an ideology that is adamantly opposed to state interference in markets. This rote understanding of neoliberalism neglects how theorists of neoliberalism frame their practice. Understanding it as an ensemble of policy choices masks the way in which neoliberal ideology actually thinks about the market as a tool for shaping malleable notions of the common good and the limits of human agency. Those who associate neoliberalism with austerity mistakenly think that it abandons a vision of the common good; according to Titolo, rather, neoliberal ideology asks us to think of the common good as "an aggregate of private, self-directed transactions" that appropriates the common good and refashions it into the "corporate good."

Once it becomes clear that the neoliberal order associates the collective good with the corporate good, implications for rights-bearing subjects flow naturally. Joshua Barkan's chapter posits a perverse twist on debates about the corporation's relationship to international human rights. While most human rights activists seek to transform the corporation into an entity with duties toward stakeholders, Barkan claims that transnational corporations seek to situate themselves as subjects of care within international law and under cosmopolitan right. Barkan argues that we can better understand the moves made by transnational corporations through their interest in being detached from specific-state responsibilities. In the fantasy of the transnational corporation, the goal is to become the subject of rights through a corporate personhood doctrine that progressively elides the difference between person and human while divesting itself of duties to specific states:

> cosmopolitan norms are designed to address populations abandoned, if you will, through the dynamics of contemporary globalization. [T]he connection between right and person that cosmopolitanism relies on and deploys reiterates, rather than breaks from, a discourse that traditionally empowered corporations in their global search for profit. In particular, cosmopolitanism's linking of right and person provides a rationale and defence for the geographic mobility of capital in its corporate form – a mobility that has been central to the disenfranchisement and displacement of the self-same populations requiring cosmopolitan protections.

In Barkan's view, emphatically strengthening the rights of refugees risks inadvertently handing rights and immunities to corporate entities as they seek to manage and take advantage of migrant labour.

In her chapter, Angela Mitropoulos sees the noble household embodied in the closely held (family) corporation. A political theorist by training, Mitropoulos considers it no coincidence that the president of the world's most powerful superpower, the United States, is also the CEO of a family corporation. Similarly, the *Hobby Lobby* case that has most upset corporate sceptics involved a closely held corporation whose case depended on the logic of *oikonomia*. The owners of Hobby Lobby argued that in a closely held corporation such as theirs, the corporation can assume the religious duties that its owners feel compelled to obey. In that case, the patriarchal ethos of the *oikos* extended such a duty to prenatal entities, though not to adult women. Mitropoulos finds that attempts by corporations to claim standing in freedom-of-religion cases enforce a patriarchal, racialized regime committed to the management and social reproduction of labouring bodies. Forced to submit to the religious duties that ostensibly flow from the clan-like interests of the corporation, human labourers are stripped of their rights, or rather forced to cede those rights in favour of the corporate body's will to reproduce itself.

1 The Corporation's Neoliberal Soul?

MATTHEW TITOLO[1]

Introduction

From its beginnings in the early British Empire, where chartered corporations colonized the New World on behalf of the Crown and investors, the corporation has become to the locus of transnational capitalism and one of the most powerful political actors in the modern world. The entrepreneurs of early settler colonialism received legal privileges in the form of charters, patents, and letters of incorporation. In exchange they acted as stand-ins for the sovereign and filled the coffers of elite investors with silver when they were profitable.[2] As William J. Novak argues, "the early corporate charter was simultaneously a tool of promotion, regulation, and control."[3] Corporations continue to provide a wide range of quasi-governmental services through government contracts.[4]

---

1 This chapter was written with the support of the West Virginia University College of Law and the Hodges/Bloom Research Fund.
2 For an excellent discussion of the role of corporations and other forms of grants from the Crown in colonizing North America, see Christopher Tomlins, *Freedom Bound: Law, Labor, and Civic Identity in Colonizing English America, 1580–1865* (New York: Cambridge UP, 2010), 157–90. See also Joshua Barkan, *Corporate Sovereignty: Law and Government under Capitalism* (Minneapolis: University of Minnesota Press, 2013. Kindle Edition), loc. 449–54: "Corporate charters were liberties held against the state that gave legal standing to corporations. From the state's perspective, the charters were grants or gifts of immunity from the sovereign, designed to strengthen the state. By granting privileges and immunities, the state encouraged groups of individuals to organize institutions such as poorhouses, religious orders, universities, cities, factories, and colonies." In Foucauldian terms, granting corporate charters to do the work of population management is a form of biopolitics.
3 William A. Novak, *The People's Welfare: Law and Regulation in Nineteenth-Century America* (Chapel Hill: University of North Carolina Press, 1996), 107.
4 Jody Freeman and Martha Minow, eds., *Government by Contract: Outsourcing and American Democracy* (Cambridge, MA: Harvard University Press, 2009).

Because of its status as a public/private hybrid, it is not surprising that the corporation is one of the most widely theorized institutions in modernity.[5] On paper, of course, the corporation is merely a convenient legal fiction, a construct that exists for specific human purposes: a vehicle for entrepreneurial aspirations, a nexus of contracts, an owner of property, a risk-distributing machine to generate, store, and distribute value on behalf of its shareholders. But political histories understand that corporations are not merely economic ciphers. As Joshua Barkan writes, "corporations are fictions, created by states, but given such social power that they threaten to undermine the political sovereignty that created them."[6] This is certainly true in our era of transnational corporations, which operate at the outer bounds of national sovereignty. The corporation, however, has been from the start a source of anxiety for modern political and social theory. Thomas Hobbes, for example, analogized the corporation to an infestation in the body of the sovereign: "Corporations are many lesser commonwealths in the bowels of a greater, like worms in the entrails of a natural man."[7] Likewise, in America's early republican imagination, the corporation could be a monstrous parasite on the body politic threatening to devour its host.[8] Our suspicions have not abated since then, with each generation inventing a new form of anti-corporate politics. As in the colonial era, corporations continue to embody delegated sovereignty, using their economic and legal power to colonize the world on behalf of state, capital and empire. The corporation's vast political power has made it excellent fodder for dystopian narratives.[9] But

---

5   For some representative corporate theory or history, see Adolph A. Berns and Gardiner Means, *The Modern Corporation and Private Property* (New York: Macmillan, 1933). Morton Horwitz supplies a classic account of the corporation as instrumental to capitalist development in *The Transformation of American Law: 1780–1860* (New York: Oxford University Press, [1978]1992), 63–139. Ronald Coase argued in a groundbreaking article that corporations were a way to organize and manage transaction costs. R.H. Coase, *The Nature of the Firm Economica*, new series, vol. 4, no. 16 (November 1937), 386–405. Examples, like corporations, could be multiplied indefinitely.

6   Barkan, *Corporate Sovereignty*, loc. 95–7.

7   Thomas Hobbes, *Leviathan*, (Penguin Classics, Kindle edition), loc 4732.

8   For an example of this, see Barkan's discussion of anti-corporate politics in the Jacksonian era, *Corporate Sovereignty*, loc. 896–961.

9   For the corporation as sociopath, see Joel Barkan, *The Corporation: The Pathological Pursuit of Profit and Power* (New York: Free Press, 2004). Science fiction, cyberpunk and transhumanist narratives often imagine corporations as the central political actors of the future. In Ridley Scott's *Alien*, for example, the plot revolves around a company that sends the hapless crew of the *Nostromo* to retrieve a deadly alien, regardless of the danger that task poses to humanity. *Bladerunner*'s Tyrell Corporation manufactures self-aware Replicants, who are given a five-year life span, but who, like Prometheus, rebel against their makers.

it is interesting to consider another perspective, one from a central political thinker in the Western tradition: G.W.F. Hegel. As Hegel understood them, corporations were collective, self-governing entities, functioning as the king's eyes and ears within civil society. They were smaller societies embedded in the larger one, which makes them useful devices for management of the polity. We have seen that Hobbes fears the corporation as an "infestation" within the body of the sovereign; for Hegel, the social ubiquity of the corporation is precisely its advantage as a governance mechanism. Hegel's corporation is an expression of the situated ethical life – *Sittlichkeit* – which enables an otherwise fragmented and self-interested bourgeois society to form a coherent ethical community oriented toward the state. To help us understand this, Hegel focuses on the governance role of corporations:

> [A] Corporation has the right, under the surveillance of the public authority, (a) to look after its own interests within its own sphere, (b) to co-opt members, qualified objectively by requisite skill and rectitude, to a number fixed by the general structure of society, (c) to protect its members against particular contingencies, (d) to provide the education requisite to fit other to become members. In short, the right is to come on the scene like a second family for its members.

Hegel was describing the guilds and civil corporations of his own day in this passage, but I want to suggest here that his analysis of the corporation's governance dimension has a wider application to the corporations of our own time. The corporation embodies a central tension within liberal capitalist governance between liberalism's commitment to individualism in theory and its need for collective decision making and resource management in practice. With its echoes of the guild or household, Hegel's corporation is an *oikos*, a basic unit of political economy within liberal capitalism.[10]

But this governance aspect of the corporation presents a puzzle for liberal democracy, which theoretically reserves governance power for the sovereign.. The corporation can exercise state-level powers but has few of the accountability mechanisms of the modern democratic state. Thus, the corporation continues to be controversial for liberalism, not least because it scrambles the polarities of public and private upon which modern liberalism depends. The corporation is always public in the simplest sense of having been created or licensed by the state and often exercising government functions. It is always undeniably private

---

10   G.W.F. Hegel, *Philosophy of Right* (New York: Cambridge UP, 1991), ¶252.

in that it acts for its own purposes, can hold property and make contracts, and to a large extent is permitted to manage its own internal affairs as if it were autonomous. The corporation is a node in an entangled public/private governance system, not reducible to the neat public/private domains that liberalism requires in order to guarantee the internal coherence of its own republican ideology.

Citizens United v. FEC nicely illustrates the fundamental ambiguity of the corporation in modern liberal politics, especially the apparent tensions between capitalism and democracy.[11]*Citizens United* ruled that limits on campaign expenditures, previously held to be constitutional, infringe First Amendment speech rights.[12] This holding upended the existing balance between public control over the democratic process and commercial speech rights.[13] There was broad outrage at the decision, rooted at least in part in the misperception that *Citizens United* invented corporate personhood out of thin air. The legal history of corporate personhood, however, is much more complicated than such rhetoric would suggest. Corporations have long enjoyed legal rights under various conceptualizations, although as I have been arguing neither law nor liberal political theory has ever really settled the issue of corporate rights once and for all.[14] Liberals claim that spending limitless corporate resources to buy elections is a corrupt practice that threatens to turn a democratic society into a plutocracy.[15] It is hard to disagree with such arguments. Many liberals understandably share Justice Ginsburg's desire to see *Citizens United* reversed: "If there was one decision I would overrule, it would be *Citizens United*. I think the notion that we have all the democracy that money can buy strays so far from what our democracy is supposed to be."[16] Justice Ginsberg, like many liberals, fears the distorting

---

11 *Citizens United v. F.E.C.*, 558 U.S. 310 (2010).

12 *Citizens United v. F.E.C.*, 558 U.S. 310, 337–57 (2010).

13 I do not address the specific legal arguments regarding how *Citizens United* is "wrong" or a bad fit for certain normative visions of American constitutional law. For a critique of *Citizens United* based on fit, see Anne Tucker, "Flawed Assumptions: A Corporate Law Analysis of Free Speech and Corporate Personhood in *Citizens United*," *Case Western Reserve Law Review* 61, no. 2 (2011): 497–548.

14 Elizabeth Pollman, "Reconceiving Corporate Personhood," *Utah Law Review* 4 (2011): 1629–75.

15 See for example Samuel Issacharoff, "On Political Corruption," *Harvard Law Review* 124, no. 1 (2010): 118–42; Richard L. Hasen, *Plutocrats United: Campaign Money, the Supreme Court, and the Distortion of American Elections* (New Haven: Yale University Press, 2016).

16 Jeffrey Rosen, "Ruth Bader Ginsburg Is an American Hero," *The New Republic*, 28 September 2014, https://newrepublic.com/article/119578/ruth-bader-ginsburg-interview-retirement-feminists-jazzercise.

effects of money and private power on democratic norms, but also the corporation's *imperium in imperio* role, a fear that was present at the beginning of the modern liberal tradition. Anti-corporate politics reflects a left-republicanism that seeks to protect democratic norms from capture by private power.[17] The concern is that courts and legislatures have been shielding the corporation from public control behind an impenetrable wall of property and speech rights. Anti-corporate politics summons to its aid the rhetoric of corruption to urge the decolonization of the political by the economic. The citizens of modern democracies watch the same process play out time and time again as corporations purchase their desired policies for pennies on the dollar every election season.

Theorists of neoliberalism were some of the first to develop systematic accounts of this dynamic. Neoliberalism has become a pivotal term in social and historical analysis in recent years, referring to a range of policy measures, political forms, and styles of management whose central feature is the "disenchantment of politics by economics"[18] and the substitution of metrics, price measures, consumer choice, and price theory for justice and the common good.[19] Wendy Brown has argued that neoliberalism has greatly

---

17   The republican critique of corporate power has been framed in the rhetoric of corruption from the very beginning of corporate personhood cases. See, for example, *Santa Clara County v. Southern Pac. R. Co.*, 18 F. 385, 437 (1883): "Great stress was laid in the arguments of plaintiffs' counsel upon the growing and overweening power and greed of corporations; and it was vehemently asserted that this is a struggle between the people and the corporations for supremacy; that corporations by corrupt means, and through their large and wide-spread influence, have obtained, and they are obtaining, control of legislatures, etc."

18   See William Davies, *The Limits of Neoliberalism: Authority, Sovereignty, and the Logic of Competition* (London: Sage Publications, 2014): "[The] central defining characteristic of all neoliberal critique is its hostility to the ambiguity of political discourse, and a commitment to the explicitness and transparency of quantitative, economic indicators, of which the market price system is the model. Neoliberalism is the pursuit of the disenchantment of politics by economics" (3). It is interesting to note that American legal scholars have until fairly recently rarely used the term. Or perhaps, this lacuna makes perfect sense: after the law and economics revolution, neoliberalism became our common policy vocabulary. We have tended to talk about neoliberalism as an event happening elsewhere, often in connection with IMF restructuring of Latin American economies and more generally as a feature of "globalization." As Jamie Peck has noted, in "North America, neoliberalism has largely remained a subterranean, critics' word." Peck, *Constructions of Neoliberal Reason* (Oxford: Oxford University Press, 2010), 2.

19   For a very good introduction to neoliberalism, see Pierre Dardot and Christian Laval, *The New Way of the World: On Neoliberal Society* (New York: Verso, 2014): "Neo-liberalism is a system of norms now profoundly inscribed in government practices, institutional policies and managerial styles ..." (15). See also Peck, *Constructions of Neoliberal Reason*; Rachel Turner, *Neo-Liberal Ideology: History, Concepts,*

damaged democratic norms of accountability that have always been fragile under liberal capitalism.[20] From this perspective, *Citizens United* reflects
the broader "corporatization" of social and political life, which accelerates
the decline of democracy into plutocracy through a jurisprudence in which
market norms colonize public governance.[21] While I believe there is a fair
bit of nostalgia for mid-century liberalism in such accounts, it is also the
case that whatever fragile restraints on corporate power once existed have
begun to unravel rapidly in the late neoliberal era.

This chapter argues that while corporate personhood and the entan-
glement of the corporation in governance are not neoliberal inventions,
it is important to understand how neoliberalism uses the corporation
to advance its own governance project, just as neoliberal jurisprudence
will instrumentalize corporate personhood for its own ends. However,
appeals to vanishing democratic norms located in an idealized past un-
derstate how central the corporation has always been to liberal governance. Critics of neoliberalism need to ground their normative critique
in a genealogy of capitalist formations to better understand how integral the corporation has been to the articulation of liberal democracy.
Indeed, corporations have been prominent features of Anglo-American
statecraft and have remained mediators of "the political" for centuries.
This point is not made in rebuttal of anti-corporate critique. Far from
it. Acknowledging the historical genealogy of the corporate form does
not downplay contemporary criticisms of corporate power. If anything,
the genealogy suggests quite the opposite: that critical left accounts of
the corporation are perhaps suggestive of a more radical revision of
economic practice than they sometimes acknowledge. At the very least,
understanding the entangled public/private history of governance
and the corporate form will suggest the openings, possibilities, and
limits for radical change given current practices. To develop a critique,
we have to begin by acknowledging that the corporation's role in the
economy is no new thing. Corporation, state, and economy have been

---

and Policies (Edinburgh: Edinburgh University Press, 2011); Philip Mirowski and
Dieter Plehwe, eds., *The Road from Mont Pèlerin: The Making of the Neoliberal Thought
Collective* (Cambridge, MA: Harvard University Press, 2009); Davies, *The Limits of
Neoliberalism*; Daniel Stedman Jones, *Masters of the Universe: Friedman, Hayek and the
Birth of Neoliberal Politics* (Princeton: Princeton University Press, 2012).

20 Wendy Brown, *Undoing the Demos: Neoliberalism's Stealth Revolution* (New York: Zone
Books, 2015).

21 See Timothy K. Kuhner, "Citizens United as Neoliberal Jurisprudence: The Re-
surgence of Economic Theory," *Virginia Journal of Policy and Law* 18, no. 3 (2011):
395–468.

mutually constitutive since the early modern era.[22] The genealogical approach adopted here suggests that the task of critiquing the present may entail a more thoroughgoing analysis of the forms of political rationality that govern our world than has been offered to date.

Corporations have been rights-bearing legal entities since the early colonial era, though of course the legal status and function of corporations has evolved in the four hundred years since the first chartered corporations began colonizing North America. Nevertheless, the corporation has enjoyed an assemblage of legal rights and has been enmeshed with sovereign statecraft since its beginnings. The corporation, in short, is deeply tied to the social ontology of liberal capitalism. Disentangling corporations from American political life is surely necessary, and that project will only benefit from the ongoing interdisciplinary analysis of neoliberalism, which is really just now getting off the ground in the English-speaking world. This chapter thus joins left critiques of *Citizens United* and corporatization more generally, but it does so with an awareness that we will need to develop an archaeology of political reason under capitalism in the coming years in order to achieve the democratic vision of the corporation's critics.

Historiography of the Corporation

The modern corporation as a legal form traces its roots back to the Middle Ages.[23] Older associational forms were borrowed from the Greek and Roman world and adapted to fit the needs of feudalism. The chartered corporation effectively functioned as the state's doppelgänger, owing its quasi-sovereignty to the state while remaining partly immune from its power through grants, charters, licences, and so on. Beginning in the seventeenth century, the English used a variety of corporate forms as vehicles to explore, colonize, and construct its empire. These corporate charters took many forms: specific grants, joint stock corporations, royal letters patent. In the early days of colonization, the corporation was a portable society, often with strong

---

22 "Modern corporate power emerges from and mobilizes apparatuses of sovereignty, discipline, and government. In this manner, corporate power and state sovereignty depend on one another, each establishing the other's condition of possibility." Barkan, *Corporate Sovereignty*, loc. 139–42.

23 For a classic account of the medieval revival of corporations see Otto von Gierke, *Political Theories of the Middle Ages*, trans. F.W. Maitland (Boston: Beacon Press, 1959); see also Frederick Pollock and Frederic W. Maitland, *History of English Law before the Time of Edward I*, 2 vols. (Cambridge: Cambridge University Press, 1923).

police powers.[24] Jurisdictional questions were sorted out in a variety of ways between the time of first colonization and the American Revolution.[25] Corporations enjoyed a vast range of political powers. They were mini-sovereigns empowered to claim territory, constitute communities, make war, make law, negotiate treaties, control populations, and render the New World productive for early settler colonialism.[26] They were both tools of statecraft and objects that constituted the state itself. Another way to make the same point is to view corporate associations as indispensable for what we can call *oikonomia*.[27] *Oikonomia*, the Greek root of economics, is essentially a theological concept that means the art of prudent household management. It has deep roots in Western political ontology. The *oikos* is a household made up of the patriarch, his property, and his dependents.[28] In the early modern project of imperial colonization, the corporation could be cast as an *oikos*, a type of proprietary governance designed to channel private economic activity toward public ends.[29] All of this suggests a rough analogy: for much of its early history, the Anglo-American corporation was effectively a system of sovereignty franchising via portable corporate households. Corporate headquarters (i.e., the Crown, which provided the licence) and the board of directors (i.e., the landowning elites who provided the capital and expected a return on investment) granted a fair degree of autonomy for the individual corporate franchisees to carry out the necessary work of governance, such as administering populations and territories, that the Crown could never have accomplished on its own. Franchisees used the corporate form to manage risks, pool resources, and capitalize on the "branding" provided by the sovereign.

By the time of the American Revolution, corporations had for many years been using monopoly grants to operate toll bridges, roads, bridges,

---

24 For a discussion of "corporation as police" see Barkan, *Corporate Sovereignty*, loc. 564–738.

25 *Calvin's Case* (1608), for example, a dispute clarifying issues of legal jurisdiction surrounding James VI's assent to the English throne, laid the groundwork for the right of oversees Crown subjects to obtain access to English law at home and local law in the King's dominions abroad. Tomlins, *Law, Labor, and Civic Identity*, 89.

26 See ibid., 67–190.

27 For an extended discussion of this concept, see Angela Mitropoulos, *Contract and Contagion: From Biopolitics to Oikonomia* (New York: Minor Compositions, 2012), 49–76.

28 For an extended discussion of the *oikos* and the modern political imaginary see Vincent P. Pecora, *Households of the Soul* (Baltimore: Johns Hopkins University Press, 1997).

29 On the early proprietary model of colonization, see Tomlins, *Law, Labor, and Civic Identity*, 166–90. "The proprietorial idea re-created mainland colonizing both in process and purpose by imposing upon it a new discourse of authority and jurisdictional relationships. From the early 1620s, English charters made palatine authority and institutions key features of the evolving design of North American colonization" (171).

colleges, mills, and so on. By the end of the eighteenth century, American state governments were beginning to encourage economic development by granting corporate charters to productive enterprises.[30] The owners of these enterprises could assert legal claims against competing enterprises, acting as a check on economic development. Existing corporate property owners asserted their rights to be free from the economic harms inflicted by competing enterprises. The theory, in other words, was that the state grant was a vested property interest whose public character entailed an exclusive franchise that forbade others from enjoying the privileges explicitly or implicitly granted in the charter. But the legal status of the corporation was never unitary. As Morton Horwitz points out, the eighteenth-century theories inherited by American law were inherently contradictory. On the one hand, the older theory of the corporation (discussed above) could trace its genealogy back to the Middle Ages. This theory was based on the status of the corporation as a type of property.[31] On the other hand, the more recent theory justified the corporation's monopoly on the ground that the exclusive charter was grounded in the public character of the corporate grant.[32] Corporations were public things doing public work. Horwitz argues in *The Transformation of American Law* that developments in the nineteenth century established a new and essentially economic theory for the existence of the corporation: "No longer primarily representing an association between state and private interests for public purposes, the corporate form had developed into a convenient legal device for limiting risks and promoting continuity in the pursuit of private advantage."[33] Horwitz traces the gradual privatization of the business corporation through the nineteenth century, theorizing that American law developed along instrumental paths that tracked the emergence of industrial capitalism.[34]

Horwitz is correct that American law developed what we would begin to call "economic" rationales for the corporation. Corporations, the theory goes, could serve the public good by developing products and markets. In liberal economic theory, securing property rights and

---

30 Horwitz, *The Transformation of American Law* 109–10.
31 Ibid., 110.
32 Ibid., 110.
33 Ibid., 136–7.
34 For the now classic view that the corporation became privatized, and on American law generally as an instrument of capitalist development see ibid. For a revisionist view of the privatization story see Novak, *The People's Welfare*, 1–113. Novak's account shows that state governments retained a lot of power and leeway over entrenched private interests during the supposed period of libertarian dominance, greatly complicating the myth of laissez-faire constitutionalism.

relations and providing a legal framework for commodity production creates value that we all share. The legal theory of the corporation, in other words, began to track our understandings of an economic sphere independent of the state. The movement from the mercantilism of eighteenth-century political economy to the self-sustaining market grounded in the "natural order" of production and consumption was at the core of classical economic theory.[35] However, Horwitz's account of the corporate privatization in the nineteenth century is unsatisfying because it relies on a conceptual dividing line between public and private spheres that doesn't reflect actual governance practices. Calling the new theory of the corporation "private" highlights the inherent instability of liberal legal theory and indeed of liberal law more generally.

Horwitz's story begins with challenges to the vested property and contract rights of colonial corporations and ends with the emergence of the rights-bearing business corporation in the late nineteenth century, after the 14th Amendment had been interpreted in a series of cases to grant a broad array of legal rights to the corporation. The movement is usually thought of as an arc from strong monopoly protections for corporations in the pre-Revolutionary period based on their public character to a shift in the rationale for corporations as an instrument of private interests. It is, in other words, a theory of law as an instrument of laissez-faire capitalism. As Robert Novak's revisionary history shows, however, that process was never linear, and a strong tradition of *salus populi* preserved the state's police powers against private interests throughout the period of laissez-faire's imagined triumph. The legal development of corporate rights in the nineteenth century was uneven: courts sometimes protected corporate monopolies and exclusive franchises and at other times upheld the power of legislatures to allow competing forms of enterprise or to abrogate vested corporate rights altogether.[36]

The classic corporation cases of the nineteenth century reflect an inherently unstable and inconclusive theory, a point evidenced by the fact that we are still fiercely debating the political status of the corporation almost two hundred years later. After the American Revolution, the public grant theory of the corporation came under pressure in a series of decisions that developed a different rationale for corporate privileges. *Dartmouth College v. Woodward* (1819), one of the early classic corporation

---

35 On natural order in eighteenth-century political economy, see Bernard Harcourt, *The Illusion of Free Markets: Punishment and the Myth of Natural Order* (Cambridge, MA: Harvard University Press, 2011, Kindle edition), loc. 1140–338.

36 See Novak, *The People's Welfare*, 1–49.

cases, concerned the charter granted by King George III in 1769, which established the college as a charitable corporation.[37] In 1816 the legislature of New Hampshire revised the 1769 charter to change the status of the school from private to public. Dartmouth then challenged the law on the grounds that it violated the Constitution's Contracts Clause. The Court was essentially asked to decide whether the original grant to Dartmouth College was public or private. In the course of deciding that question in favour of a private right that could not be disturbed by the legislature, Justice Marshall began with general observations about the nature of the corporation: "A corporation is an artificial being, invisible, intangible, and existing only in contemplation of law. Being the mere creature of law, it possesses only those properties which the charter of its creation confers upon it, either expressly, or as incidental to its very existence."[38] Note that even in this early case, the corporation's status as a unitary entity with legal rights was limned, albeit in fairly general terms: "Among the most important [features of the corporation] are immortality, and, if the expression may be allowed, individuality; properties, by which a perpetual succession of many persons are considered as the same, and may act as a single individual."[39] When Justice Marshall writes "if the expression may be allowed," his qualification suggests that he knows he is advancing a novel theory. An "individual," after all, is not exactly a person in the legal sense; that development would take more than sixty years to come to fruition.[40] Still, it demonstrates that corporations were beginning to be viewed as rights-bearing entities in the new constitutional order, just as Horwitz argues. The private theory is also evidenced, of course, by the fact that Dartmouth College won the case on a private rights theory under the Contracts Clause.[41]

---

37 17 U.S. 518.

38 636. This essentially reaffirms Blackstone's view that when the members of a corporation "are consolidated and united into a corporation, they and their successors are then considered as one person in law: as one person, they have one will, which is collected from the sense of the majority of the individuals ... for all the individual members that have existed from the foundation to the present time, or that shall ever hereafter exist, are but one person in law, a person that never dies." 1 William Blackstone, *Commentaries* 468 (7th ed. 1775).

39 17 U.S. 518, 636.

40 The corporation is also called a "real person" in another early corporation case *Bank of the United States v. Deveaux*, 9 U.S. 61, 88 (1809): "As our ideas of a corporation, its privileges and its disabilities, are derived entirely from the English books, we resort to them for aid, in ascertaining its character. It is defined as a mere creature of the law, invisible, intangible, and incorporeal. Yet, when we examine the subject further, we find that corporations have been included within terms of description appropriated to real persons."

41 17 U.S. 518, 652–4.

But narratives of corporate privatization tell only part of the story. Even within the *Dartmouth College* decision there was never a clean break with the corporation's public character. To see this, consider the rich seam of semantic ambiguity contained in the concept "public."[42] On the one hand, there is the question of whether the state can control the inner workings of the corporation, which earlier grant theory had said it can do: what the state gives, it can take away. This was the State of New Hampshire's argument: we can radically revise the college's charter because there is always an implied power for public authorities to control public things. The Court seemingly rejects that theory when it holds that the college charter is a type of private right protected from interference by the Contracts Clause. But we need to read the case in full. The Court in *Dartmouth College* only *seems* to banish corporate publicness with its invention of corporate private rights. The private corporate rights were protected here only because the existing charter failed to include a clause reserving the sovereign's right to revoke or alter the charter. Private contractual rights gifted to the charter recipient could be legislatively abrogated by the simple device of placing language reserving such legislative power in the charter itself.[43] So in the heart of this early "privatization" decision there was clear protection for legislative powers.

On the other hand, the Court in *Dartmouth College* also adverts to a more expansive sense of publicness, one that includes the *positive social benefits of the corporation*. This emergent utilitarian conception of publicness is key to understanding the corporation's modern role as biopolitical institution that manages affairs of state that will increasingly be seen as problems of population management, infrastructural development, and so on. This sense of publicness is reflected in the Court's puzzlement over a key theoretical issue in the case: the question of contractual requirement for consideration. In order for the corporate charter to fit into the ambit of the Contracts Clause, it would need to be a contract as traditionally understood. And for this to be the case, there would need to be an exchange. As every first-year law student knows, today we call that quid pro quo exchange "consideration." In an ordinary commercial contract, the consideration is usually easy to see: seller parts with a bushel of wheat and buyer parts with $20. The wheat and the $20 are each consideration; they form the basis of the bargain. But how does consideration work in a corporate grant? In a corporate grant, it is obvious that the grantee is receiving something of value: the exclusive corporate franchise. But what does the sovereign receive in return?

---

42   616–17.
43   712.

The answer is that the sovereign receives net social utility, in our modern terms. This sense is reflected in Justice Marshall's comment that "[t]he objects for which a corporation is created are universally such as the government wishes to promote. They are deemed beneficial to the country; and this benefit constitutes the consideration, and in most cases, the sole consideration of the grant."[44] The problem with the corporate privatization story is that it focuses too narrowly on liberal law's own theoretical account of the private corporation, from which it draws very broad conclusions about the laissez-faire nature of American law. *Dartmouth College* established a private theory of the corporation, but that tells us very little about the corporation's social role within capitalism, nor does it even solve the narrower legal problem of when private rights are operative when challenged by the police power. It does not account for the social function of the corporation, or rather, for the fact that the economic function of the corporation relates not just to its private rights within capitalism, but also to its role in social provision via public/private *oikonomia*.

Charles River Bridge (1837) shows a similarly conflicted public/private theory of the corporation.[45] The holding of *Charles River Bridge* seemingly changes course dramatically from the private-rights theory of the corporation announced in *Dartmouth College*. The original grant in *Charles River* was given to the corporation in 1785 in order for it to build and operate a bridge. Massachusetts created a corporation in 1828 to build another bridge very close to the Charles River Company bridge that the original grantees claimed would destroy the value of their contract and would thus violate the Contracts Clause.[46] The Court begins with the public nature of the original grant and reasons that "public grants are to be construed strictly."[47] The 1785 grant did not imply a right to be free from any potential economic competition caused by future development. The corporation, in other words, did not have the right in perpetuity to enjoy a monopoly that could be implied by the exclusive nature of the original grant. The police power of the state had to trump the claims of the corporate proprietor or else the business of constructing a national infrastructure would essentially be impossible:

> But the object and end of all government is to promote the happiness and prosperity of the community by which it is established; and it can never be

---

44 637.
45 38 U.S. 420.
46 38 U.S. 420, 537.
47 38 U.S. 420, 546.

assumed, that the government intended to diminish its power of accomplishing the end for which it was created. And in a country like ours, free, active and enterprising, continually advancing in numbers and wealth, new channels of communication are daily found necessary, both for travel and trade, and are essential to the comfort, convenience and prosperity of the people.[48]

This hymn to the infrastructural public interest is not surprising. It was during the 1830s that the first real push for public/private corporate infrastructure development would get under way.[49] One thing is clear, however: Justice Taney's legal resolution of the conflict between existing grantees and newcomers is no resolution at all. It tells us nothing in its own terms about when existing private rights must yield to the exigencies of public interest. But it does tell us that the liberal narrative that the corporation was privatized in the laissez-faire nineteenth century needs revision.[50]

Modern corporate capitalism emerged at the turn of the twentieth century.[51] It was well understood that the large business corporations that were beginning to dominate American life were primarily vehicles for shareholder profit.[52] At the same time, however, the political status of corporations continued to cause controversy. The overwhelming concern for Progressive Era thinkers and politicians was the existence of a concentrated and unchecked private power that threatened to subvert democracy, which is precisely the argument proffered by twenty-first-century critics of the corporation. Louis Brandeis, striking the usual republican chords, railed against corporate oligarchy and the money power, the same subversion by which "Caesar became master of Rome. The makers of our own Constitution had in mind like dangers to our political liberty when they provided so carefully for the separation

---

48 38 U.S. 420, 547.
49 John Lauritz Larson, *Internal Improvement: National Public Works and the Promise of Popular Government in the Early United States* (Chapel Hill: University of North Carolina Press, 2001), 233–40.
50 See Novak, *The People's Welfare*, 105–13.
51 See Martin Sklar, *The Corporate Reconstruction of American Capitalism, 1890–1916: The Market, the Law, and Politics* (Cambridge: Cambridge University Press, 1988).
52 See for example *Dodge v. Ford Motor Co.*, 170 N.W. 668, 684 (Mich. 1919): "A business corporation is organized and carried on primarily for the profit of the stockholders. The powers of the directors are to be employed for that end. The discretion of directors is to be exercised in the choice of means to attain that end and does not extend to a change in the end itself, to the reduction of profits or to the nondistribution of profits among stockholders in order to devote them to other purposes."

of governmental powers."[53] Indeed, the effects of corporate power on the democratic process, on the vanishing world of small-producer capitalism and on the larger consumer marketplace, led a generation to develop Progressive regulatory law. There was no question that the business corporation was a brute fact of social and political life under modern capitalism. But in terms of developing a theoretical framework for taming the corporation, liberal law was no closer to a final resolution of the public/private question than it had been at the time of the Marshall Court, despite the development of corporate personhood at the end of the nineteenth century. In retrospect, for example, the *Lochner* case seems to have been a rearguard action within the emerging Progressive theory of state-based governance and the primacy of public over private rights. There was no principled legal line to be drawn between the private rights of contract and the state's regulation of the public good under its police powers, a point made succinctly in Justice Holmes's *Lochner* dissent.[54]

As twentieth-century law advanced, pragmatists and legal realists attacked the private-rights theory associated with Lockean liberalism with a remodelled regulatory approach intended to counter claims that broad regulatory powers were per se illegitimate. Everywhere nominalism and formalism were under attack. Writing in the legal realist period, for example, John Dewey argued against the conceptual metaphysics that sought an unchanging essence for corporate personhood in "natural entity" theories.[55] Corporate personhood, he flatly stated, "signified what the law makes it signify" and is grounded in the underlying social relations that law exists to advance.[56] Metaphysical speculation about the true nature of corporate personhood was beside the point. Legal realist attacks on the sanctity of property and contract led to new theoretical formations that opened space to develop theories of private power, something that classical liberalism typically rejects as a matter of principle outside of very narrow cases of force and fraud.[57]

In 1932, Adolf A. Berle and Gardiner Means theorized that the modern business corporation was revolutionizing the property system by

---

53 D.L. Brandeis, *Other People's Money and How the Bankers Use It* (New York: Frederick A. Stokes Company, 1914), 6.

54 *Lochner v. New York*, 25 S. Ct. 539, 546–7 (1905).

55 Dewey, "The Historic Background of Corporate Legal Personality," *Yale Law Journal* 35:6 (1926), 655–73.

56 Ibid., 655.

57 See Robert Lee Hale, "Coercion and Distribution in a Supposedly Non-coercive State," *Political Science Quarterly* 38, no. 3 (1923): 470–94; Morris Cohen, "Property and Sovereignty," *Cornell Law Quarterly* 13, no. 1 (1927): 8–30.

dividing corporate ownership and control.[58] Berle and Means' corporation separated corporate ownership from control and asserted that the primary responsibility of managers is to shareholders. But in frankly acknowledging the social nature of the corporation, their account opened the door to the corporate social responsibility movement, which triggered bouts of apoplexy in early neoliberals such as Milton Friedman.[59] Nonetheless, since the emergence of the transnational corporation in the mid-twentieth century, the personified corporation has generated its own vast philosophical literature on corporate social responsibility, which asks this question: If the corporation is a person, what are its obligations?[60] Despite attempts to depersonalize the corporation by reframing it as merely a "nexus of contracts" and nothing more, it is clear that the corporation in its many guises is the institution that governs our lives.[61]

Neoliberalism, the Entrepreneur, and Human Capital Theory

This section brings these questions into sharper relief by focusing on contemporary neoliberalism, in particular on the idea of the entrepreneur as a central feature of neoliberal social ordering. Joshua Barkan argues that recent critiques of corporatization viewing it as a creature of neoliberalism are missing the deep and long-standing public/private entanglements this chapter has been mapping out.[62] This point is especially relevant to our current anti-corporate rhetoric that frames the problem as "corporations versus democracy." The problem is that anti-corporate critiques often rely on a binary model of state and market, where neoliberalism is represented as a straightforward displacement of the former by the latter.[63] The view that neoliberalism is

---

58 A.A. Berle and G.C. Means, *The Modern Corporation and Private Property* (New York: Transaction Publishers, [1932]2008).

59 Milton Friedman, "The Social Responsibility of Business Is to Increase Its Profits," *New York Times Magazine*, 13 September 1970, 32–3, 122–4.

60 There is a well-developed literature on corporate personhood and corporate responsibility. See for example Peter French, "The Corporation as a Moral Person," *American Philosophical Quarterly* 16, no. 3 (1979): 207–15; Michael J. Phillips, "Corporate Moral Personhood and Three Conceptions of the Corporation," *Business Ethics Quarterly* 2, no. 4 (1992); William S. Laufer, *Corporate Bodies and Guilty Minds: The Failure of Corporate Criminal Liability* (Chicago:: University of Chicago Press, 2006).

61 Melvin Eisenberg, "The Conception That the Corporation Is a Nexus of Contracts, and the Dual Nature of the Firm," *Journal of Corporation Law* 24 (1999): 819–36.

62 Barkan, *Corporate Sovereignty*, loc. 2347–70.

63 Ibid., loc. 2360; see also Philip Mirowski, *Never Let a Crisis Go to Waste: How Neoliberalism Survived the Financial Meltdown* (New York: Verso, 2014), 16–18.

a straightforward project of laissez-faire deregulation, however, needs to be abandoned. Neoliberalism has led not to an unregulated world, but rather to its reregulation under alternative forms of political control and force.[64] I have been arguing that corporations have deep roots in Anglo-American political rationality that suggest a much longer trajectory than the neoliberal timetable, with its emphasis on the Reagan/ Thatcher years, typically allows. Corporate and political sovereignty have been "ontologically linked" since the earliest moments in political economy.[65] The linkages can be traced throughout the early modern period, beginning with British imperialism, colonization, and the franchise model of sovereignty discussed above. In the eighteenth and nineteenth centuries, it can be traced through the many forms of enterprise that built American infrastructure, exercised police powers, and ultimately morphed into the large-scale enterprises that now dominate our world. But neoliberal theories and practices have changed how the individual, the state, and the corporation relate to one another. They've done so not least by gradually redefining a state-based redistributive idea of the public good that had taken hold during the late nineteenth to the mid-twentieth centuries and transforming it into a price theory of the consumer good organized around utility maximization and efficiency.

The key to understanding the continuing social role of the corporation and the corporate colonization of everyday life is to grasp that neoliberalism's claims to be a system of laissez-faire cannot be taken at face value. Neoliberalism does not abandon the idea of the common good; rather, neoliberalism *redefines* the common good as an aggregate of private, self-directed transactions integral to the functioning of a liberal market state. The corporation is an institution of governance to advance the public good under neoliberalism, but in the sense that neoliberalism considers capitalism to be in the public good. To put it another way, it is a mistake to think that neoliberalism has abandoned the idea of the public good. It retains a belief in the collective good but now as a corporate good, which it frames in the putatively value-free reasoning characteristic of positive economics. It is important to remember that the neoliberal colonization of the political by the economic has its origins in a principled mid-century project, developed in the shadow of fascism and totalitarianism: to pre-empt the emergence of populist resentments that for neoliberalism (then and now) lead us down

---

64 Ibid., 57: "In practice, 'deregulation' always cashes out as 'reregulation,' only under a different set of ukases."

65 Barkan, *Corporate Sovereignty*, loc.92.

a "road to serfdom."[66] For neoliberals, when corporations maximize profits they are advancing the public good in the only way that can guarantee long-term political stability and prosperity. Unlike the caricatured view of neoliberalism, it does not offer just a stale laissez-faire defence of private power and the negative state. Instead, neoliberalism offers a principled defence of the vitality of the marketplace as the most important mechanism for advancing individual and collective welfare. For neoliberalism, capitalism *is* democracy. To ensure the flourishing of consumer democracy, however, political democracy and legislative power must be kept in check. Thus when public choice theorists attack the "rent-seeking" tendencies of the state, for example, they offer the inherently competitive marketplace as a ready-made cure.[67]

To remake an emerging corporate capitalist order into the final word on the meaning of "democracy" would require a radical reconstruction of liberal theory. It was precisely this vision that an international group of intellectuals began to develop in the 1930s.[68] The early neoliberal theorists understood that people would need to be prepared to face the risks and uncertainties of the capitalist marketplace. This project would involve a *principled* economization of society and would scuttle the dangerously "totalitarian" idea of a public interest that is not reducible to the consumer marketplace. Neoliberalism substitutes metrics and price theory for normative politics in the belief that only a technocracy and a very thin procedural definition of democracy can offer proof against fascist and totalitarian temptations. A central innovation of Chicago School neoliberalism was to replace normative judgment, "about which men could only fight," in Milton Friedman's words, with positivist social science and quantitative methods.[69] Technocracy promises a value-neutral methodology grounded in utilitarian welfare economics. The neoliberal future would be corporate in the sense that the dominant discourses of the future would transform all non-economic rationales into economic ones, but they would do so in a principled way by banishing destabilizing normative questions to the margins as a matter of sound social management. Reducing the political to the economic is a moral stance that purports to serve the wealth-maximizing rationale at the heart of liberal utilitarianism. This project has largely succeeded in

---

66   F.A. Hayek, *The Road to Serfdom* (Chicago: University of Chicago Press, [1944]2007).

67   See Matt Titolo, "The Jargon of Corruption," *Southwestern Law Review* 43, no. 4 (2014): 591–603.

68   Mirowski and Plehwe, *The Road from Mont Pèlerin*, 1–42.

69   Milton Friedman, *Essays in Positive Economics* (Chicago: University of Chicago Press, 1953), 328.

capturing public policy discourse, but not without leaving a troubling remainder or residue of irreducible normativity in its wake.

Part of the principled economization of politics would be rational choice methodology.[70] Neoclassical economics is at the centre of this project. Classical liberalism is built on the split between economy and society, with economics treating social phenomena as exogenous to the market. As William Davies argues: "Neo-classical economics, which rests on the assumption that value resides in the optimal satisfaction of stable and exogeneous individual preferences, has been one of the foremost techniques via which economization has proceeded, especially thanks to the work of the Chicago school of economics. Various other techniques of social and political audit, quantification and risk management have followed in its wake."[71] Among other things, neoliberal theory is a radical and utopian rethinking of the subject.[72] It has involved a disenchantment of private and public life by economic rationality. And it has involved a shift in corporate sovereignty that does not so much anthropomorphize the corporation (this was present long before neoliberalism) as it does "corporatize" the individual and its household – its *oikos*.

Perhaps, then, it is not only that the corporation has become a person that is objectionable to the left-liberal account, but also that the person has become a corporation. Turning the *oikos* into a competitive enterprise modelled on the corporation requires a radical reframing of life, a new ontological picture of capitalism and of the individual's relationship to market, the state, and society. The neoliberals want to neutralize destabilizing normative and political questions by turning them into questions of measurement. Thus, positivism grounds the neoliberal enterprise and serves as its mechanism for displacing normative questions to the margins (from which, as I mentioned earlier, they continue to haunt neoliberalism.)[73] One might say in this regard that neoliberalism is a Weberian innovation within capitalism in which instrumental rationality becomes a model for human life in general, in which all activities are revealed to be market activities, a logic that is then aggressively injected into previously uncolonized areas (love, marriage,

70 For a general account of public choice and rational choice theory, see S.M. Amadae, *Rationalizing Capitalist Democracy: The Cold War Origins of Rational Choice Theory* (Chicago: University of Chicago Press, 2003).
71 Davies, *The Limits of Neoliberalism*, loc. 604.
72 See Michel Foucault, *The Birth of Biopolitics: Lectures at the Collège de France: 1978–1979*, ed. Michel Senellart, trans. Graham Burchell (New York: Picador, 2008), 101–231.
73 Davies, *The Limits of Neoliberalism*, 429–59.

religion, etc.) once thought to be the province of enchantment.[74] But where Max Weber saw disenchantment as a condition to be born with resignation, neoliberals will scrub it of its negative valence. The disenchantment of the lifeworld and of politics is grounded in a utopian theory of technocratic management and individual empowerment.

Neoliberal theory will not need to succeed fully in this utopian project of disenchantment. It needs to be "just good enough" to provide ready-made explanations for contemporary problems.[75] So for example neoliberal executive power will save financial capitalism by invoking a "state of exception" that abolishes financial competition for a time by fiat even if its hypercompetitive logic cannot justify doing so in an internally consistent way.[76] As we saw vividly illustrated in the bailouts and restructurings of 2008, democratic protocols take a back seat to financial institutions when necessary to save the system, just as Hayek would have wanted. Rankings, metrics, and price become the machinery of value. Explanations can be crafted around exigencies.

Neoliberal theory will approach this task by developing the linkages between self, family, and firm, anchoring them in the risk-bearing private project of entrepreneurial enterprise. One such node in that network of ideas is Gary Becker's "human capital theory," a concept that has been smoothly incorporated into neoliberal analysis and has now made its way out into everyday business talk.[77] Another is the entrepreneur, a concept that migrated from Schumpeter's economic sociology to the "managerial vulgate" in the 1970s and '80s.[78] Indeed, the entrepreneur dominates the neoliberal social vision, redefining personhood, political agency, and citizenship. In its starkest form, neoliberalism strives to reduce as much of life as possible to entrepreneurial striving and competition. On this view, to be a person is to be engaged in a lifelong project of self-making via the educative process of the market.[79] To be responsible subjects, we must invest our human capital in productive enterprises centred on the self-sufficient household. The bundle of characteristics we once quaintly called the self will be refigured as our "human capital portfolio," which we will be required by the capitalist state to manage as entrepreneurial pioneers of our own enterprises. Neoliberalism is not simply laissez-faire

---

74   Ibid., loc. 266–338.
75   Ibid., 266–338.
76   Ibid., loc. 3633–4.
77   Gary Becker, *Human Capital: A Theoretical and Empirical Analysis, with Special Reference to Education*, 3rd ed. (Chicago: University of Chicago Press, 1993).
78   Dardot and Laval, *The New Way of the World*, 118.
79   Ibid., 111.

rebooted, an attitude of indifference to private life. Nor is it an unqualified form of market fundamentalism. It has always been a state-centred project that has recruited the corporation for the work of managing populations on behalf of capital. Indeed, from the perspective of elite policy, one might say that neoliberalism in the twentieth century was a program for capturing the state for the purpose of saving capitalism from democratic and collectivist challenges on the left and the right.

One irony in neoliberalism's pragmatic use of the entrepreneur to anchor capitalism in the household is that Schumpeter himself was not so optimistic that the corporation would save capitalism. Big, bureaucratic corporations are a problem for neoliberalism. Schumpeter worried that the large business corporation would smother innovation and ultimately doom the generative power of capitalist creativity to bureaucratic mediocrity. *Capitalism, Socialism, and Democracy* (1942) advanced a dire prognosis: under conditions of modern corporatism, the spiritual zeal and generative power of capitalism would be crushed under the power of corporate administration.[80] To put it another way, the efficient administration of corporate capitalism would lead to mediocrity and stagnation, stifling the entrepreneur's creative/generative power.[81] Schumpeter's entrepreneur is a dying breed of Nietzschean aristocrat on the verge of extinction by mass society, bureaucratic socialism, and intellectual resentment. Schumpeter's view is ultimately tragic: the vigorous creative energies of the true adventurer would disappear into the Weberian iron cage of modern capitalist rationality, of life administered by statist corporations. Contemporary neoliberalism, by contrast, favours an optimistic business boosterism that would democratize the entrepreneur: "Every individual has something entrepreneurial about them and the distinguishing feature of the market economy is that it liberates and stimulates human 'entrepreneurship'... This struggle is contagious. People imitate the best, become ever more alert."[82] The entrepreneur serves as a social ethic, the marketplace as the site of *agon* and struggle through which we test ourselves, thereby making us more successful in work, love, family, religion, and so on. By implication, any failures are our own.

So perhaps the old radical slogan is correct: the personal *is* political, just not always in the way that radicalism had hoped. The neoliberal self and its *oikos*, like the entrepreneurial corporate firm, is adaptable and resilient,

---

80   Josef Schumpeter, *Capitalism, Socialism and Democracy* (New York: Harper and Brothers, 1942).
81   For an overview of Schumpeter's thought, see Jerry Z. Muller, *The Mind and the Market: Capitalism in Western Thought* (New York: Anchor Books, 2002), 288–316.
82   Dardot and Laval, *The New Way of the World*, 111, 113.

on the lookout for new opportunities and always ready to internalize failure. To believe otherwise is to accept moral hazard and mediocrity. Risk-taking, and trial and error over many iterations, reduce the unknown to the manageably uncertain.[83] The important point for neoliberalism is that entrepreneurial habits must be ingrained and unconscious. This requires an ongoing project of ideological education: "To enable everyone to become genuine subjects of the market presupposes combating those who criticize capitalism. This battle, incumbent on intellectuals, is indispensable in that ideologies have a major influence on the orientation of individual action."[84] Like any enterprise, our personal firms must be adaptable, flexible, and mobile: always responsive to constant change. We must invest in our corporate enterprise as a going concern, always ready to accept risk and uncertainty as part of the natural order of things. Under human capital theory, the self is reduced to a résumé, a portfolio of endowments to be profitably invested. Here, neoliberalism offers us a devil's bargain: if we are willing to internalize market norms and to naturalize the protocols of the corporation, we will not experience alienation from our labor. The self-as-corporation is just part of the order of things in our social contract.

One source for anti-corporate critique is a deep revulsion for this way of life, the permanent hustle. Living the life of perpetual entrepreneurial competition is not natural, as public choice has always made clear in its image of man as rent-seeker, always on the lookout for a sinecure. We must be constantly prompted to be competitive. Our natural tendency, neoliberals tell us, is to insure ourselves against the worst risks by letting other people bear them in the form of "confiscatory" schemes of redistribution and state capture (a concern held over from classical liberal theory's antipathy to mercantilism). Without proper neoliberal management in the form of the entrepreneurial firm, it's rent-seeking all the way down. If we are to run our own corporate firms, our *oikos*, we must be bred to a life of uncertainty, exactly as Walter Lippmann had argued in *The Good Society*, a 1937 book that helped launch the "neoliberal thought collective."[85] The new liberalism that Lippmann and his cohort mapped out would be a positive, active force, manufacturing new subjects able to live harmoniously with the rhythms of capitalist life.[86]

---

83 Frank Knight, *Risk, Uncertainty, and Profit* (Mineola: Dover, [1921]2006).
84 Dardot and Laval, *The New Way of the World*, 114.
85 Mirowski and Plehwe, *The Road from Mont Pèlerin*, 4–6.
86 "Neo-liberalism was based on the dual observation that capitalism had inaugurated a period of permanent revolution in the economic order, but that human beings were not spontaneously adapted to this changing market order because they had been formed in a different world." Dardot and Laval, *The New Way of the World*, 65.

By the 1920s, the early neoliberals understood that theories of the negative state failed to capture the everyday work of governance. The state could not be treated as an afterthought. Liberalism simply hadn't kept pace with historical changes since the time of Adam Smith. To govern modern populations within a framework of capitalism, a new liberalism would need a new anthropology. As Lippmann wrote:

> The economy requires not only that the quality of the human stock, the equipment of men for life, shall be maintained at some minimum of efficiency, but that the quality should be progressively improved. To live successfully in a world of the increasing interdependence of specialized work requires a continual increase of adaptability, intelligence, and of enlightened understanding of the reciprocal rights and duties, benefits and opportunities, of such a way of life."[87]

A new theory of capitalism would embrace an evolutionary process through which people learn the moral discipline required to live as self-regulating economic subjects. In a sense, Lippmann was attempting to confront the collapsed fortunes of liberalism in the 1930s by reviving eighteenth-century *doux commerce* theory.[88] But there is a key difference: in this new theory, markets and commerce still civilize people, but now they will require an active corporate state, which will work to transform us into neoliberal subjects. To believe otherwise is to abandon "the social" to dangerous populist forces.

This means that the neoliberal state cannot be hands-off. It must integrate subjects and head off socialized unhappiness and discontent with the liberal order. A well-functioning corporate enterprise will not be alienated in any aspect of its life. It must learn to love the things that make it miserable. Ideally, it must learn not to be made miserable by them at all.[89] The macro and micro corporations that constitute our version of the social are compelled to be happy and healthy. For us, happiness is not optional: it is a mandate. Perhaps this is our version of the long-standing metaphor of the health of the body politic. Every

---

87 Walter Lippman, *An Inquiry into the Principles of the Good Society* (Boston: Little, Brown, 1937), 213.

88 Dardot and Laval, *The New Way of the World*, 69–70 (locating Lippmann in the tradition of Hume and Ferguson and the theory that commerce civilizes people). For a classic statement of *doux* commerce theory, see Albert O. Hirschmann, "Rival Interpretations of Market Society: Civilizing, Destructive, or Feeble," *Journal of Economic Literature* (1982): 1463–84.

89 William Davies, *The Happiness Industry: How the Government and Big Business Sold Us Well-Being* (New York: Verso, 2015).

macrosystemic problem must be framed as one that can be solved by correct corporate entrepreneurial planning and by responsiveness to ever-changing conditions. The thought that perhaps we can master the conditions themselves through collective action is taken off the table as either impractical or morally undesirable. Better for the entrepreneurial *oikos* to manage its portfolio of assets and price the risks of life as much as possible as an autarkic enterprise. After all, any other result would distort incentives by introducing moral hazards into social life. We can see this logic at work in the various neoliberal reform movements of our time: welfare reform, social security reform, education reform. Everywhere the neoliberal declares: Average is over! Competition is universal![90] So to the extent possible neoliberalism dismantles systems that "hide" or displace social risks and costs elsewhere in the system. Welfare reform is an urgent moral necessity for neoliberals because removing state support and encourages the poor to be responsible investors in their own human capital funds. Public goods are fragmented into countless personal investment options, and learning to embrace the risk inherent in that model is an existential ethic in itself. These risks should be finely calibrated to make us, like the capitalist firms we must become, responsible for our fortunes so that we internalize as much as possible the cost of our own material reproduction. We are all corporations now.

Conclusion

The left should continue to fight for the decolonization of social life by economizing logic, for which the corporation has become convenient if sometimes misleading shorthand. It should also build movements to recapture the state and to challenge concentrated private power and the erosion of democratic norms, even if these had always really been honoured in the breach under liberal capitalism. Challenging neoliberal hegemony, however, is more than a matter of depersonalizing the corporation or reviving republican rhetoric. Anti-corporate critique will need to develop an historical approach that comprehends how intermingled corporate forms and economizing logic are with our everyday lives. My focus in this chapter has been on the experience of the United States. Many more stories could be told, of course, not only about the American experience, but also about the uneven and contradictory

---

90 Tyler Cowen, *Average Is Over: Powering America beyond the Age of the Great Stagnation* (New York: Dutton, 2013).

mapping of neoliberalism across the globe.[91] If we follow the example of American critics such as Wendy Brown for whom democracy is an aspirational answer to the neoliberal problematics represented by *Citizens United*, corporatization, privatization, and so on, we will need to think in a more sustained way about how neoliberalism has become a way of life for us.[92]

If recapturing the state from neoliberal elites is a long-term goal for the left, anti-corporate rhetoric will have its uses as a mobilizing electoral force, as it has since the nineteenth century. But mobilizing rhetoric must yield to sustained genealogical analysis where the question is how extensive and deeply rooted neoliberal governance strategies really are. Households, selves, and entire economies have been remade along neoliberal lines. When we view ourselves as competitive selves, as risk-bearing managers of our *oikos*, we reproduce in our everyday lives the macropolitical world we hope to challenge. My view is that anti–laissez-faire rhetoric, with its implication that more legal regulation provides a counterweight to neoliberalism, really misses the extent to which neoliberalism has always been a project of reregulating society through various institutions, such as corporations, not a project of "letting alone." Radical critics of neoliberalism and corporatization will need to think about how the building blocks of neoliberal *oikonomia* have insinuated themselves into our everyday lives and whether in the last instance the urgent task of recapturing the democratic process and the state from neoliberal elites will, without a larger social revolution, really achieve the promise of democracy.

---

91 See Ahwa Ong, *Neoliberalism as Exception: Mutations in Citizenship and Sovereignty* (Chapel Hill: Duke University Press, 2006).

92 William Connolly, *The Fragility of Things: Self-Organizing Processes, Neoliberal Fantasies, and Democratic Activism* (Durham: Duke University Press, 2013).

2 Cosmopolitanism, Sovereignty, and the Problem of Corporate Personhood

JOSHUA BARKAN

In a moment when the geopolitical order is experiencing a crisis associated with refugees and migrants, Hannah Arendt's formulation of the "perplexities" of rights remains as timely as ever.[1] Arendt, writing in the aftermath of the Second World War, famously characterized the predicament of marginalized minority populations rendered stateless during the interwar period as one in which the "depravation of a place in the world which makes opinions significant and actions effective"[2] established the conditions of possibility for stripping people of human rights, including the right to live. Because rights in Western political and legal thought, at least since the eighteenth century, have been guaranteed through the constitutions of nation-states, denationalization policies and the expulsion of individuals from constituted political orders set those individuals not only outside of territorial borders, but also outside spheres of right and law. Additionally, the fact that nation-states failed to guarantee rights that were everywhere

---

1 Hannah Arendt, *The Origins of Totalitarianism* (New York: Harcourt, 1968). On the current migration crisis stemming from the wars in Syria, Afghanistan, and Iraq and variously qualified as "European," "Greek," or "Syrian," see Melissa Fleming, "Statement by UN High Commissioner for Refugees, António Guterres on refugee crisis in Europe," UNHCR Press Release, 4 September 2015, http://www.unhcr.org/en-us/news/press/2015/9/55e9459f6. Major media outlets, including the *New York Times*, the BBC, the *Financial Times*, the *Washington Post*, *The Economist*, the *Wall Street Journal*, and *The Guardian*, among others, have picked up the UNHCR's language of crisis. See for instance "Countries under the Most Strain in Europe's Migration Crisis," *New York Times*, 28 August 2015; Anemona Hartocollis, "Traveling in Europe's River of Migrants," *New York Times*, 27 August–1 September 2015; "Migrant Crisis Divides Europe," *Wall Street Journal*, 3 September 2015; "Europe's Boat People," *The Economist*, 25 April 2015; "How to Manage the Migrant Crisis," *The Economist*, 6 February 2016.
2 Arendt, *The Origins of Totalitarianism*, 296.

proclaimed to be self-evident, inalienable, and grounded in human nature portended, in Arendt's estimation, future problems. Unable to legally distinguish "what is right" from "the notion of what is good,"[3] Arendt demonstrated that grounding law in humanity, which had by that point "assumed the role formerly ascribed to nature or history"[4] as the self-authorizing justification of legal authority, still contained the possibility to abandon individuals or even whole populations for the sake of the community. Putting the perplexity of rights bleakly, she warned that "it is quite conceivable, and even within the realm of practical political possibilities, that one fine day a highly organized and mechanized humanity will conclude quite democratically – namely by majority decision – that for humanity as a whole it would be better to liquidate certain parts thereof."[5]

Given that contemporary geopolitics remains haunted by the spectre of this liquidation, prominent political and legal theorists have turned toward concepts of cosmopolitan rights and norms of justice as a way of responding to the paradox Arendt outlined. For scholars like David Held, Daniele Archibugi, Kwame Anthony Appiah, Ulrich Beck, James Bohman, and Seyla Benhabib, among others, cosmopolitanism offers a mechanism for protecting vulnerable populations.[6] These academic discussions have broken through to the popular press. For instance, Zygmut Bauman, discussing the current refugee crisis in the *New York Times,* argued that the crisis is "humanity's" and advocated cosmopolitan political and legal reforms as necessary for ameliorating the conditions of refugees.[7] The appeal of cosmopolitanism rests

---

3 Ibid., 299.
4 Ibid., 298.
5 Ibid., 299.
6 David Held, *Democracy and the Global Order: From the Modern State to Cosmopolitan Governance* (Stanford: Stanford University Press, 1995); Daniele Archibugi and David Held, eds., *Cosmopolitan Democracy: An Agenda for a New World Order* (Cambridge: Polity Press, 1995); Daniele Archibugi, ed. *Debating Cosmopolitics* (London: Verso, 2003); Kwame Anthony Appiah, *Cosmopolitanism: Ethics in a World of Strangers* (New York: W.W. Norton, 2006); Ulrich Beck, "Cosmopolitan Manifesto," *New Statesman* 127, no. 4337 (1998); Ulrich Beck, *Cosmopolitan Vision* (Cambridge: Polity Press, 2006); James Bohman, "Republican Cosmopolitanism," *Journal of Political Philosophy* 12, no. 3 (2004): 336–52; James Bohman, *Democracy across Borders: From Dêmos to Dêmoi* (Cambridge, MA: MIT Press, 2007); Seyla Benhabib, *The Rights of Others: Aliens, Residents, and Citizens* (Cambridge: Cambridge University Press, 2004); Seyla Benhabib, *Another Cosmopolitanism* (Oxford: Oxford University Press, 2006).
7 Brad Evans and Zygmut Bauman, "The Refugee's Crisis is Humanity's Crisis," *New York Times*, 2 May 2016, http://www.nytimes.com/2016/05/02/opinion/the-refugee-crisis-is-humanitys-crisis.html.

on the promise of institutionalized legal rights for persons irrespective of their citizenship or geographic location. As Seyla Benhabib has framed it, "cosmopolitan norms of justice, whatever the condition of their legal origination, accrue to individuals as *moral and legal persons* in a worldwide society."[8] Such institutionalization is important because, particularly under contemporary dynamics of globalization, social relations and social processes often transcend the territorial boundaries of nation-states. Thus, confronted with the growth of displaced persons, refugees, and other populations that state-based systems of law and right have failed to protect, cosmopolitans ask how the universal moral norms granted to people based solely on their status as moral agents or persons can be transformed into claims that establish legal rights and obligations beyond the territorial boundaries of existing jurisdictions.

The difficulty that remains is how to square universal moral norms with democratic processes of self-determination that are often spatially or territorially delimited. Contemporary democratic theorists have addressed the disjuncture between the bounded nature of democratic de liberation and the transnational demands for justice from a variety of angles. For some, global interconnectedness has led to new spheres of deliberation. David Held, for instance, has advocated a cosmopolitan democracy resembling the Kantian vision of a confederated system of republican nation-states with democratic processes operating within political and legal institutions at both national and international levels.[9] Others suggest that globalization has changed the nature of political community itself. Iris Marion Young has argued that economic globalization creates new forms of responsibility shaped not by the contours of state boundaries but based on our differently situated relations to the structures of the global economy.[10] James Bohman has argued for a cosmopolitan vision of democracy in which plural *dêmoi* emerge in reaction to the multiple situations of domination associated with globalization.[11] Still others suggest that cosmopolitanism cannot resolve the tension between territorially circumscribed deliberation and universal moral commitments to people. Instead, cosmopolitan norms "mediate" between irresolvable commitments to moral universalism and political and ethical particularism.[12]

---

8   Benhabib, *Another Cosmopolitanism*, 16.
9   Held, *Democracy and the Global Order*.
10 Young, "Responsibility and Global Labor Justice," *Journal of Political Philosophy* 12, no. 4 (2004): 365–88.
11 Bohman, *Democracy across Borders*.
12 Benhabib, *Another Cosmopolitanism*, 19–20.

Although these issues have dominated the discussion of cosmopolitanism, there are other ways in which the cosmopolitan commitment to persons comes into conflict with the spatio-political boundaries of the *demos*. This chapter examines cosmopolitism, not through the normal figures by which theorists address the subject (The Foreigner or The Stranger in philosophical languages; The Refugee or Asylum Seeker in the idioms of politics and law), but through another type of ambiguous legal person: the corporation. I argue that, inasmuch as cosmopolitan norms are designed to address populations abandoned, if you will, through the dynamics of contemporary globalization, the connection between right and person that cosmopolitanism relies on and deploys reiterates, rather than breaks from, a discourse that traditionally empowered corporations in their global search for profit. In particular, cosmopolitanism's linking of right and person provides a rationale and defence for the geographic mobility of capital in its corporate form – a mobility that has been central to the disenfranchisement and displacement of the self-same populations requiring cosmopolitan protections.

To make this argument, I begin with the theories grounding contemporary articulations of cosmopolitanism. From a historical standpoint, contemporary discussions of cosmopolitan right are intertwined with concerns about economic globalization. Yet as I demonstrate, concepts of global trade, commerce, and economy were already internal to the eighteenth-century theories on which modern cosmopolitanism hinges. Cosmopolitan theorists, of course, recognize this complication. For this among other reasons, I argue, contemporary cosmopolitanism has come to focus even more intensely than its eighteenth-century predecessors on the notion of personhood. Yet personhood scarcely resolves the problem. Although personhood promises a universal extension of right, personhood also contains within itself a relationship to sovereignty that allows for the exclusion of those deemed either to be lacking aspects of personhood or to pose threats to the polity. Part II of this chapter thus engages Italian philosopher Roberto Esposito's notion of depersonalization as a means of complicating cosmopolitan notions of the rights of persons. In Part III, this critique is extended specifically to corporate personhood, demonstrating that, as with cosmopolitan theory in general, personhood has long been connected to visions of trade and economic exchange, as well with certain geographical imaginations of the market. Corporate personhood matters for the types of depersonalization associated with cosmopolitanism inasmuch as cosmopolitanism presents itself as a response to and solution for displacements produced through economic globalization. Thus, the chapter concludes by showing how the corporation, as a legal embodiment of capital, complicates cosmopolitan norms of justice.

I. Economic Globalization and the New Cosmopolitanism

Cosmopolitanism has a long history, but in the 1990s a new discourse of cosmopolitanism emerged as an important element in debates over global justice among members of the democratic left. This discourse responded to the increasing salience of economic globalization and the pervasive argument that the transnational nature of the economy had undermined nation-states' abilities to govern their domestic economies and international affairs. Associated with issues ranging from migration and environmental protection to transnational production and cross-border finance, a number of books in the mid-1990s foretold the decline of national economic regulation.[13] As subsequent work on globalization made clear, such positions proved to be radically overstated. Yet they also highlighted a disjuncture between territorially ascribed political rights and the transnational aspects of the economy. At the same time, the new interest in cosmopolitanism flourished amid the declining viability of communist or socialist projects in the aftermath of the Cold War. As Timothy Brennan has pointed out, the new cosmopolitanism resonated with other notions of globalism, but supplanted concepts of internationalism connected with communist and socialist political movements.[14]

This context was readily apparent in the programmatic statements that attempted to shape the cosmopolitan political project. For instance, when Daniele Archibugi made the case for "cosmopolitical democracy" in the pages of the *New Left Review*, he argued that new approaches to regulation and justice were necessary because "many of the problems of the political organization of contemporary society go beyond the scope of the nation-state."[15] He identified three. First, he argued that states are forced to grapple with economic, environmental, and biophysical problems that fall across territorial boundaries, giving examples such as, "the US Federal Reserve's decision to raise the interest

---

13 See for instance, Kenichi Ohmae, *The End of the Nation-State: The Rise of Regional Economies* (New York: The Free Press, 1995); Manuel Castells, *The Rise of the Network Society* (Malden: Blackwell, 1996).

14 Timothy Brennan, "Cosmopolitanism and Internationalism," in *Debating Cosmopolitanism*, ed. D Archibugi (London: Verso, 2003).

15 Daniele Archibugi, "Cosmopolitical Democracy," *New Left Review* 4 (2000): 137–51, reprinted in Archibugi, ed. *Debating Cosmopolitics*, 3.

rate may provoke a substantial rise in unemployment in Mexico; the explosion of a nuclear power station in the Ukraine can trigger environmental disasters throughout Europe; the lack of prompt information about the diffusion of AIDS in Nigeria may cause epidemics throughout the world."[16] Second, Archibugi noted movements within states for "autonomy" – including the national liberation movements of the Palestinians and the Kurds, or, alternatively the post-socialist break-ups of Yugoslavia and Czechoslovakia.[17] Third, he suggested that states were troubled by mass migration to the West, which he characterized as "Turks in Berlin, Chinese in Los Angeles, Arabs in Paris, Bangladeshis in London, Vietnamese in Montreal."[18] Cosmopolitical democracy responded to these issues with attempts "to create institutions which enable the voice of individuals to be heard in global affairs, irrespective of their resonance at home."[19] Elsewhere, writing with David Held, he characterized cosmopolitics as "a model of political organization in which citizens, wherever they are located in the world, have a voice, input and political representation in international affairs, in parallel with and independently of their own governments."[20] Archibugi's vision thus involved three levels or scales of political processes and institutions – "within states, between states and at a world level"[21] – with cosmopolitics corresponding to the primacy of the world scale connecting individuals directly to international or global institutions.

As a general outline, Archibugi's brief introduction brings three elements into relief. First, it illuminates the causal processes that initiated the renewed interest into cosmopolitanism. Forms of cosmopolitan thought predate contemporary economic globalization, but almost all accounts of cosmopolitanism from the 1990s onward link problems with existing international institutions to globalization and the changing dynamics of the capitalist world system. Although not a subject of sustained empirical investigation for Archibugi in that essay, economic globalization is implicitly presented as the reason why US monetary policy impacts unemployment in Mexico and why Turkish migrants are arriving in Berlin. Others cosmopolitan theorists echo this claim. For instance, Ulrich Beck has distinguished the empirical event of cosmopolitanism from our philosophical apprehension of it, asserting that

---

16 Ibid.
17 Ibid., 4.
18 Ibid.
19 Ibid., 8.
20 Archibugi and Held, *Cosmopolitan Democracy*, 13.
21 Archibugi, "Cosmopolitical Democracy," 8.

globalization has already made us cosmopolitan, even if our legal and political institutions, or the undergirding philosophies on which they rely, have yet to recognize this fact or embrace it.[22]

Second, Archibugi's narrative converges with others in emphasizing the triadic structure of rights and treating cosmopolitanism as a level or scale above the nation-state's, one that connects people directly to international institutions. Seyla Benhabib too has described

> three interrelated but distinct levels of "right" in the juridical sense of the term. First is domestic law, the sphere of posited relations of right, which Kant claims should be in accordance with a republican constitution; second is the sphere of rightful relations among nations, resulting from treaty obligations among states; third is cosmopolitan right, which concerns relations among *civil persons* to each other as well as to organized political entities in a global civil society.[23]

Moreover, as Benhabib stresses, cosmopolitanism is distinguished by the notion that persons, rather than states or other collective bodies, have a globally valid legal standing. Nancy Fraser also treats the focus on the person as the unique reserve of cosmopolitan justice, contrasting it, on one hand, with liberal nationalist visions of justice (associated with the work of John Rawls), for whom bounded political communities like nation-states remain the primary venue for justice claims, and, on the other hand, with egalitarian internationalists, who see international obligations as primarily pertaining to political communities. For cosmopolitans, Fraser notes, "egalitarian distributive norms apply globally, among individuals, irrespective of nationality or citizenship; thus, impoverished individuals in, say, the Sudan have moral standing *qua* persons to make transborder claims for economic justice upon their fellow inhabitants of the globe."[24]

Third, the similarities in contemporary arguments for cosmopolitanism hearken back to a common origin in the political philosophy of Kant, and in particular his discussion of cosmopolitan right in two of his later works: his 1795 essay *Toward Perpetual Peace* and the third section on public rights in *The Metaphysics of Morals*, published in 1797. Both accounts maintain the triadic and interlinked structure of public

22 Beck, *Cosmopolitan Vision*.

23 Benhabib, *Another Cosmopolitanism*, 21.

24 Nancy Fraser, *Scales of Justice: Reimagining Political Space in a Globalizing World* (New York: Columbia University Press, 2009), 33–4. See also John Rawls, *The Law of Peoples* (Cambridge, MA: Harvard University Press, 1999).

rights and some semblance of the concept that peoples maintain rights irrespective of geography or jurisdiction. More interesting, however, is the content of and justification for Kantian cosmopolitanism. For Kant, cosmopolitanism established not just norms, but *rights*, entailing duties and enforceable claims. Strangers or foreigners were thus authorized to rights of hospitality when they "arrive on someone else's territory," although Kant defined this right as less than the right of "a guest to be entertained" and more simply as the absence of hostility.[25] Accordingly, one does not have to enjoy the stranger's company either morally or legally, but hosts are prohibited in both senses from treating the stranger as an enemy and exercising violence against them. Kantian cosmopolitan rights are, thus, minimal. Kant stipulated little beyond noting that we all have the ability to initiate interactions with others; and the language of possibility and potential runs throughout his account. Foreigners are entitled to "attempt" to enter into relations with hosts, and everyone has a right "*to try to* establish community with all and, to this end, to *visit* all regions of the earth."[26]

Kant justified this right – along with its attendant duties and obligations – on the basis of the "communal possession of the earth's surface which the human race shares in common."[27] By sharing the space of the globe, Kant argued, humanity has begun a process leading toward a universal community. Benhabib usefully captured Kant's orientation to the future: "hospitality is a right that belongs to all human beings insofar as we view them as *potential* participants in a world republic."[28] As Kant argued, given the limited space of the globe, cosmopolitan rights have the possibility of creating spaces for positive social, political, moral, and economic interactions: "continents distant from each other can enter into peaceful mutual relations which may eventually be regulated by public laws, thus bringing the human race nearer and nearer to a cosmopolitan constitution."[29] For this reason, his vision of a cosmopolitan system did not suggest a unified world-state, but rather a federation of republics with growing legal obligations to strangers. Kant left open the question of how such obligations come to have legal force within the federation of republican states, an issue that has preoccupied democratic theorists working in the Kantian tradition.

---

25 Immanuel Kant, "Perpetual Peace: A Philosophical Sketch," in *Kant: Political Writings*, ed. H.S. Reiss (Cambridge: Cambridge University Press, 1970), 105.
26 Immanuel Kant, *The Metaphysics of Morals* (Cambridge: Cambridge University Press, 1996), 121.
27 Kant, "Perpetual Peace," 106.
28 Benhabib, *Another Cosmopolitanism*, 24.
29 Kant, "Perpetual Peace," 106.

Given that much cosmopolitan theory responds to and hinges on assessments of economic globalization, it is important to stress that one of the models for cosmopolitan right was commerce. The market, the economy, and commercialism were all internal to Kant's formulation of cosmopolitan right in a number of ways. At the most basic level, Kant's theory of cosmopolitan right turns on the proprietary relationship persons and people have to territory. Moreover, the view of peoples as owners of the earth structures Kant's account of commerce. In one sense, Kant treated the term "commerce" as synonymous with "interaction." Thus, in *The Metaphysics of Morals,* he argues that, because we inhabit a shared globe, all nations "stand in a community of possible physical *interaction (commercium),* that is, in a thoroughgoing relation of each to all the others of *offering to engage in commerce* [*Wechselwirkung*] with any other, and each has a right to make this attempt without the other being authorized to behave towards it as an enemy because it has made this attempt."[30] Commerce, here, connotes general social exchanges, but it also carries the more specific meaning of trade. This is evident not only in the passage above, which references the conditions of Europeans engaged in international trade, but also in the movement back and forth between two German words for commerce: *Wechselwirkung*, the general term for interaction, and *Verkehr*, the more technical term for trade, commerce, or traffic.[31]

Yet Kant's ideas about trade and right were complex. For many commentators, trade is the essence of cosmopolitanism. Jeremy Waldron reads cosmopolitanism in everyday events of transnational economic linkages, such as "postal and telephone conventions, airline safety and navigation standards, the law of international trade, the practices that define the convertibility of currencies, transnational banking arrangements, weights and measures, time zones, international quarantine arrangements, and so on."[32] Sharon Byrd and Joachim Hruschka go further, arguing that "cosmopolitan law for Kant is indeed the idea of a perfect World Trade Organization."[33] But Kant's discussions of commerce

---

30 Kant, *The Metaphysics of Morals*, 121. See also Kant, *Metaphysik der Sitten,*ed. J.H. von Kirchman (Berlin: Verlag von L. Heimann, 1870), 197–9.

31 Kant, *The Metaphysics of Morals*, 121, note b. See also Pauline Kleingeld, *Kant and Cosmopolitanism: The Philosophical Ideal of World Citizenship* (Cambridge: Cambridge University Press, 2012), 75.

32 Jeremy Waldron, "Cosmopolitan Norms," in Seyla Benhabib, *Another Cosmopolitanism*, R. Post, ed. (Oxford: Oxford University Press, 2006), 83.

33 B. Sharon Byrd and Joachim Hruschka, *Kant's Doctrine of Right: A Commentary* (Cambridge: Cambridge University Press, 2010), 7.

were more nuanced than these comments suggest. In the first supplement to *Perpetual Peace*, Kant lauded commerce as the model for world peace, suggesting that as states pursue their self-interest "the spirit of commerce sooner or later takes hold of every people, and it cannot exist side by side with war."[34] But the passages on cosmopolitan right in both *Perpetual Peace* and the *Metaphysics of Morals* also note the violence of eighteenth-century international trade and attempt to differentiate just commercial interactions from unjust ones. Kant's distinction hinges on violence, as cosmopolitan right established no rights of foreigners to settlement (*ius incolatus*), and legitimate or just settlements can only be established through contract.

Kant's formulation rebuked the violence of European colonization. He criticized "the *inhospitable* conduct of the civilized states of our continent, especially the commercial states," for "visiting foreign countries and peoples (which in their case is the same as *conquering* them)."[35] Kant railed against the colonization of the Caribbean, calling it the "stronghold of the cruellest and most calculated slavery"; even worse, it did "not yield any real profit."[36] He also chastised Dutch and British colonial incursions into India, noting that "foreign troops were brought in under the pretext of merely setting up trading posts [but] this led to oppression of the natives, incitement of the various Indian states to widespread wars, famines, insurrection, treachery and the whole litany of evils which can afflict the human race."[37]

Yet if cosmopolitan rights challenge the violence of European commercial imperialism, they also entail another relation to economy, not in terms of commerce but in terms of *oikonomia*, the law of the household, which, Derrida has argued, reading these same passages, governs the host's relation to his territory.[38] I use the gendered pronoun "his" advisedly. Derrida notes that Kant discusses the cosmopolitan right of hospitality using both the Latin term *hospitalität* and, in parenthesis, its German equivalent, *Wirtbarkeit*. For Derrida, the *Wirt* (host) in *Wirtbarkeit* is linked with the *Wirt* in *Wirtschaft* (meaning economy or an inn or pub): "economy and, thus, *oikonomia*, law of the household – where it is precisely the patron of the house – he who receives, who is master in

---

34   Kant, "Perpetual Peace," 114.
35   Ibid., 106.
36   Ibid., 107.
37   Ibid.
38   Jacques Derrida, "Hostipitality," *Angelaki: Journal of the Theoretical Humanities* 5, no. 3 (2000): 3–18. See also Derrida, *On Cosmopolitanism and Forgiveness* (New York: Routledge, 2001).

his house, in his household, in his state, in his nation, in his city, in his town, who remains master in his house – who defines the conditions of hospitality or welcome."[39] This relation of patriarchal power and mastery marks the *aporia* of hospitality, which Derrida accentuates through the neologism "hostipitality." Combining hospitality with hostility, Derrida emphasizes the ways in which unconditional giving is always conditioned by the need to maintain the relation of authority between host, as master, and guest, as supplicant.[40] It is also for this reason that hospitality, a specific type of economic relation based on hierarchies within the household, threatens to turn into its doubling opposite of hostility once those lines of authority are crossed.

Finally, it's worth noting that for other cosmopolitan theorists working in the tradition of deliberative democracy, the tension within this economy of power, in which the patriarchal model of territorial authority unravels the universal compunction to provide hospitality, has been framed not as an *impossibility* (as Derrida argues) but as a *paradox* concerning how to balance state sovereignty, particularly republican notions of self-government, with cosmopolitan norms of justice. For scholars like Benhabib, the point is not to resolve the paradox. Rather, she suggests that cosmopolitan rights gain legitimacy as they are articulated, enacted, and iterated through the legal claims of individuals. These iterations change the meaning and content of right, while also resetting the normative threshold of democratic legitimacy.[41]

Thus, to summarize, contemporary cosmopolitanism responds to conditions of globalization by articulating a minimum set of rights universally guaranteed to individuals on the basis of their personhood. The Kantian model for these rights was based substantially on the image of international trade and commerce, but it also critiqued the violence of European colonization. This tension – between commerce and colonization – is only one of the contradictions and paradoxes structuring cosmopolitan right; others include relations between hospitality and hostility, conditional versus unconditional rights, and republican self-government versus universal norms. Advocates of cosmopolitanism nonetheless argue that it establishes a normative framework for rights claims based on the universal moral standing of strangers that can move toward both democratic legitimacy and positive law.

---

39 Derrida, "Hostipitality," 4.
40 Ibid; See also Derrida, *On Cosmopolitanism and Forgiveness*; Bonie Honig, "Another Cosmopolitanism? Law and Politics in the New Europe," in Benhabib, *Another Cosmopolitanism*, ed. Post.
41 Benhabib, *Another Cosmopolitanism*; Benhabib, *The Rights of Others*.

The Rights of Persons

Part of cosmopolitanism's appeal is that it speaks to the rights, not of states, but of persons. Although contemporary theories look back to Kant, he gave relatively minimal attention to personhood as a legal category in his formulation of cosmopolitan right. Kant certainly had a concept of moral personhood connected to the use of reason. Famously, in the *Groundwork of the Metaphysics of Morals*, Kant distinguished persons as "rational beings" from things "without reason"[42] and connected the concept of the person to one of his key formulations of the categorical imperative: "act that you use humanity, whether in your own person or in the person of any other, always at the same time as an end, never merely as a means."[43] In the sections on cosmopolitan rights in *Perpetual Peace*, however, Kant primarily focused on rights accruing to foreigners or strangers, rather than the more abstract notion of persons. Kant implicitly attributed some moral agency to all peoples, recognizing the communal ownership of the earth as well as the potential of all peoples to enter into commercial exchanges.[44] Likewise, Kant's criticism of European colonization and conquest reasserted the categorical imperative, centring on the failure of European powers to recognize that "the peoples of the earth have thus entered in varying degrees into a universal community, and it has developed to the point where a violation of rights in *one* part of the world is felt *everywhere*."[45] Yet in these passages Kant ascribed reason to peoples rather than to individual persons. This focus on collectivities is likewise maintained in the discussion of cosmopolitanism in *The Metaphysics of Morals*, where cosmopolitan right is considered as a division of public right and refers to laws governing public rather than private order. Kant, again, referred to universal capacities to own land and enter into commerce, in particular describing valid and invalid forms of settlement on the "the lands of another nation."[46] But the language throughout refers to groups as opposed to individuals, incorporating peoples – including "shepherds or hunters (like the Hottentots, the Tungusi, or most of the American Indian Nations)"[47] – into the universal community, which

---

42 Immanuel Kant, *Groundwork of the Metaphysics of Morals*, ed. and trans. M. Gregor, (Cambridge: Cambridge University Press, 1998), 37.

43 Ibid., 38.

44 Kant, *Perpetual Peace*.

45 Ibid., 107–8.

46 Kant, *The Metaphysics of Morals*, 121.

47 Ibid., 122.

racist European anthropological discourses (including in Kant's earlier work) had denied.[48]

Personhood, however, became a central concern of the renewed cosmopolitan theories of the late twentieth century as a means of addressing the problems associated with statelessness and displaced persons that Arendt identified. Because, as Arendt demonstrated, statelessness was a potential that was always already contained within the frameworks of nation-states and their models of citizenship and liberal sovereignty, Arendt argued that the state-based international order was incapable of ensuring "the right to have rights" – a basic precondition for inclusion in "humanity."[49] It is in this respect that cosmopolitan discourses have converged with conceptions of human rights as a way of thinking about justice claims. In cosmopolitan theories, personhood addresses an abstract subject of right, free from the constraints of time and place as well as any social bonds that shape individuals. Personhood attempts to reach through the particulars of socially embedded lives to get at rights that inhere in our humanity rather than in our political subjectivity. As Samuel Moyn has claimed, this conception of rights for persons – rather than citizens or peoples, much less states – has arguably become the key feature of the modern human rights regime.[50] Thus, when contemporary theorists appeal to cosmopolitanism as a response to the conditions of refugees, they advocate universal legal frameworks protecting the lives of all persons in general,

---

48 On Kant's shifting notions of race see Kliengeld, *Kant and Cosmopolitanism*, esp. 111–17.

49 Arendt, *The Origins of Totalitarianism*, 296–8.

50 Samuel Moyn, *The Last Utopia: Human Rights in History* (Cambridge, MA: Harvard University Press, 2010). Moyn argues that this regime, with its focus on the rights of humans irrespective of citizenship, came into being in the 1970s with the rise of non-governmental institutions like Amnesty International, and not in 1948, with the UN Universal Declaration of Human Rights, or in the late eighteenth century, with the Enlightenment discourses of the rights of man. My claim that the focus on the rights of humans or persons is *arguably* the central element of the modern human rights regime reflects my ambivalence about Moyn's contention that the 1970s marked an epochal and basically linear transformation in the concept of rights in the international sphere. As Pheng Cheah has shown, Moyn is incorrect that the human rights of persons can be neatly demarcated from state sovereignty. See Pheng Cheah, "Human Rights and the Material Making of Humanity: A Response to Samuel Moyn's *The Last Utopia*," *Qui Parle* 22, no. 1 (2013): 57–61. Moreover, multiple renderings of rights – as combinations of privileges and duties that inhere in humans, in citizens, or in personified states – existed prior to the 1970s and continue to have their advocates today. Moreover, these tangled, rather than linear, histories are what make questions of rights and personhood interesting from a genealogical perspective.

including the vulnerable, rather than addressing the specific historical processes that produce any particular group of refugees.

Yet if personhood is central to the hopes of human rights, it is also a more complex and fraught category than contemporary cosmopolitans and advocates of human rights suggest. One could note, for instance, that even as human rights has become institutionalized in the apparatuses of international law, the number of refugees and internally displaced people has continued to increase, reaching the unprecedented total of more than 65 million people in 2015.[51] Some might respond that this simply means we have not gone far enough in ensuring the human rights of the person. Italian philosopher Roberto Esposito, however, argues exactly the opposite: "the essential failure of human rights, their inability to restore the broken connection between rights and life, does not take place in spite of the affirmation of the ideology of the person but rather *because* of it."[52] For Esposito, human rights are only the latest iteration of what he terms "the *dispositif* of the person"[53] – the apparatus of power and knowledge by which the concept of the person has come into being in fields as diverse as law, theology, anthropology, philosophy, and biology.

Tracing the genealogy of this *dispositif*, Esposito has argued that the thread running through the diverse articulations of personhood has always been a reoccurring form of separation that the person both posits and annuls. As such, personhood is one of the central categories by which Western thought has produced, grappled with, and assimilated hierarchical forms of difference. This can be seen in the Aristotelian discussion of political life with its separation between *bios* and *zoe*, famously elaborated upon by Giorgio Agamben, in which political life is treated as a category over and above that of bare life or pure animal existence.[54] But Esposito also traces the presence of this *dispositif* elsewhere: in the Roman concept of *personae* (in which personhood was connected not with the physical body but with the mask that served as a secondary representation of the individual); in Christian theology

---

51 UNHCR, *Global Trends: Forced Displacement in 2015* (Geneva: UN High Commission for Refugees, 2016).

52 Roberto Esposito, *Third Person: Politics of Life and Philosophy of the Impersonal*, trans. Zakiya Hanafi (Cambridge: Polity Press, 2012), 5.

53 See Roberto Esposito, "The *Dispositif* of the Person," *Law, Culture, and the Humanities* 8, no. 17 (2012): 17–30; Esposito, *Third Person*; Esposito, *Persons and Things: From the Body's Point of View* (Cambridge: Polity Press, 2015).

54 See Aristotle, *Politics.*, 2nd ed. ed. and trans. C. Lord (Chicago: University of Chicago Press, 2015); Giorgio Agamben, *Homo Sacer: Sovereign Power and Bare Life* (Stanford: Stanford University Press, 1998).

(connected with concepts such as the unity of the Holy Trinity or the totality of body and soul); in Cartesian rationalism (and the distinction between *res extensa* and *res cogitans*); and in racist nineteenth- and twentieth-century social biology (where racialized national bodies attempted to immunize themselves by excising and exterminating those parts deemed unfit).[55] In each case, Esposito argues, personhood establishes a hierarchical distinction between a base, physical, or animal aspect of the person and a rational or spiritual element that is, subsequently, prioritized as the essential element of personhood.[56] As such, personhood carries within itself aspects of *depersonalization* that enable the division of living bodies into differing groups and classes.[57]

This *dispositif* is also central to state sovereignty. As Esposito avers, "the notion of the person is what introduces and defines that of the sovereign state." Medievalist historian Ernst Kantorowicz recognized as much as far back as the 1950s when he examined the relations between personification and sovereignty in his magisterial study of medieval political theology, *The King's Two Bodies*.[58] Because sovereignty was a power that extended beyond the life of individual rulers, *the person* came to represent sovereignty – of, first, the Catholic Church, and, later, the secular state – in a corporate capacity, combining individuals and territory both across space and through time. Kantorowicz traced the doubling of the sovereign's body in legal texts, theological arguments, iconographic representations, and popular maxims, arguing, for instance, that even popular chants such as "Le roi est mort! Vive le roi!" captured the essentially dual nature of the sovereign's person.[59] Individual monarchs might come and go, but the king, as the corporate body of the sovereign – its *body politic* – lived on.

Esposito articulates the importance of personhood for sovereignty, not through the medieval texts and images that fascinated Kantorowicz, but by focusing on the double nature of personhood in Thomas Hobbes's account of the Leviathan. Esposito makes essentially two claims about sovereignty and personhood. First, he emphasizes the way Hobbes's account of personhood turns on issues of representation. Whereas

---

55 Esposito, "The *Dispositif* of the Person"; Esposito, *Third Person.*
56 Ibid.
57 See also Timothy Campbell and Adam Sitze, "Introduction to the Symposium on Esposito's *Dispositif* of the Person," *Law, Culture and the Humanities* 8, no. 1 (2012): 11–12.
58 Ernst Kantorowics, *The King's Two Bodies: A Study in Medieval Political Theology* (Princeton: Princeton University Press, 1957).
59 "The King is dead! Long live the King!" Ibid., 410.

in the state of nature, personhood coincides perfectly with one's living being, the passage from the state of nature into civil society initiates not one, but two new concepts of personhood, both of which are characterized by relations between interests, on the one hand, and their political representation, on the other. Thus, within civil society, Hobbes distinguishes *natural persons*, who speak for themselves and represent their own interests, from *artificial persons*, who represent "the words and actions of an other."[60] Crucially for Esposito, however, both types of personhood are never simply coextensive with living flesh-and-blood human beings. Indeed, recalling the Roman *personae* as a mask worn over the face of an actor, the central element in Hobbes's account is the way personhood always functions as a representation, whether of the self or another.

Second, by treating personhood as a representation, Hobbes is able to elevate artificial personhood – and specifically the artificial personhood of the sovereign – over all other types of persons. Given Hobbes's association with social contract theory, we might normally think of the natural person as the primary category of personhood, with the contract between natural persons temporally preceding the creation of the sovereign. Esposito argues, however, that Hobbes inverts the relation. Because all persons (including natural persons) are representations, and the sovereign, once constituted, represents all persons, the sovereign, in Hobbes's account, becomes a kind of perfect representation. Using metaphors from the stage, Hobbes presents individuals as authors that have authorized the sovereign to act as a representative in their interests. Once authorized, however, the sovereign becomes its own entity: an artificial person "entirely autonomous from the control of the authors who initially set him in place."[61] Artificial personhood becomes central to Hobbes's argument that individuals have no recourse to challenging the sovereign's decrees, as flesh-and-blood individuals are wholly "subject *to* an actor who, in interpreting their role, strips them of any decision making capacity."[62] As such, the sovereign is free to parse and qualify life between those elements that support and intensify sovereign power and those that threaten or undermine sovereignty.

In focusing on the way that personhood empowers the sovereign to distinguish between qualified political life and unqualified or

---

60 Thomas Hobbes, *Leviathan*, 2nd Edition, ed. R. Tuck (Cambridge: Cambridge University Press, 1996), 111. See also Esposito, *Third Person*, 84.
61 Esposito, *Third Person*, 86.
62 Ibid.

threatening forms of depersonalization, Esposito's notion of sovereignty mirrors both Foucault's discussion of "state racism"[63] and Agamben's analysis locating sovereign power within "the camp."[64] Much like Foucault and Agamben, Esposito links sovereign power to an immunitary paradigm in which the sovereign exposes certain elements of society to death in order to foster the health and welfare of the commonwealth.[65] But whereas Foucault located this dynamic in the broad formations of discipline and government used to intervene in the population, and Agamben found it in the increasingly normalized states of emergency producing legally authorized exemptions from law, Esposito locates the immunitary paradigm within the concept of personhood – more specifically, in the processes of depersonalization as individuals subsume their interests under the artificial person of the sovereign. Esposito thus characterizes the sovereign as "the principle of depersonalization ... What he removes from the other persons is what the very core of their personality resides in."[66] Reflecting back on Arendt's fear of a democratically authorized liquidation of some parts of "humanity" by its "fully mechanized" self, Esposito identifies the conditions of possibility for this exposure to death in the processes and logics that elevate the artificial person of the sovereign and his desires over the depersonalized individuals that authorized its creation.

That this *dispositif* structures not just theories of sovereignty but also the practices of territorial states is now readily apparent.[67] It also illuminates the relationship between sovereignty and right, showing how tenuous a category personhood remains for human rights claims. As Timothy Campbell and Adam Sitze have explained, "the 'person' is less a *foundation* than a *trap-door*: it is the hinge in and through which every positive affirmation of the rights of the human will pivot into an administrative discourse that turns the human inside out, cutting up and distributing the plane of living being it presupposes into lesser and greater

---

63 Michel Foucault, "Society Must Be Defended," in *Lectures at the Collège de France, 1975–1976* (New York: Picador, 2003).

64 Agamben, *Homo Sacer.*

65 On the relation of the immunitary paradigm and politics see also Roberto Esposito, *Bios: Biopolitics, and Philosophy,* trans. T. Campbell (Minneapolis: University of Minnesota Press, 2008).

66 Esposito, *Third Person,* 85.

67 For an overview of some of the geographic and interpretive social science literature examining the ways in which sovereignty functions in relation to Foucault's and Agamben's arguments, see Joshua Barkan, "Sovereignty," in *The Wiley Blackwell Companion to Political Geography,* ed. J. Agnew, V. Mamadouh, A. Secor, and J. Sharp (Malden, MA: Wiley Blackwell, 2015), 48–60.

quantities ... of rights-bearing substance."[68] Campbell and Sitze indicate that the *dispositif* of the person excludes categories of being deemed not fully rational (such as animals, children, and the insane) while at the same time including artificial persons (including the sovereign, corporations, and other political bodies) within the sphere of right.[69] Cosmopolitan theories of the person similarly function within this general apparatus inasmuch as they base the extension of rights, in Benhabib's phrasing, on theories of "moral and legal"[70] personhood. The intention of cosmopolitan theorists is to universalize rights to all individuals irrespective of geography; yet basing cosmopolitan norms of justice in moral personhood – whether figured as Benhabib's capacity to enter into conversations and, thus, democratic deliberation, or as Kant's interest in the shared dominion of the world – only underscores the exclusion of those depersonalized elements while simultaneously including artificial persons such as states and corporations. In this regard, far from being antithetical to sovereignty, cosmopolitan norms of justice extend the paradox of sovereignty and its biopolitical implications around the globe.

II. Corporate Personhood and the Cosmopolitanism of Capital

The importance of Esposito's account can be readily seen in the cosmopolitan desires of corporations. I have argued elsewhere that the biopolitical dynamics of personhood underpinning sovereignty not only structured the corporate bodies of secular states but also those lesser corporate entities – such as hospitals, almshouses, universities, academic societies, and churches, as well as corporations for commerce, trade, manufacturing, and transportation – that are genealogically linked to the modern business corporation.[71] These were the entities that early modern liberal states chartered, often through special acts of legislatures, so as to empower them to discipline and govern populations, territories, and their interrelations – or what Foucault termed "the complex of men and things."[72] Here too, the conceptualization

---

68 Campbell and Sitze, "Introduction," 12.
69 Ibid., 11–12.
70 Benhabib, *Another Cosmopolitanism*, 16.
71 Joshua Barkan, *Corporate Sovereignty: Law and Government under Capitalism* (Minneapolis: University of Minnesota Press, 2013); Barkan, "Roberto Esposito's Political Biology and Corporate Forms of Life," *Law, Culture, and the Humanities* 8, no. 1 (2012): 84–101.
72 Michel Foucault, *Security, Territory, Population: Lectures at the Collège de France, 1977–1978*, ed. M. Snellart, trans. G. Burchell (New York: Palgrave Macmillan, 2007), 96.

of personhood was paramount, as charters established corporations as juristic persons. Through the chartered grant, corporations came to take on a standardized legal status as an artificial person empowered to undertake some specific project. Personhood allowed any corporation to represent itself as a unified entity that could sue and be sued and operate under a common seal. As corporations came to be used for trade, manufacturing, and other types of capitalist business enterprise, personhood was also central to limiting the liability of investors. It was the juridical person – the corporation – that held property and capital, rather than the individual shareholders.

In the United States, the personhood of corporations came to be more and more pressing as a political-legal issue with the rise of a national corporate capitalist economy in the nineteenth century. US corporations were (and continue to be) chartered by states rather than the federal government, yet the US government, and the courts in particular, have at various times extended protections to corporations as legal persons. Infamously, the reconstruction amendments, passed in the aftermath of the Civil War and meant to extend the rule of law to freed slaves, was first applied not to freedmen but to corporations. The hinge that enabled these claims was the 14th Amendment of the US Constitution and its language of "the person," holding that no state shall "deprive any person of life, liberty, or property, without due process of law; nor deny to any person within its jurisdiction the equal protection of the laws."[73] In the late nineteenth and early twentieth centuries, corporations used the 14th Amendment to challenge state actions, such as specific corporate taxes, or to protect corporations from illegal searches and seizures.[74] Since the 1970s, the resort to personhood to establish rights against the state has intensified, with corporations now claiming rights to free speech, recognized most recently in the US Supreme Court's *Citizens United* decision, as well as rights to religious freedom, recognized for closely held corporations in the US Supreme Court's *Hobby Lobby* decision.[75]

Understandably, political concerns about corporate personhood have focused on these extensions of rights. Less commented on, however, is that corporate personhood has also been central to the geographic mobility of corporations. For instance, in the United States, corporations

---

73 US Constitution, Amend. 14, sec. 1.
74 See Morton Horwitz, "*Santa Clara* Revisited: The Development of Corporate Theory," *West Virginia Law Review* 88, no. 2 (1985): 173–224.
75 *Citizens United v. Federal Election Commission*, 558 U. S. 310 (2010); *Burwell v. Hobby Lobby Stores, Inc.*, 573 U. S. ___ (2014).

were created by individual states and thus only recognized within the territorial jurisdictions of those states. As Justice Taney noted in the 1839 US Supreme Court case of *Bank of Augusta* v. *Earle*, "[a] corporation can have no legal existence out of the boundaries of the sovereignty by which it is created. It exists only in contemplation of law, and by force of the law; and where that law ceases to operate, and is no longer oblig-atory, the corporation can have no existence. It must dwell in the place of its creation, and cannot migrate to another sovereignty."[76] Of course, even in the 1840s corporations did cross jurisdictional boundaries, and when they did so, it was on the basis of comity, variously interpreted as a custom or right, but always connected with the deference one sover-eign shows to another. Although comity (especially when interpreted as a custom) could potentially limit the ability of corporations to trans-act business, the system, at least by the mid-nineteenth century, was almost always deployed to facilitate the legal standing of corporate per-sons outside of their home jurisdiction.[77]

With the rise of liberal general incorporation laws in states like New Jersey and, later, Delaware (which made incorporating a pro forma process and the benefits of limited liability widely available),[78] debates began to emerge about both the location of corporations and the justi-fications of and limitations on territorial forms of regulation. Because the charter had traditionally served as the mechanism for government oversight, what did it mean when almost all business corporations were chartered in states with liberal incorporation laws? Were corpo-rations only to be regulated under the laws of states like New Jersey? What rights did the places in which corporations were headquartered have to regulate? And what about the far-flung jurisdictions where shareholders resided?

In response, early twentieth-century legal realists looked for new in-tellectual foundations that could support businesses that transcended territorial boundaries. Calling their approach to the problem a "liberal theory" of corporate regulation (in contrast to Taney's model based on comity, which they derisively called the "restrictive theory"), scholars like Gerard Henderson, E. Hilton Young, and Walter Cook suggested – in

---

76 *Bank of Augusta v. Earle* 38 U.S. 588 (1839).

77 For a fuller account of this history, see chapter 4 on "territory" in Barkan, *Corporate Sovereignty*; as well as Gerard Henderson, *The Position of Foreign Corporations in American Constitutional Law* (Cambridge, MA: Harvard University Press, 1918).

78 On different state models of shareholder liability see William Roy, *Socializing Capital: The Rise of the Large Industrial Corporation in America* (Princeton: Princeton University Press, 1997).

a formulation that bears a striking resemblance to the discourses of cosmopolitanism – that we should dispense with philosophical debates over the nature of corporate personhood and that corporate persons should be recognized as persons universally, across jurisdictions, reflecting the increasingly trans-jurisdictional nature of business.[79] Advocates of the liberal theory noted that corporate persons, like persons generally, had a certain type of moral standing or will, connected with accomplishing the enterprise they were created to undertake.[80] This will gave a corporation the right, like other persons and like the person in cosmopolitan theory, to attempt to initiate commerce in foreign jurisdictions, restricted only by the limits of what is necessary for the juridical person to fulfil its purpose or functional capacity.

Realists grounded their argument in the fact of the economy. Recognizing corporations in multiple jurisdictions was simply pragmatic in an economy that was national and, increasingly, international in scope. But scholars also relied on philosophical notions that, as in the Kantian formulation, connected commerce and cosmopolitanism, treating both as public goods and thus as deserving of universal recognition. Young, like other realists, admitted that "the primary purpose in the creation of commercial associations is not the public welfare, but private gain," but he also argued that private gain itself produced a universal benefit: "It is in the interest of all nations alike to promote international commercial intercourse. Capital is cosmopolitan, and commercial associations are associations rather of capital than men."[81]

The realist dream of a unified liberal theory of the corporation in international law never materialized, as lawyers from the advanced capitalist countries shifted attention away from the structure of the corporation and toward the legal frameworks of the trading system and international markets in the second half of the twentieth century. Nonetheless, the notion of corporations as the paradigmatic cosmopolitan person persisted in discussions about multinational corporations, free trade, and globalization. In these discussions, efficient global markets depended on the abilities of multinationals to scour the world looking

---

79   Henderson, *The Position of Foreign Corporations*; E. Hilton Young, *Foreign Corporations and Other Corporations* (Cambridge: Cambridge University Press, 1912); E. Hilton Young, "The Status of Foreign Corporations and the Legislature – I and II," *Law Quarterly Review* 23, nos. 2–3 (1907): 151–64, 290–303; Walter W. Cook, "The Logical and Legal Basis of the Conflict of Laws," *Yale Law Journal* 33, no. 5 (1924): 457–88.

80   Ernst Freund was the primary advocate of the will theory of the corporation in US law. See Freund, *The Legal Nature of Corporations* (Chicago: University of Chicago Press, 1897), as well as Morton Horwitz, "*Santa Clara* Revisited."

81   Young, "Status of Foreign Corporations," 158.

for lower-cost factors of production, including raw materials and infrastructure, but most importantly cheap labour. Advocates for free trade globalism thus emphasized the ways that the needs of the world market superseded national regulatory frameworks. For instance, US diplomat George Ball, speaking in 1967 to the British National Committee of the International Chamber of Commerce on free trade and the European Economic Community, argued that the EEC marked a positive step toward a "world corporation."[82] Ball referred to this corporation euphemistically as "Cosmocorp" and advocated a plan of "denationalizing" the regulation of multinationals "to avoid being increasingly hamstrung and emasculated by national restrictions."[83] Ball's plan depended on the creation of an "international companies law" that would be a first but by no means only step in making Cosmocorp an effective "citizen of the world."[84]

Corporate Persons and the Politics of Cosmopolitan Right

There is more to be said about the free traders' dreams of unfettered capitalism, the ways corporations move into and out of jurisdictions looking for cheaper factors of production, and the theories of law, government, and regulation that enable and constrain the movements of corporate persons. Yet I would like to conclude this discussion from a slightly different angle, asking what it means, particularly today in an era rife with anti-immigrant sentiments and renewed ethnic nationalisms, to ground progressive politics in cosmopolitan right. In what ways does the cosmopolitanism of the corporate person throw the broader basis of cosmopolitan right into question? Or, to put it even more directly, given the reactionary forces arrayed against any ascription of rights to strangers and foreigners, what good can come from interrogating cosmopolitan political imaginaries that are arguably already on the defensive? Considering the continuities between renewed ethno-racial and economic nationalisms across many of the centres of the capitalist world system, what other resources are available for critiquing capital's dream of the cosmopolitan corporation outside of these increasingly nationalist frameworks?

There are at least two reasons that we should continue to query cosmopolitanism, even today. The first concerns what I think of as

---

82 Reprinted as George Ball, "Cosmocorp: The Importance of Being Stateless" *Columbia Journal of World Business* 2 (1967): 25–30.
83 Ibid., 29.
84 Ibid.

cosmopolitan theory's spatial problem. Democratic theorists look toward cosmopolitanism as a protection for those made vulnerable by the dynamics of globalization. In doing so, cosmopolitans seek to resolve the problem of rights within nation-states by universalizing rights and drawing a direct connection between the global and the person. Universalism, here, is synonymous with the international, and in this regard, cosmopolitanism offers a scalar politics, jumping from the national to the global scale as a means of resolving tensions irresolvable within or between nation-states.[85] This misconstrues the nature of the international, which, as political geographers have stressed, rather than being a smooth and undifferentiated space, has always been striated by uneven networks of power.[86] It also fails to pinpoint the problem that Arendt first identified and that Esposito takes up and radicalizes, which was never solely about the scale of rights claims or even the tension between geographically circumscribed processes of democratic deliberation within nation-states and universal rights. Rather, as they both show, the conditions of possibility for liquidating, depersonalizing, or, more simply, exposing some part of humanity to death in the name of collective welfare have always been internal to rights themselves. Inasmuch as personhood was meant to bridge the relation between political rights and simple human existence, it only did so by internalizing the hypostatized split between the rational elements of the person worthy of rights and the base or animal aspects that remained depersonalized. If Arendt and Esposito are correct, the globalization of rights of the person that cosmopolitanism advocates intensifies and spreads, rather than deactivates, the desubjectifying and depersonalizing tendencies within the apparatus of rights and the corresponding *dispositif* of the person.

Second, and more pertinently, the focus on the corporate person illuminates a particular form of depersonalization within cosmopolitan theories of right. Although corporations have long connections with spheres of international law,[87] what has always been cosmopolitan

---

85   There is a long discussion in the geographic literature on globalization concerning the politics of scale and "scale-jumping." See Neil Smith, "Geography, Difference, and the Politics of Scale," in *Postmodernism and the Social Sciences*, ed. J. Doherty, E. Graham, and M. Malek (London: Macmillan, 1992), 57–79; Eric Sheppard, "The Spaces and Times of Globalization: Place, Scale, Networks, and Positionality," *Economic Geography* 78, no. 3 (2002): 307–30.

86   For a comprehensive presentation of this argument see Doreen Massey, *For Space* (London: Sage, 2005).

87   These relations go back at least to Grotius. See Richard Tuck, *The Rights of War and Peace: Political Thought on the International Order from Grotius to Kant* (Oxford: Oxford University Press, 1999).

about the corporate person is the way it has functioned as a legal embodiment of mobile capital. This was clear to advocates of standardization and universalization in international corporate law such as Young and Ball. What they failed to address, however, was the ways in which the extension of rights to corporate persons – as with rights in general – also carries with it a particular depersonalization. Corporations have been recognized as moral actors with wills that can enter into potentially beneficial contracts. In this regard, they are considered worthy of cosmopolitan rights. But this also draws a connection between right and profitability that makes the latter the metric of the former. As such, the personalization of the corporation is coextensive with the depersonalization of individuals, communities, and places seen as tools important for profitability but without inherent value in themselves.

In this regard, we can see how modern discourses of cosmopolitan right unwittingly bleed into a celebration of global entrepreneurialism, which is cosmopolitan rather than parochial in outlook and sensibility. Rather than an incidental conflation, however, cosmopolitan right becomes entrepreneurial because its formal philosophical and legal languages are partly founded in and imbricated with the cosmopolitanism of commerce and capital. This is true not only because of the dual meaning of commerce in Kant or because the ancient *Lex Mercatoria*, like the modern trade regime, constitutes, in the words of Gunther Teubner, "a global law without a state."[88] It is also true because the liberal legal category of person has long been used to represent and foster the global movement of capital in its corporate form.

This renders personhood a difficult category for combating corporatization. At the end of her Tanner Lectures on Human Values, the eminent political theorist Seyla Benhabib captured the predicament succinctly, writing that "the fraying of the social contract and the dismantling of sovereignty suggest that the transcendence of the nation-state is occurring hardly in the direction of cosmopolitanism but more in the direction of privatization and corporatization of sovereignty. These trends endanger democracy and popular sovereignty by converting public power into private commercial or administrative competence."[89] Her lectures provide one response to this condition, emphasizing her concepts of democratic iterations and cosmopolitan norms of justice as a solution to "the corporatization of sovereignty." As she put it, "with the concept of 'democratic iterations,' I wanted to signal forms of popular

---

88 See Gunther Teubner, ed., *Global Law without a State* (Aldershot: Dartmouth, 1997).
89 Behabib, *Another Cosmopolitanism*, 177.

empowerment and political struggle through which the people themselves would appropriate the universalist promise of cosmopolitan norms in order to bind forms of political and economic power that seek to escape democratic control, accountability and transparency."[90]

Although I remain sympathetic to Benhabib's stated objective, the problem I have attempted to outline is that, inasmuch as cosmopolitan theories of right hinge on concepts of personhood, the persons composing the "people themselves" that Benhabib hopes will appropriate the universal promise of cosmopolitanism are difficult to distinguish from those making up the corporations dismantling democracy and converting public power into private commercial or administrative competence. To make such a distinction would mean grounding our theories of cosmopolitan justice in something different than the person, with its long history of desubjectifying and depersonalizing individuals, places, and things. What such a politics, much less a system of right or law, looks like and how it would attend to the needs of the most vulnerable remain daunting questions that, unfortunately, the critique offered here cannot answer.[91] But it can, at the very least, suggest an alternative starting point: not in the abstract rights inhering in our personhood but in the concrete forms of violence and power that continually cleave and qualify the lives of individuals and populations, threatening some for the salvation of others.

---

90 Ibid.
91 Esposito, for his part, offers a range of possibilities focused on "impersonal" forms of life as they emerge in contemporary French critical thought. The impersonal or non-person ranges from the third person in Benveniste's linguistics to the Levinasian Other to Deleuze's plane of immanence. Again, Esposito only gestures at the sociopolitical implications of these linguistic, ethical, and philosophical formulations. For his full account, see Part III of *The Third Person*, 104–51.

3 Watched Over by Assemblages of Providential Grace

ANGELA MITROPOULOS

I. The Art of Law's Nature

Justitia is one part of the medieval iconography of the Roman cardinal virtues, blindfolded sometime in the fifteenth century, invariably holding the scales of equity and the sword of decision. What matters in this ubiquitous statuary pantheon is not resemblance or the chronicling of a person's life but, to the contrary, composition and perspective – the invitation to a judicial gaze, "that place," as Foucault might interject, "which is completely inaccessible because it is exterior" to the image, "yet is prescribed by all the lines of its composition."[1] Was Justitia's blindfolding the implication of law's impartiality, or indifference, toward those who appear before it; or was it the arrangement of medieval aesthetics, emblematic of a theological dichotomy between the impaired eye of human nature and an all-seeing divinity, as it was for Aquinas?[2] Is there wisdom in knowing that the blindfold is really a "bandage [that] hides festering sores," as Langston Hughes proposed?[3] Perspective, composition, gnosology, and the range of

---

1 Michel Foucault, *The Order of Things: An Archaeology of the Human Sciences* (London: Routledge, 1970), 15.

2 Dennis Curtis and Judith Resnik, "Epistemological Doubt and Visual Puzzles of Sight, Knowledge, and Judgment: Reflections on Clear-Sighted and Blindfolded Justices," in *Genealogies of Legal Vision*, ed. Peter Goodrich and Valérie Hayaert (New York: Routledge, 2015), 219–60; Bennett Capers, "On Justitia, Race, Gender, and Blindness," *Mich. J. Race & L.* 12 (2006): 203; Thomas Aquinas, *Summa Theologiae: Questions on God* (Cambridge: Cambridge University Press, 2006), II.I. q.100, art. 9. ad. 261.

3 Langston Hughes, "Justice," in *Scottsboro Limited: Four Poems and a Play in Verse* (New York: Golden Stair Press, 1932), 8.

the visible all matter in aesthetics, as in law; in the case of Justitia organize the contemplation of a metaphysics of nature presented by an idealized woman's body fixed in stone or bronze; a metaphorical cascade that may draw the eye up to a face that cannot return the gaze, and down to medieval law's bedrock naturalist claim, often pointedly, as bare feet standing on a bare rock. Whether corporations emerge from something foundational, or are conjured up by legislation, or are inscribed in readable documents of incorporation and trademarks signed and filed and stamped and filed again is, however, a long-standing dispute situated between what can be seen and the theoretical imagination and desire of and for legitimate *corpora*; a metaphysics and microphysics of legal bodies replete with assumptions about properties and property rights whose derivation is as disputed as their consistency and warrant. Since the late nineteenth century in the United States, corporate personhood rulings have pressed forward an economic definition of the corporation. In contrast to prior characterizations, the corporation has been defined as both a real and a natural entity, bearing a substantive and legal resemblance to the familial estate's heritable property, from which – as it happens – an emerging economics in the eighteenth century sourced its presumably primordial creation and etymological root by basing itself on an awkward combination of *nomos* and *oikos*, the law of the household, or *oikonomia*.[4] The point, here, is this: corporate personification is a powerful counter to the empiric incertitude of properties and property rights; it insists that those rights derive not from a jumble of changing laws and their enforcement but instead are revealed; that they do not reflect the art of law's naturalism, either, or the rough historical semblance of legitimacy and force, but rather the reappropriation of nature – that troublesome, fugitive, and disobedient object of an unseen and unaccountable gaze.

Within legal history, the definition of the corporation in corporate personhood rulings has involved a series of overlapping shifts: from an artificial entity, to an aggregate of real persons, to a singular, natural entity regarded as having "a separate existence and [assigned with] independent rights."[5] It would be tempting to render corporate personification as a spurious conflation of existent people and

---

4 Angela Mitropoulos, *Contract and Contagion: From Biopolitics to Oikonomia* (Wivenhoe: Minor Compositions, 2012).

5 Anne Tucker, "Flawed Assumptions: A Corporate Law Analysis of Free Speech and Corporate Personhood in Citizens United," *Case W. Res. L. Rev.* 61 (2010): fn. 16.

corporations. From there, the reliance of corporate personhood rulings on the 14th Amendment might be denounced as a "brazen historical forgery," treated as grimly ironic, as an anthropomorphic distortion or, more simply, a mystery[6] – as analytically incomprehensible, in other words, as the ubiquitous statuary presentation of justice in the figure of a woman, from a time and in a place when no woman could be a judge, serve on a jury, or possess property, but where many could be property. It may also be the case that subsequent interpretations of the headnote appended to *Santa Clara County v. Southern Pacific* involved inordinate reaching and mischief.[7] Yet the circumstances in which corporate personhood rulings arose, and which "traumatized legal thinking," did not involve the appearance of large corporations, or joint stock trading companies, or even the eclipse of agriculture by large-scale industry and the decline of agrarian economies, as some have argued.[8] Explaining the historical coincidence of corporate personhood rulings and the abolition of slavery as a debasement of naturalist representation neglects the aesthetic apparatus of realism that this presupposes and, not least, a shared recourse by proponents of plantation slavery and corporate personification to the assumptions and appeal of natural economy. Arguably, the abolition of slavery contributed to the crisis and restructuring of agriculture by wiping out the value of enslaved people as a distinct class of plantation assets, and may not have been unrelated to Southern Pacific Railroad's attempt to limit the valuation of taxable property in that case. However, the 15th Amendment's nullification of the horrific 1857 decision of the United States Supreme Court in Dred Scott's case – the ruling that no enslaved person or their descendants could be a citizen, and that slavery could not be

---

6   Howard Jay Graham, *Everyman's Constitution: Historical Essays on the Fourteenth Amendment, the "Conspiracy Theory," and American Constitutionalism* (Wisconsin: Wisconsin Historical Society, 1968), 417; Anna Grear, "Human Rights – Human Bodies? Some Reflections on Corporate Human Rights Distortion, The Legal Subject, Embodiment, and Human Rights Theory," *Law and Critique* 17, no. 2 (2006): 171–99.

7   The headnote reads: "The defendant Corporations are persons within the intent of the clause in section 1 of the Fourteenth Amendment to the Constitution of the United States" (118 USSC 394, 1886).

8   Gregory A. Mark, "The Personification of the Business Corporation in American Law," *University of Chicago Law Review* 54, no. 4 (1987): 1445. Similar to Mark but emphasizing the historical schema of Polanyian moral economy, Ritu Birla argues that the joint stock company is the exemplar of corporate personhood, in "Maine (and Weber) against the Grain: Towards a Postcolonial Genealogy of the Corporate Person," *Journal of Law and Society* 40, no. 1 (2013): 92–114.

constitutionally prohibited[9] – also heightened the reactionary purchase of an agrarian romanticism concerning "the natural course of things" on which both defenders of slavery and corporate personhood drew to make their case.

Therefore, as convenient as denunciations of corporate personhood as a violation of a presumably natural order of things and persons might seem, this is not the approach taken here. Such accounts gloss over the turn to descriptions of corporations as natural entities at the very moment in which the trade in enslaved people would be both prohibited and integrated into an expanded wage labour market and penitentiary system as the administration of uncertainty. It is at this moment that definitions of the corporation and of the law that creates them begin to pull away from the then-prevailing tendency – as in William Blackstone's *Commentaries* and Thomas Hobbes's *Leviathan* – to describe corporations as an extension of sovereign authority.[10] The rise of a natural metaphysics of bodies predicated not on political power but, instead, on "the natural course of things" – Adam Smith's most enduring epistemological expression – rearranged the selective mechanisms of legal decision and the weighing of justice by emphasizing an economic and providential link between contingency and necessity.[11] As to a spurious anthropomorphism, legal personhood and existent persons within a jurisdiction have never coincided. There was no unequivocal prohibition on slavery or the extension of citizenship: the 14th Amendment involved a crucial caveat to the abolition of slavery that would become the route to its antebellum, *de facto* restoration through criminalization, in turn creating a path to disenfranchisement and segregation.[12] Further to this, the 14th Amendment's guarantee of equal protection was not extended to women until a century after its ratification.[13] In other

---

9   *Scott v. Sandford*, 60 US 19 How. 393 393 (1856).

10 William Blackstone, *Commentaries on the Laws of England*, vol. 1 (Chicago: University of Chicago Press, 1979); Thomas Hobbes, *Leviathan, or The Matter, Forme, & Power of a Common-Wealth Ecclesiasticall and Civill*, ed. Richard Tuck (Cambridge: Cambridge University Press, 1996).

11 Adam Smith, *An Inquiry into the Nature and Causes of the Wealth of Nations*, ed. R.H. Campbell, A.S. Skinner, and W.B. Todd (Oxford: Clarendon, 1976), III, passim; Mitropoulos, *Contract and Contagion*, 25–7, passim.

12 For a more comprehensive discussion of legal personhood, see Cheryl I. Harris, "Whiteness as Property," *Harvard Law Review* 106, no. 8 (1993): 1707–91; Margaret Jane Radin, "Property and Personhood," *Stanford Law Review* 34, no. 5 (1982): 957–1015.

13 Ralph A. Rossum and G. Alan Tarr, *American Constitutional Law: The Bill of Rights and Subsequent Amendments*, 4th ed., vol. 2 (New York: Routledge, 1995), 431–2.

words, treating natural law as if its object and method implied a correspondence to and representation of an independently existing natural world is implausible when the emergence of natural law's pivotal theory of contingency illustrates the extent to which it does not assume such a correlation because it is, above all, a method of subtraction and selection – the encoding, in other words, of the law of the household in a normative epistemic ascent to the ideal.[14] In any case, it is unclear how the assumption that there is an ideal correlation between existent persons and legal personhood can serve to bolster the expansion of civil rights while it neglects a critical analysis of the pattern of their non-correspondence in favour of scrambling history into a cautionary tale of nature's desecration that proponents of corporate personhood have themselves emphasized.

In summary, the theoretical and historical approach here is as follows. First, corporate personhood rulings have advanced an economic definition of the corporation as a singular and natural entity, such that the *corpora* at issue is treated as analogous with the *oikos*. As with a nascent economics of the eighteenth century, this treatment harks back to the ancient, archaic texts of Xenophon and Aristotle on "the art of managing the household" though, more so, the arguments of Augustine on the interaction of desire and divine predestination, and the medieval texts of Thomas Aquinas in which *oikonomia* was understood as a tenet of prudential conduct.[15] From these and other Christian texts, economics derived an understanding of the source of legal and moral authority, autonomous from positive law, and emphasizing a contingent but providential interaction between natural and divine law. Economics, in turn, influenced readings of Christian texts. Adam Smith was as much concerned with elaborating a theory of natural jurisprudence in his *Theory of Moral Sentiments* as he was in putting forward a purportedly natural measure of wealth and prosperity in *The Wealth of Nations*.[16] Second, this is by no means a continuous development in at least two notable respects. Corporate personhood is unlike a prior,

---

14 Angela Mitropoulos, "Encoding the Law of the Household and the Standardisation of Uncertainty," in *Mapping Precariousness, Labour Insecurity, and Uncertain Livelihoods: Subjectivities and Resistance*, ed. E. Armano, A. Bove, and A. Murgia (London: Routledge, 2017), 210–26.

15 Aristotle, *Complete Works: Revised Oxford Translation*, ed. Jonathan Barnes, vol. 2 (Princeton: Princeton University Press, 2014), "Politics," 1253b; Aquinas, *Summa*, passim; Augustine, *On the Free Choice of the Will, on Grace and Free Choice, and Other Writings*, ed. Peter King (Cambridge: Cambridge University Press, 2010).

16 Adam Smith, *The Theory of Moral Sentiments* (Penguin, 2010); Smith, *Wealth of Nations*.

conventionalist understanding of the law, or *nomos* – an understanding to which Aristotle subscribed, but to which the medieval neo-Aristotelianism of Aquinas and an Augustinian Neoplatonism did not.[17] The novel contribution of Neoplatonist and neo-Aristotelian approaches was that they attempted to reconcile what they saw as a profoundly uncertain and fallen material world with their adherence to a divinely ordained natural, hierarchical order. In this sense, law is understood as the facilitation of divine omniscience in conditions of radical, human uncertainty – for Augustinian Neoplatonists, a deference to God's incomprehensible grace. The point is that a providential understanding of contingency as the assistant of teleological or deterministic necessity is the very the meaning of "free market" or "marketplace of ideas" stressed in corporate personhood rulings. It is neither individualistic in any general sense, not amoral by its own definition. The most emphatic version, involving a theory of predestination and an incomprehensible divine law, is important to understanding the course and implications of legal cases such as *Burwell v. Hobby Lobby* and *National Institute of Family and Life Advocates v. Becerra* since both of these overtly link corporate personhood with religious freedom.[18]

Furthermore, the nation-state and concepts of a national culture are no more archaic phenomena than is the conjuncture of *nomos* and *oikos*. Eighteenth-century economics both influenced and reflected contemporaneous translations of Christian scripture from the Greek and Latin – as in the increasing use of the phrase "wealth of nations" in biblical text and apocalyptic verse from the sixteenth century, and the hermeneutic emphasis on dispensations of economic orders or *oikonomia* in the *Scofield Reference Bible*.[19] On the one hand, this bound the notion of constitution and the sword of original decision to an appeal to a singular, mythic people and the limits of a defined citizenship. On the other, it set the scales of justice in such a way that money served as a natural, providential metric for weighing the prudence of choices. For Platonism, this meant the rational governance of the soul; for Aristotelianism, the auto-catalytic and teleological realization of intrinsic potential – both

---

17 Angela Mitropoulos, "Oikonomia," *Philosophy Today* 63, no. 4 (2019): 1025–36.

18 *Burwell, Secretary of Health And Human Services, et al. v. Hobby Lobby Stores, Inc., et al,* 573 USSC (2014); *National Institute of Family and Life Advocates, dba NIFLA, et al. v. Becerra, Attorney General of California, et al,* 585 USSC (2018).

19 Jordan J. Ballor, "An Inquiry into the Origins of 'The Wealth of Nations': Exploring a Myth Concerning the Relationship between Adam Smith and Scripture," in *History of Economics Society* (East Lansing, Michigan, 2015); Charles C. Ryrie, *Dispensationalism* (Chicago: Moody, 2007); Cyrus Ingerson Scofield, *The Scofield Study Bible: English Standard Version* (New York: Oxford University Press, 2006).

implying a version of formal or categorical reasoning from ideal properties according to the right proportions or the *rectaratio*.[20] Yet the shift from a conventionalist to a natural economic account of *nomos* – the turn of Neoplatonisms and neo-Aristotelianism – is a result of the impossibility of empirically verifying the existence of an essentially unchanging physical world while, at the same time, treating the material world of transactions as the precarious scene of performative redemption. Whether the emphasis falls on traditionalist iterations of a patriarchal sequence that links the familial estate with the corporation or on the market as a mechanism of moral judgment, corporate personhood rulings have effectively combined both of these in an elaborate imaginary of legal *corpora*, through specific legal cases, and in a metaphysics of heritable property as the ideal ground of natural right. The combined registers of natural economy and contingency, treated as facilitative of a prudential disposition toward necessity, are key to the following analysis of corporate personhood. Corporate personhood rulings are indicative of one influential line of anxiety about and hostility toward the perceived trespass of expanded civil and labour rights on the private and commercial jurisdiction of a purportedly natural servitude. Another such line is the elaboration of fetal personhood cases, in which pregnancy becomes a matter of criminal law and abortion is treated as "a crime against their master's property."[21] The broader yield is a narrowing of legal personhood: the emergence of a doubtful, precarious legal subject navigating a restricted, uninsured, uninformed, and interdicted range of choices in a "free market," liable to the policing and criminalization of conduct and bracketed on either side by an expansion of immunities, protections, and the limitation of liabilities afforded to prenatal and incorporated legal subjects.

So as to situate and illustrate the theoretical approach taken here, the following discussion is structured around an analysis of three legal cases and a critical reading of Foucault's writings and lectures on the

---

20   Plato, *The Republic*, ed. G.R.F.Ferrari, trans. Tom Griffith (Cambridge: Cambridge University Press, 2000), 430d–445e; Aristotle, *Complete Works*, vol. 2:"Metaphysics," vii. 4; Angela Mitropoulos, "The Commons," in *Gender: Nature*, ed. Iris van der Tuin (Farmington Hills: Macmillan, 2016), 166, passim.

21   Elizabeth Fox-Genovese, *Within the Plantation Household: Black and White Women of the Old South* (Chapel Hill: University of North Carolina Press, 1988), 324. See also recent cases such as *Azar v. Garza* (584 USSC, 2018); and the proposed revision of Title X of the Public Health Service Act "to ensure compliance with ... the statutory requirement that none of the funds appropriated for Title X may be used in programs where abortion is a method of family planning" (Department of Health And Human Services, 42 CFR Part 59, HHS-OS-2018-0008).

clinic, *parrhesia* ("the right to speak one's mind freely"), and biopolitics or the transformation of economic liberalism by population theory. The second section of this chapter briefly tracks the belated and at times ambivalent rise of an economic definition of the corporation. The third section reads *National Institute of Family and Life Advocates v. Becerra* – which recently overturned stipulations on disclosure by "crisis pregnancy centers" as likely infringements on their free speech rights – alongside Foucault's discussion of the birth of the clinic. The fourth section comprises a very brief discussion of *Citizens United v. Federal Election Commission* and Foucault's understanding of *parrhesia*.[22] The fifth section analyses *Burwell v. Hobby Lobby* along with Foucault's discussion of population theory. It delves into the evangelical theology of Hobby Lobby's owners and suggests that Foucault's remarkable neglect of Malthusian catastrophism and neo-Malthusian nationalism occludes the connections between neoliberalism and religious conservatism. The final section returns to the implication of Neoplatonist concepts of contingency in the conjuncture of *oikos* and *nomos* – which is to say, the reckless consequence of imbuing the happenstance of birth, place, and heritable property with a providential and deterministic meaning that implies not the "politicization of life" but, to the contrary, a kind of corporatist state by way of the transformation of politics by a corporatism rendered analogous to the *oikos*.[23]

II. Economic Corpora and "the natural course of things"

The order of things that necessity imposes ... promoted by the natural inclinations of man.

– Adam Smith, *The Wealth of Nations*

Order manifests itself in depth as though already there.

– Michel Foucault, *The Order of Things*

In Blackstone's *Commentaries* (1765) and Hobbes's *Leviathan* (1651), corporations were artefacts of sovereign power, and sovereignty, in turn, was an "Artificiall Man" who utters law as a "word, without substance."[24] By this view, corporations were a sovereign grant or charter.

---

22 558 USSC 310 (2008).
23 This extends the critical comparison of Foucault's and Hannah Arendt's treatments of biopolitics and *oiko*-politics respectively, see Mitropoulos, *Contract and Contagion*, 59–62. It also links the argument in *Contract and Contagion* regarding the *oikonomic* nexus of family, race, and nation to its political iteration.
24 Blackstone, *Commentaries*; Hobbes, *Leviathan*, 184, 245.

But in tandem with the growth of merchant wealth through grants of monopoly over colonial trade and administration, economics emerged as a search for a mythic, archaic authority independent of the Crown, and definitions of the corporation would slowly begin to shift. In 1793, in his *Treatise on the Law of Corporations*, Stewart Kyd defined the corporation as "a body, united." It was still conceived as a creation of sovereign or positive law. Yet in contrast to Edward Coke's 1612 opinion in the case of *Sutton's Hospital*, Kyd insisted that the corporation could be "seen by all but the blind."[25] In the early twentieth century, the translation and republication of Otto Gierke's argument that the corporation was derived from the German medieval law of fellowship presented a different view altogether. There, the corporation was deemed to be neither a fiction, nor a symbol, nor a "piece of the State's machinery" or even a "collective name for individuals, but a living organism and a real person."[26] Gierke was determined to add the fraternal association to natural philosophy's dichotomous repertoire of *oikos* and *polis*. Yet in the mythological sweep of transatlantic resonance and approximation to the Athenian noble household and Roman latifundia that animated the Renaissance classicism of the American plantation economy, and at the disciplinary intersections of an emerging sociology and economics, the vernacular analogue of this individuated, naturalist personification of the corporation was the master of the familial estate.[27]

Notwithstanding these archaic allusions, corporate personhood has been a long time in the making. A contemporary naturalist metaphysics of *corpora* involves the semblance of an economic definition of the corporation through categorical analogy to the *oikos* as well as through legal cases that, increasingly if not at the very outset, have related to family-owned companies or so-called non-profits, involving limited disclosure and regulatory requirements with additional taxation exemptions derived from charitable or faith-based status. In the first of these cases, a decade after Reconstruction had ended with the removal

---

25 Stewart *Kyd, A Treatise on the Law of Corporations* (J. Butterworth, 1793), 16; Edward Coke, "The Case of Sutton's Hospital," in *Selected Writings of Sir Edward Coke*, ed. Steve Shepherd, vol. 1, 3 vols. (Indianapolis: Liberty Fund, 2003), 347–77.

26 Otto Friedrich Von Gierke, *Political Theories of the Middle Age* (Cambridge: Cambridge University Press, 1900), xxvi.

27 According to Max Weber, "the primeval form of 'administration' is represented by patriarchal power, i.e., the rule of the household." In Weber, *Economy and Society: An Outline of Interpretive Sociology*, vol. 1 (Berkeley: University of California Press, 1978), 645. For a brief discussion of the history of sociology in influencing understandings of neoliberalism and fascism, see Mitropoulos, "'Post-Factual' Readings of Neoliberalism, Before and After Trump," *Society and Space*, 5 December 2016.

of troops from southern states and the commencement of transcontinental railway construction, the petitioners in *Santa Clara County v. Southern Pacific Railroad Company* had the character of a hybrid public/private entity.[28] Southern Pacific was a private holding company operating under a public grant, a partnership between Leland Stanford, Collis P. Huntington, Charles Crocker, and Mark Hopkins. But it was nevertheless the legal and financial creation of a succession of Pacific railroad acts passed by Congress between 1862 and 1874. That legislation specifically named and "erected [Southern Pacific, among others] into a corporate and politic in deed and in law," and issued advantageous mortgage bonds and leases over land for the construction of rail lines.[29] The more recent and watershed corporate personhood cases discussed below, by contrast, have not involved corporations established by specific government grant, as with Southern Pacific Rail, nor are they subject to the disclosure rules faced by companies publicly trading on central exchanges such as Wall Street, nor have they been established by name in laws passed by Congress. They have, instead, been private companies, family-owned or closely held, in some cases as non-profits – thereby strengthening the implication of an *oikonomic* definition of the corporation and, at the same time, loosening the measure of value from the strictures of efficiency and cost-benefit analyses.[30]

The rise of an economic understanding of the corporation was one of the outcomes of early modern conflicts between ecclesiastical authority and royal power, out of which a concept of economics as an autonomous domain of moral reckoning and natural jurisprudence emerged in the eighteenth-century writings of Smith, influenced in no small way by the moral economy of his teacher, Francis Hutcheson.[31] Indeed, Smith's theory of natural jurisprudence drew from natural law theology in its redescription of the corporation as a natural entity that had spontaneously evolved from Scottish familial clans, of exchange as

---

28 118 USSC 394 (1886).
29 Pacific Railway Act (US, 2 July 1864).
30 Bernard Harcourt's argument concerning the different tracks of self-regulated financial markets guided by efficiency and a punitive, penitentiary system are an important antidote to superficial analyses of the history of economic liberalism. But it does not deal with the increasing legal and political prominence of private companies, the eclipse of utilitarian principles, or the link between concepts of natural economy and the *oikos* that would explain overlapping iterations of class, race, and gender. Harcourt, *The Illusion of Free Markets* (Cambridge, MA: Harvard University Press, 2011).
31 Francis Hutcheson, *Collected Works: A System of Moral Philosophy*, vol. 5 (Basel: Georg Olms Verlag AG, 1969).

a sophisticated development of the bartering between familial estates, and of national economies as analogous to households. Hutcheson's inalienable rights doctrine – written in firm opposition to Hobbes's conventionalist account of legal authority – furnished the description of "the economy" as an aggregate of self-regulating entities (households), whose immunities from royal power were derived from a higher law – which is to say, from God, who had established "the very constitution of the rational mind" and therefore the capacity to "assent or dissent solely according to the evidence presented, and naturally desires knowledge."[32] In basing themselves on the concept of an *oikos*, Hutcheson's oeconomics and Smith's economics carried forward the couplet of natural liberty and natural slavery integral to natural law concepts of *oikos* and *nomos*. In the *Nicomachean Ethics*, Aristotle argues that natural law dictates a political equality; at the same time, he contends the inoperability of an unqualified measure of justice and equality in the *oikos*: "What is just for the master and for the father are not," in relation to other members of the *oikos*, subject to arithmetical rules of equality and justice because "there is no unqualified injustice in relation to what is one's own, and," he proceeds, "a man's property [is] ... as it were, a part of him, and no one rationally chooses to harm himself." Aristotle's argument in the *Politics* furnishes the classical link between the *oikos* and the definition of a slave as a "living possession," incapable of self-movement: "in the arrangement of the family," he writes, "a slave is a living possession, and property a number of such instruments; and the servant is himself an instrument for instruments."[33] Slaves, by Aristotle's definition, did not have an inherent capacity for the rationality that was deemed the condition for self-movement, teleological becoming, and therefore the exercise of freedom. Nor did they have the capacity for the prudential foresight that weighs moral or any definition of risk: "the slave has no deliberative faculty at all; the woman has, but it is without authority, and the child has, but it is immature."[34]

This was the configuration of natural liberty, natural slavery, and natural servitude that natural philosophy bequeathed to a Smithian jurisprudence of economic sentiments. It would be modified in time by the foregrounding of uncertainty, which is to say, the uncertainty as to whether people were in their "proper place" and the corollary difficulty of inferring the existence of an eternal, natural order from empirical observation – which is to say, the hand of God becomes, as in

---

32 Hutcheson, *Collected Works*, 5:295.
33 Aristotle, *Complete Works*, vol. 2: "Politics," 1253b28–1254a14.
34 Ibid., 2:1260a–10–15.

Adam Smith's most famous trope, "invisible" to human perception.[35] This combination of epistemic and historical uncertainty spurs the abandonment of Aristotle's conventionalist account of *nomos*, binding *oikos* to *nomos* by relaunching a Neoplatonist formalism – implicit in Smith's argument that "[t]he order of things that necessity imposes in general, though not in every country, is in every country promoted by the natural inclinations of man."[36] Smith's epistemology of a natural order arising from complexity is reliant on the persuasive method of imagined scenarios of a natural economic industriousness, insistent on the constitutive incompleteness and fallibility of a multiplicity of worldly perspectives and the inaccessibility of eternal truth other than through signs and portents (prices and markets). It need not carry forward a profuse description of empiric complexity to normative prescriptions, of the variety of existent households and desires; it need only appeal to an idealized, fraternal account of "moral sentiments."[37]

In any case, empiric variety and change will remain troublesome for economic liberalism. Under the pressure of uprisings and revolutions, the classical jurisdictional dichotomy of natural liberty operating in commerce and politics and a natural servitude within the natural economy will blur. As a consequence, economic theories of natural jurisprudence will vacillate between, on the one hand, a fortunate Smithian emphasis on commanding "diligent" labour through the internalized, prudential guidance of the presumably natural price of corn and, on the other hand, an unfortunate, correctional insistence in the expedited enforcement of frugality and industriousness through starvation and the elimination of parish welfare, urged on by the Malthusian imagination of biblical catastrophe. Where Aristotle had classically emphasized demand as the harmonic mechanism of exchange between equal and free male citizens, Smithian neoclassicism emphasized desire guided by an invisible, providential hand – in its macroeconomic sense, the application of the "maxim of every prudent master of a family" in aggregate.[38] The additional shift from a Smithian emphasis on the providential interaction between the moral divination of signs and the aggregate of desires to Malthusian sermons against a ruinous hedonic calculus is far less philosophical than it marked a shift in emphasis in precise circumstances – vividly, the revolution and uprisings in France and

---

35 Smith, *The Theory of Moral Sentiments*, IV. 1.
36 For a discussion of Aristotle's conventionalist definition of *nomos*, see Mitropoulos, "Oikonomia." Smith, *The Wealth of Nations*, III. 1.
37 Smith, *The Theory of Moral Sentiments*.
38 Smith, *The Wealth of Nations*, IV. 2. 11.

its colonies, and more broadly, a reaction to the movement of people outside the ostensibly natural order of the *oikos* prompted by rural-to-urban migration and the perceived moral hazard of welfare disconnected from properly productive and reproductive work. By way of comparison, the stipulation in *Plessy v. Ferguson* "that no person shall be permitted to occupy [places] other than the ones assigned to them, on account of the race they belong to," the means by which a "separate but equal" judgment could elude the 14th Amendment's definition of the deprivation of liberties, echoes the resegregationist call arising from the theory of ideal properties and proper places in Plato's *Republic*.[39]

Yet in the years prior to the revolution in France and the uprisings of enslaved people in the French colonies, a decade before the American war of independence broke out, as Blackstone prepares his lectures on common law, the jurisdictional dichotomy of politics and economics is ambiguous with respect to the distinction between public and private law. But it remains largely intact as a distinction between the public policing of a moral economy, grounded in and accompanied by the common law tenet of the inalienable possession of heritable property, and the conventionalist, sovereign grant of the corporation that administratively links colonial power to colony. For Blackstone, slavery appeared as a tyrannical violation of the inherent freedoms granted to propertied individuals, yet he deemed it proper to the relations between master and servant in the domain of "private economical relations."[40] Corporations, by contrast, he understood to include a range of civil, voluntary organizations such as universities, ecclesiastical bodies, and mercantile associations established by sovereign consent: "The founder of all corporations in the strictest and original sense is the king alone," by extension, established by an act of Parliament. In the final chapter of the first book of the *Commentaries*, Blackstone defines bodies corporate as an "artificial person ... for the advancement of religion, of learning, and of commerce" that "never dies"; however, his discussion of them does not suggest that they evolved from the familial estate.[41] Where Blackstone does discuss the economy, it is to define the role and the scope of the "public police," as a familial trope for and extension of sovereign power, and in giving an account of miscellaneous offences and felonies – not to characterize corporations. "By the public police and economy,"

---

39 163 US 537 (1896); Plato, *Republic*, 561d–562b.

40 Blackstone, *Commentaries*, 1:123, 410–11; Teresa Michals, "'That Sole and Despotic Dominion': Slaves, Wives, and Game in Blackstone's Commentaries," *Eighteenth-Century Studies* 27, no. 2 (1993): 195–216.

41 Blackstone, *Commentaries*, 1:468, 455–6.

Blackstone says, "I mean the due regulation and domestic order of the kingdom: whereby the individuals of the state, like members of a well-governed family, are bound to conform their general behavior to the rules of propriety, good neighborhood, and good manners"; to which he adds: "and to be decent, industrious, and inoffensive *in their respective stations.*"[42] These miscellaneous felonies include offences against public health, polygamy and the religious monopoly on the issuing of marriage licences, sumptuary laws, the criminal conduct of indigents and idle wanderers, and disorderly inns and bawdy houses. The *Commentaries* also hint at the way in which the economy is at once carved out from and ensured by public political authority, in a discussion of wills and whether the owner of an estate might be declared *non compos mentis* ("insane, or not in one's mind") and therefore incapable of bearing testament. The rights of persons, Blackstone affirms, if ambivalently, include "using their own property as they please," limited only by the narrow principle of *sic utere, tuo ut alienum non-laedes,* or "use your property not to injure that of another."[43] In this, Blackstone repeats Aristotle's tenet that it is impossible to damage one's private property. The distinctions between insanity, clinical deviancy, and an aristocratic eccentricity came later – in the United States, by no means unrelated to the changing strictures of antebellum and postbellum genealogy, marriage, and slavery.[44]

With corporate personhood, however, Blackstone's categorical difference between the public policing of disorderly (and oftentimes intimate) conduct and the self-regulation of private, heritable property shifts toward the self-governance of corporations deemed analogous to the familial estate operating in a providential market. The emphasis on market freedom reflects economic liberalism's derivation from moral economy – one outcome of which is that "the free market" is understood as the scene of a cautionary experience that admonishes fallen, disobedient persons and underscores for them the necessity of moral conduct. It treats immunities from positive law as a deference to a divine, unknowable omniscience. Corporate personhood, by this reading, is an effort to preserve a metaphysical concept of properties and property rights of economic *corpora* in material circumstances understood as contingent, and in which political authority is considered

---

42 Ibid., 1:162.
43 Blackstone, *Commentaries,* 1:295.
44 Susanna L. Blumenthal, "The Deviance of the Will: Policing the Bounds of Testamentary Freedom in Nineteenth-Century America," *Harvard Law Review* 119, no. 4 (2006): 959–1034.

unreliable and as deviating from its otherwise natural course – the echo of Augustinian Neoplatonism that, in the late nineteenth century, would re-emerge as an explicit "lifeboat" theology of evangelical Christianity and the "lifeboat ethics" of a neo-Malthusian ecological nationalism. The extension of citizenship and the franchise renders political authority suspect according to a metaphysics of the natural "order of things." Thus the locus of decision and metrics of authority shift to the market, in tandem with the rise of a corporatist polity emphasizing the intimate intersection of "public police and economy," the penitentiary and plenary powers that might restore a purportedly natural order. The implications of corporatism in politics will be discussed briefly in the conclusion. For now, this chapter turns to a discussion of corporate personhood as an entitled means for setting the reach of insurable actions, immunities, and liabilities, determining the extent to which some transactional risks and desires are underwritten (or not), and setting forth the differential between the providential "free market" of natural liberty and the policing of natural servitude in a material world understood as fallen.

III. The Birth of the Clinic – Born Again in Uncertainty

At the time of writing, the most recent and far-reaching corporate personhood case in the United States is the Supreme Court's 2018 ruling in *National Institute of Family and Life Advocates v. Becerra* (the California Attorney General, Xavier Becerra).[45] Few might immediately describe this as a corporate personhood ruling. Yet as with *Citizens United v. FEC* in 2010,[46] the petitioners in *NIFLA v. Becerra* were private, sometimes non-profit corporations making a claim that disclosure requirements and conditions on licensing and operation would violate their rights to freedom of speech. NIFLA describes itself as an organization that provides "pro-life pregnancy centers and medical clinics with legal counsel, education, and training," and boasts that it has enabled hundreds of faith-based, anti-abortion facilities to undertake "a successful conversion to medical clinic status" under the moniker of "crisis pregnancy centers" or CPCs.[47] The Supreme Court reversed and remanded the decision of a lower court, finding that the California Reproductive

---

45   585 US (2018).
46   558 US 310 (2010).
47   "National Institute of Family and Life Advocates," nifla.org, accessed 27 June 2018, https://nifla.org.

Freedom Act (FACT ACT)[48] had likely violated the freedom of speech of faith-based corporations in stipulating that they must notify clients where they are not a licensed clinic, and in obliging those facilities to inform their clients of the full range of health care options in California, including free or low-cost abortion services. In the opinion supported by a narrow majority, Justice Clarence Thomas set aside informed consent and licensing considerations by arguing that "professional speech" is not a separate category of speech or liable to the burden of disclosure and full information on a topic over which there is controversy, such as abortion. On this basis, Thomas went on, as contended in the dissenting opinion, to nullify the conditions of informed consent. By way of noting the shifting position of the majority on the Supreme Court over almost thirty years, in *Planned Parenthood v. Casey* Justice Thomas had joined the dissenting opinion, which stated that "Roe [v. Wade] was wrongly decided, and that it can and should be overruled consistently with our traditional approach to *stare decisis* in constitutional cases."[49] Yet even as the Constitution links the event of birth to the assumption of rights, the objectification of the law's "compelling interest" in the "potentiality of human life" in *Roe v. Wade*[50] has been successively interpreted to ratify a narrowing pattern of restraints on privacy and the dispensation of immunities in furtherance of "the State's interest in preserving unborn life."[51] This is a far cry from Edward Coke's 1612 opinion in *Sutton's Hospital*, in which the private hospital is described as an artificial, invisible aggregate without a soul, and therefore incapable of arrogating to itself a definition and calculation of risk through recourse to claims of religious freedom.[52] It is however indicative of a line of argument in which immunities from positive law yield a selective catalogue of individual rights ironically invoked against "paternalism" in some cases, as in Thomas's disagreement with *Green v. County Board of Education*,[53] and the affirmation of group rights in the case of corporations that, in practice, eliminate the rights of employees and patients by way of privileging the ostensibly natural law of property's legitimate possession and administration.

---

48   Freedom, Accountability, Comprehensive Care, and Transparency Act, 123470–1234073 California Health and Safety § (2015).
49   505 USSC 833 (1992)
50   410 USSC 113 (1973).
51   505 USSC 833 (1992), 840, sec. 5.
52   Coke, "The Case of Sutton's Hospital."
53   Scott Douglas Gerber, *First Principles: The Jurisprudence of Clarence Thomas* (New York: NYU Press, 1999), 49.

In writing his opinion, Justice Thomas used a fragment from an argument for the right of patients to unbiased medical advice so as to, in effect, conclude the inverse. That is, the rights of the quasi-medical consulting corporation displaced those of the pregnant person and quasi-patient, and therefore the circumstances and stakes of informed consent in any clinical or quasi-clinical discussion of choices available to the latter. In that opinion, Thomas cited Paula Berg on the manipulation of "the content of doctor-patient discourse" to increase state power and suppress minorities," as with doctors in Germany during the period of National Socialist government who "were taught that they owed a higher duty to the 'health of the Volk' than to the health of individual patients." Promptly, he went on to conclude that placing conditions on the content of quasi-clinical speech fail to "preserve an uninhibited marketplace of ideas in which truth will ultimately prevail." As it happens, Berg had argued that "viewpoint-based regulation of doctor-patient discourse" eliminated the conditions of rational choice theory – the very theory that underpins claims that the "marketplace of ideas" functions as a rational mechanism of selection. According to Berg, "viewpoint-based regulation of medical speech distorts medical decision making, and thus infringes on patients' constitutional right to determine the destiny of their bodies."[54]

Berg's contention involves a criticism of the distorting effects of state involvement in the privacy of doctor–patient discussion. Thomas's opinion effectively voided the specification of full and unbiased information on which, ideally, patient consent takes shape in conventional accounts of rational choice and contract theory. In the natural law jurisprudence to which Thomas subscribes, however, the practical formation of patient consent defers to the conduct rule of faithful assent to divine authority, based on an assumption that the economy is a natural order administered by divine omniscience. According to natural law understandings of the economy, the political stipulation of complete and unbiased knowledge in informed consent is an impertinent encroachment on divine authority and an infringement on God's providential operation in an uncertain world – what Adam Smith had called "the highest impertinence."[55] Here as elsewhere, Thomas's argument echoes the rise of eighteenth-century economic liberalism from moral economy, which would have it that the proper source of knowledge and rationality – the scales of equity that weigh choices and guide

---

54 Paula Berg, "Toward a First Amendment Theory of Doctor–Patient Discourse and the Right to Receive Unbiased Medical Advice," *BuL ReV.* 74 (1994): 237.

55 Smith, *The Wealth of Nations*, II. iii. 36/346.

the sword of decisions – is not government. Nor is it afforded to every person as an unqualified assumption of risk-bearing and rationality in lieu of declarations of faith that furnish the first principles of a purportedly rational definition and calculus of risk. Nor does it originate in hypothetical principles of exchange, which might otherwise dictate the consistent, non-discriminatory application of the principles of efficiency, equality, and the unbiased empowerment of choice and speech. On the contrary, legitimacy is derived from religious authority – according to Thomas, from the interaction between "natural rights and higher law,"[56] understood by Aquinas as rational man's participation in but not usurpation of God's wisdom and judgment, in this case, as represented by faith-based facilities.

In The Birth of the Clinic, Foucault suggested that "clinical experience represents a moment of balance between speech and spectacle," an epistemological implication of correspondence between the visible and the expressible, but one where complete "description is a present and ever-withdrawing horizon" because a generalized claim of transparency "leaves opaque the status of the language that must be its foundation." And so, Foucault argues, a deficiency in eighteenth-century empiricism entails a redescent "from the exigency of calculation to the primacy of genesis," where the clinic becomes, in its pedagogical function, the scene of an initiation "into true speech."[57] Tacitly attributed to the eighteenth-century philosopher Étienne Condillac, in the main this forms part Foucault's argument concerning an aetiological and techno-scientific transformation in the causal priority of clinical experience, experiment, and the rise of the empirical gaze. If there is a concept of time in Condillac's writings, however, it is as a conjectural history, at once biblical and anthropological, of developmental transitions from natural sounds to conventional signification to natural law. In that respect, Foucault explains Condillac's theory of language less by describing him as an empiricist who happens to fall back on metaphysics and more by echoing Kant's distinction between practical and speculative reason – a distinction that could easily be mistaken for a substantive dichotomy between, rather than a theoretical conjugation of, empiric observation and divine revelation. Indeed, Condillac was a conservative monarchist who entered a Catholic order and was appointed abbot in commendam of the Norbertine abbey in Mureau in the

---

56 Clarence Thomas, "The Higher Law Background of the Privileges or Immunities Clause of the Fourteenth Amendment," Harv. JL & Pub. Pol'y 12 (1989): 63.

57 Michel Foucault, The Birth of the Clinic: An Archaeology of Medical Perception, trans. Alan Sheridan (London: Tavistock, 1973), 115–17.

years prior to the French Revolution. Condillac was more Augustinian than Thomist; nevertheless, his writings were similarly preoccupied with furnishing a concept of eternal natural law and the selective preservation of property in highly uncertain circumstances through inductive reasoning from experience. Unlike Thomas Aquinas, his method involved emphasizing the approximate, analogical reasoning of case precedents rather than the fixed categorical of canon within the history of natural law jurisprudence – and he was far more influential in shaping early Smithian economic liberalism for all that.

Moreover, far from aspiring to epistemic completeness as Foucault suggests, Condillac advises staying "within the bounds that are marked out for" human knowledge – a restricted and austere economy of abstract signs, perceptive of an abundant, sensory empiricism – and, at the same time, eschewing a "chaotic" profusion through, as in his economic writings, a proto-marginalist embrace of a theory of natural scarcity. By this view, language is the pivot between experiential, inductive reasoning and the restatement of a foundational metaphysics of prime causes and divine omniscience. Thus Condillac does not hold to an unrestricted radical empiricism; instead, his language is the performative, anthropological connection between, on the one hand, a material world he characterizes as "an assemblage or collection of things" or "a multitude of substances" in a fallen world of "disobedience," and, on the other, the revelation of a divine moral and natural law to the developed senses and experience. Condillac's empiricism does not, as Foucault seems to imply, claim or aspire to a total clinical gaze or knowledge in which the status of language is left opaque. It is the explicit iteration of a restricted, fallen condition in a chaotic world: "when I say 'that we do not have any ideas that do not come from the senses,' it must be remembered that I speak only of the state we are now in after the Fall."[58] The claim of opacity concerns not the status of language but rather the unknowable characterization of "the mind of God." The existence of the controversy to which Thomas refers obliges a performative deference to the revealed wisdom of God – not a scientific knowledge resting on claims of the existence of complete knowledge, or even what can be known to a degree of certainty, or the range of historically available information concerning a complex empirical reality, but the performative utterance of a devotional and obedient faith in first principles, the elementary division between believer and non-believer: "The first

---

58 Etienne Bonnot De Condillac, *Condillac: Essay on the Origin of Human Knowledge*, trans. Hans Aarsleff (Cambridge: Cambridge University Press, 2003), 1, I sec. 6, sec. 8.

natural law," Condillac wrote, "is to worship God."[59] In Smithian economics, this is rendered as the theory of subjective utility (desire) interacting providentially with a grammar of natural prices (signs) and is grounded in the assumption of an endogenously ranked self-government of the *oikoi*.[60]

Still, Condillac has not been alone in his description of material entities in a fallen, uncertain world as "an assemblage or collection of things." With or without deference to a Platonist metaphysics of non-spatial, at-emporal forms and the corruption of the material world, this could be pressed toward analytical philosophy, phenomenology, a radical histor-icism or empiricism, the positive law jurisprudence of John Austin, or Herderian linguistic nationalism.[61] Relevant to this discussion, however, is the emergence of a concept of the corporation imbued with person-hood and therefore, in landmark cases, religious freedoms. Condillac's theory of speech turned toward the performative manifestation of an unknowable, invisible divine law and the material assemblage finds an echo in the Pentecostal revivalism and apostolic evangelism of Dwight L. Moody and the establishment of the Assemblies of God in the United States in the early twentieth century, in which uncertainty was rede-scribed as the circumstance of preparing for salvation through the gift of tongues, in a fallen world, and in preparation for the end of days.

IV. *Parrhesia* – Aristocratic and Performative Speech

In *Citizens United v. Federal Election Commission*, the Supreme Court de-clared in an opinion supported by a narrow margin, and written by

---

59 Étienne Bonnot De Condillac, "Traité des animaux," in *Oeuvres philosophiques de Condillac*, ed. Georges Le Roy and Mario-Louis-Guillaume Roque (Paris: Presses Universitaires de France, 1951), 122b, 1.

60 Indeed, the argument in Condillac's *Commerce and Government: Considered in Their Mutual Relationship* (Indianapolis: Liberty Fund, [1776] 2008) is remarkably similar to that in Smith's *Wealth of Nations* published a year later.

61 An "assemblage of many properties" is Marx's description of use-value of Smith-ian economics in *Capital: A Critique of Political Economy*, vol. 1 (Moscow: Progress Press, 1978), 43. It has also been prominent in the writings of Gilles Deleuze and Felix Guattari, cf. *Two Regimes of Madness: Texts and Interviews, 1975–1995*, ed. David Lapoujade (New York: Semiotext(e), 2006), 176–9. In these accounts, the empha-sis is on a radical historicism and radical empiricism of forms, where abstraction is understood as historical or, as in Whitehead's, processual. For a discussion of simultaneously metaphysical and physical assemblages, cf. Mitropoulos, "Ar-chipelago of Risk: Uncertainty, Borders, and Migration Detention Systems," *New Formations* 84, nos. 84–5 (2015): 163–83; Mitropoulos, "Art of Life, Art of War: Movement, Un/Common Forms, and Infrastructure," *E-Flux*, no. 90 (April 2018).

Justice Anthony Kennedy, that Section 441(b) of the Bipartisan Campaign Reform Act of 2002 was unconstitutional. According to Justice Kennedy, it would allow the government to allocate free speech rights to speakers based on a distinction between corporations and persons as well as enable the government to ban the political speech of media corporations; moreover, suppression of corporations' political speech would interfere with the "marketplace of ideas." The ruling invalidated Section 441(b) of the Federal Election Campaign Act of 1971 and Section 203 of the Campaign Reform Act and overturned precedential Supreme Court rulings in *Austin v. Michigan Chamber of Commerce* and *McConnell v. Federal Election Commission*.[62] *Austin v. Michigan Chamber of Commerce*, for instance, had condemned "the corrosive and distorting effects of immense aggregations of wealth that are accumulated with the help of the corporate form." *Citizens United* was the culmination of a campaign to expand the rights of corporations in their opposition to the presidential candidacy of Senator Hillary Rodham-Clinton. The documentary comprised a series of interviews with conservative figures such as Ann Coulter and outlined a catalogue of scandals that Hillary Clinton had purportedly been involved in, such as Whitewater. It was produced by David Bossie, who would go on to serve as Donald J. Trump's deputy campaign director in 2016. The case itself arose in 2008, when Citizens United, a conservative, private non-profit corporation, released a documentary titled *Hillary: The Movie* during the primaries for the Democratic nomination and, around the same time, sought an injunction in a district court claiming that any possible application of Section 203 would be unconstitutional because the film did not fit the definition of electioneering communication. The district court ruled against Citizens United. The Supreme Court overruled the lower court in 2010.

"The Court," Kennedy opined, "has thus rejected the argument that political speech of corporations or other associations should be treated differently under the First Amendment simply because such associations are not 'natural persons,'" but ought to be treated as "natural persons" because "speech cannot be distinguished based upon the presence or lack of economic motive." To do so, Kennedy argued, "would eliminate most speech from first amendment coverage. Likewise, if one eliminates the right to association from economically interested groups, one would eliminate most groups, with the possible exception of the purest religious groups." "Distinguishing wealthy individuals from corporations," Kennedy argued, "based on the latter's special advantages of,

---

62   558 USSC 310 (2010); 494 USSC 652 (1990); 540 USSC 93 (2003).

e.g., limited liability, does not suffice to allow laws prohibiting speech." He then reasoned without evidence that "[t]here is ... little evidence of abuse that cannot be corrected by shareholders 'through the procedures of corporate democracy'" and the expansion of communication by way of the internet.[63] As Anne Tucker points out, this is naively contrary to the actual assumptions and organization of corporate ownership[64] – and, it might be added, to the operations of online platforms. Almost a decade later, the debate over "distortion" has shifted its focus to the use of low- or no-cost online media as a boombox for inflammatory speech, the raising of foreign money for domestic political campaigns and the leverage arising from the resultant financial debts, and the silent harvesting of megadata from online platforms such as Facebook, by companies such as Cambridge Analytica, as a means to gin up (or suppress) undecided voters through microtargeting. The most prominent criticism of *Citizens United*, however, has reiterated the arguments of overturned precedent, *Austin v. Michigan Chamber of Commerce*, namely that accumulated wealth distorts the ostensibly rational functioning of the so-called marketplace of ideas.

In a series of lectures since published under the title *The Government of Self and Other*, Foucault distinguishes between performative speech acts and *parrhesia* in terms of knowledge and risk. "In a performative utterance," Foucault says, "the effect which follows is known and ordered in advance, it is codified," whereas *parrhesia* "opens up an unspecified risk," an "undefined or poorly defined risk for the subject who speaks." It is the statement of a truth to which the subject is bound, come what may, one that emphasizes "his own freedom as an individual speaking" indifferent to status. Simply put, Foucault characterizes *parrhesia* as an act of "courage."[65] By this account, the speech of *Citizens United v. FEC*, operating under conditions of corporate limited liability and shaped by the standing of "wealthy individuals," is not *parrhesia*. There is no courage involved in a prior limitation of and immunity from consequences; there are no unforeseeable risks to which the subject of speech might become liable or fears that might constrain that subject. Nor can the speech of *National Institute of Family and Life Advocates v. Becerra* be described as an instance of *parrhesia* by extension, since it is turned toward the restriction of choices and a determination to calculate risks to

---

63   558 USSC 310, sec. 2.c.1, sec. 3 (2010).
64   Tucker, "Flawed Assumptions."
65   Michel Foucault, *The Government of Self and Others: Lectures at the Collège de France 1982–1983*, trans. Graham Burchell (Basingstoke: Palgrave Macmillan, 2010), 62–7.

which the speaker is not liable, but which the listener is obliged to bear in costly deference to the "marketplace of ideas."

The distinction Foucault makes between the demonstrative and selective condition of performative speech and the ostensibly undefined risks of *parrhesia* is, however, untenable. To be fair, elsewhere he admits the defined conditions on the latter so as to effectively dismiss them as constitutive of the conceit of courageously speaking the entire truth to power. But he does so in order to affirm the bravery of the aristocratic speaker who risks becoming a slave as a consequence, but whose very capacity to speak is predicated on not being enslaved. In his lectures at Berkeley in 1983, Foucault raised Plato's disparaging characterization of *parrhesia* as "chattering," or "saying any or everything one has in mind without qualification," and whose "meaning is also found more frequently in Christian literature where such 'bad' *parrhesia* is opposed to silence as a discipline or as the requisite condition for the contemplation of God."[66] Foucault's omission of performative speech in Christianity, or the more demonstrable speech of Pentecostal *glossolalia*, is as notable as his silence on the implication that Plato's disparagement relies on characterizing speech without qualification as effeminate – which combines in the prohibition on female clerics, presumptuously linking the process of content-selection to the ostensibly natural qualifications of sex and gender. The broader set of limitations on the conditions of *parrhesia* is continuous with these. "This is not to imply," Foucault suggests, "that anyone can use *parrhesia*," to which he adds:

> most of the time the use of *parrhesia* requires that the *parrhesiastes* know his own genealogy, his own status ... One must first be a male citizen to speak the truth as a *parrhesiastes*. Indeed, someone who is deprived of *parrhesia* is in the same situation as a slave to the extent that he or she cannot take part in the political life of the city ... Where one speaks to the assembly, the *ekklesia* – one must be a citizen; in fact, one must be one of the best among the citizens, possessing those specific personal, moral, and social qualities which grant one the privilege to speak.[67]

Still, Foucault mostly proceeds to depict *parrhesia* as if it were the exemplar of courageous speech and not the preserve of entitled speech whose ultimate risk is the foreseeable loss of its aristocratic premise.

---

66 Michel Foucault, "Discourse and Truth: The Problematization of Parrhesia" (November 1983), 3, foucault.info/downloads/discourseandtruth.doc.
67 Ibid., 5.

When seen in this light, it is perhaps unsurprising that freedom of speech has become an irredentist catch-cry that is directed not from "above," as Foucault puts it, but to the contrary, from below. Moreover, the above conflation of assembly, ecclesiastical gathering, and the political life of citizenship in the above quote is not trivial. It does not depict, for instance, the prohibition on the political establishment of a religion, nor does it ponder the implications of a restricted enfranchisement for the life of the city. It does, however, describe the performative assembly of apostolic, evangelical Christianity that is genealogically grounded in and rises up from but also exclusive of most of the inhabitants of both the *oikos* and the city.[68] Because most commentary on *Citizens United* has focused on campaign financing, it might be supposed that it is unlike the cases involving NIFLA and Hobby Lobby. However, *Citizens United* itself makes no distinctions between economics and the putative health, welfare, and security of populations, describing its mission as "reassert[ing] the traditional American values of limited government, freedom of enterprise, strong families, and national sovereignty and security."[69]

V. Lifeboat Theology – Crafting Dominion and Dispensing Salvation

I look on this world as a wrecked vessel. God has given me a life-boat and said to me, "Moody, save as many as you can."
— Dwight Lyman Moody. "Our Lord's Return."[70]

The harsh ethics of the lifeboat become harsher when we consider the reproductive differences between rich and poor.
— Garrett Hardin, "Lifeboat Ethics:
The Case Against Helping the Poor"

In *Burwell v. Hobby Lobby Stores, Inc.*, the US Supreme Court ruled by a narrow majority to apply what it described as "the familiar legal fiction

---

68 The point holds not only for Christianity, but also more broadly for a resurgent religious nationalism, one that eschews the "politicization of life" in deference to the restoration of the noble household. On Foucault's seemingly inexplicable response to theocratic rule in the wake of the Iranian Revolution, see Janet Afary and Kevin B Anderson, *Foucault and the Iranian Revolution: Gender and the Seductions of Islamism* (Chicago: University of Chicago Press, 2010).

69 "Citizens United," Citizens United, accessed 27 June 2018, http://www.citizensunited.org/who-we-are.aspx.

70 Dwight Lyman Moody, *New Sermons, Addresses, and Prayers* (Ohio: Henry S. Goodspeed, 1877), 535.

of including corporations within RFRA's [the Religious Freedom Restoration Act's] definition of 'persons,'" thereby extending a religious exemption to the health care mandate in the Affordable Care Act of 2010 (ACA) to "merchants" so as to protect "the free-exercise rights of closely held corporations [and] the religious liberty of the humans who own and control them." The court decided that the ACA's mandate had violated "the sincerely held religious beliefs of the companies' owners."[71] In a series of legal cases that culminated in *Burwell v Hobby Lobby*, Hobby Lobby and two related and similar companies had sought an exemption from the ACA's regulatory mandate that insurance coverage be extended to all FDA-approved contraceptive methods, sterilization procedures, and patient education and counselling. Closely held corporations are private companies that may trade shares but do so outside of central exchanges such as the NYSE and are often family-owned companies, as with Hobby Lobby Stores. The Court's description of corporate personhood as a "familiar legal fiction" rests on a theory of the corporation as an extension and aggregate of real proprietors, in this case a private company whose ownership structure is patrilineal, where all of the voting stock is held in family trusts and all trustees have signed a statement of adherence to Christian evangelism, called a "Trust Commitment." More patriarchal-familial than familiar, this understanding of corporate personhood declared against the capacity of Hobby Lobby's employees to define and calculate risk, rendering the cost of the range of available reproductive choices prohibitive and narrowing those choices by subjecting reproductive rights to employer prerogative. As Justice Ruth Bader Ginsburg pointed out in dissent, the price of "an IUD is nearly equivalent to a month's full-time pay for workers earning the minimum wage." David Green, the founding father of Hobby Lobby, makes few distinctions between religious assembly, household, and firm. According to Green, "Hobby Lobby has always been a tool for the Lord's work."[72] Dawn Johnsen, one of the authors of an amicus brief in support of the Obama administration's case, argues that the majority opinion illustrated a failure of empathy that may, following Ginsberg, "reflect less a lack of understanding of the parties' perspectives than a choice of which party is considered."[73]

---

71 573 USSC (2014).

72 S. Kyle Duncan et al., "Verified Complaint, Jury Demanded. Case 5:12-Cv-01000-HE" (United States District Court for the Western District Of Oklahoma, September 9, 2012), sec. II. 40.

73 "Hobby Lobby Symposium: Corporations Who Worship – 1, Women Who Work – 0," SCOTUSblog, 1 July 2014, http://www.scotusblog.com/2014/07/hobby-lobby-symposium-corporations-who-worship-1-women-who-work-0.

In this sense, Green's instrumental view of the corporation – as "a tool for the Lord's work" – resolves into an instrumental understanding of its employees, not its owners, who are granted liberty in the conflation of apostolic mission and proprietorship that privileges a theological calculus of moral risk. In treating immunities from non-discriminatory stipulations in the provision of health, welfare, and services on the grounds of moral hazard, conservatives have echoed Augustine's epiphany over the Pauline injunction to "make no provision for the flesh in its concupiscence."[74]

God, according to then-president of Hobby Lobby Steven Green, has "given us the ability to be very successful in our business." To this he added, "I think to some degree it's providential."[75] Furthermore, "Hobby Lobby is basically a ministry."[76] Hobby Lobby is also one of the largest investors in evangelical education and ministries in the United States and around the world, partnering with Wallbuilders, a Christian nationalist organization whose head runs the Providence Foundation. David Green founded Hobby Lobby Stores in 1972. He was the only one of six children who did not become a pastor as their father had been in the Church of God of Prophecy, otherwise known as the Assemblies of God. The Brethren movement replaced the idea of churches with that of assemblies (at times referred to as "households of faith"), as in the Assemblies of God. The Assemblies of God states its belief in "the whole Bible rightly divided" – a reference to the dispensationalism of C.I. Scofield's *Rightly Dividing the Word of Truth*.[77] Developed by John Nelson Darby during the 1820s in Dublin, Ireland, dispensationalism gained followers across the Atlantic through the Bible Conference movement of the 1880s and '90s and the proselytizing of Dwight L. Moody and Scofield.

Dispensationalism is an explicitly historiographic and futurist *oikonomic* doctrine in which historical and biblical time is divided into discrete ages called *oikoi*, each with its own set of administrative principles, or *nomoi*. In a dispensationalist text on economics, McDowell restates the first premise as follows: "there is a God who created all things, including man – and God is concerned about the economy, about how we

---

74   Augustine, *The Confessions*, trans. J. G. Pilkington (Edinburgh: T & T Clark, 1876), 8.12.29.
75   Joel Baden and Candida Moss, "Can Hobby Lobby Buy the Bible?," *The Atlantic*, 2016.
76   Aaron K. Ketchell, *Holy Hills of the Ozarks: Religion and Tourism in Branson*, Missouri (Baltimore: Johns Hopkins University Press, 2007), 218.
77   C.I. Scofield, *Rightly Dividing the Word of Truth* (Grand Rapids: Zondervan, 1973).

manage our household and our nation."[78] For each stage of *oikos* there are *nomoi* pertaining to the proper management of the *oikos* – in other words, the stages are "rightly divided." In Scofield's reading, there are accordingly seven dispensations or *oikonomia* in the Bible. "Each of the Dispensations," Scofield argued, "may be regarded as a new test of the natural man, and each ends in judgment – marking his utter failure."[79] Each *oikos* culminates in crisis, and all tend toward the rapture and the end of days.[80] As Michael Phillips points out, dispensationalism presented a Manichaean view of redemption and salvation, one in which Jews were granted an honorary whiteness in millennial conflict, as a philo-Semitic reading of divine selection – a sentiment that had its scientific parallel in eugenicist depictions of "history as heading towards Armageddon in which white civilization squared off against colored savagery" and a literal Antichrist.[81] Since the 1980s, Scofield's premillennial concept of seven dispensations has been adapted to a postmillennial mandate doctrine of Christian Reconstructionism by groups such as the New Apostolic Reformation and the National Christian Charitable Foundation.[82] The first of these articulates the dispensations as a "divine mandate ... to do whatever is necessary, by the power of the Holy Spirit, to retake the dominion of God's creation which Adam forfeited to Satan in the Garden of Eden," an aim that obliges the transfer of wealth to priests and divinely anointed kings so that they might fulfil their divine commission.[83] This is one iteration of so-called dominionist theology. It is coupled with the strict view that government provision of health care, welfare, or insurance is an infringement on moral law and best carried out by faith-based organizations or the family, since to do

---

78 Stephen K. McDowell, *The Economy from a Biblical Perspective*, vol. 23 (Charlettesville: Providence Foundation, 2009), 2.

79 C.I. Scofield, "Dispensational Premillennialism," in *Evangelicalism and Fundamentalism: A Documentary Reader*, ed. Barry Hankins (New York: NYU Press, 2008), 60.

80 H.A. Ironside, *A Historical Sketch of the Brethren Movement* (Chicago: Wholesome Words, 2014), 3, 16.

81 Michael Phillips, *White Metropolis: Race, Ethnicity, and Religion in Dallas, 1841–2001*, 16.

82 Frederick Clarkson, *Eternal Hostility: The Struggle between Theocracy and Democracy* (Monroe.: Common Courage Press, 1997); Julie Ingersoll, *Building God's Kingdom: Inside the World of Christian Reconstruction* (New York: Oxford University Press, 2015), 33.

83 C. Peter Wagner, "Letter," 31 May 2007, in René Holvast, *Spiritual Mapping in the United States and Argentina* (Boston: Brill, 2009), 161; C. Peter Wagner, *The Great Transfer of Wealth: Financial Release for Advancing God's Kingdom* (New Kensington, Whitaker House, 2015).

otherwise risks moral hazard and the facilitation of sin.[84] In their book *America's Providential History*, Mark Beliles and Stephen McDowell resort to a hermeneutical gloss to contend that "scripture makes it clear that God is the provider, not the state, and that needy individuals are to be cared for by private acts of charity."[85] They espouse both the dominionist tenet of the absolute and unlimited rights of property owners and the view that economic success is a sign of God's grace – the doctrine of prosperity.

There are historical parallels to restrictions on the scope and definition of insurable conduct and dominion. There is also a legislative context that extends beyond that of evangelicalism but that nevertheless similarly implies a Neoplatonist metaphysics of ideal forms as souls whose material existence is regarded as inherently imperfect and corrupted, and that, as in Plato's *Republic*, hold a potential for salvation. In contrast to positive injunctions to a rigid, omniscient classification of the objective sciences discussed by Foucault, the emphasis falls on an essence or potential accessible through a combination of intuition and revelation.[86] Increasingly, that has involved a combination of a narrowed sentiment and the inferential leap to ontological revelation through the use of ultrasound technologies.[87] The interaction between the performative gaze of empirical observation in the clinic and the unseen perspective of the law that constitutes the conditions of the former is a legacy of the limits on the legal personhood of women, who have no authority in the *oikos* and are liable to disobedience. As Jean Schroedel and colleagues have observed, *Roe v. Wade* did not legalize abortion so much as it ruled that the privacy right under the 14th Amendment's due process clause may be applied to a woman's decision about whether to have an abortion but, crucially, this would hereafter be "balanced" against the state's right to claim a "compelling interest" in "the potentiality of

---

84 Angela Mitropoulos, "Dispensing God's Care," *The New Inquiry*, 12 June 2017, https://thenewinquiry.com/dispensing-gods-care.

85 Mark A. Beliles and Stephen K. McDowell, *America's Providential History: Including Biblical Principles of Education, Government, Politics, Economics, and Family Life* (Charlottesville: Providence Foundation, 1989), 187.

86 Simona Forti makes a similar argument in "The Biopolitics of Souls: Racism, Nazism, and Plato," *Political Theory* 34, no. 1 (February 1, 2006): 14.

87 Joanne Boucher, "Ultrasound: A Window to the Womb? Obstetric Ultrasound and the Abortion Rights Debate," *Journal of Medical Humanities* 25, no. 1 (March 1, 2004): 7–19; Julie Palmer, "Seeing and Knowing: Ultrasound Images in the Contemporary Abortion Debate," *Feminist Theory* 10, no. 2 (1 August 2009): 173–89.

human life."[88] As to the actuarial handling of postnatal property imbued with potential for redemption and subject to absolute dominion, for early nineteenth-century slaveholders faced with increasingly high insurance premiums, the trend of "replacing 'mutual duties and responsibilities' with impersonal market relations" encouraged a pooling of the downside risks of contracting and managing an increasingly mobile, fugitive, and disobedient labour. At the same time, however, the insuring of slaves was anxiously viewed as a means of "divorcing the slave from the 'natural discretion and prudence' of the owner."[89] Where risk-pooling between the owners of enslaved people was indicative of a broader historical turn to welfare and insurance (for the most part undertaken by private, dedicated insurance companies and schemes), it also signalled a growing conflict over the futurial stakes of speculation, a conflict whose allocative tensions would, in time, be increasingly resolved through recourse to more or less tacit rulings on legal personhood and the imputed categorical properties of legitimate *corpora,* the insurability of disobedient, insurrectionist slaves, and the stigmatization of fugitive property.[90]

In *The Order of Things*, Foucault describes the Smithian emphasis on the interaction between contingency and necessity obliquely. He characterizes it as "the interior time of an organic structure which grows in accordance with its own necessity and develops in accordance with autochthonous laws – the time of capitalist production." For Smith, however, that meant the rule of subjective preference operating as fraternal interaction in exchanges between "[m]en [who] ... experience needs and desires" and the objective, ideal norm that subjects those exchanges to a "great exterior necessity."[91] While Foucault claims that this diminished the centrality of the family, it is, to the contrary, a theory of the *oikos* as a moral economic version of population theory, in which natural and divine law are understood to be interactive mechanisms of providential selection precisely because there is no empirical correlation between

88 Jean Reith Schroedel, Pamela Fiber, and Bruce D. Snyder, "Women's Rights and Fetal Personhood in Criminal Law," *Gender Law and Policy* 7 (2000): 91–2.

89 Sharon Ann Murphy, "Securing Human Property: Slavery, Life Insurance, and Industrialization in the Upper South," *Journal of the Early Republic* 25, no. 4 (2005): 625.

90 Anita Rupprecht, "Excessive Memories: Slavery, Insurance and Resistance," *History Workshop Journal* 64, no. 1 (2007): 6–28. See also Carol E. Henderson, *Scarring the Black Body: Race and Representation in African American Literature* (Columbia: University of Missouri Press, 2002); Stephen S. Best, *The Fugitive's Properties: Law and the Poetics of Possession* (Chicago: University of Chicago Press, 2004).

91 Foucault, *The Order of Things*, 244–5.

the *oikos* as the basal unit of a nascent economics and the "bodies in motion" first objectified by Hobbesian theories of sovereignty as the personification of well-defined aggregates motivated by appetites and fears. The parallels between Smith's moral economy and Augustinian theodicy have been pointed out by others as a shared theory of "natural selection" that propels human evolution toward "an ideal limiting case."[92] This is not quite Darwin's theory. While it recalls Darwin's theory of "natural selection" in that both purport to discover the one great law or mechanism governing life's evolution, it is nevertheless unlike Darwin in emphasizing not the increased range of chances made possible by diversity but, to the contrary, the selective conservation of properties and their redemption through uncertain and catastrophic circumstances.[93] Yet in his later writings and lectures, Foucault treats this mechanism as if it were derived from a political ratio, reversing the order of Hannah Arendt's argument that politics is reshaped by the principles of the *oikos* so as to arrive at the claim that population theory indicates a biopolitical "politicisation of life."[94] Additionally, Foucault mischaracterizes the rise of population theory as a shift away from pastoral power and eschatological time.

Indeed, despite the importance he placed on the concept of population in yielding this transformation, Foucault rarely engaged with the writings of the eighteenth-century Protestant cleric Thomas Robert Malthus – arguably the most influential if not the most original of population theorists.[95] Nor does he discuss neo-Malthusians such as

---

92 A.M.C. Waterman, "Economics as Theology: Adam Smith's *Wealth of Nations*," *Southern Economic Journal* 68, no. 4 (2002): passim; Jerry Evensky, *Adam Smith's Moral Philosophy: A Historical and Contemporary Perspective on Markets, Law, Ethics, and Culture* (Cambridge: Cambridge University Press, 2005), 25.

93 Briefly, Darwin doubted the Neoplatonist premise of ideal perfection as the striving toward a hierarchical, orderly universe, that the evolutionary significance or the advantage of attributes at any given or catastrophic moment could be meaningfully derived from their present or past functions, or even that "the term species, [was other than] ... arbitrarily given for the sake of convenience." Darwin's view of classification is as a convenience, and it does not rest on a subtle concept of divine purpose as the link between genesis and destiny crucial to teleology. *On the Origin of Species* (Peterborough: Broadview Press, 2003), 127.

94 Mitropoulos, *Contract and Contagion*, 60; Hannah Arendt, *The Human Condition* (Chicago: University of Chicago Press, 1998), 28.

95 Ute Tellmann makes a similar point in "Catastrophic Populations and the Fear of the Future: Malthus and the Genealogy of Liberal Economy," *Theory, Culture, and Society* 30, no. 2 (2013): 135–55. On discussions of Malthus by Foucault's contemporaries, compare Jacques Donzelot, *The Policing of Families*, trans. Robert Hurley (New York: Pantheon, 1979).

Garrett Hardin, who rose to prominence with the publication of "The Tragedy of the Commons" in the decade prior to Foucault's lectures on population, and whose later essay "Lifeboat Ethics: The Case against Helping the Poor" is contemporaneous with those lectures at the Collège de France.[96] Instead, Foucault follows the archaeologist Paul Veyne in proposing an archaic history of the decline of ecclesiastical-pastoral power, which he argues underwent a crisis in the fifteenth and sixteenth centuries and gave way to a "new historical perception no longer polarized" around eschatology, less inclined to resort to coercion, but "open to an indefinite time for the struggle for survival" administered by a tenuous equilibrium wrought through international treaties. Put simply, Foucault describes as the circumstantial rise of population theory and the biopolitical "management of state forces" as an eclipse of ecclesiastical authority.[97]

Yet eschatology and biblical catastrophism are key to the writings and arguments of Malthus and Hardin.[98] In a lengthy footnote on Malthus, Marx bluntly points to the close correspondence between moral economy, eschatology, and population theory: "with this very 'Principle of Population,'" he writes, "struck the hour of the Protestant parsons." The counter-revolution in the history of economic liberalism, according to Marx, was situated in the wake of the French Revolution, "in the midst of a great social crisis," and "greeted with jubilance by the English oligarchy as the great destroyer of all hankerings after human development."[99] Hardin, for his part, borrowed the analogy of "lifeboats" from the evangelical sermons of Dwight L. Moody.[100] He did so in making a series of Manichaean, ultra-nationalist arguments against the rule of international treaties and the United Nations and in favour of regulating sexual conduct and closing the borders of the United States to immigrants – urged on by the imagination of an impending ecological apocalypse. Unlike Smith, whose writings predate the French Revolution, there is no proposition of an economic equilibrium in population

96 Garrett James Hardin, "The Tragedy of the Commons," *Science* 162 (1968): 1243–8; Hardin, "Lifeboat Ethics: The Case against Helping the Poor," *Psychology Today*, September 1974.

97 Michel Foucault, *Ethics, Subjectivity and Truth: Essential Works of Foucault 1954–1984*, ed. Paul Rabinow, vol. 1 (London: Penguin, 1997), 67–71.

98 T.R. Malthus, *On Population: Three Essays*, ed. Frederick Osborn (New York: New American Library, 1960).

99 Karl Marx, *Capital: A Critique of Political Economy: The Process of Capitalist Production*, vol. 1 (Moscow: Progress Press, 1978), 578n1.

100 Moody, *New Sermons, Addresses, and Prayers*, 535.

theory. There is instead the imagining of a simultaneously economic and moral hazard that warrants a turn to harsh and coercive measures of selection so as to avert a catastrophe akin to divine judgment and the end of days – specifically, both Malthus and Hardin advise the punitive regulation of sexual conduct and reproduction in view of a theory of natural scarcity or natural limits. This is the Neoplatonist "governance of souls" turned into a principle of preserving, through coercion or immunities from positive law, the properties of legitimate *corpora* through recourse to a myth of property's origins and the animating aesthetics of its providential, eschatological end of days.

VI. His Majesty the Accident

It is a widespread assumption that neoliberalism emphasizes individual rights at the expense of collective rights and diminishes the role of the state in relation to the market. The first supposition cannot account for the qualified, categorical patterning of provisions and immunities, or the corporation as the personification of aggregates; the second cannot furnish an explanation for how it has transformed but not diminished state power and the reliance on mechanisms of selection. Foucault's fleeting remarks on biopolitics contribute to these assumptions insofar as his theory of biopolitics and neoliberalism is understood as continuous with a classical sociological claim that, with the onset of a modern rationality, life and natural economy are altered by a distinctly political ratio and calculus.

   Corporate personhood, however, is one aspect of a broader modification of legal reasoning, in which the twinned assumptions of uncertainty and determinism become a premise of inaccessible knowledge that, at the intersection of political and corporate administration, veers into the selective organization of speech, visibility, accountability, and disclosure. The trope of an inaccessible divine purpose finds its secular parallel in the unknowable intentions of the powerful, which are no longer evidenced by objective measures of performance as Oliver Wendell Holmes had argued.[101] Such a purpose can only be intuited through presumably opaque sentiment or feelings whose intersubjective meaning and implications drift off in assertions of Manichaean controversy. As has been widely reported, in 2005, Donald J. Trump brought a $5 billion libel suit against Timothy L. O'Brien, the author of *Trump Nation: The Art of Being*

---

101   Mitropoulos, *Contract and Contagion*, 39–40.

Donald Trump.[102] At issue was not Trump's characterization in the book, which was for the most part laudatory, but whether O'Brien's efforts to specify the dollar value of Trump's companies indicated "malice." In depositions, Trump was asked, "Have you always been completely truthful in your public statements about your net worth of properties?" Trump responded: "My net worth fluctuates, and it goes up and down with markets and with attitudes and with feelings, even my own feelings, but I try." Trump was prompted to elaborate: "The net worth goes up and down based upon your own feelings?" "Yes," Trump replied.[103] The point here is not that evaluations do not involve sentiments, including of self-evaluation, although the shift to contingent accounting methods is one aspect of this.[104] It is what this entails for politics and governance, and in a circumstance where politically influential corporations are less those highlighted by Occupy Wall Street than those which are incorporated as private, family-owned companies, trading in private, unsecured, and often unregulated markets, and privy to a broader range of immunities.

As in Gierke's writings, mentioned at the beginning of this chapter, continental European theories of political and corporate personification have long been accompanied by a corporatist theory of the state. There are different views on what, in politics, corporatism means – whether it is a rigid version of pluralism, a variant of authoritarian populism, or something closer to fascism. In any case, corporatism is presented as an alternative to the perceived instability of parliamentary democracy, and its ideal prototype is the political combination of the medieval estates in a stable, organic unity.[105] The point here is not to resolve these debates but to outline the implication of the above analysis of corporate personhood for politics and governance, as theory of and reaction to uncertainty, in which decision and measure are mechanisms of selection.

In classical philosophy, that method proceeds as a metaphysical definition and as distinctions between essence, ephemera, and accident, which is to say, the contingent. What happens, then, when contingencies are incorporated into measures of value and ground a decision as if they are its essential properties, or when contingency is transformed

---

102 Timothy L. O'Brien, *TrumpNation: The Art of Being The Donald* (New York: Warner Business Books, 2005).

103 *Donald J. Trump v. Timothy L. O'Brien, Time Warner Book Group, Inc., and Warner Books, Inc.* (Superior Court of New Jersey, Appellate Division 2011).

104 Angela Mitropoulos, "Archipelago of Risk: Uncertainty, Borders, and Migration Detention Systems," *New Formations* 84 (2015): 163–83.

105 Leo Panitch, "The Development of Corporatism in Liberal Democracies," *Comparative Political Studies* 10, no. 1 (1 April 1977): 61.

into an inexorable necessity?[106] In his "Critique of Hegel's Doctrine of the State," Marx describes Hegel's corporatist theory of the state, which preserves and personifies a purportedly universal ethic, as the invention of an "independent private person," the "abstract embodiment" and personified synthesis of state and civil society resting on the aggregate of the "independent private capital" of private, familial estates and therefore, by Hegel's reasoning, presumably incorruptible by bribery and independent of particular interests. Hegel's proposal for the refoundation of political authority according to "the natural principle of the family" means, according to Marx, that "this class [of landed property] is summoned and *entitled* to its political vocation by *birth* without the hazards of election." "Hegel has failed to prove," Marx writes, "that the right of this landowning class is based on the natural principle of the family unless by this he means landed property is acquired by inheritance." As such, Hegel's investment of property with a spiritual dimension devolves into a vulgar materialism that, contemptuous of nature, links birth to the presumably indisputable and ahistorical arrangement of heritable property rights.

As such, Marx underscores the selective conflations and synthetic abstractions on which rest Hegel's dialectical version of Neoplatonism, as well as his definition of corporate personification: "The *false* identity, the fragmentary, intermittent identity of nature and spirit, body and soul, becomes manifest here as *embodiment, incorporation*," in which "the nobility takes a natural pride in its blood," and "political qualifications appear ... as *the property of landed property*, as something directly arising from the *purely physical earth* (nature)." By Marx's reading, Hegel's corporatist state rests, in short, on a doctrine of blood and soil. It alters political tenets of equality, and it proposes the restriction of the franchise, which Hegel affirms, in line with the ostensibly organic properties and property rights derived from natural economy. In Hegel's ideal historiography, this reverses the disunity of the state in the wake of the decline of its unified monarchical embodiment, while retrieving the semblance of a presumably eternal hierarchy and natural order at a "higher" level. The corporatist state is a syncretism of the noble household, understood in eugenic terms, and the contingency of the market, understood as providential – their combination, in "the natural course of things," resolves the division between ecclesiastical authority and monarchical power in an organic unity. The result, in Marx's view, is

---

106   Mitropoulos, *Contract and Contagion*, 48, passim.

however not a peaceful order but the profound reign of contingency, one that, by seemingly incomprehensible turns, is benevolent, brutal, and erratic: "The two moments," Marx writes of Hegel's ideal state, "are the *accident of will*, caprice," exemplary in the exceptional plenary power to pardon as an act of grace, "and the *accident of Nature*, birth – and so we have *His Majesty the Accident*."[107]

---

107 Karl Marx, *Early Writings*, trans. Rodney Livingstone and Gregor Benton (London: Penguin, 1984), 172–7, 94. Emphases in original.

.

PART TWO

The Social Theory of the Corporation

In *Supercapitalism: The Transformation of Business, Democracy, and Everyday Life*,[1] Robert Reich examines the myriad ways that corporate power corrodes democracy and political norms in the United States. Critics of corporate personhood doctrine who invoke human rights do not restrict themselves to discussions of whether *Citizens United* and *Hobby Lobby* were incorrectly argued. Rather, they join Reich in pointing to the corrosive effects of the corporation's expanding rights and privileges on social and political life. In this section, the contributors examine how corporate rights insert themselves into social life beyond the corrosion of democracy. They devote particular attention to the impact of corporations on our distributions (public welfare) and on our institutions of social reproduction and social cohesion (public education and social media).

Andrea Matwyshyn has characterized the corporation as a cyborg, one that conceals its artificial personhood by adorning itself with a human face that it hopes is not off-putting. Applying actor–agent–network theory, Matwyshyn has shown how corporations interact with human society through a perfidious mix of humanized corporate branding and dehumanized internal corporate affairs: "Internally, a corporation conceptualizes itself as a type of machine – a series of overlapping information networks, both human and technological. Externally, a corporation seeks to be viewed as a trusted (human) friend to maximize its goodwill. Internal corporate information flows are increasingly mechanized through computerization; externally, however, corporations work to maintain a human face to build brand and customer loyalty."[2] In their

---

1 Robert B. Reich, *Supercapitalism: The Transformation of Business, Democracy, and Everyday Life* (New York: A.A. Knopf, 2007).
2 Andrea M. Matwyshyn, "Corporate Cyborgs and Technology Risks," *Minnesota Journal of Law, Science, and Technology* 11, no. 2 (2010): 575.

chapter, David Golumbia and Frank Pasquale take up the impact of this cyborg figure on education, social media, and the linguistic resources of human selves. They read the dystopian young adult novel, *Feed*, by M.T. Anderson, to explore the implications of granting for-profit educational institutions untrammelled 1st Amendment rights to design the curriculum of a grade school. In the process, educational technologies overpower traditional sources of the self. Liability for corporate actions, the relations of individuals to corporations and of corporations to the state, and, ultimately, the way we understand the rights of the corporate person, are all transformed.

If corporations have launched a hostile takeover of the rights of natural persons, however, they have not done so entirely through attaining expressive rights. Perversely, corporations have posited themselves as the true subjects of welfarism because they lack the moral fallibility of natural persons, and also as a consequence of their economic power – aid to corporations will flow to workers and consumers more efficiently than aid to the impoverished. In his contribution to this volume, Richard Hardack posits corporations as beneficiaries of social welfare precisely *because* as neoliberal subjects they are superior to actual human beings who suffer from deprivation and inequality. He coins a term for this ascendance of the corporation over the individual – negative individualism: "the various iterations of negative individualism that suffuse US society mirror the inverted structure of corporate personhood; in legal and practical terms, individual persons assume most blame and liability, while corporate persons remain almost categorically immune from them." Corporate legal doctrine paves the way for this unequal treatment of corporations and individuals by making it difficult to penalize corporations, as collective entities, even as innocent individuals – those who had no part in the making of decisions, including shareholders, employees, and contractors – are punished vicariously. Furthermore, neoliberal ideology holds that the collective nature of corporations means that bestowals on corporations benefit individuals in the corporation and individuals in the market more efficiently. Hardack uses the Maussian logic of the gift to argue that corporate persons are cast as deprived, but deserving, in contrast to actual humans. They are deserving because their participation in public/private partnerships and wealth creation makes them better caretakers of humans than human entities themselves. Hardack is correct to say that in the current ideological regime and under our legal systems, individual existence opens one up to greater legal liabilities and public deprivations than those associated with corporate persons.

4 From Public Sphere to Personalized Feed: Corporate Constitutional Rights and the Challenge to Popular Sovereignty

DAVID GOLUMBIA AND FRANK PASQUALE[1]

Government, Natural Persons, and Corporate Rights

The mutual co-constitution of self and society has been an enduring theme of social thought.[2] Individualistic approaches to modelling human experience have rested on atomistic (and behaviouristically monadic) representations of human consciousness,[3] whereas social scientists and humanists with broader historical and cultural perspectives have always emphasized the way society shapes selves.[4]

There is a normative paradox implicit in the descriptive logic of mutual co-constitution. Basic norms of conscience, freedom, and autonomy suggest that all human beings enjoy the right to question critically any institution they are a part of once they reach legal adulthood. At the same time, the very norms one might use to question one institution may themselves be the product of some other institution. Outside the

---

1 The authors wish to thank Tamara Piety, Sharif Youssef, and other readers for helpful comments on the law, policy, and normative framework of this chapter. All remaining errors and omissions remain our responsibility.
2 George Herbert Mead, *Mind, Self, and Society* (originally published 1934; "definitive edition," Chicago: University of Chicago Press, 2015); William H. Poteat, *Polanyian Meditations: In Search of a Post-Critical Logic* (Durham: Duke University Press, 1985).
3 See, for example, James S. Coleman, *Foundations of Social Theory* (Cambridge, MA: Harvard University Press, 1990), importing rational actor model from economics to sociology.
4 Charles Taylor, "Atomism," in *Philosophy and the Human Sciences: Philosophical Papers 2* (New York: Cambridge University Press, 1985), 187–210; Joseph Raz, *The Morality of Freedom* (New York: Oxford University Press, 1979), arguing that autonomy is only possible given a flourishing background of choices of paths of life to take; further explained in Frank Pasquale, "Two Concepts of Immortality: Reframing Public Debate on Stem-Cell Research," *Yale Journal of Law and the Humanities* 14, no. 1 (2002), http://digitalcommons.law.yale.edu/cgi/viewcontent.cgi?article=1250&context=yjlh, esp. 110–11.

Rousseauvian fantasies of evolutionary biologists, there is no stepping outside this embeddedness to some primal uncovering of bare instinct.[5] Yet this acknowledgment should not be seen as a dismissal of, or even a radical questioning of, personal autonomy. Liberalism, democracy, and human rights have helped ensure a civil society vibrant enough to support diverse values and ways of life. The tension between individual and group has been productive, however much liberals and communitarians may argue about potential recalibrations of its balance in particular scenarios.[6]

There are signs, though, that critical aspects of this balance are in danger.[7] In the non-governmental realm, for-profit corporations have moved from a *primus inter pares* role to one of domination.[8] They are demanding that once stalwartly independent features of the social landscape (such as non-profit universities, hospitals, and churches) submit themselves to business logics of managerialism, competition, and profit maximization.[9] As one type of institution crowds out other modes of organization, the

---

5 For an example of such sociobiological unveiling, see Tucker Max and Geoffrey Miller, *Mate: Become the Man Women Want* (New York: Little, Brown, 2015).

6 Stephen Mulhall and Adam Swift, *Liberals and Communitarians*, 2nd ed. (Malden: Blackwell, 1996).

7 We draw on a metaphor of balance to correct the functionalism and quietism of equilibrium-oriented theories of economics. While equilibrists are quick to spot dynamics of diminishing returns that preserve a status quo, other social theories (particularly conflict theories) emphasize how quickly equilibrium can be upset. See Roger Boesche, "Why Could Tocqueville Predict So Well?," *Political Theory* 11, no. 1 (February 1983), 79–103: "Tocqueville expresses the ancient belief that a society resembles a fabric in which the elements are interwoven and interdependent ... Perhaps a more precise image surfaces in modern language; society seems to resemble a delicately balanced mobile in which every aspect settles into its position as a result of the composite influence of every other. Laws, religion, art, architecture, economic considerations, manners, language, literature, and so forth, lean upon one another. Although the image of a mobile may be modern, the idea supporting this image is at least as old as Plato, who feared that changing only the music would transform all of society" (82).

8 Elizabeth Anderson, *Private Government* (New York: Princeton University Press, 2017); K. Sabeel Rahman, *Democracy Against Domination* (New York: Oxford University Press, 2016).

9 This is in keeping with Niklas Luhmann's systems theory, which disaggregated society into a series of systems, each trying to translate the others into its own terms, and insisting on that translation once it had attained sufficient power. Michael Walzer offered a normative critique of such a process in *Spheres of Justice: A Defense of Pluralism and Equality* (New York: Basic Books, 1984). Luhmann's rival in social theory, Jürgen Habermas, may have become so concerned about developments like genetic engineering in the late 1990s because he realized the descriptive power of Luhmann's vision: economic/corporate pressures squeezing people into ever more Procrustean self-shaping. Habermas sincerely believed in democratic will formation as a "steering" mechanism for society as a whole, but such steering becomes impossible if entities as powerful as for-profit corporations refuse to submit to it.

space of institutions relative to individuals undergoes two transformations corrosive of individual autonomy. First, that space becomes normatively monocultural, as neoliberal logics of productivity, marketization, and wealth maximization crowd out other means of assessing and guiding human conduct.[10] Second, the dominant corporate entities in the institutional field become far more powerful than most individuals, since those individuals would need some alternative institutional identity to mount a plausible, enduring challenge to for-profit corporations.

For-profit corporations have deployed a powerful rhetorical tool to deflect attention from these developments, by arguing that a corporation is nothing more than a collection of people. This is the "aggregate" theory.[11] While Margaret Thatcher's famous insistence that "there is no society, only individuals and families" was meant to discredit a more holistic, common-good–oriented politics, the rhetoric of corporate reductionism is more a trick meant to replicate semantically what liability limits accomplish pragmatically: to hide the power and responsibility of corporations as such, by diverting attention to individuals. It is a verbal Ring of Gyges.

To be sure, given the extraordinary ways that individuals and boards can manipulate the corporate form, it may seem natural to try to "pierce

---

10 In the case of hospitals, for example, non-monetizable activities (such as community service or some forms of research) may be pushed aside in order to maximize quarterly returns. See Frank Pasquale, "Ending the Specialty Hospital Wars: A Plea for Pilot Programs as Information-Forcing Regulatory Design," in *The Fragmentation Of U.S. Health Care: Causes And Solutions*, ed. Einer Elhauge (Oxford University Press, 2010, 235–77). In universities, performance may be boiled down to some ratio of cost-of-attendance and graduates' starting salaries – demoting classic university goals of research, disinterested inquiry, community service, and encouragement of students' exploration of diverse vocational opportunities and avocational pursuits. See Frank Pasquale, "Synergy and Tradition: The Unity of Research, Service, and Teaching in Legal Education," *Journal of the Legal Profession* 40, no. 1 (2015), 25–49. We leave aside for now another form of "takeover": corporate influence over government. See Pasquale, *The Black Box Society: The Secret Algorithms That Control Money and Information* (Cambridge, MA: Harvard University Press, 2015), on the "blob"-like character of government capture.

11 See Brandon L. Garrett, "The Constitutional Standing of Corporations," *University of Pennsylvania Law Review* 163 (2014), 95–164, http://papers.ssrn.com/sol3/papers.cfm?abstract_id=2330972, on the historical alternation between the "aggregate" and "artificial entity" theories of the corporation; Anne Tucker, in "Flawed Assumptions: A Corporate Law Analysis of Free Speech and Corporate Personhood in *Citizens United*," *Case Western Reserve Law Review* 61:2 (2011), 495–548, http://papers.ssrn.com/sol3/papers.cfm?abstract_id=1805932; and Elizabeth Pollman, "Reconceiving Corporate Personhood," *Utah Law Review* 4 (2011), 1629–75, http://papers.ssrn.com/sol3/papers.cfm?abstract_id=1732910, critique the ad hoc application of these competing theories in US Supreme Court jurisprudence.

the corporate veil" to identify certain key players as the ultimate motive sources of action.[12] Yet the power, dominance, and endurance of leading firms – particularly in an era of centripetally accumulating data and money among Silicon Valley's and Wall Street's leading companies – suggest that we are entering a phase change in the balance between individual and institution. That transition features a new ontological priority for corporations: sovereigns' recognition that their prerogatives, affirmed legally as the natural rights accruing to corporate personhood, trump individual prerogatives, even when those individual prerogatives are themselves also rights.[13]

This volume offers an opportunity to reflect on the consequences of this transition. Under concession theory, the privileges of corporate formation had an explicitly public-regarding rationale: charters would not be granted unless applicants for them could meet certain basic requirements of public service. At present, this approach is subordinate to a private law modelling of the corporation as little more than a nexus of contracts. This thin conceptualization of the corporation gives its controllers flexibility and obscures its nature. The large multinational corporation can be all things to all people: a heroic CEO for the technology press; thousands of tax-paying workers for politicians; a board and management for regulators. But without a clear charter of obligations and goals, there is little reason to attribute real value to such a protean entity.

A reductionist narrative – one that reduces corporations to the persons running or working at them – strategically occludes this problem by hailing each advance in the rights of a corporation as a vindication of the rights of certain persons running it. But for every corporate right won in court, there are individual losers. Hobby Lobby's right not to pay for contraceptives trumps at least some aspects of its employees' reproductive rights.[14] After *Citizens United*, residual democratic abilities to cabin the time, place, manner, and amount of corporate speech

---

12 For an excellent primer on how such manipulation has evolved, see William W. Bratton and Adam J. Levitin, "A Transactional Genealogy of Scandal: From Michael Milken to Enron to Goldman Sachs," *Southern California Law Review* 86 (2013): 783–868, http://papers.ssrn.com/sol3/papers.cfm?abstract_id=2126778; on piercing, see Nancy Krieger, "Epidemiology and the Web of Causation: Has Anyone Seen the Spider?," *Social Science and Medicine* 39, no. 7 (October 1994): 887–903.

13 There are particular dangers in the possibility that technology can be used to shape human values, rather than being shaped by these values. For an account of how this process may occur, see Pasquale, "Technology, Competition, and Values," *Minnesota Journal of Law, Science, and Technology* 8, no. 607 (2007): 607–22.

14 Jennifer Taub, "Is Hobby Lobby a Tool for Limiting Corporate Constitutional Rights?," *Constitutional Commentary* 30, no. 403 (2016): 403–29.

were sharply curtailed, severely diminishing the worth of citizens' basic liberties in the same contexts.[15] In cases like these and many others, corporate rights conflict with the rights of many aggrieved individuals. As corporate rights to free expression gain momentum, the future regulability of a great deal of commerce will depend on whether individual rights (to, say, consumer protection, privacy, antitrust protection, anti-discrimination protections, and many others) can survive the Lochnerizing onslaught of a corporatized 1st Amendment.[16]

At this point the 1st Amendment has been opportunistically deployed in so many contexts, and 1st Amendment litigation by corporations has so eclipsed that by individuals,[17] that it is imperative to contemplate what it means for corporate rights to have ontological priority over other rights claims. At what point are corporations the entities in our social universe that *really exist*, that are *fundamental*, as opposed to other, more ephemeral and less important entities (such as human beings)?[18]

Scholars have observed the formal immortality of many corporations (which have no natural span of existence) and the sociopathic

---

15 See the discussion of Rawls's work on the value of liberties in Pasquale, "Reclaiming Egalitarianism in the Political Theory of Campaign Finance Reform," *University of Illinois Law Review* 2008, no. 1 (2008): 599–660, http://www.illinoislawreview.org/wp-content/ilr-content/articles/2008/2/Pasquale.pdf.

16 John C. Coates, IV, "Corporate Speech and the First Amendment: History, Data, and Implications," *Constitutional Commentary* 30, no. 2 (Summer 2015): 223–76, http://papers.ssrn.com/sol3/papers.cfm?abstract_id=2566785; Neil M. Richards, "Why Data Privacy Law Is (Mostly) Constitutional," *William and Mary Law Review* 46, no. 4 (April 2015): 1501–33, http://wmlawreview.org/sites/default/files/17-Richards.pdf. Tamara Piety has been prophetic in anticipating the full force and shape of this onslaught. See, e.g., Piety, "*Citizens United* and the Threat to the Regulatory State," *Michigan Law Review First Impressions* (2010), at http://repository.law.umich.edu/cgi/viewcontent.cgi?article=1022&context=mlr_fi; Piety, "Brandishing the First Amendment," at 30 ("Business was back, this time brandishing claims to freedom of speech rather than freedom of contract as a weapon against governmental attempts at regulation .... With the *Citizens United* decision, we may be seeing a replay of the Lochner drama").

17 Documented in Coates, "Corporate Speech."

18 Nicole Dewandre has demonstrated that neoliberal discourse all too often takes business interests as fundamental, while disregarding the interests of individuals. Dewandre, "Political Agents as Relational Selves: Rethinking EU Politics and Policy-Making with Hannah Arendt," *Philosophy Today* 62, no. 2 (Spring 2018), at 512 ("Instead of being part of the European society, with a normal constraint of profitability coupled with a sense of belonging to a wider ecosystem, corporations became dangerous zombies driven by the pursuit of an ever-increasing profitability. Under the cover of growth and jobs, EU policies prioritised the needs of these irresponsible zombies over the needs and vital necessities of European human beings.").

implications of profit maximization as a corporate instantiation of naked self-interest as *telos*.[19] We wish to convey the urgency of the present conjuncture in a different way. What might a society look and feel like in which corporate rights gain priority over individual rights? And how might the altogether plausible acceleration of current trends toward corporate personhood lead to a social reality in which for-profit corporations were, in a very real sense, the only persons granted meaningful agency and capacity for planning?

In our chapter, we take each of these questions in turn. The first section makes the case that many aspects of American legal culture pave the way to such a world. The second section introduces the setting of M.T. Anderson's *Feed*, a dystopian novel with surprisingly rich insight into the habits of mind and character that would naturally thrive in a world even more dominated by for-profit corporations than our own.[20] We conclude by reflecting on the fragility of the current diversity of sources of the self.[21] Given the extraordinary power of for-profit corporations over the American political system, further grants to them of rights could end legislative efforts to limit their domination of schooling, church, family, health care, and professional guidance – indeed, of every sphere of human experience now (at least partly) shielded from pecuniary motivations.[22] There could be no clearer case

---

19 Harvey Cox, "The Market as God," *The Atlantic Monthly* 283, no. 3 (March 1999): 18–23; Daniel Warner, "An Essay on the Market as God: Law, Spirituality, and the Ecocrisis," *Rutgers Journal of Law and Religion* 6 (2004), http://lawandreligion.com/sites/lawandreligion.com/files/Warner.pdf.

20 M.T. Anderson, *Feed* (Somerville: Candlewick Press, 2002). On the degree of domination now prevailing, see David Korten, *When Corporations Rule the World*, 3rd ed. (Oakland: Berrett-Koehler, 2015).

21 Charles Taylor, *Sources of the Self: The Making of the Modern Identity* (Cambridge, MA: Harvard University Press, 1992); William Connolly, *The Fragility of Things: Self-Organizing Processes, Neoliberal Fantasies, and Democratic Activism* (Durham: Duke University Press, 2013). As the COVID crisis shows, even in an already corporatized landscape, crisis is likely to further entrench the power and reach of the largest corporations.

22 For example, the extraordinary profits of Walmart and Microsoft have helped fuel the Walton and Gates Foundations, which promote charter schools throughout the United States. The wealthier these foundations become, the more direct influence they seek over school districts – and the less restricted their electoral spending is, the better they can attain such influence. Similarly, funds from private student lenders have helped the Lumina Foundation fund research that promotes further privatization of education finance. Pasquale, "Democratizing Higher Education: Defending and Extending Income-Based Repayment Programs," *Loyola Consumer Law Review* 28 (2015): 1, 13n50. The Walton, Gates, and Lumina Foundations dominate education philanthropy in the United States, profoundly shaping research and policy.

of a development touted as an expansion of freedom instead eroding its very conditions of possibility.

Corporate Constitutional Rights and the US Constitution

In a wide-ranging and insightful analysis of the long history of the US Constitution and its application to the corporate form, legal scholar Daniel Greenwood argues that in the

> great liberal division between citizen and state – end in itself and mere tool – corporations obviously belong on the state side. Like governments, corporations are human institutions made by humans and authorized by states, for human purposes. Like governments, they are critical to our happiness and prosperity, but like governments, they can threaten us as well. On first principles, a People that founds its government in a distinction between human beings "endowed by their Creator with natural rights" and human institutions should have no trouble seeing corporations as no more sacred than the governments that empower them.[23]

However compelling Greenwood's position is as a matter of logic, it has been spurned by American courts. They view corporations as rights-bearing entities, despite the fact that neither the Constitution nor the Bill of Rights mentions them.[24] A bizarre and conceptually (but not empirically) implausible legal environment has emerged as a result. Corporations have rights, but citizens have no constitutional prerogative to, say, prevent a corporation from censoring employees' speech

---

23 Daniel J.H. Greenwood, "Do Corporations Have a Constitutional Right to Bear Arms? and Related Puzzles in Post-National Jurisprudence" (2013), draft posted to https://people.hofstra.edu/Daniel_J_Greenwood/pdf/2dADRAFT.pdf, 11; see also Greenwood, "Person, State, or Not: The Place of Business Corporations in Our Constitutional Order," *University of Colorado Law Review* 87 (2015) 101–85; Greenwood, "Should Corporations Have First Amendment Rights," *Seattle Law Review* 30 (2007): 875–926.

24 Along with other scholars, including some in this volume, Greenwood offers several different angles of analytical attack on the question of whether what we today call corporations are really the same kind of entities that we referred to in similar terms in the past, noting for example that the most familiar corporate form in the Constitutional period was the one taken by many local governments, and therefore would have been redressable by democratic mechanisms. The crucial point for our analysis is the recent development of corporations as institutions that can portray themselves as bearers of the rights most see as attaching to natural persons, itself at least on the surface a reversal of the relationship between persons and institutions usually entailed by talk of human rights.

or invading their privacy. "The spirit of the eighteenth century liberal constitution," Greenwood writes, "might demand giving citizens rights against corporations ... but it cannot justify giving corporations unwritten rights against us and our elected representatives."[25] The Bill of Rights was explicitly intended to protect citizens (both as individuals and as groups) against overweening power vested in their institutions; even as the institutions of government under liberal theory literally are the people, and earn certain powers of the people vested in them whose use must be checked by rights protections. Thus the powers of government and the rights of citizens exist in a delicate balance that requires persistent checking through all parts of the political apparatus. Greenwood argues that the contemporary corporation occupies a status – neither government nor individual, but with many of the powers and few of the responsibilities of both – that the Founders could not have anticipated.

As the power of for-profit corporations has expanded, in a manner that few have even recognized despite its pervasiveness, a new and unbalanced status quo has taken hold. Jurists have adopted theories of corporate personhood, enabling corporations *qua* corporations to assert rights, including some of those included in the Bill of Rights (either textually or as part of constitutional jurisprudence).[26] As Greenwood explains, this has shifted the balance of power, on which the framers spent so much energy, in an unexpected and untenable direction. Rights primarily ought to protect individuals from institutional power, not the other way around. The lack of balance emerges directly from this subtle but profound revision of Constitutional thought. Laws and constitutions exist to construct institutional power, and rights exist in part to protect individuals from overweening use of those powers. When institutions, including corporations, are able to take advantage of the rights accorded to individuals, this situation hampers (and may well end entirely) individuals' hope for recourse against corporate misuse of power. Thus the typical rights arrangement of the legal system – wherein individuals use rights language to protect themselves against abuses of state power – gets turned on its head. When individuals use the courts or even the legislatures to combat abuses of corporate power, corporations resist those restrictions through the invocation of rights, leaving individuals with no structural recourse against that invocation. Rather than asserting their rights against corporate bad actors, individuals must rely on institutional laws and regulations;

---

25 Greenwood, "Do Corporations Have a Constitutional Right to Bear Arms?," 18.
26 Tamara R. Piety, "Why Personhood Matters," *Constitutional Commentary* 30, no. 101 (2016): 361–90.

meanwhile, corporations assert rights to protect themselves against those actions; individuals have no such recourse. Citizens cannot sue private corporations for the abridgement of their freedoms (say, of expression or religion), but corporations can sue the citizenry's democratically elected representatives on just those grounds – indeed, they have had success in doing just that.

The best-known recent extension of corporate rights against those of individuals is of course *Citizens United*, in which the US Supreme Court ruled that corporate expenditures in the particularly central field of political campaigns were speech for the purposes of 1st Amendment jurisprudence. Decisions like *Citizens United* (which expanded the scope of corporate speech rights) interact synergistically with decisions like *Thompson v. Western States Medical Center* (which intensified the force of 1st Amendment protections by limiting the FDA's authority to proscribe advertising by compounding pharmacies).[27] Here, again, corporations use rights talk to limit citizens' ability to constrain their power, despite this being exactly the reverse of the balance of power intended by the framers of the Constitution and the Bill of Rights.

Absolute Corporate Speech Rights in *Feed*

Corporate influence over the rules of American politics has become self-reinforcing. A series of cases, dating back at least to *Buckley v. Valeo* (1976) and *First National Bank of Boston v. Bellotti* (1978), have opened the floodgates to corporate spending, not merely in legislative and executive races, but also in judicial elections. The result has been the gradual accumulation of power by the Republican Party (which at this writing controls the Senate, the presidency, the Supreme Court, and a clear majority of state legislative chambers and governorships), as well as the hollowing out of much of the Democratic Party's ostensible commitment to egalitarian social policies. It is entirely possible that, following the lead of Turkey, Hungary, and Poland, the United States will never see the pendulum of political power "swing back" in a more egalitarian direction and will instead intensify its politico-economic commitment to entrenching and extending corporate power. What will such a future look like?

---

27 Christopher T. Robertson, "A Trojan Horse? How Expansion of the First Amendment Threatens Much More Than the Regulation of Off-Label Drugs and Devices," *Ohio State Law Journal* (forthcoming, 2017) ("Courts should tread carefully when using 10 words from a 240-year old document to dismantle a key part of the modern regulatory state").

To imagine it, we turn to a work of fiction, a genre that frees authors to extrapolate from current trends to thick descriptions of the futures they portend. Corporations and governments often use scenario analysis to understand a range of possible futures to prepare for, but such analyses tend to eschew the visceral, subjective, and psychological insights that good fiction embodies. A novelist can imagine the ways in which the minds of individuals both reflect and reinforce their social environment. These considerations are just as worthy of policy-makers' attention as the economic and political models that now dominate discussions of corporate rights.

Choosing a particular novel to think through corporate power is both an easy and an uneasy task. Uneasy because the question of representation is real: why is any given person's narrative worthy of sustained attention? Easy, because the field of literary criticism has long generated skilled appreciation of resonant works: those that "ring true" by offering insight into modes of interiority, conversation, self-deception, and self-understanding.

Moreover, novels may offer insights on far more than the personal. "Fiction is about transformation through conflict," the novelist Richard Powers argues. He typologizes "three general levels of dramatic conflict: the battle within a person (psychological), the battle between people (social or political), and the battle between people and non-people (environmental)." Powers complains that "while the challenge to our continued existence on Earth has never been greater or clearer, literary fiction seems to be retrenching into an obsession with the challenges of private hopes, fears, and desires."[28] He commends "three-level stories," which address the psychological, social, and environmental crises of our time. Without such a comprehensive outlook, Powers fears, literature will fail to offer its richness of perspective, descriptive acuity, and deep insight to a world desperately in need of each.

M.T. Anderson's 2002 young adult novel *Feed* (a finalist for the National Book Award, and winner of other awards) offers such a "three-level story," staging many of the issues at the heart of battles over corporate rights in startling and disturbing relief.[29] *Feed* is a dystopian novel set in a near-future in which the ability of governments to regulate corporations has all but vanished. As such it paints a picture that is not very many

---

28 Richard Powers, interviewed by Everett Hamner, *L.A. Review of Books*, 7 April 2018, at https://lareviewofbooks.org/article/heres-to-unsuicide-an-interview-with -richard-powers.

29 Anderson, *Feed* (originally published 2002; we refer to the reissued edition, Somerville: Candlewick Press, 2012). Hereafter referred to parenthetically in the text by page number preceded by the letter F.

steps away from the normative vision of hundreds of already powerful politicians in the United States. But like all dystopian fiction, *Feed* is also a symbolic refashioning of current society, and this aspect of the novel, less immediately obvious from its surface, may be even more disturbing. *Feed* shows repeatedly that the construction of corporations as rights-bearing entities erodes the most fundamental notions of democratic and liberal governance. Thus the "solution" to the problems *Feed* describes is not to chip away at the edges of corporate power or to prevent the development of the specific and disturbing technology on which Anderson focuses – a version of networked computing located in cranial implants, the "Feed" which gives the novel its name – but instead to challenge the foundations on which our current corporate-political world is built. In depicting current phenomena from climate change, to the degradation of the environment and health, to the wholesale revising of the education system toward corporate desiderata, Anderson's novel illuminates a world in which the unchallengeable primacy of the corporate form, and its associated invocation of rights that were meant to be reserved for individuals, turns the democratic project on its head.

Feed is set at an unspecified point in a future United States that, while appearing to maintain something of its current political structure, nevertheless has ceded virtually all important social functions to corporations. The titular Feed of the novel is entirely the product of a massive corporation, FeedTech, and despite the fact that nearly everything in society is dependent on access to the Feed, "only about seventy-three percent of Americans have Feeds" (F 112). The book is largely structured as a romance between the narrator, Titus, and a girl named Violet whom he meets during a trip to the moon, which has become a tourist destination. Titus has a Feed and presumes everyone does, but Violet's family "didn't have enough money" (F 112–13), so unlike others in the novel did not get the Feed implanted until the age of seven, which turns out to have advantages but also to entail significant risks.

Alone among the novel's main characters, Violet has some general knowledge of history and politics, due to her having been home-schooled rather than attending the completely corporation-owned School™ of the other characters. The narrator Titus writes of that educational system using Anderson's characteristically sarcastic argot of futuristic terminology, teen speak, and studied misapplication of current standard English, along with a kind of Orwellian doublespeak that nods strongly at current usage:

> I don't do too good in School™. We were back in School™, so I was reminded pretty often that I was stupid.
>
> School™ is not so bad now, not like back when my grandparents were kids, when the schools were run by the government, which sounds

completely like, Nazi, to have the government running the schools? Back
then, it was big boring, and all the kids were meg null, because they didn't
learn anything useful, it was all like, da da da da, this happened in four-
teen ninety-two, da da da da, when you mix like, chalk and water, it makes
nitroglycerin, and that kind of shit? And nothing was useful?

   Now that School™ is run by the corporations, it's pretty brag, because
it teaches us how the world can be used, like mainly how to use our feeds.
Also, it's good because that way we know that the big corps are made up
of real human beings, and not just jerks out for money, because taking care
of children, they care about America's future. It's an investment in tomor-
row. When no one was going to pay for the public schools anymore and
they were all like filled with guns and drugs and English teachers who
were really pimps and stuff, some of the big media congloms got together
and gave all this money and bought the schools so that all of them could
have computers and pizza for lunch and stuff, which they gave for free,
and now we do stuff in classes about how to work technology and how to
find bargains and what's the best way to get a job and how to decorate our
bedroom. (F 109–10)

In many ways this setting of the educational scene forms the critical
backdrop for the world depicted in *Feed*, since so much of the novel
turns out to depend on the characters' lack of critical thinking skills
and ignorance of fundamental issues of history and politics. Like much
of the novel, it also parodies very sharply current American corporate
political initiatives regarding education, which often indicate a desire
to reshape education in much the way School™ is described here.
Corporate advocates in the "edtech" space present the rapid introduction of computers to early childhood education as a foundation for
future workforce development. In *Feed,* this tactic is taken to its logical
extreme – neural interfaces, almost always implanted near the time of
birth – and has quite different results. Most of the students we hear
from in the novel seem to be entirely incompetent as future workers.
But they are ravenous consumers, so predictable in their buying habits
that firms can calculate their lifetime value as shoppers. They may suggest the future role of education in a nearly entirely automated world in
which few work but all are entitled to a universal basic income.

   Anderson's students have internalized the disparagement of the
education system's humanistic goals – goals that are arguably tied in
the most direct way to the rights of individuals. Their corporate school
teaches them to regard public schools as "Nazi," suggesting a broader
dismissal of government power and a complete trust in corporate
power. The word "Nazi" has clearly lost its referential capacity in the

world of *Feed*, so much so that Titus can describe an educational program that is actually committed to teaching history and politics as the worst possible form of ideological indoctrination, even as he himself is expressing delight at being indoctrinated in a different but no less ruthless fashion.

The emphasis Titus places on "usefulness" in education reflects contemporary corporate-educational ideology. In the decades since *Feed* was published, the voices of corporate actors, the think tanks they fund, and the government appointees they influence have only grown louder. The perspectives they offer starkly reject what are arguably the fundamental goals of education in the American system (arguably, in any democratic system). As one of the main early proponents of public education in the United States, Thomas Jefferson, wrote:

> The most effectual means of preventing [the perversion of power into tyranny are] to illuminate, as far as practicable, the minds of the people at large, and more especially to give them knowledge of those facts which history exhibits, that possessed thereby of the experience of other ages and countries, they may be enabled to know ambition under all its shapes, and prompt to exert their natural powers to defeat its purposes.[30]

So for Jefferson the purpose of public education is perched exactly at the intersection of self and society, in a profoundly interactive fashion. Society, if it is to be just and free, must guarantee the enlightenment of the citizenry. Titus says that under this form of education students "didn't learn anything useful," but one notes how Jefferson and other early developers of the American education system always emphasized the civic role of education over the practical one. Of course they also promoted the practical ends of education, but those practical ends were secondary to the social ones.[31] It is suggested in *Feed* that

---

30 Thomas Jefferson, "Diffusion of Knowledge Bill," FE 2, no. 221, Papers 2:526 (1779), http://famguardian.org/Subjects/Politics/thomasjefferson/jeff1350.htm.

31 These social ends have even been recognized by some courts. See Danielle Allen, "What is Education For," *Boston Review*, https://bostonreview.net/forum/danielle -allen-what-education (9 May 2016) "In 2006, the highest court in New York affirmed that students in the state have a right to civic education ... 'Capable' civic participation, Judge Leland DeGrasse ... ruled, includes, for instance, the ability to make sense of complex ballot propositions and follow argumentation about DNA evidence at trial. The court agreed that 'meaningful civic participation' and prospects for 'competitive employment,' not simply minimum-wage employment, demanded a twelfth-grade level of verbal and math skills and similarly advanced competence in social studies and economics. The court ordered New York City to increase school funding with these goals in mind."

individuals benefit from the reconfiguration of education as primarily about vocational training, yet that benefit emerges – as *Feed* shows repeatedly – only when the corporate social form takes primacy over the representative governmental one. The view that in the republican system, governmental power alone expresses the "will of the people" and therefore must be tended to and guarded over in the most vigilant fashion, and that concentrations of capital were one of the primary targets of democratic revolutions, has been lost entirely. The corporate control of language – exemplified in the trademark (™) symbol following the generic term School – meshes with the corporate control of thought and governmental power. With regard to the triumvirate of individual, governmental, and corporate power, *Feed* posits that corporations can use rights as a tool to negate the rights and duties that are said to accrue to individuals and governments, perhaps intuiting Greenwood's insight that the existence of corporations outside constitutional foundations allows them eventually to become the only locus of powers and immunities robust enough to be deemed rights.

Violet, the home-schooled character who was implanted with the Feed as a child (instead of during infancy) due to her parents' relative poverty and their hesitancy about the Feed based in part on her father's late Feed implantation and her mother's lack of a Feed altogether, serves as the reader's proxy for the values that corporatism has displaced. Titus, for most of the narrative Violet's boyfriend, plays a key role in the narrative because, unlike most of his peers, he is apparently to some degree capable of seeing through the ideological screen created by corporate power. Titus says he feels "stupid" in School™, like all his friends, but that after meeting Violet he begins to think about "some conversation we were having where I was dumb": "dumb" both because his Feed has been turned off due to sabotage and because Violet knows so much more than he does:

> Like she was always reading things about how everything was dying and there was less air and everything was getting toxic. She told me about how things were getting really bad with some things in South America, but she couldn't really tell exactly how bad, because the news had been asked to be a little more positive. She said that it made her frightened to read all this kind of thing, about how people hated us for what we did. So one time I said to her that she should stop reading it, because it was just depressing, so she was like, *But I want to know what's going on*, so I was like, *Then you should do something about it. It's a free country. You should do something.* She was like, *Nothing's ever going to happen in a two-party system.* She was like, *da da da, nothing's ever going to change, both parties are in the pocket of big business, da da da*, all that?

So I was like, You got to believe in the people, it's a democracy, we can change things.

She was like, It's not a democracy.

I hated it when she got like this, because then she wasn't like herself, I mean, she wasn't like this playful person who drags me around the mall doing crazy shit, she was suddenly like those girls in School™ who sit underground and dress all in black with ribbing and get an iron fixture for their jaws and they're like, "Capitalist fool – propaganda tool," holding up both their hands, etc. When she said things like *It's not a democracy*, suddenly I couldn't stand to be having this whole conversation. I was like, *Oh, yeah*, and she was like, *It's not*, and I was like, *Oh, okay*, and she said, *No, it's not a democracy*, and I was like, *Yes it is*, and she was like, *No it isn't*, and I got sarcastic, so I was like, *No, sure, it's all fascist, isn't it? We're all fascists?*

Then she was like, really gently, No, please, I'm not trying to be an asshole. It's not a democracy.

I was like, Then what is it?

A republic. It's a republic. (F 110–11)

Like most aspects of *Feed*, this conversation takes pieces of current political discourse and twists them just a little into ironic absurdity. Yet it is remarkable to reflect on how small those twists are, and that in some social contexts in the United States today this conversation would be almost entirely realistic.

The election of Donald Trump as President of the United States in 2016 has only made clearer the ongoing relevance of Anderson's work. As a candidate that year, Trump could say obviously and demonstrably false things (such as: Barack Obama founded ISIS), as could his spokesperson (who claimed that Obama was responsible for presidential decisions that were made before he took office). He could, and still does, make overtly racist, sexist, and Islamophobic comments. He could, and still does, propose economic policies that redistribute resources to the wealthiest. And he may well be re-elected, despite a disastrously belated, partisan, and ideological response to the COVID-19 pandemic.

The Freedom to Predict and the Freedom to Resist

Once a constitutional principle like "free expression" is twisted beyond all recognition, new forms of order emerge. In the America of *Feed*, the government so cynically dismissed in Titus's reverie on civics has not only abandoned the education sector but also stopped paying for health care. A "cash on the barrel," purely transactional health care system is harsh to imagine, even in dystopian science fiction. A "safety net" does persist in *Feed*, but purely as a form of retail financialization. When Violet needs new neural equipment, she must look not to insurers but to some algorithmically improvised set of retailers who model whether the discounted present value of the profits they would make from her future stream of purchases from them would be greater than the investment they would need to make now in order to save her.

Standing alone, this would be a chilling enough policy (though one with some clear antecedents in the present, including CBO "scoring models" that count earlier deaths of unvaccinated Medicare patients as a budgetary gain for the United States).[32] But the reason *Feed* gives for Violet's denial of health care is even more disturbing. As a form of civil disobedience through "culture jamming," Violet had purchased items randomly, to make her actions harder to model via consumer profiling (a practice very similar to ones recommended in works like Brunton and Nissenbaum's *Obfuscation*).[33] Without a standard pattern of purchases to trace, the modellers could not reliably project an income flow from her. So she was doomed to die from an easily preventable condition.

What's remarkable here is an expansion of E.P. Thompson's concept of eliminationism, and Saskia Sassen's social theory of expulsion, from the poor to the unpredictable.[34] The rules of health care in *Feed* obviously disadvantage those without much purchasing power. Where predictive analytics might have once projected likely labour income in a world of employer-sponsored insurance, now purchasing power alone is critical. And someone who cannot demonstrate a likelihood of sufficiently exercising that power on behalf of entities with some greater purchasing power is calculatively excluded from concern.[35]

Violet's dilemma – render oneself legible or be rendered untouchable – recalls a premise of William Bogard's penetrating book *The Simulation of Surveillance: Hypercontrol in Telematic Societies*.[36] The simultaneous

---

32 Tim Westmoreland, "Standard Errors: How Budget Rules Distort Lawmaking," *Georgetown Law Journal* 95 (2007): 1555–610. Allocating health care on the basis of ability to pay, rather than need, means that "even as the U.S. lags in quality indicators in many forms of basic medical care, it is excelling at a range of services designed to make people 'better than well.'" Pasquale, "Access to Medicine in an Era of Fractal Inequality," *Annals of Health Law* 19 (2010): 284.

33 Finn Brunton and Helen Nissenbaum, *Obfuscation: A User's Guide for Privacy and Protest* (Cambridge, MA: MIT Press, 2015).

34 Peter Frase, *Four Futures: Life after Capitalism* (New York: Verso, 2016); Saskia Sassen, *Expulsions: Brutality and Complexity in the Global Economy* (Cambridge, MA: Harvard University Press, 2014).

35 For contemporary examples, see David G. Beer, *Metric Power* (London: Sage, 2016).

36 William Bogard, *The Simulation of Surveillance: Hypercontrol in Telematic Societies* (New York: Cambridge University Press, 1996).

neologism and archaism of "telematic" suggests a startling premise of the book: that surveillance is meant just as much to control the future as it is to record the past. Media studies scholar Richard Grusin has referred to this practice as "premediation."[37] We are surrounded by systems of *surveillance and control*. It is supervision via a "super vision" far beyond the abilities of the subjects it shapes[38] – something that should be foremost in the minds of jurists who hear corporate pleas that their efforts to invade privacy are merely ways of "knowing" their customers, and the world, better.

In *Feed,* modelling consumer behaviour is a way to stop particularly bad acts, but it is also a means to *shape* behaviour through messages and enticements each waking minute. The better the surveillance gets, the better those behind the surveilling eye can plan, behaviouristically, matrices of penalties and rewards to reinforce acceptable behaviour and deter terror, crime, antisocial behaviour, suspicious activities, lack of productivity, laziness – because once some financialized scorecard or dashboard becomes the *Grundgesetz* or principle of order, all threats can be placed on a continuum.[39] Thus, replicating captured patterns of past behaviour is the only safe way to evade suspicion, stigma, and detention. Even ceasing to shop could be a national security threat, since military advantage is epiphenomenal of taxation of a vast and growing national economy. Anti-consumerism undermines economic growth and, indirectly, military might.

Kate Crawford captures the larger cultural dynamic:

If we take [the] twinned anxieties – those of the surveillers and the surveilled – and push them to their natural extension, we reach an epistemological end point: on one hand, the fear that there can never be enough data, and on the other, the fear that one is standing out in the data. These fears reinforce each other in a feedback loop, becoming stronger with each turn of the ratchet. As people seek more ways to blend in – be it through normcore dressing or hardcore encryption – more intrusive data collection techniques are developed. And yet, this is in many ways the expected

---

37 Richard Grusin, *Premediation: Affect and Mediality after 9/11* (New York: Palgrave Macmillan 2010).

38 John Gilliom and Torin Monahan, *Supervision: An Introduction to the Surveillance Society* (Chicago: University of Chicago Press, 2012).

39 Jathan Sadowski and Frank Pasquale, "The Spectrum of Control: A Social Theory of the Smart City," *First Monday* 20, no. 7 (2015), at http://firstmonday.org/ojs/index.php/fm/article/view/5903/4660. "The overall pattern of relationships in the smart city results in a seamless spectrum of control, with meritorious or merely creepy technologies directly imbricated with deeply disturbing ones."

conclusion of big data's neopositivist worldview. As historians of science Lorraine Daston and Peter Galison once wrote, all epistemology begins in fear – fear that the world cannot be threaded by reason, fear that memory fades, fear that authority will not be enough.[40]

Even present technology is not merely recording; it is also trying to catch creative dissimulation like Violet's. Emotion detection start-ups are using databases of millions of faces and expressions to find "fakers" of emotion. As Anderson so presciently and depressingly illustrates, attempts to "resist the feed" are themselves anticipated in the Feed itself and too easily rebound on the resister, to his or her own severe detriment.

The logic of accumulation in *Feed* works against Violet in still another way. She was vulnerable to damaging sequelae after a hacking attack in part because her parents waited to buy her a direct neural interface with the Feed. In 1st Amendment jurisprudence, the classic case vindicating their right to raise their child without many forms of modern technology is *Wisconsin v. Yoder*, which addressed the free exercise claims of members of an Amish community. *Feed* gives us a glimpse of a future where the untrammelled exercise of corporate speech rights may effectively nullify choices granted via free exercise. Just as it is almost impossible to operate in many contexts today without a smartphone, the world of *Feed* presents brutal network effects in which even the most basic communications and commerce are wired into direct neural interfaces. The price of deliberating over whether to accept the Feed is a medically perilous future.

Feed captures the uneasy mix of acceleration and ossification so characteristic of corporatized modernity.[41] Violet's sickness and disability reflect the pressure on parents to adopt technology into their progeny, lest they be "left behind" (to adapt a millenarian theological category to the singularitarian eschatology increasingly popular among Silicon Valley elites).[42] Yet the corporate messages accelerated and intensified by the Feed seem merely to entrench the existing social order. Whoever owns significant shares of the leading firms will enjoy more wealth and power in the future.[43] A "Matthew Effect" is thus designed into

---

40 Kate Crawford, "The Anxieties of Big Data," *The New Inquiry*, 30 May 2014, http://thenewinquiry.com/essays/the-anxieties-of-big-data.

41 Hartmut Rosa, *Social Acceleration: A New Theory of Modernity* (New York: Columbia University Press, 2015) (commenting on this juxtaposition of speed and quiescence).

42 See the analysis of the *Left Behind* series in Michael Standaert, *Skipping Toward Armageddon: The Politics and Propaganda of the* Left Behind *Novels and the LaHaye Empire* (Brooklyn: Soft Skull Press, 2006).

43 A future also anticipated in Robin Hanson, *The Age of Em* (New York: Oxford University Press, 2016).

the communicative infrastructure. "Citizens" either fit into some stable pattern of behaviour capable of predictably supporting some subset of ruling firms, or are left to die at the first opportunity.

Note, too, that such opportunities to conform in *Feed* are coming more and more quickly: even the youngest characters in the novel are suffering from skin lesions, presumably caused by some combination of pollution and chemical exposure. Astonishingly, even the horror of decaying flesh is autopoetically repurposed by the Feed to spur new consumer activity: fashion gurus deem the lesions new beauty marks, to be adorned with make-up or replicated with cosmetic surgeries. The system is able to convert a fundamental degradation of human experience (pollution so bad it corrodes skin) into a commerce-enhancing trend, once the Feed has enough control over public perceptions. That may seem transparently absurd, but consider how much dominance today's *real-life* Feed – Facebook – exerts over popular perceptions. When the firm itself sponsored research to argue that it merely reflected its own user preferences, not many news outlets demurred.[44] In the near future, most young people will be getting their news from Facebook (or some later iteration of social media), and the platform's power to shape public understanding of its own dominance will be overwhelming.

Unless, of course, the state steps in. There are already nascent movements for "algorithmic accountability" that would require Facebook to be more forthcoming about how it constructs its feed, or would regulate how it and other internet giants arrange stories (or grant or deny their users the capacity to arrange their own feeds).[45] Sadly, activists are almost always confronted with "1st Amendment arguments" against state intervention, at least in the United States.[46] Facebook claims that it "speaks" its feed to users and therefore enjoys the right to select and arrange material in any way it wishes. Here, again, the 1st Amendment stands less for the "robust, uninhibited, and wide open" public debate decreed one of its primary purposes in *N.Y. Times v. Sullivan*, than for a reflexively deregulationist approach to

---

44 For a rare exception, see Alexander B. Howard, "Facebook Study Says Users Control What They See, But Critics Disagree," *Huffington Post*, 14 May 2015, http://www .huffingtonpost.com/2015/05/12/facebook-study-polarization_n_7245192.html.

45 For a collection of potential classifications of social media, see Pasquale, "Platform Neutrality," *Theoretical Inquiries in Law* 17 (2016): 487–513, at 507.

46 Eugene Volokh and Daniel M. Falk, "First Amendment Protection for Search Engine Search Results," *Journal of Law, Economics, and Policy* 8, no. 4 (2012): 883–99, http:// www2.law.ucla.edu/volokh/searchengine.pdf. For excellent responses to Volokh's 1st Amendment arguments against privacy regulation, *see* Neil M. Richards, "Reconciling Data Privacy and the First Amendment," *UCLA Law Review* 52, no. 4 (April 2006): 1149–212.

the very entities that ought to be regulated to ensure that they are in fact reflecting these values.[47] Facebook should be seen as more akin to a telephone company or cable network (an intermediary) than to a direct speaker, yet an increasingly pro-corporate judiciary stands poised to strike down even modest regulation of social media as an infringement on free speech – however much such regulation may be necessary to preserve true freedom of thought and expression for the vast majority of citizens.[48]

Slouching toward Oligarchy

An entrenchment of obvious imbalances in communicative power is even more evident in campaign finance law.[49] When the Supreme Court hears cases on campaign financing, fundamental dynamics of democratic theory should be at the core of its concerns. Justice Elena Kagan reflected them in the opening of her brilliant dissent in *Arizona Free Enterprise Club's Freedom Club PAC v. Bennett*, decided 5–4 at the end of the 2011 term.[50] But she and Justices Sotomayor, Breyer, and Ginsberg were sidelined by a cynical and incoherent majority committed to freezing into place inequalities in voice and influence.

In *Bennett*, a PAC challenged an Arizona law offering additional funding to publicly funded candidates if their privately financed opponents exceeded a certain spending threshold. As Justice Roberts's majority opinion explained, "[d]uring the general election, matching funds are triggered when the amount of money a privately financed candidate receives in contributions, combined with the expenditures of independent groups made in support of the privately financed candidate or in opposition to a publicly financed candidate, exceed the general election

---

47   For an entirely different approach, see the French case where a woman successfully sued to force Facebook to allow her to post images of artworks that the site's decency policy had censored. Associated Press, "Nude painting furore: court rules Facebook can be sued in France," *The Guardian*, 12 February 2016. In the United States, the 1st Amendment right of the platform, Facebook, would almost certainly trump any such challenge.

48   Jack Balkin, "The Political Economy of Freedom of Speech in the Second Gilded Age," *Balkinization*, 4 July 2018, at https://balkin.blogspot.com/2018/07/the-political -economy-of-freedom-of.html.

49   This section is based on the article by Pasquale, "First Amendment Freeze Play," *University of Pennsylvania Law Review Online* 164 (2016): 215–22, https://www .pennlawreview.com/online/164-U-Pa-L-Rev-Online-215.pdf.

50   *Ariz. Free Enter. Club's Freedom Club PAC v. Bennett*, 131 S. Ct. 2806, 2829 (2011) (Kagan, J., dissenting). The case's technical veneer has obscured its fundamental importance to the future of campaign finance jurisprudence.

allotment of state funds to the publicly financed candidate."[51] One could easily imagine a similar rationale for regulation to make future "feeds" more reflective of public values by, for example, mandating sponsorship disclosures or ensuring some modicum of promotion of public interest programming.

Note that the Arizona matching funds statute did not limit the spending of privately financed candidates, even while imposing several limits on candidates who accepted public financing (including a limit on their expenditure of personal funds of $500, as well as an overall expenditure cap). Nevertheless, Roberts's majority opinion described the statute as unconstitutionally burdensome on the privately financed candidates' speech:

> Once a privately financed candidate has raised or spent more than the State's initial grant to a publicly financed candidate, each personal dollar spent by the privately financed candidate results in an award of almost one additional dollar to his opponent. That plainly forces the privately financed candidate to shoulder a special and potentially significant burden when choosing to exercise his First Amendment right to spend funds on behalf of his candidacy.[52]

By the Court's reasoning, state aid to the publicly financed candidate suddenly deters the privately financed candidate's speech once it goes above the initial allotment. But why allow *any* public funding, under that logic? As soon as there is *any* public financing, a privately financed candidate may decide not to run at all.[53] That is precisely the type of

---

51 *Id.* at 2814 (majority opinion). "Once matching funds are triggered, each additional dollar that a privately financed candidate spends during the primary results in one dollar in additional state funding to his publicly financed opponent (less a 6% reduction meant to account for fundraising expenses)." Matching funds were only provided up to three times the initial allocation of state funding.

52 *Id.* Note that the speculative harms to privately financed speech, taken so seriously in *Bennett*, should now drive a complementary worry in a more liberal court – that without a scheme like Arizona's matching funds, candidates who would add to speech by running with public financing may never materialize. That rationale alone should be grounds for overruling *Bennett*, given the weakness of the Court's other arguments, and its failure to even consider the mirror image of its "discouraged candidates" rationale for striking down the matching funds. What is sauce for the goose is sauce for the gander, and two can play at the game of extrapolating dire consequences with barely a passing reference to social scientific literature (either domestic or international) on campaign financing.

53 As Justice Kagan's dissent observed, "privately funded candidates may well find the lump-sum system *more* burdensome than Arizona's (assuming the lump is big enough)." *Id.* at 2838 (Kagan, J., dissenting).

speculative harm to speech that Roberts's opinion takes seriously, however implausible it may be as a matter of genuine democratic theory or empirical research.

The Roberts opinion aggressively expanded the Court's already activist approach to striking down opportunity-promoting election law. Prior campaign finance jurisprudence – strained as it was – had at least paid lip service to the ideal of promoting more speech in that it struck down expenditure and contribution limits. In *Bennett*, the Court declared that even that goal could be trumped by another, higher purpose:

> [E]ven if the matching funds provision did result in more speech by publicly financed candidates *and more speech in general*, it would do so at the expense of impermissibly burdening (and thus reducing) the speech of privately financed candidates and independent expenditure groups. This sort of "beggar thy neighbor" approach to free speech – "restrict[ing] the speech of some elements of our society in order to enhance the relative voice of others" – is "wholly foreign to the First Amendment."[54]

From an ordinary language perspective, Roberts has strained the meaning of "restrict" beyond all recognition. The Arizona matching funds law did nothing to restrict the speech of private speakers. All it did was slightly rebalance the playing field once they had spent above a certain threshold. Roberts's reading comprehension is also strikingly weak here. He is elevating a *specification* of the anti-restriction principle from its source in *Buckley v. Valeo*[55] (i.e., "do not restrict some persons' speech *in order to* promote others") into its own independent 1st Amendment principle.

Justice Kagan rightly expressed bafflement at the majority's opinion in her stinging dissent. She rightly treated "equalizing campaign speech" as the type of government interest that can help *justify* public funding, not render it suspect.[56] However, there is a silver lining in Justice Roberts's agonistic misreading of *Buckley*:[57] the majority has once and for all dispensed with a naively "deliberativist" conception of campaign

---

54 *Id.* at 2821 (emphasis added) (majority opinion).
55 *Buckley v. Valeo*, 424 U.S. 1 (1976).
56 *Id.* at 2845. See Ellen D. Katz, "*Hobby Lobby* and the Pathology of *Citizens United*," *Duke Journal of Constitutional Law and Public Policy* 9, no. 1 (2014): 23–36, http://papers.ssrn.com/sol3/papers.cfm?abstract_id=2437958, on the Court's "misreading of precedent" (26) in *Buckley* and other cases involving corporate constitutional rights.
57 The idea has been applied in legal settings where the form of respect for precedent is maintained while the substance is drained from it – a point Justice Kagan makes repeatedly in her dissent regarding the majority's treatment of *Davis*, the "millionaire's amendment" case that it said controlled *Bennett*.

finance law. Both democratic theory and legal theory took a long detour into "deliberative democracy" and "republicanism" (respectively) from the 1980s to the 2000s as an allegedly non-partisan, neutral rationale for many forms of election regulation – including restrictions on campaign finance.[58] Going back to the work of Alexander Meiklejohn, it is easy to see how structure and rules can lead to better public debates. But deliberativism was, by and large, a dead end, since it could so easily be hijacked into a rationale for deregulation. Virtually every deregulatory campaign finance case up to *Bennett* agonized over the state's efforts to shape the public sphere, and proudly declared that, in striking down campaign finance limitations, the majority was guaranteeing "more speech." *Bennett* finally let that mask drop and revealed the ugly face of campaign deregulation: a Court committed to freezing into place extant disparities in resources. Thus existing runaway inequality and extreme wealth concentration have created a pattern of self-reinforcing advantage among those connected enough to convert money into power, and vice versa, ad infinitum.[59] In *Feed*, the self-recreating pattern is substantively different but structurally similar: money creates ad messages that induce purchases and thereby generate more profit.

Bennett's obsession with striking down "relative voice" regulation has dire implications for other aspects of the public sphere. In the same year as *Bennett*, the Supreme Court decided *Sorrell v. IMS Health*, which struck down a modest attempt by the state of Vermont to limit a data broker's use of prescribing data to enhance pharmaceutical firms' marketing campaigns.[60] The logic of *Sorrell* is expansive, potentially undermining any data regulation aimed at equalizing the influence of various competitors in the marketplace of ideas. Like *Bennett*, it ultimately stands for the proposition that existing imbalances in communicative resources are to be respected, not corrected, even if they make a mockery of prior 1st Amendment jurisprudence's commitment to preserving a "robust, wide-open, and uninhibited" public sphere.

The nightmarish vision of *Feed*'s corporatized public sphere is underwritten by the normative principles that have guided leading 1st

---

58 Pasquale, "Reclaiming Egalitarianism."
59 Gilens and Page, "Testing Theories of American Politics," analysing work on voice and class in American democracy; Paolo Liberati, "The World Distribution of Income and its Inequality, 1970–2009," *Review of Income and Wealth* 61, no. 2 (2015): 248–273, http://papers.ssrn.com/sol3/papers.cfm?abstract_id=2605259, comparing Gini Coefficient worldwide over time.
60 Kevin Outterson et al., *William H. Sorrell, Attorney General of Vermont, et al. v. IMS Health Inc., et al. – Amicus Brief in Support of Petitioners*, http://papers.ssrn.com/sol3/papers.cfm?abstract_id=1770524.

Amendment cases of the Roberts Court. In its 1st Amendment jurisprudence, corporations must have access to the minds of consumers,
untrammelled by regulators. Even when they dominate a communicative space, the state cannot attempt to level the playing field without
provoking the "strict scrutiny" of a hostile court. In the near future,
automated messages, based on deep psychological profiling, may be
treated exactly the same as a speech in a park on a soapbox.[61] These
are all natural consequences of a long-term ideological crusade to treat
corporations as persons.

Corporate Constitutional Rights: Toward the Long View

Given a narrow enough horizon of time (and social concern), corporate
rights may appear to be a good (or at least innocuous) idea. The corporation may be seen as a "technology" of law, as vital to self-expression
for its owners as a computer or cellphone is to the expression of average
individuals. Those alarmed by some forms of corporate speech rights,
arguably, are welcome to form their own corporations in order to
enhance their own messages.

But careful attention to actually existing social realities belies each
prong of this quietist affirmation of corporate free speech rights. While
computing capacity varies by machine, the owner of the best computer
on earth does not (by virtue of that fact) suddenly possess a means of
communicating millions or billions of times more potent than that of
his rivals or enemies with more ordinary technology. In the corporate
world, that scenario of vast power differentials can indeed obtain: some
firms are hugely more powerful than their rivals (let alone non-profit
corporations or persons). Counter-speech in that skewed environment is an unconvincing remedy for power imbalances. Without a
strong democratic government capable of standing independent from
massive firms, the communicative environment will be deeply (and
increasingly) skewed.

Yet this skewing happens slowly, over years or decades. Each step
toward it may seem like little more than an extension of a reality we
have already become acclimated to and lulled to accept as inevitable.
The arresting power of a novel like *Feed* is that it plays out the logical
extension of these incremental advances in a scenario of the future that
bears eerie similarities to current American life. But its meaning goes

---

61 Pasquale, "Automated Arrangements of Information: Speech, Conduct, and Power"
    Concurring Opinions, 25 June 2012, http://concurringopinions.com/archives/2012
    /06/automated-arrangement-of-information-speech-conduct-and-power.html.

far beyond any simple moral or rule. As James Boyd White observes (when discussing "the way one engages with a literary text, or other artifact to be read in a humanistic way"):

> The central question one asks is about its meaning, to the maker and to us. This is not reducible to a summary or other propositional statement but lies in the experience of the original: it is specific to its form, to its materials, to its language, to its cultural and even to its physical context. The makers of a Gothic cathedral, for example, could not say in words what their building meant – for that they needed stone and space, light and dark – and much the same is true of the musical composition, the drama, the poem. The meaning of such a text cannot be reproduced in other terms without loss.[62]

The startling insights revealed in the language of *Feed* – particularly in the words and thoughts attributed to its characters – offer us a picture of a society where some embers of humane aspirations and virtues persist despite the crushing weight of a commercial apparatus concerned only with channelling desire into its most profitable forms. Some evocations of this theme are darkly comic (for example, a date at a beach so contaminated the lovers must wear hazmat suits to frolic near the waves). Others are heart-rending – for example, Titus's agonized (if brief) thoughts on the moral meaning of his calculated indifference to Violet's suffering, punctuated by descending percentage measurements of her remaining cognitive function. We are left with little doubt that the world of *Feed* is headed toward disaster – yet in the midst of this slow violence, the more conscientious characters can glimpse the conditions of a better future, even if they have no clue as to how to achieve it.[63]

A similar sensibility might fruitfully inform today's struggles against excessive corporate power. Most jurists are, like most characters in *Feed*, conditioned to respect and reinforce the status quo. But some occasionally glimpse deeper principles and ethical obligations. Reading a novel like *Feed*, they might have a better sense of what a future public sphere dominated by the most profitable corporations asserting themselves as primary rights-bearing entities might look like. The concrete and shocking vision of a novel like *Feed* should be at least as influential as the vacuous aphorisms used to justify too many decisions expanding

---

62 James Boyd White, "What Can a Lawyer Learn from Literature," *Harvard Law Review* 102, no. 8 (1989): 2014–47.
63 Rob Nixon, *Slow Violence and the Environmentalism of the Poor* (Cambridge, MA: Harvard University Press, 2010).

corporate rights and the 1st Amendment. While jurists would almost never cite a novel to directly support an interpretation of law, they may do well to counterbalance the thousands of commercial messages we are all exposed to with a sustained reflection on their potential outcome. *Feed* and speculative works like it can contribute to such a humane sensibility. As long as books like it can be written and be read, persons have some hope of remaining the main beneficiaries of civil rights. But we must work to maintain that hope; otherwise, as Adrian Piper's haunting work "Everything #21," echoing the chilling final words of *Feed*, warns: "everything will be taken away."[64]

---

64   Adrian Piper, "Everything #21," 2010-2013, chalk on vintage blackboards.

5 Exceptionally Gifted: Corporate Exceptionalism and the Expropriation of Human Rights

RICHARD HARDACK

In this chapter I address case law, US culture, and gift theory to trace how the idea of corporate personhood has, since the late nineteenth century, developed at the expense of human rights. In prior publications, I argued that corporations, both ontologically and under US *stare decisis*, should be considered incapable of producing any speech beyond commercial speech. Whatever "personhood" or rights a corporation has are intrinsically delimited by and pertain entirely to the domain of commerce: in other words, a corporation can possess only commercial, not human, personhood. The perverse abnegation of these limitations is all the more ironic given the Court's recent equation of money with speech in *Citizen's United v. Federal Election Commission*,[1] which, among other things, fails to differentiate, even in terms of the Court's own precedents, between free speech and commercial speech. Though now attributed with something resembling human personhood, corporations still cannot act with univocal personal intention or human agency. I argue that as a result of many such anomalies, corporations are increasingly structured to expropriate personal rights while avoiding aggregate liability.

Because the argument I develop here relies on several claims I made previously, I briefly summarize these points here. I coined the term corpography to connote the limited forms of self-representation – such as advertisements, filings, and corporate histories – that corporations can generate as speech.[2] I proposed that personhood is a zero-sum game and that the more "personhood" and human rights corporations attain, the less of those traits and rights people retain. In the final necessary

---

1 558 U.S. 310 (2010).
2 See, generally, Richard Hardack, "New *and* Improved: The Zero-Sum Game of Corporate Personhood," *Biography: An Interdisciplinary Quarterly* 37, no. 1 (2014): 36–68.

inversion – created by the displacement of human personhood and human rights by corporate personhood and corporate rights – corporations don't just become people; people must become like corporations. In other words, the logic that allows corporations to become persons is inextricable from and predicated on a logic that requires persons to begin to take on the attributes of corporate entities. This process, which I treat as a kind of negation of gift-giving or the potlatch, both documents and further precipitates a redistribution of wealth in a kind of polarizing feedback loop, but the more consequential and less examined aspect of the expansion of corporate personhood pertains to its effects in ontological and epistemological terms. In many ways, the current, ever-increasing wealth gap in the United States is actually a personhood gap.

Because the issue of corporate personhood is so expansive, one way to chart its development is to focus on the critical relationship between the artificial corporate "person" and its cultural opposite, the living poor person. In cyclical waves since the late nineteenth century, people who receive public assistance have been demonized as parasites on the public good – as if they were not part of the public/*polis* – while large corporations that receive assistance or corporate welfare are treated as beneficiaries of the public good. In terms of rights and ontology, the deserving corporate person is constructed as the polar opposite of the undeserving person on welfare. Much of the press and the public chastised some banks for receiving government bailouts during the financial crisis that began in 2008, yet little was done to question the assumption that banks, not individuals, needed, by necessity or right, to be bailed out. Corporations, with their evolving form of personhood, are assumed worthy until proven otherwise; the poor, and especially welfare recipients and those carrying subprime loans, are assumed unworthy until proven otherwise. I argued in "Bad Faith: Race, Religion, and the Reformation of Welfare Law" that the concept of the gift – the form by which goods or services are offered for discretionary or unspecifiable return as part of the basic system of social interaction – plays a critical role in the economics and sociology of both the corporation and the welfare system, and helps contextualize the constitutional status of social insurance in American capitalism.[3] Here, I argue that as the ontological status of corporations and people becomes conflated, corporations are attributed with personal histories and beliefs, and rights

---

3 See Richard Hardack, "Bad Faith: Race, Religion, and the Reformation of Welfare Law," *Cardozo Public Law, Policy and Ethics Journal* 4, no. 3 (2006): 539.

attendant to them, while human beings come to be identified primarily in terms of their commercial value and to resemble personal ads. The most critical redistribution involves not money in the abstract – the wealth that has been directed not just to the 1 per cent, but to corporations – but the redistribution of welfare and rights from people to corporations.

In this chapter, I contrast case law that treats corporations as deserving of some form of public assistance with case law that treats the poor as undeserving, and analyse how these cases implicitly presuppose or develop a theory of human rights. In the United States, private corporations have over a long period commingled incommensurate aspects of the private and the public and become recipients of public rights and gifts in inverse proportion to the way individuals, and especially the poor, have lost access to them or become ineligible for public benefits. I briefly invoke gift theory to address how corporations, in claiming exceptional status in an exceptional nation, pervert notions of public welfare, the common good, and democratic rights. In numerous contexts, *Citizens United*, and the increasingly pervasive attribution of personhood and rights to corporations, codifies a zero-sum game between corporations and the poor (and ultimately between corporate personhood and personhood itself).

As Thom Hartmann notes via Paul Hawken, corporations are actually consumers or exploiters of rather than contributors to the tax base.[4] (I would add that they here function much like red states – especially when one considers the resources and infrastructure that corporations use without paying for them, the harms they cause the environment, and other rarely examined social externalities – in axiomatically opposing the very federal system of taxation they are exploiting.) Since the 1970s, corporations also have become consumers of rights as well as resources. Through the 1970s, welfare did not merely redistribute a fixed pie to poor people – that is, reducing benefits to some to increase them to others in a zero-sum game – but expanded the funds available to all and the rights recipients had. Such an approach was wholly undermined beginning with Reagan's welfare "reforms" and continued in force under Clinton.[5] As Lucy A. Williams indicates, these reforms generally "return[ed] to state and local government the discretion to define

---

4 Thom Hartmann, *Unequal Protection: The Rise of Corporate Dominance and the Theft of Human Rights* (San Francisco: Berrett Kohler), 2002.

5 See William H. Simon, *Rights and Redistribution in the Welfare System*, 38 Stan.L. REV. 1431, 1498 (1986).

who among the poor are sufficiently worthy to receive benefits."[6] The ethos inducing such reforms has helped redefine human personhood against corporate personhood in a process that – in tandem with the criminal justice system – has redefined the black welfare recipient as less than human, and the corporate person as more human than human.

My primary goal is to trace a teleology of corporate exceptionalism and examine how various legal conceptions of personhood in the United States – from those attributed to fetuses to those denied to non–US citizens and enemy combatants – have come to be predicated on exigently artificial conceptions of corporate personhood and rights. For example, corporations now counter-sue human rights lawyers, such as Terence Collingsworth, for libel, as if corporate entities had personal qualities or human characters one could libel.[7] Inhuman things are increasingly using personal discourses against people, and the approach is systemic. I argue that because we have no coherent definition of personhood in our culture, corporations have been able to hijack and co-opt the very notion of human identity and rights and have helped precipitate and benefited from an inchoate patchwork of laws and cultural beliefs regarding human and corporate personhood, rights, speech, and agency. Corporations have perpetrated the greatest identity theft in history.

Though the trajectory is not entirely linear, and has been tempered by countervailing progressive agendas, courts since the Civil War have codified a notion of corporate personhood that has tended to expand in inverse proportion to the rights afforded to the poor. In the overarching trajectory I chart, corporations are always seeking not just deregulation but a consolidated form that combines an increasing array of personal rights and privileges with an increasing number of impersonal immunities. The corporate version of the zero-sum game has unique and exceptional rules; paradoxically, for example, the more human traits the corporation claims, the less human liability it faces.

Finally, I also explore how the "fictions" or artificial attributes of the corporate identity warp the definitions of human personhood on which they are ineluctably based. In part because the corporation is theoretically an immortal collective, locatable nowhere as an agent, yet operating everywhere, it has been able to claim the legal right to elide most individual human limitations regarding continuity, embodiment,

---

6 Lucy Williams, *The Ideology of Division: Behavior Modification Welfare Reform Proposals,* 102 *Yale L.J.* 719, 725 (1992).

7 Harry Meier,"Companies Turn Tables on Human Rights Lawyers," *New York Times,* 6 March 2015, B1–2.

inheritance, criminal liability, and agency. These considerations also help explicate a principle of corporate exceptionalism, which then precipitates a number of other inversions, polarities, and ontological exchanges; a corporation is exceptional, for example, because it can be multinational or transnational in ways people and most other institutions cannot. Under *World-Wide Volkswagen Corp. v. Woodson*,[8] a case addressing which jurisdictions a corporation can be haled into, a corporation is considered to exist or reside virtually anywhere its products enter the stream of commerce. (Such a holding initially helps consumers, who are able to sue corporations in whatever location they have been injured; but in the long term, it brings with it unexpected deleterious effects, because it helps validate key components of corporate personhood, especially the idea that corporate personhood is a kind of invisible network that cannot be curtailed, scaled, or delimited. In many ways, that jurisdictionally omnipresent corporation takes the place of universal, divine nature in American culture – it takes on the function not just of the impersonal commons, but of a transcendental regulatory system that is uniform, ubiquitous, and finally quasi-numinous.[9] Many U.S. naturalists, especially Emerson, broadly believed in the unity and universality of nature, as formulated by naturalists such as the German Alexander von Humboldt. Here, the idea of universal, uniform Nature served as a harbinger of worldwide trade, globalization, and technologies of communication and travel, such as the World Wide Web, that link, homogenize, and effectively franchise all places. But where individuals derive almost all their rights through national citizenship, corporations transcend national boundaries and have acquired not only international but supra-national rights.

Not only are the rights of US citizens effectively held in opposition to those of corporations, the very contrast itself can obscure the wider system in which such rights are allocated. "First World" personhood is in many ways substantiated by its disparity with "Third World" personhood, but all human personhood is increasingly substantiated by its disparity with corporate personhood, particularly as corporate rights become naturalized and human rights come to be seen as relative constructs. In various races to the bottom, the corporation has the right to hire people anywhere it can pay the lowest wages; produce goods wherever it can find the weakest regulations or environmental laws; and relocate in or outsource to countries that do not tax its earnings,

---

8 444 U.S. 286, 297 (1980)

9 See generally Richard Hardack, *Not Altogether Human: Pantheism and the Dark Nature of the American Renaissance.* (Amherst: University of Massachusetts Press, 2012).

offer few human rights protections, or can exploit "illegal" immigrants or guest workers. While a discourse of rights carries the danger of locking people into determinate preferences, a discourse of discretionary benefits – which often comports with postmodern and post-human theories of the indeterminacy and constructedness of identity – can lock them out of the system altogether. A system that legitimates corporate personhood occludes the "naturalized" but epistemologically and morally bizarre and unjustifiable fact that the United States, as one example, treats people who aren't US citizens as having few or inferior rights – in the most extreme instance, they often have less or no right to due process and can be subjected to torture and rendition, especially if they reside or are held outside US territory. In parallel ways, the corporation can usually pick and choose malleable rights by location, in ways people cannot. When rights are local and malleable – that is, when they are contingent on and change according to fantasies of national borders – corporate personhood more easily becomes universal and determinate.

Here, gift theory is consistent with a notion of determinate human rights that cannot vary across borders, cultures, economies, and so on – these rights are not fungible. Throughout this chapter I intentionally conflate the gift with the human right, because I argue that human rights are kinds of gifts – they cannot be rationalized on the basis of equivalent or contractual return, but only as the basis for the social contract itself. Gift theory in some ways comports with a notion that basic human rights to food, water, shelter, education, health care, and freedom from violence and torture should be universally guaranteed, in effect, as social gifts "repaid" simply by being a member of society. A refusal or inability epistemologically, ontologically, and legally to define the invariable, public parameters of human personhood and rights cedes the definition to private corporations, which collectively form the closest thing to an international rule-making body that the world now has. (And of course such parameters will almost surely be identified using a specific and questionable set of Western premises; but not to adopt such parameters means adopting or continuing to rely on an existing set of even more problematic, largely corporate notions of personhood. Our failure to develop such standards also reflects a failure of Western will and belief in its own values). Such a notion of universal rights, cast against the rights of corporations, will perhaps raise significant problems with multicultural notions of rights; but refusing to consider such a determinate notion of rights, I argue, lets the corporation serve as the model for personhood. While a discourse of rights carries the danger of reifying determinate preferences, a discourse of discretionary rights and benefits can exclude people from the system altogether. *Homo sacer* has become the opposite of the corporation.

Finally, I briefly invoke critical theory to address how corporate personhood distorts the premises of human personhood. The contemporary corporation represents the apotheosis of a post-human identity – that is, the corporation is not tethered to any "natural" or traditional notion of a human identity and need have no biological body, no personality, limitations, and so on. A post-human theory of identity can embrace new concepts of personhood, including nomadism, animality, artificial intelligence, and so on, but it also can reify the concept of artificial corporate personhood. In Paul Giles's estimation, post-humanism "does not mean the end of the human or of humanity," but questions

> comfortable liberal assumptions about the sovereignty of the human subject. If the emergence of postmodernism can be attributed contextually to the aftermath of the Second World War, when the collapse of grand modernist narratives centered on a utopian state paved the way for the liberal agendas of multiculturalism and diversity, the provenance of posthumanism can be traced to more specific concerns around the mid-1980s about the extent to which a politics of human identity might ontologically be differentiated from other categories of scientific and biological existence. Such anxieties were impelled partly by rapid developments in information technology.[10]

Changes in the conception of corporate personhood are both cause and effect of such transformations in information technology, and the corporate form exploits technology to undermine human privacy, identity, and rights. The corporation is a truly post-human entity; it acts without having an actor, agency, or intention; in some ways it is analogous to a post-structuralist text produced without an author. In unexpected ways, Republican ideology in such contexts often seems commensurate with aspects of post-human and postmodern relativism and indeterminacy; while Republicans tend to be absolute about certain human rights – for example, those of gun owners and fetuses – they tend to challenge facts and scientific theories whose implications they dislike and effectively to reverse-engineer artificial rights for artificial persons such as the corporation. (That is, these rights are designed after the fact to meet the economic demands of corporations, not on the basis of any

---

10 Paul Giles, "Sentimental Posthumanism: David Foster Wallace," *Twentieth Century Literature* 53, no. 3 (2007): 327–44.

coherent or legitimate theory of personhood, save insofar as the corporation becomes the repository for the rights transferred from persons.)

Much as workers often become irrelevant to the corporation – that is, corporations at least symbolically often strive to have fewer and fewer people actually work for them – human personhood becomes irrelevant in the wake and context of corporate personhood. For Walter Benn Michaels, on ontological grounds, "corporations must be persons even if persons aren't"; the corporation must have a body and a soul and represent a new kind of man (205–6). That new kind of person is again post-human: a disembodied agent that cannot speak, have intent, or bear true liability yet is afforded or can attain unlimited speech, presence, and "mass" as well as unprecedented social, economic, and political influence. (Perhaps most incongruously, impersonal corporations are responsible for much of contemporary culture, telling people what it means to act like a human, love, be loved, desire, and so on. Speech is itself a human right, and corporations, which now have a virtually unfettered ability to monopolize speech in every register – including almost all broadcast media and publishing – again appropriate this right from individuals.) The corporation is a kind of computer simulation that mimics people and nature; it might appear to act as a human being, but because of the corporate form, one can rarely as a structural matter ever trace a corporate act to a specific person or intention. The corporation is a series of effects without causes, and its personhood is a series of accumulated thefts and now gifts that codify its legal exceptionalism, which only escalates as corporations hoard rights at the expense of persons.

The above considerations helps contextualize how individuals, and especially the poor, tend to be blamed for making choices that necessitate public assistance, while corporations are largely shielded from inquiry into decision-making agency. For example, Anna Grear observes that corporations are effectively agents when it comes to acting and formulating some fictional form of intent (and rights), but escape liability because they are disembodied; under our criminal justice system, there is no body/corpus to produce to hold accountable – and, I would add, more problematically, no intent to be uncovered.[11] Notwithstanding the media's distracting focus on celebrity CEOs, the corporation is legally and ontologically a decentralized network that can function only as an impersonal system that does not rely on human succession, personality,

---

11 *See* Anna Grear, *Redirecting Human Rights: Facing the Challenge of Corporate Legal Humanity* (New York: Palgrave Macmillan), 2010, 91.

or attributes. Grear proposes that "corporate rights, animal rights, the rights of eco-systems, 'post-human' rights and human rights need not be reduced to one monolithic category," and, in fact, as Grear intimates, the conflation of non-human rights with human rights is based on faulty premises.[12] The problem is that the cultural logic embedded into our current ethos seems to be generated by that non-existent corporate person in a kind of automated program. In some ways, our consistent, remarkable failure to hold corporations accountable for ostensibly legalizing a remarkably consistent culture of fraud and exploitation reflects our unconscious acceptance that no specific agency resides behind the corporation – that it functions like some kind of collective id or daemon. One can find an accessible colloquial example that illustrates how corporate impersonality generates a specious corporate intention in almost any diurnal interaction with a corporation: when an automated corporate phone message tells you "your call is very important to us," or a recorded airline announcement "thanks" you for choosing to fly with that airline, there is no person and no intent behind the message (even if a human, rather than a tape, conveys the message and happens to believe it). Much as shareholders by ineluctable design cannot represent a corporation, these speakers, when they even exist, can't represent a corporate person or intention. The very nature of the corporation is that there's no their there. This scenario illustrates the way the corporation serves as what Žižek, via Lacan, calls the Big Other – it is a repository for ideological fantasy. The issue is that we give rights to this Big Other as if it could be a person, when it functions like an idol.

Created by public charter, US corporations were initially designed to have only those delimited rights conferred upon them by law, rather than any natural rights: they existed through some form of the consent of the sovereign or *polis* and were formulated to reflect not only their exceptional uses but their potential dangers, particularly with regard to their concentration of power. In *Dartmouth College v. Woodward*, Chief Justice John Marshall declared that "[b]eing the mere creature of law, [the corporation] possesses only those properties which the charter of its creation confers upon it, either expressly or as incidental to its very existence." This rhetoric mirrors the language of Article I, Section 8 of the US Constitution, which establishes the delimited, enumerated powers of the federal government and the complex relationship between US exceptionalism and US notions of personhood.

But recent Court holdings have inverted the original conception of the chartered corporation, as Gregory A. Mark notes in related contexts:

---

12 Ibid. at 47.

"In *First National Bank of Boston v. Bellotti*, the Court rejected and characterized as "extreme" the view that "'corporations, as creatures of the State, have only those rights granted them by the State.'"[13] This naturalization and personification has been an ongoing process in which corporations, if sometimes haphazardly, accreted and retained more and more aspects of personhood. Because the corporation has exceptional, extra-human traits – including immortality and exceptional forms of immunity – it has achieved not just *more* rights than human beings, but *enhanced* rights whose very existence are incompatible with and antagonistic to individual rights. Those exceptional corporate rights are manifested in ontological, deontological, and practical contexts, in the latter case in the ways corporate lobbying, spending, and speech are treated as if they were undertaken by mere individuals, and in the bewildering array of tax exemptions and economic incentives uniquely awarded to corporations.

Originally, as various courts have noted, "[t]he fiction of corporate personhood [was] a convenient way to capture the essence of the principle of limited liability."[14] But ultimately, the enhancement of corporate personhood stems from the "separation" of personhood: "The many benefits of limited liability (for society as well as for the shareholders) are built on the idea that every corporation is a distinct legal person from its parent or subsidiary corporations and from its various shareholders."[15] Courts have been gradually eradicating that distinction in terms not of liabilities, but of benefits; that fiction has now become a means of bestowing extraordinary rights on corporations. Ironically, the most recent, immediate impetus for this further extension of the parameters of corporate personhood has been the desire of owners to use the corporate form to argue that their business entities have personal rights, and sometimes – at least in symbolic terms – to allow them to influence employees' choices and options regarding reproduction. In other words, the inhuman corporate thing has at least figuratively reached a point where it can affect the literal creation of persons.

On the one hand, courts continue to offer corporations protections because they are putatively impersonal contrivances pointedly separate

---

13   435 U.S. 765, 778 n.14 (1978); Gregory A. Mark, "The Personification of the Business Corporation in American Law," *University of Chicago Law Review* 54, (1987): 1441.

14   *Beiser v. Weyler*, 284 F.3d 665, 670 (5th Cir. 2002).

15   Throughout this article, I invoke cases whose logic is emblematic – that is, I chose cases less for their current precedential value than for the way they illuminate the assumptions and premises that make corporate personhood possible. *NAF Holdings, LLC v. Li & Fung (Trading), Ltd.*, 772 F.3d 740, 751 (2d Cir. 2014).

from their shareholders, operators, and employees; unless they effectively act personally – on frolics of their own or beyond the sanctioned scope of their duties – corporate actors remain protected by the veil.[16] But these limitations on liability were created with attendant limitations on rights, which have been largely removed. Many courts still do reassert the obvious but necessary point that corporations have no feelings to be injured or personal sentiments to express. As a result, corporations should be able to sue only for factual misrepresentations (e.g., if one published a claim that Coke is made of carcinogenic acid, though that might represent an improvement on its actual contents), and never for representations of its "traits": one can libel or defame only a person. Any other form of defamation is commercial or involves some other ontological category. Yet the corporation that has no emotions or thoughts per se has been given a set of rights based on personhood (the final irony is that if the corporate person cannot vote, the single ballot it cannot cast is irrelevant in light of the millions of votes corporations can influence and the legislation they can effectively write themselves). The fundamental derangement of the attribution of rights to corporate persons is to forget that the corporation can engage only in commercial behaviour and produce only commercial speech; as such, all its acts are regulable, and it cannot have rights outside the context of the commercial realm, or "opinions" or beliefs about anything beyond that realm.

Yet courts now routinely grant corporations exceptional rights and exemptions based purely and precisely on "personal reasons." As Judge Rovner observes in her dissent in *Korte v. Sebelius*[17] addressing the religious claims of a corporate person, "[t]he court extends a highly personal right to a secular corporation, a man-made legal fiction that has no conscience enabling belief or worship." Judge Rovner logically asks:

What if, for example, one of a corporation's two equal owners is Catholic and the other is Protestant, Muslim, Jewish, or an atheist – are the beliefs of one or both attributed to the corporation, and if the beliefs of only one count, which does? Are the beliefs a conglomeration or neither? Or suppose that both owners are Catholic, but only one of them claims that his beliefs are burdened by some legal requirement (like the mandate at issue

---

16 See, for example, *Cross v. Gen. Motors Corp.*, 721 F.2d 1152, 1156 (8th Cir. 1983) (noting that overcoming the corporate personhood issue [sic] requires that individual defendants have "acted outside the scope of their employment or for personal reasons"). *Baugh v. Ozarks Area Cmty. Action Corp.*, 2010 U.S. Dist. LEXIS 31888, 10 (W.D. Mo. 2010).

17 *Korte v. Sebelius*, 735 F.3d 654, 688 (7th Cir. 2013).

here) imposed on the company, whereas the other professes either indifference or support for that requirement.[18]

Judge Rovner concludes:

> To say, as the court does today, that the right to exercise one's religious faith may be asserted on the same terms by a legal construct – an incorporated currency exchange, accounting firm, or automobile repair shop, for example – as by a human being, is, to my mind at least, irreconcilable with the very essence of religious faith and, for that matter, humankind.[19]

If a corporation can have no feelings to hurt, how can it have faith to defend? In fact, corporate personhood and rights writ large are irreconcilable with their human counterparts.

Courts generally maintain the distinction between corporations and owners and shareholders when addressing liability, but increasingly erase the distinction between corporations and owners when it comes to rights:

> It is true that a corporation is a fictional entity, separate and apart from its association of individuals, and it enjoys certain privileges benefitting both the association as a whole and the individuals alike. But the individuals are the real parties that make up the association and these individuals bring with them certain rights that, unless incompatible with the corporate form, should not be relinquished. It cannot be said here that the exercise of religion by an individual in association with other individuals is incompatible with any of its corporate privileges, whether we speak of the privilege of a shareholder to enjoy limited liability or the privilege of a corporation to exist in perpetuity. Put simply, an individual's right to freely exercise religion includes the right to exercise religion in association with others under the corporate umbrella.[20]

Of course, the court does not consider what happens when those speech rights conflict, or that it is privileging the religious rights of *some* owners over others and of an impersonal corporate person over human

---

18 *Id.* at 704.
19 *Id.* at 701–2.
20 See generally *Citizens United v. Fed. Election Comm'n*, 558 U.S. 310, 392. "But the individual's right to speak includes the right to speak *in association with other individual persons*" (emphasis in original). See also *Beckwith Elec. Co. v. Sebelius*, 960 F. Supp. 2d 1328, 1342 (M.D. Fla. 2013).

employees. Claiming that an "association's" (corporation's) right and ability to speak are equivalent to an individual's is as specious and fatuous as claiming that an individual litigant's rights and abilities in a lawsuit are equivalent to a corporation's.

Courts unwittingly reveal the ulterior logic of the ways corporations hide behind veiled inhuman impersonality in achieving immunities, yet simultaneously claim the privileges of personal rights under the very same regime: "Similarly, the facts in this case show that Beckwith Electric *is inculcated with the beliefs of its owner* and CEO. Beckwith manages the day-to-day operations of Beckwith Electric and is responsible for establishing all its operational policies."[21] If such is the case, the corporation has been infiltrated by or commingled with the personal assets of an owner, and the corporate form should be dissolved or pierced. The whole rationale of the corporate form (which has its own attendant problems) is to be impersonal and preclude any such "consanguinity" between owners and operators under the corporate form. In reality, CEOs such as Beckwith and the Green family that owns Hobby Lobby are almost irrelevant distractions – the problem isn't that the owners of a few anomalous corporations have been given the ability to impose their (no doubt sometimes problematic) human beliefs on their corporate enterprises. It's that the overwhelming majority of corporations have been given the right to impose their personhood on the vast majority of people. As I argue in more detail in "New *and* Improved,"[22] the corporation by charter can speak and act only impersonally, but the newly empowered personed corporation relies on a series of impersonations and contrivances to simulate human personality.

In the next sections, I develop a necessarily compressed discussion of the history of corporate welfare in the United States as it relates to these issues of human rights and personhood. The development of the railway in the United States was intimately connected to the expansion of corporate personhood and the extension of public benefits and rights to the corporate form – most prominently through the notorious judicial bootstrapping that used uncitable precedent, dicta, and headnotes in *Santa Clara County v. Southern Pacific Railroad Co.*[23] to codify the notion of corporate personhood. Peter Lyon contends that "the iron horse was fed and watered at the public trough for more than fifty years ... [For

---

21 *Beckwith*, 960 F. Supp. 2d at 1344 (emphasis added).
22 "New *and* Improved: The Zero-Sum Game of Corporate Personhood." Special Issue on Life-Writing and Corporate Personhood, *Biography: An Interdisciplinary Quarterly* 37, no. 1 (2014): 36–68.
23 *Santa Clara County v. Southern Pacific Railroad Co.*, 118 U.S. 394 (1886).

example], a committee of the New York state legislature would later reckon that the state and various cities had given New York railroad companies, among other goodies, $40,039,496.82 either in cash or by investment, and that only about one quarter if this sum had ever been repaid."[24] Though Congress intended the railways "to promote the public interest and welfare" and tried to curtail monopoly, the propensity of the corporation is to consolidate what should be public resources – for example, natural resources, airwaves, access to the legislative process – into private gain and redefine such private gain as a public good.[25]

Alfred Chandler Jr., among others, observes that the railway was "the nation's first big business": "the size and complexity of [its] operations required new ways and new forms. The financial requirements of the railroads caused the centralizing and institutionalizing of the nation's investment market" and the development of "modern ways of finance, management, labor relations, competition, and government regulation" – in other words, the modern corporation (9). Numerous fields – especially transportation, energy, media, and education – lent themselves to the corporate co-option of the public good and public resources and rights. Frank Donoghue notes that Sinclair Lewis, in his 1920s work *The Goose-Step: A Study in American Education*, was already documenting the ways many American universities had become corporate entities (Lewis designated Columbia the university of J.P. Morgan and asserted that you could not differentiate its trustees from the owners of the New York Central Railroad [14]). This same conflation of private and public trusteeship applies with even greater dissonance to many contemporary corporations, from Comcast to Walmart, that are functional monopolies, or behemoths that have outstripped the government that chartered their form and first gave them rights. The very concept of rights becomes untenable when rights holders become more powerful than the system that regulates rights.

As Brook Thomas documents, in the early nineteenth century, when the country's new market economy required great expenditures, common law that required private corporations to serve a public good was changed to favour first developers, effectively turning chartered limitations into special privileges and rights (259). Court opinions regarding corporate personhood also reflect the shifting cultural assumptions of antebellum and postmodern approaches to the public welfare in general and actual forms of welfare specifically. I address the following

---

24 Peter Lyon, *To Hell in a Day Coach: An Exasperated Look at American Railroads* (Philadelphia: J.P. Lippincott),1968, 5, 12.
25 *Id.* at 30.

cases as illustrative of representative court positions rather than as necessarily precedential in legal terms. In general, courts considered gifts
to (white) civic entities to be acceptable, where aid to individual (often
black) recipients was not; in this inversion, the "public" interest was
identified with wealthy white private corporations and the "private"
interest with the public poor. Corporations were already beginning to
become people, effectively at the expense of the poor. In *Kentucky Live
Stock Breeders' Ass'n v. Hager*,[26] 120 Ky. 125 (1905), an emblematic pre–
New Deal case discussing the idea of "the gift," the court of appeals
reversed the lower court's decision regarding the illegality of a "public
purpose": it was

> the contention of the State that the appropriation in question was not, and
> is not, for a public purpose or use, but that it is a gift pure and simple,
> by the toiling masses of this Commonwealth, through the same, and un-
> der cover of law, to advance the interests of the Kentucky Breeders' As-
> sociation, and that the Legislature had no constitutional right to levy a
> tax upon the people of Kentucky, in order to raise funds for this private
> corporation.[27]

The irony that this case involved subsidies for breeding or reproduction
should not be overlooked; endemically, corporations are celebrated
for their production, even when subsidized by public largesse, while
women of colour have been constitutively demonized for "breeding"
in supposedly irresponsible ways. In our culture, in various formulations since the period of Reconstruction, the person most diametrically
opposed to the corporate person is the single black mother, whose offspring were originally valued only as chattel/slaves and later devalued as public dependents. Whether a state disbursement was classified
as an illegal gift or a valid economic or contractual disbursement depended largely on the personhood of the recipient.

The appeals court in *Kentucky Live Stock* here reversed the lower court
to hold that what we might consider a private business enterprise is
itself a public good: what is good for the Kentucky Breeder's Association is good for America, and it would have been hard for the court to
see how state fairs designed to promote a particular business do "not
equally [serve] a public purpose."[28] But most substantive subsidies,

---

26 *Kentucky Live Stock Breeders' Ass'n v. Hager*, 120 Ky. 125 (1905).
27 Lexis Summary of Counsel's Argument, *Ky. Live Stock*, 120 Ky. at 129.
28 *Ky. Live Stock*, 120 Ky. at 133.

according to David Johnston, "are available only to corporations and those individuals rich enough to own a substantial business. Everyone, however, is forced to finance these bounties ... [F]rom a national perspective, those [subsidized] jobs, [e.g., through which government subsidizes the health care, benefits, taxes, and so forth of corporations such as most fast food restaurants] are a drag on the American economy because they cost more than they are worth."[29] Ironically, while a strain of federalism initially opposed the notion of a centralized government using public funds to subsidize the wealthy – and while many Republicans and Tea Party members claim to repudiate the principle of corporate favouritism – the system the Republican Party embraces is entirely beholden to a corporatism that subsidizes rich shareholders and corporate enterprise at taxpayer expense.

For the most part, under a pervasive though never absolute cultural logic that courts use to differentiate what we might call gifting down from gifting up, gifts to the poor remain handouts to undeserving private entities, while gifts to the wealthy more often represent necessary and deserved public expenditure. (This logic should sound familiar since it overlaps with Republican talking points that situate billionaires and corporations as job creators and corporations as people, my friends, when they are takers and fictions). The largely overlooked critical issue now is whether the corporate person is a private or public entity. American society has historically weighed whether and who among the poor deserve welfare and considered the poor as a class as pointedly separate from the public interest and hence ineligible for "gifts." Recent welfare reforms continue to target these unworthy, "undeserving poor," especially those whose personal behaviour does not conform to putative middle-class norms. Susan Sterett documents that the justification for much state expenditure that we now view as part of a security net – including state pensions and social security – relied on "a contract justification for a return for service."[30] In other words, recipients who had paid into a system had a right to get something back; they were not given gifts, and had no rights to subsistence, but were receiving only returns on a kind of investment.

The ever-expanding legal, religious, and civic rights of the corporate person can best be understood when measured against those of the poor. William H. Simon argues that "the substantive rights theme has had a peculiarly conservative influence in liberal welfare discourses"

---

29   Davis Cay Johnston, *Free Lunch: How the Wealthiest Americans Enrich Themselves at Government Expense (and Stick You with the Bill)* (New York: Penguin), 2007, 7.

30   Susan Sterett, "Serving the State," 22 LAW & SOC. INQUIRY 311, 329 (1997).

because it has inhibited efforts at redistribution: "Right was a term to be invoked against redistribution."[31] Ironically, the rights corporations now invoke serve to justify ongoing redistribution to the rich. Again, historically, welfare benefits and other social expenditures could be defended only under a contract theory, not as a matter of right, and any rights the poor retained were of a "lower normative status" than those rights acquired by contract.[32]

A similar logic applies in elevating the rights of corporate persons over those of actual persons. Because they exist almost exclusively in the realm of contract, corporations are considered generally under the law to operate beyond good and evil – they are virtually defined as deserving within that framework, which again treats corporations as, in effect, categorically exempt or non–*compos mentis* in terms of moral responsibility, but exceptional in terms of rights. By contrast, citizens with needs often are subjected to a bewildering array of inspections to evaluate whether they are morally deserving, from drug tests to assessments of their characters, sexual behaviour, laziness, and so on.

Contrary to Simon, I would argue that only a rights approach can circumvent the current legal framework that has inverted the status of people and corporate things. Simon asserts that Charles Reich's shift in his influential article "The New Property,"[33] "from contract to property seems related to the goal of turning public assistance benefits into rights ... [and mistakenly failed to distinguish] between Social Security as contractual and therefore a right and public assistance as noncontractual and therefore not a right."[34] Such an analysis validates the premises of corporate personhood and treats persons as if they were business entities and human rights as if they were earned or awarded only after one fulfils an economic contract. Simon also elsewhere observes that

> Progressive attacks undermined the basic classical distinction between individual right and collective or state power. They portrayed many of the forms of power threatening individual independence as arising from citizens engaged in activities classicism characterized as the exercise of rights. The most prominent example was the large corporation, which the Progressives described as a concentration of power rather than as a rightholder. Conversely, the Progressives showed that many of the welfare and

---

31   William H. Simon, "Rights and Redistribution," *38* STAN. L. REV. at 1432, 1435.
32   *Id.* at 1438.
33   See Charles Reich, "The New Property," *73* YALE L.J., 733 (1964).
34   *Id.* at 1487.

regulatory activities of the state could be described – even if one started with the basic moral premises of the classicists – as rights enforcement.[35]

The recent trends again invert the Progressive perspective by situating the corporation as our culture's pre-eminent rights holder – having the right to unlimited spending, speech, religious expression, and affect itself – and effectively denying that individuals have any rights other than those formulated through economic contract.

As part of a series of critical polarizations or inversions, the concept of corporate personhood has helped aggregate economic and even human rights to the owners of corporations, and left, at the opposite end of the spectrum, the single poor woman as an isolated *homo sacer* increasingly divested of rights. Lisa Crooms contends that

> if "the welfare-dependent single mother is ... the shortest possible shorthand for the pathology of poor, urban, black culture," then the single motherhood welfare encourages is the single motherhood of black women ... The new welfarism is concerned with the single motherhood of all poor women who act like black women – those who bear children outside the confines of traditional two-parent families because welfare pays them to do so.[36]

A similar logic applies to tax credits and breaks – the rich and the corporate person *deserve* tax breaks and incentives because they are lionized as job creators, while the poor, who are denigrated for allegedly failing to pay any taxes, deserve their fate. According to a conservative research centre, for example, "no able adult should be allowed to voluntarily take from the common good without also contributing to it."[37] Corporate personhood is part of a cultural economy that radically has redefined the poor in opposition to the "common good" and that has situated welfare not as a right but as a drain on the common good. Dorothy E. Roberts notes that even "maternalist rhetoric [allowing remittances to the deserving poor] has no appeal in the case of Black welfare mothers because society sees no value in supporting their domestic service."[38] Similarly, Tonya L. Brito documents that society has typically

---

35 William H. Simon, "The Invention and Reinvention of Welfare Rights," 44 MD. L. REV. 1, 12–13 (1985).

36 Lisa Crooms, "Don't Believe the Hype: Black Women, Patriarchy, and the New Welfarism,"*Howard Law Journal* 38, no. 3 (1995): 611, 613.

37 Andrew Hacker, *Two Nations: Black and White, Separate, Hostile, Unequal* (New York: Scribner), 1992, 90.

38 Dorothy E. Roberts, "The Value of Black Mothers' Work," *Connecticut Law Review* 871 (1994): pp. 873–4.

deemed the work black mothers provide as mothers as "pathological and unworthy of subsidy."[39] This racialized rhetoric of pathology, which might seem removed from the concept of corporate personhood, is inexorably connected to it. At stake is the definition of personhood. For example, as Joel Barkan notes, via Noam Chomsky, the corporation's drive to privatize is coterminous with an attempt to enforce its "particular conception of humanity," which Barkan aptly describes, via Mark Kingwell, as being modelled after itself – "an artificial person made in the image of a human psychopath."[40] Corporate personhood has turned the profile of an extreme, antisocial private individual, elevated into a legal archetype, into a model of public personhood and rights.

Some of the shift in the allocation of rights reflects our changing definition of social worth: as the poor become less deserving and less worthy, corporations become almost proportionately more deserving and worthy. While it has become acceptable to call for almost any recipient of state benefits (or public employee) to be drug-tested, micromanaged, and subjected to often purposefully humiliating scrutiny – typically at the behest of right-wingers who fulminate about personal liberty – it has become unacceptable to place almost any constraints on corporations that need bailouts, destroy ecosystems, routinely lie to regulators, or cause significant harm to consumers though fraud. US case law is rife with assumptions regarding how the poor represent private, unworthy interests, while private businesses represent the public good. Most state courts in the late nineteenth century held that the state could not offer credit to businesses, but also that aid, gifts, or disbursements made for individual welfare, even when presented to groups, were by definition unconstitutional: "The Legislature shall have no power to give or to lend, or to authorize the giving or lending of the credit of the State ... in aid of or to any person, association or corporation ...; nor shall it have power to make any gift, or authorize the making of any gift, of any public money ... to any individual" (Cal. Const., art. VI, 6). Though in practice aid to business entities could be rationalized as constitutional investments, the overriding ethos was that state expenditures for targeted ends, including specific corporations, were prohibited. Such provisions are commonly cited as dispositive in cases from the Civil War to the New Deal – courts' definition of a public purpose precluded gifts

---

39   Tonya L Brito, "From Madonna to Proletariat: Constructing a New Ideology of Motherhood in Welfare Discourse," *Villanova Law Review* 44 (1999): 415, 434.

40   Joel Barkan, *The Corporation: The Pathological Pursuit of Profit and Power* (New York: Simon and Schuster), 2005, 135–6.

unless they were made to certain delimited forms of corporate entities: "We have established, we think, beyond cavil that there can be no lawful tax which is not laid for a public purpose" (*Loan Ass'n v. Topeka*).[41]

Discussing "a subsidy to a private sawmill, [in] *Weismer v. Village of Douglas* [64 N.Y. 91 (1876)]," Susan Sterett notes that courts did restrict which business endeavours could be viewed as offering public benefits, under statutes that required state expenditures to serve a public purpose:

> Public purpose allowed the state to pay for a "benefit or convenience to the public." That statement embodied limits on state spending; it did not mean the legislature could decree anything was of public benefit. Sawmills, for example, were not. Judge Folger rather neatly stated the categories of legitimate payments. States could pay for service, which was distinct from charity. Payments for both were legitimate. But different responsibilities prompted the payments: gratitude motivated payments for service, while charity was a feeling distinct from gratitude and "no other than a moral obligation." The prohibition on gifts covered all payments states might try to make that were not of a general public benefit – that is, were not an expression of gratitude for service or an expression of charity.[42]

For Sterett, "by interpreting constitutional provisions regarding what was a public purpose, state appellate courts provided articulation of desert in social spending programs"; but their definition of desert "made spending more readily available to those who could be construed as having served the state in work," which again situated the disbursement under a form of contract law rather than as a gift or right.[43] As we erode the distinction between public and private, and imagine that private good is a public good – for example, that billionaires are job creators or public benefactors – we also redefine the concept of rights, as attached to the definition of a person and personhood.

The definition of public purpose was always implicitly intertwined with the definition of personhood, because it included normative and regulatory standards to determine one's social standing and worth. In *Auditor of Lucas County v. The State, Ex Rel. Boyles*, the court in part addressed an Ohio Act of 1904 that provided for "relief for [the] worthy blind" (internal quotation marks omitted) (quoting An Act to Provide Relief for the Worthy Blind, 1904 Ohio Laws 392). Like many similar

---

41 *Loan Ass'n v. Topeka*, 87 U.S. 655, 664 (1874).
42 *Serving*, 22 LAW & SOC. INQUIRY at 320–321 (1997).
43 *Id.* at 351.

statutes, the Act provided guidance for how to ascertain who was "worthy" of assistance. The court iterated several common distinctions between the public and private good, and the worthy and unworthy poor.

Lucas then weighed whether a public gift made for "private" or special ends could comport with the state constitution. Counsel challenging the statute argued that

> Article VII of the Constitution of the State of Ohio, provides: "Institutions for the benefit of the insane, blind and deaf and dumb, shall always be fostered and supported by the state" ...
>
> [But] The words "due process of law" as used in Article V of the Amendments to the Constitution of the United States, have been held to prohibit the levy of taxes for any other than public purpose.[44]

The petitioners also alleged that "the purpose and object of the law in question in this case, is purely private and for the benefit of the individual and not for a public purpose, nor for the welfare of the general public."[45] As in *Kentucky Breeders*, corporate subsidies could be situated as benefits to the public welfare, while subsidies for the poor became "private" indulgences. In addition, the court tellingly accepted the argument that the expenditure at issue "is simply a gift, and one which is forbidden not only by the Constitution, but by good morals. If such a classification is to be permitted, its possibilities are without limitation. There is no place where we may call a halt."[46] Therefore, the individual does not represent the public good, but the corporation does – again, what's good for the corporation is good for the US. This logic of proto-corporate personhood defines people as contractual entities, not as civic, political, or moral beings. Society is held together by an options, not a social, contract.

The *Lucas* court held that the Act impermissibly sanctioned an expenditure of public funds for private purposes, yet it also warned that private individuals should not be allowed to become "public charges": "it must be said that the act under consideration is without precedent in this state and that no provision is made in the act to insure the application of the money to the support of the individual, or to prevent him from becoming a public charge, or in any manner to control its use

---

44 *Auditor of Lucas County v. State ex rel. Boyles*, 1906 Ohio LEXIS 328 (1906), Lexis Summary of Counsel's Argument at 3.
45 *Id.* at 4.
46 *Id.* at 4–5.

by him."[47] In the court's reasoning, if the state is to confer benefits on one class of people, such as the blind, "then why not upon other classes who for various reasons may be unable to support themselves? And if these things may be done, why may not all property be distributed by the state?"[48] Of course, the states and the federal government have always distributed distinct benefits to different classes, from veterans to the elderly: the problem is often with the states' definition of rights, public and private good, and personhood itself.

The *Lucas* court found that "the controlling question then is, whether the disbursement of the public funds provided for by the act in question is for a public purpose."[49] For *Lucas*, the disbursement could represent only "an indeterminate gratuitous annuity, a gift pure and simple, and, being so, the Legislature is without authority to make it from the public funds."[50] That pure and simple gift is made precisely for a public purpose, but courts often conflate public and private. The for-profit corporation in its modern guise is pointedly a private entity, but it frequently transposes itself onto public and human hosts. The encroachment of corporate personhood on human personhood has helped divest many classes and aspects of society from being considered part of the public, which also means they end up with little voice in politics or media (especially relative to the corporate voice). While the specific reasoning and discourse the court used here will likely seem archaic to us, many of the same premises apply in modern contexts to corporate personhood, with the result that corporations have become legally and culturally validated as exceptional super-persons with more rights than any individual can possess either categorically as finite mortals or under our current legal regime.

The *Lucas* court dismisses the "incidental public benefit" provided to the blind or the poor as irrelevant: "The merchant, the mechanic, the innkeeper [*sic*], the banker, the builder, the steamboat owner are equally promoters of the public good and equally deserving of the aid of the citizens by enforced contribution."[51] A similar rationale explicates why, despite bridling, the public generally holds government bailouts for criminal or criminally negligent banks, or subsidies to purely commercial organizations, ultimately to represent a benefit to the public

---

47 *Lucas*, 78 N.E. at 956.
48 *Lucas*, 78 N.E. at 955.
49 *Lucas*, 78 N.E. at 956.
50 *Id.* (emphasis added).
51 *Lucas*, 78 N.E. at 956–7.

welfare, while aid or "bailouts" even to the "innocent" remain a form of private gift.

Throughout the late nineteenth century, and generally before the New Deal, courts invalidated many forms of public assistance as illegal disbursements of gifts that effectively contravened the public interest: "New York had a similar anti-gift constitutional provision dating from 1874.... . The prohibition on gifts covered all payments states might try to make that were not of a general public benefit," which initially precluded payments to business. [52] But that proscription ultimately was inverted to preclude not gifts to public corporations, but those to any "special" class, especially the poor.[53] Courts here tend to rely on a logic of negative individualism; the putatively dependent individual, and especially the poor person, is held responsible for his or her own status, while corporations – which typically deny any dependence on infrastructure, laws, and other civic systems – reap the benefits of myriad direct and indirect public expenditures, incentives, and expiations. The recent furore over Obama's remarks that "you didn't build that" – perhaps inartfully referring to the fact that all entrepreneurs and businesses succeed only by relying on infrastructure and social contexts that belie libertarian claims to absolute autonomy – partly emanates from the misperception that the corporate person is self-sufficient: in fact, it is closer to a parasite. The various iterations of negative individualism that suffuse US society mirror the inverted structure of corporate personhood; individual persons assume most blame and liability, while corporate persons remain almost categorically immune from liability. (Though it occupies a different register, the fact that so many failed CEOs – who are themselves impersonators of the corporate personhood that impersonates human personhood – walk away from failure or scandal with huge payouts reinforces the liability structure of corporate personhood).

A similar logic elevates the rights of corporate persons over real ones. As Jennifer Jorczak suggests, in *Burwell v. Hobby Lobby Stores, Inc.*[54] – which addressed the right of the owners of a closely held corporation to deny their employees birth control because it ostensibly offended the religious beliefs of the corporation itself – the Court had "to raise the corporations' newfound statutory rights above the constitutional rights of their employees" in order to conclude that the corporation's religious

---

52 Susan Sterett, "Serving the State: Constitutionalism and Social Spending," *1860s–1920s*, 22 LAW & SOC. INQUIRY 311, 320–1 (1997).

53 *Id.*

54 *Burwell v. Hobby Lobby Stores, Inc.*, 134 S.Ct. 2751 (2014).

rights trumped the rights of employees to contraception.[55] That case –
whose implications go far beyond the ruling, which should, at most,
have applied only to other closely held corporations – unwittingly has
codified the rules of the zero-sum game between corporate and human
personhood. According to Jennifer S. Taub, the *Hobby Lobby* decision
reflects the Court's belief that the "free-exercise rights of corporations
protect the owners as opposed to the employees or other human stakeholders."[56] But as I argue, human owners are largely distractions and
always mere stand-ins for the non-existent personhood of the corporation; "protecting" owners is a cover for protecting corporate personhood, and the unwitting owners are actually being used.

It was effectively necessary for the Court to consider a closely held
corporation – that is, an anomalous, relatively small corporation – in
order to grant the corporate form religious rights. It would have been
(even more) ludicrous for the Court to consider whether Coca-Cola has
religious beliefs, but its holding provides another rationale for granting
all commercial entities personal rights – that is, to treat their commercial
speech as free or political speech, and to treat their impersonal limitations as personal rights across a broad spectrum. As I suggested earlier,
it is the exigent impersonality of the corporation that allows it to become exceptional and that affords it the ability to speak, avoid liability,
and attain the effect of a kind of mass consciousness in the culture. But
the corporation is an empty cipher that siphons and aggregates human
traits and rights in ways that increasingly lend it to a kind of uncanny,
artificial voice and persona. What is most disturbing is that the creation
has overtaken the creator, so that corporations are now regulating the
states that once chartered them.

In rejecting individual assistance while validating an array of corporate subsidies, courts often alleged that legislatures intended to distinguish and allow for a variety of kinds of aid: "'Aid in assisting' a
business for co-operative self-help, whether to found it or to continue
it, need not necessarily be wholly by gift ... It is reasonable to suppose
that Congress intended that such associations, engaging in business,
would have business-like, as well as purely gratuitous, aid from the
government, gifts when they were necessary, temporary loans to carry

---

55 Jennifer Jorczak, "'Not Like You and Me': Hobby Lobby, the Fourteenth
    Amendment, and What the Further Expansion of Corporate Personhood Means For
    Individual Rights," *Brooklyn Law Review* 80 (2014): 285, 315.
56 Jennifer Taub, "Is Hobby Lobby a Tool For Limiting Corporate Constitutional Rights?,"
    Constitutional Commentary 30 (2015): 403, 420.

it during non-productive seasons when they were sufficient."[57] During and after the New Deal, courts did become more flexible in evaluating the legality of gifts, though still often in corporate contexts. The more progressive reasoning that would help sustain businesses in times of crisis could also be applied to individuals as equally representative of the public.

But the approach could have unintended consequences. For example, in *Goodall v. Brite*, a California court observed that "[a]s our civic life has developed so has the definition of 'public welfare' until it has been held to embrace regulations 'to promote the economic welfare, public convenience and general prosperity of the community.'"[58] Here, the court was evaluating whether the rationale of public welfare could justify increased access to hospital care, and gauging whether expenditures in that context could be considered "for a public purpose and not gifts to a private individual."[59] *Goodall*'s analysis, which emphasized not only "human progress" but the idea that need-based expenditures could fulfil a public purpose, could serve as a kind of corrective to the approach in *Lucas*.[60] The problem is that, especially over the past four decades, the corporation has come to represent both the public good and a public person, while the poor have been deemed private persons who represent nothing but themselves. In other words, the "gift theory" of the New Deal has been perverted to serve the interests of corporate personhood.

While handouts to corporations might represent a relatively minor outlay of public funds in direct terms, our political, economic, and ontological infrastructure writ large is designed to provide corporations with special rights and incentives. In an example of the logic used to treat corporations as exceptional, the court in *Frostburg v. Jenkins*[61] validated the use of industrial bonds to increase local employment as a specific form of justifiable "gift": "The answer admitted the facts alleged in the bill, and further [justifiably] alleged that the issuance of the bonds 'will be for the benefit of the citizens and residents of the City of Frostburg and that the issuance of such bonds are for a public purpose and are necessary to obtain industrial sites for the purpose of giving employment to the residents of the City of Frostburg.'" Under such logic, if it benefits some citizens, or provides some jobs or even marginal taxes,

---

57 *In re Dissolution of Cmty. Co-Operative Indus., Inc.*, 273 N.W. 287, 289 (Mich. 1937).
58 11 Cal. App. 2d 540, 546 (1936).
59 *Id.* at 547
60 *Id.* at 547–8.
61 *Frostburg v. Jenkins*, 136 A.2d 852, 853–4 (Md. 1957).

then any corporation can be held to serve a public purpose. The kind of tax breaks and incentives invoked in *Frostburg* are inherently subject to cronyism and corruption, in that they offer select industries benefits without any real oversight or consistency.

Corporate welfare favouritism often has been justified by claims that it provides an overarching public benefit. Recent cases that validate corporate welfare – almost always implicitly or explicitly against individual rights – even resort to the circular logic that if a constitutional amendment appropriates funds for a corporation, that action must reflect the public will and therefore not only reflect a public benefit but be *a priori* democratically sanctioned. In *State ex rel. Burton v. Greater Portsmouth Growth Corp.*[62], a "Relator attack[ed] the validity of Section 13, Article VIII of the Ohio Constitution, which provides for public aid to private corporations for the purpose of creating new employment, and Section 1724.10, Revised Code, enacted pursuant to the provisions of Section 13, Article VIII." According to the court,

> [b]oth parties seem to have missed the salient point. Here we are not concerned with a legislative act. The problem before us is an amendment to the Constitution by the people of Ohio. If the people think that aid to private enterprise serves a public purpose and amend the Constitution to so provide, barring some infringement of the federal Constitution, such determination by the people becomes the law of the state. The people have spoken through their fundamental document.[63]

The court was perhaps correct insofar as public disbursements to corporations did not technically violate any Ohio laws since the state Constitution itself provided a corporate loophole – but they did violate the premise of the corporate charter. Such cases, and recent Court decisions, indicate that we have little separation between corporation and state and that the corporation has become a quasi-numinous entity in its cultural functions.

In consonant terms, while courts often show no such restraint when determining that expenditures for the poor are ill-advised, they typically defer to legislative determinations that corporate assistance serves the public welfare:

---

62 *State ex rel. Burton v. Greater Portsmouth Growth Corp.*, 7 Ohio St. 2d 34, 36 (Ohio 1966).

63 *Id.* at 38–9.

[T]he law is well settled that the wisdom of legislative and executive action may not be reviewed by the courts. Whether any project is based on sound economic theories is not within the scope of judicial review. Such considerations are matters of legislative and executive judgment and do not necessarily affect the constitutionality of the conduct.[64] Our role is not that of a super legislature. Our only function is in the interpretation of the acts of the other branches of government in the light of the Constitution, existing legal precedents and the legislation itself.[65]

With a familiar disingenuousness, the court here has dismissed concerns that one person's definition of public good or purpose might differ radically from a corporate person's (both as agent and object):

Section 3 of the Constitution prohibits separate privileges except in consideration of public services and Section 171 is closely related to it because it provides the taxes shall be collected and levied only for public purposes ... The precise meaning of the two different words "public services" and 'public purpose" should not be unduly troubling. There is an absence of exact general definition or definition in the context of the Constitution. Common sense dictates that the words are totally compatible. This Court has recognized previously that the sections are closely related. [66]

Corporations were initially chartered in the United States as semi-public entities under the proviso that they served the public welfare, and the exceptional rights they were granted – and never naturally possessed – were held only on the condition that they benefit society (and sometimes accomplish more specific ends). Since corporations now serve their shareholders' interest and not the public's, the *Hayes* court's atavistic rationale is subject to numerous forms of misprision. Emblematically, *Hayes* seems to indicate that direct aid to the poor would not serve the public interest, while direct aid to corporations that would (presumably) then help some people obtain employment serves an entirely public purpose:

The relief of unemployment is a public purpose within the purview of the case law and the constitution. The important point is whether the purpose is public and not whether the agency through which it is dispensed is

---

64 See *Dalton v. State Property and Buildings Com'n*, Ky. 304 S.W.2d 342 (1957).
65 *Hayes v. State Property & Bldgs. Comm'n.*, 731 S.W.2d 797, 799 (Ky. 1987).
66 *Id.* at 801 (citation omitted).

public. The appropriation is not made for the agency or company but for the public purpose or object which is to be served ...

The fulfillment of the intent of the law will undoubtedly accord private industry considerable profit yet the ultimate objective of the act and its declared purpose is not only to alleviate unemployment but also to foster the prosperity of the people of the State as a whole.[67]

We can see subtle ways in which, in the zero-sum game of personhood, such decisions reify the notion that the corporate person can and does almost automatically stand for the public, while the poor person has to prove him- or herself deserving in order to be granted circumscribed rights. Again inverting both empirical and ontological data, the court in effect is asserting that while disbursements made to individuals would be subject to cronyism, those made to corporations are impersonal and by definition – since they serve a public benefit – cannot be illegal gifts:

The purpose of this section is to prevent special privileges, favoritism and discrimination in order to ensure equality under the law. This statute authorizes the financing of industrial development projects by the state for the use of industrial entities in order to provide for valid public purposes such as the elimination of unemployment. The law is not directed to the Toyota project although the availability of such a project obviously ignited interest in this method of financing.[68]

The problem is not just that what's good for Toyota as a quintessential corporate entity becomes good for America – it's that it becomes less and less clear where one begins and the other ends. Gifts are somehow treated as impermissibly personal, while most issues related to the corporate person – with the notable exception of its religious and speech rights – are treated as impersonal. But any public good a corporation generates is a contingent tangent to its function, in much the way that the owners are, in legal terms, mere side-effects of corporate personhood.

By contrast, the dissent in *Hayes* stresses that under the majority's logic, all businesses would represent the public good, and that the holding effectively eviscerates the distinction between public and private good. Under the court's reasoning,

so long as the Governor and General Assembly perceive the need, there are no constitutional restraints on the power of state government to raise

---

67 *Hayes*, 731 S.W.2d at 801–802 (citation omitted).
68 *Id.* at 797.

and spend money for the benefit of a private business. Although the economic activity generated by Toyota will, hopefully, confer a public benefit as an incident to carrying out its private purpose, Toyota will perform no function of government. Its future contribution to the general welfare, if any, will be only indirect in the same sense that the public benefits more or less from the economic activity generated by every successful private business, the by-products of which are taxes, employment and a general increase in the level of economic activity.[69]

Locating the widespread cultural logic that conflates corporate purposes and actions with their potential and often hypothetical by-products, the dissent adds that

> [t]he constitutional concept of payment from the state treasury for "public services" in § 3 does not permit payment from the Commonwealth for those benefits to the general welfare which flow incidentally from the profit making activity of a private corporation. The Commonwealth cannot pay a private corporation for conducting its business in Kentucky unless it is performing a service directly for the government. The economic activities of the Toyota Corporation are not performed as services to the government, but are conducted for a private purpose. They benefit Toyota Corporation and not the State of Kentucky except in the same general sense that applies as well to the productive activity of all private individuals and corporations within this state. The fact that a by-product of this private economic activity is an incidental benefit to other citizens, through providing employment or otherwise, does not change the character of Toyota's economic activity from private to public.[70]

Most business incentives will be offered to the "public" with the same constraints – individuals, and usually small businesses, never have any access to such benefits. As the dissent concludes,

> [r]eduction of unemployment may well satisfy the requirement of § 171 that taxes must be levied and collected for "public purposes," but public purpose in § 171 requires that the method utilized to attack unemployment be through public means, not private means. A supplement to selected private businesses does not qualify. This is so because under § 3 the only persons entitled to public emoluments are those performing services for the Commonwealth. Although such persons need not be public

---

69 *Hayes*, 731 S.W.2d at 805, J. Leibson, dissenting.
70 *Id*. at 813.

employees, the services must be those that are directly performed on be-half of the government, not those services which indirectly, incidentally or remotely benefit the public.[71]

Even most dissents are constrained by a kind of endemic corporate definition and derogation of the gift and welfare as corruptions, rather than implementations, of the public good. As the second dissent in *Hayes* succinctly remarks, "the transaction with Toyota is a gift."[72] Lumping corporate giveaways with individual rights, gifts, or benefits tends to reduce rights and benefits to the level of the giveaway, rather than elevate the giveaway to the level of a human ontological right. As the final dissent in Hayes adds, "the financing agreement devised for the Toyota project is a donation of land to Toyota, pure and simple, and is in violation of § 177 of the Kentucky Constitution. I also believe that the interpretation of § 177 by the majority in such a manner as to approve the Toyota agreement, in reality, renders § 177 null and void to a significant degree."[73] Such a view of the corporate gift would invalidate corporate entitlements; unfortunately, it also could help invalidate *all* gifts. All sides' derogatory use of the phrase "a pure and simple gift" pinpoints the problem with how we view the concept: we're looking a gift-horse in the entirely wrong part of its anatomy.

In another fairly recent case, *Dannheiser v. City of Henderson*, the court considered "whether a city can determine that the enhancement of economic development by promoting employment is a valid public purpose and whether KRS 82.082 prohibits a City from entering into the business of industrial development on an individual basis."[74] In acknowledging the limitations the state Constitution placed on public expenditures, the court effectively again redefined and inverted what represented the public good. The court first observed that

> [s]imilar limitations are placed on state government by means of Section 177 of the Constitution which provides that "the credit of the Common-wealth shall not be given, pledged or loaned to any individual, company, corporation or association, municipality, or political subdivision of the State; nor shall the Commonwealth become an owner or stockholder in,

---

71 *Id.* at 814 (citation omitted).
72 731 S.W.2d at 816, J. Stephenson, dissenting.
73 *Id.* at 818, J. Vance, dissenting.
74 *Dannheiser v. City of Henderson*, 4 S.W.3d 542, 543 (Ky. 1999).

nor make donation to any company, association or corporation; nor shall the Commonwealth construct a railroad or other highway."[75]

The court then broadly validated virtually *any* expenditure made on behalf of or to a corporation (whose size effectively takes it out of the realm of the private that small businesses might inhabit):

> *Hayes* stated that as long as the expenditure of public money has, as its purpose, the effectuation of a valid public purpose, Section 177 is not offended even in situations where the conveyance of publicly financed property to a private business occurs without consideration. Applying the *Hayes* doctrine, we must conclude that the actions by the City in this case did not violate either Section 177 or Section 179 so long as they were undertaken for a valid public purpose.[76]

Whenever states or cities give tax breaks to corporations, they are effectively giving gifts to private entities at public expense, under the rationale that they are serving a public purpose. But they are also transferring personhood from the poor, and constituents in general, to the corporate form.

The reasoning in *Dannheiser* makes virtually any public expenditure for corporations a public benefit: Kentucky courts have consistently approved such undertakings as legitimate public purposes as long as they are for the promotion of economic welfare, relief of unemployment, and stimulation of industry.[77]

The logic of corporate personhood is here laid bare: direct aid to individuals who are unemployed would be a private gift and can only be legitimated in limited circumstances as return on an insurance contract; direct aid to an individual corporation is for the public benefit. Again, such reasoning relies on the same logic that billionaires and the Republican Party use to depict tax evaders as job creators – every corporate claim that it cannot pay benefits; that it is acceptable for its working employees to need public assistance to survive; that raising taxes or the

---

75 *Id.* at 544–5.
76 *Id.* at 545.
77 Cf. *Stovall v. E Baptist Inst, Ky.*, 375 S.W.2d 273 (1964). See also *Indus. Dev. Auth. v. E. Ky. Reg'l Planning Com'n, Ky.*, 332 S.W.2d 274 (1960), which holds that fostering industrial development to alleviate unemployment is a public purpose. *Stovall, supra*, also holds that a public purpose exists if the end to be achieved bears a reasonable relation to the public interest or welfare and is within the scope of legitimate government activity. See also *Dannheiser*, 4 S.W.3d at 545 (citation omitted).

minimum wage or benefits or maintaining workers' rights will reduce
shareholder profits, are all legitimated under this claim that the corporation is providing a public benefit by offering employment, and obfuscates the fact that private shareholders reap all the profits while the
public pays for all the externalities. In the way of British public schools,
the term shareholder is exceptionally ironic because corporate personhood represents the antithesis of sharing and public responsibility.

Cumulatively, court decisions regarding the legitimacy of welfare
and gifts have helped create deeply ingrained images of the "deserving
corporation" or billionaire and the "undeserving poor" (often emblem-
atized by single women of colour). Even the terminology in *Dannheiser*
suggests the way the corporation takes over the human form, identities, and accoutrements, first through language itself, for example by
designating a business site as a park and an impersonal legal fiction as
a person:

> Kentucky has repeatedly recognized that economic development is a valid
> public purpose. [citations omitted] ...
>
> The public purpose that provided constitutional validity in the *Hayes*
> case is identical to the public purpose in the *City of Henderson* case. The
> only difference is that the *Hayes* case applied to a very large project that
> had obvious state-wide implication, the *Henderson* case applies to local
> activities. The City's sole purpose in developing the corporate park was
> to foster economic development by attempting to retain existing industry
> as well as to attract new industry to its local community. The incidental
> benefits provided to private industry are permissible under Kentucky law
> as noted in *Industrial Development Authority* and *Hayes*.[78]

A corporate park is to park what corporate personhood is to human
personhood.

Again, under the logic of such cases, any public spending that directly
or indirectly benefits corporations can be considered a public benefit,
and this premise corrodes the division between public and private, and
corporation and person,. *Dannheiser* stands for the proposition that a
corporation need only invoke the prospect of economic benefit to justify being granted exceptional rights and exemptions that individuals
could never receive. In this sense, the court merely grants a formal legal
sanction to a common practice of many state governors and legislators,
which is to solicit corporations by offering them exceptional rights:

---

78 *Dannheiser*, 4 S.W.3d at 546.

Kentucky precedent shows that the City must only prove that the development bears a reasonable or sufficient relationship to the purpose of economic growth as long as there is a sufficient relation to the accomplishment of a legitimate public purpose, there is no necessity for the courts to interfere with the determination of public purpose. [citation omitted] The question of high unemployment should not be the sole basis for action by a legislative body and it need not be established pursuant to the clear and convincing evidence standard.[79]

Dannheiser concludes with an astonishingly broad, virtually *a priori* endorsement of any act a government entity would undertake to subsidize a corporation: "As noted in *Hayes,* any time new industry is brought into Kentucky or existing industry is persuaded to stay in Kentucky, the entire state benefits although indirectly."[80]

When courts engage in these kinds of specious exegeses, which validate foregone conclusions, they virtually never ask what the corporate subsidy could have been used for instead (e.g., education that would provide much greater economic opportunity), or why corporations need or should get such welfare. Typically, after asserting that the expenditures at issue are providing economic benefits, courts suddenly claim that any analysis of the wisdom, efficacy, or even purpose of spending is outside their purview or would make judges activists:

Hayes teaches that whether a project is based on sound economic theory is not within the scope of judicial review. Such considerations are matters of legislative and executive judgment and do not necessarily affect the constitutionality of the conduct. The question of the propriety of a particular legislative or executive decision is for the electorate as the voting public to accept or reject at the next appropriate public election.[81]

Parsing the evaluation of "sound economic theory" from the evaluation of the economic purpose of a disbursement, or from the evaluation of gift theory, is wholly disingenuous. The dissent in *Dannheiser* again teases out the ulterior reasoning of the majority:

Dannheiser presented evidence from which a trier of fact could have believed that the City lacked a sufficient public purpose. The City Council neglected to obtain guarantees from the private buyers that the City

---

79 4 S.W.3d at 546–7.
80 *Id.* at 547.
81 *Dannheiser,* 4 S.W.3d at 547–8.

would be assured of repayment of the taxpayers' money or receive any benefit whatsoever. The City Council did not undertake any fact-finding to show that the private buyers would indeed bring economic opportunities to the City. The City sold some [of] the land in its industrial park at prices less than fair market value, often for as little as $1,500 per acre, the price the City paid for the land in its unimproved state. Statistics from the Kentucky Department for Employment Services indicated that the unemployment rate in the area was not significantly higher than the state or national rate. This evidence was sufficient to create an issue of fact as to whether the City's industrial park served a proper public purpose. That question should have been fully litigated.[82]

But corporations are rarely treated or regulated in the context of data, because they are ideological constructs of fantasy. As evident in the frenzy to pass the Republican corporate tax bill in 2017, actual findings have become virtually irrelevant when it comes to corporations, which have become quasi-numinous objects of faith. In perhaps the ultimate irony, courts in some sense are channelling and unwittingly acknowledging the underlying narrative of corporate personhood; data, facts, and evidence might indeed be inapposite in evaluating the corporations, because they are and have always been the protagonists of a legal fiction.

---

82 *Dannheiser*, 4 S.W.3d at 549–50, J. Lambert dissenting.

PART THREE

Discipline and Guardianship

Discipline and guardianship are two sides of the same coin. There is growing agreement among human rights scholars that corporate persons ought to be subjects of international rights, not because they believe the corporation ought to be eligible for human rights, but rather so that international law may subject corporations to legal remedies for human rights violations. The European Convention on Human Rights is exceptional in imposing duties upon corporations to protect human rights – but only in specific provisions: "other treaty systems have largely rejected the idea."[1] Statutory anti-discrimination laws and laws penalizing other violations of human dignity often spring from the inefficiencies of tort law. It was thus a sign of ingenuity and desperation when human rights activists turned to the United States' Alien Torts Statute (ATS) to attempt to mitigate the harm inflicted by corporate atrocities. Ultimately, however, in the 2013 decision in *Kiobel v. Royal Dutch Petroleum*, the United States Supreme Court barred the case on the basis that the ATS does not have extraterritorial application. The minority opinion does leave some slight room open for the statute's use in cases on American territory involving American national interests and an American national, since the ATS does not specify whether the American national must be a natural person. According to Donald Childress, "at bottom, foreign plaintiffs will only be able to proceed under the ATS when they are injured in the United States or when substantial activities occur in the United States that violate the law of nations, even though the injury is ultimately felt abroad. As such, the Court has substantially limited the ability of plaintiffs to file ATS cases in federal

---

1 Julian G. Ku, "The Limits of Corporate Rights under International Law," *Chicago Journal of International Law* 12, no. 2 (Winter 2012): 754.

court."[2] With the waning of ATS as a means for redressing atrocities, Nora Mardirossian argues, although the ATS will not resolve disputes between third parties, the tort law of transnational corporations' home states can still be used to penalize them for their negligence: "by applying tort law duties of care to parent corporations, home States will improve access to remedy for victims of human rights impacts who might have no alternatives due to deficiencies in the justice system of the host State."[3] While tort law may remain a viable alternative for holding transnational corporations responsible for corporate human rights violations, the use of international human rights law for the same purposes faces additional complications.

Some have sought soft alternatives, such as the invocation of corporate social responsibility, in hope that corporations could be obliged to act as if they were governmental bodies and tasked with enforcing human rights obligations. The South African Constitution binds corporate power under such an imperative to respect and protect human rights. The justification for doing so is that corporations are a unique type of person: corporations wield extensive economic and political power, and they are required to abide by provisions not to infringe upon human rights as well as actively to promote the rights of natural persons. One could say that the South African Constitution posits corporations as quasi-state entities. Anglo-American jurisprudence has also treated corporations as quasi-states. This model of the corporation's governmental relationship to humans turns on transfiguring property rights to alter the terms of the relationship between governing authority and property owners. Larissa Katz argues against the libertarian view that strong, formalized property rights protect owners from government interference. Rather, spelling out the principle of "governing through owners," she writes, "the formalization of private property rights actually makes owners more vulnerable to the state and enhances the state's governance powers over them. When property rights are formalized, the state gains the power to define the scope of those rights. This, in turn, provides the state with opportunities to impose significant burdens on owners."[4]

---

2 Donald Childress, *Kiobel Commentary: An ATS Answer with Many Questions (and the Possibility of a Brave New World of Transnational Litigation)*, SCOTUSblog (18 April 2013, 5:03 PM), https://www.scotusblog.com/2013/04/kiobel-commentary-an-ats-answer-with-many-questions-and-the-possibility-of-a-brave-new-world-of-transnational-litigation/.

3 Nora Mardirossian, "Direct Parental Negligence Liability: An Expanding Means to Hold Parent Companies Accountable for the Human Rights Impacts of Their Foreign Subsidiaries" (7 May 2015). Available at SSRN: https://ssrn.com/abstract=2607592.

4 Larissa Katz, "Governing through Owners: How and Why Formal Private Property Rights Enhance State Power," *University of Pennsylvania Law Review* 160 (2012): 2030.

This governance could take the form of statutes that require companies to clean public sidewalks in front of their businesses, or it could, as US Supreme Court Justice Black argued in his ruling of *Marsh v. Alabama* (1946), hold that corporations, as rights-bearing property owners, are bound not only to respect the 1st Amendment rights of others, but also to assume responsibilities consistent with their property-owning status: "we do not think it makes any significant differences as to the relationship between the rights of the owner and those of the public that here the State, instead of permitting the corporation to operate a highway, permitted it to use its property as a town, operate a 'business block' in the town and a street and sidewalk on that business block."[5] Effectively, Black argued that corporate power derives from the state and that, in behaving with the scope of a municipality, a corporation must be subject to the same restrictions as a municipality. Black's decision invokes the artificiality of the corporation as a legal fiction whose rights have been granted by the state and then amends those rights in accordance with its expansive ("unnatural") economic power.

We open this section with Stefan Padfield's defence of the corporate death penalty. Padfield returns to debates about whether corporations should be the subject of rights, a vehicle for their enforcement for human individuals, or a subject of accountability for criminal wrongs, to show that our answer depends almost entirely not on legal or moral principles but on what theory of the corporation is at play. Padfield finds that in recent US Supreme Court cases, judgments have failed to take the opportunity to define corporations strategically. Courts do not take up the special nature of the corporation to ascertain its eligibility for specific rights, nor do they consider models of corporate theory that can render it punishable – even to the death.

In this volume, Angela Fernandez points out that, as corporate power increases and its accountability diminishes, the gains made by other non-human entities who might be eligible for the rights of persons have been more tentative. Of late, models of corporate personhood have become especially significant in rethinking the relationship between rights and personhood for a range of non-human entities that bear little or no resemblance to the traditional corporation: indigenous intellectual property; natural entities that are inextricably tied up with local cultural practices; non-human animals; and art objects. In his landmark essay "Should Trees Have Standing? Towards Legal Rights for Natural Objects,"[6] Christopher D. Stone posited that environmentalists can

---

5   "Marsh v. Alabama 326 U.S. 501 (1946)," 508.
6   Now anthologized in Stone, *Should Trees Have Standing?*

foment resistance to the exploitation of natural resources by seeking juridical personhood for these resources and by appointing guardians who would be given the legal standing to represent their interests. Stone relies heavily on a comparison of non-human entities to children, who are legal persons who cannot represent themselves in court. Stephen Wise uses a similar "guardianship" logic in his writings on animal legal personhood, contesting what he calls the "Great Legal Wall," the founding distinction made in Roman law (notwithstanding the history of slavery) between property and persons. As Fernandez recounts in her article for this volume, Wise's Nonhuman Rights Project seeks to extend the category of persons to non-human animals in part by contesting the understanding of animals as property, in part by recognizing the similarities to humans of higher-order mammals such as chimps and bonobos, and in part by appealing to a very basic form of analogical thinking – one that directly calls out the corporation: as Fernandez puts it, "a living, breathing mammal is closer to a natural person than either rivers or corporations." Fernandez joins others in critiquing some of the legal moves necessary to extend personhood to animals (or trees) in this way: the limitation of legal advocacy to higher-order mammals; the repeated comparison of non-human entities in such arguments to marginalized and disenfranchised human groups such as prisoners and the differently abled; and the problem of the ostensible declining coherence of the category of personhood (if it ever had any coherence) as environmental justice and animal rights activists argue for the extension of the term to an ever broader array of non-human creatures and entities.

6 Killing Corporations to Save Humans: How Corporate Personhood, Human Rights, and the Corporate Death Penalty Intersect

STEFAN PADFIELD[1]

I. Introduction

There is a growing sense of frustration among certain groups that the attribution of rights and responsibilities to corporations is evolving in a manner contrary to the best interests of natural persons. In the United States Supreme Court, for example, we have recently seen an expansion of corporate free speech rights in *Citizens United*[2] and religious free exercise rights in *Hobby Lobby*,[3] while arguments for holding corporate actors accountable for complicity in human rights violations were rejected in *Kiobel*[4] and *Jesner*.[5] A primary justification for expanding corporate rights is the belief

---

1 Professor, University of Akron School of Law (BA, Brown University; J.D., University of Kansas). Thanks to Professor Jody Greene and Sharif Youssef for asking me to contribute this chapter to their book, *Human Rights after Corporate Personhood: An Uneasy Merger?* This paper was presented at a faculty workshop at the University of Akron School of Law on 2 March 2016, and I am grateful to all the participants who provided helpful feedback. Finally, thanks to the University of Akron School of Law for supporting this project with a research grant.

2 *Citizens United v. Fed. Election Comm'n*, 558 U.S. 310, 365 (2010) (holding that "the Government may not suppress political speech on the basis of the speaker's corporate identity").

3 *Burwell v. Hobby Lobby Stores, Inc.*, 134 S. Ct. 2751, 2772 (2014) (concluding that "a for-profit corporation [can] engage in the 'exercise of religion' within the meaning of [the Religious Freedom Restoration Act]"). Cf. *Masterpiece Cakeshop, Ltd. v. Colorado Civil Rights Comm'n*, 138 S. Ct. 1719, 1731 (2018) (ruling in favour of incorporated baker who refused to bake a wedding cake for a gay couple because "the Commission's treatment of Phillips' case violated the State's duty under the First Amendment not to base laws or regulations on hostility to a religion or religious viewpoint").

4 *Kiobel v. Royal Dutch Petroleum Co.*, 133 S. Ct. 1659, 1669 (2013) (applying presumption against extraterritoriality to deny relief under the Alien Tort Statute because, among other things, "[c]orporations are often present in many countries, and it would reach too far to say that mere corporate presence suffices" for jurisdiction).

5 *Jesner v. Arab Bank, PLC*, 138 S. Ct. 1386, 1407 (2018) ("the Court holds that foreign corporations may not be defendants in suits brought under the ATS").

that corporate rights should essentially track the rights of the natural persons who own or manage them, which is a position often equated with the aggregate or real entity theory of corporate personhood.[6] Meanwhile, one of the justifications for limiting corporate responsibility is a feared loss of the economic benefits that corporate status bestows on society as a whole in the form job creation, innovation, and so on. This fear of lost productivity is also prominent in discussions surrounding the "corporate death penalty."

This book chapter will argue that the corporate death penalty and corporate personhood are connected in the context of corporate accountability for human rights violations because the fear of the negative consequences of corporate accountability embodied in resistance to the corporate death penalty strengthens arguments in favour of corporate personhood theories that support expanding corporate rights, while those same corporate personhood theories support limiting corporate accountability, including accountability via the corporate death penalty. The arguable paradox here is that what begins as a justification rooted in benefiting humans ends up justifying harming humans without consequences. Finally, a number of arguments that challenge both the pro-rights corporate personality theories and the anti-accountability fears triggered by threats of a corporate death penalty will be discussed, thus providing a reasonable starting point for activists seeking greater corporate accountability for human rights violations as a means to challenge the current perceived trend toward greater corporate rights and less corporate accountability.

Part II of this chapter discusses the unique impact that corporations can have on human rights. Part III then discusses the corporate death penalty, and Part IV introduces the reader to the primary theories of corporate personhood. Part V seeks to pull all the foregoing together to explain how the corporate death penalty, human rights, and the theories of corporate personhood intersect. Part VI addresses some criticisms of the proposition that corporate personality theory can or should constitute a lever to improve the impact of corporations on human rights. Finally, Part VII offers concluding remarks.

II. Corporations and Human Rights

Most readers will likely need little convincing that corporations – at least large, multinational corporations (MNCs) – can have a unique impact on human rights. One commonly cited data point is the participation of the

---

6 See Virginia Harper Ho, *Theories of Corporate Groups: Corporate Identity Reconceived*, 42 *Seton Hall L. Rev.* 879, 893–94 (2012) ("Like the aggregate view, the 'real entity' view developed in response to the decline of state chartering, as corporate activity came to be seen as private rather than public, and corporate persons came to be viewed as sharing many of the rights and obligations of natural persons").

I.G. Farben Corporation in Nazi war crimes, which led to imposition of the corporate death penalty in the form of dissolution.[7] It seems that more recent controversies also abound, including cases alleging the involvement of oil companies in kidnapping, torture, and murder to protect pipelines in Central and South America,[8] and others alleging companies' involvement in child slavery[9] and war crimes.[10]

7   See Beth Stephens, "Are Corporations People? Corporate Personhood under the Constitution and International Law: An Essay in Honor of Professor Roger S. Clark," 44 *Rutgers L.J.*, 32 (2013) ("In the aftermath of World War II, the United States Military Tribunal in occupied Germany found that the I.G. Farben Corporation had violated international law prohibitions against pillage and plunder as it built a chemical empire in the service of the Nazi expansion into neighboring countries."); Michael Bazyler and Jennifer Green, *Nuremberg-Era Jurisprudence Redux: The Supreme Court in* Kiobel v. Royal Dutch Petroleum Co. *and the Legal Legacy of Nuremberg*, 7 *Charleston L. Rev.* 23, 35 (2012) ("[T]he Allied Control Council, the multinational body that the Allies created after their defeat of Hitler, to govern occupied Germany ... dismantle[ed] I.G. Farben"). *But see Jesner*, 138 S. Ct. at 1400 ("Although the Military Tribunal 'used the term "Farben" as descriptive of the instrumentality of cohesion in the name of which' the crimes were committed, the Tribunal noted that 'corporations act through individuals.' Farben itself was not held liable") (internal citation omitted).
8   See generally, Mary Carson, Adrian Gatton, Rodrigo Vázquez, and Maggie O'Kane, "Colombian takes BP to court in UK over alleged complicity in kidnap and torture," theguardian.com, 22 May 2015 ("his captors ... claimed they were paid to protect the pipeline by the oil companies"), http://gu.com/p/495em/stw.
9   "SCOTUS Decides Not to Review 9th Circuit's Controversial *Doe v. Nestle* Decision," U.S. Chamber Institute for Legal Reform, 12 January 2016) ("three American companies [Nestle USA, Archer Daniels Midland, and Cargill] ... are alleged to have aided and abetted acts of child slavery by cocoa farmers in Cote d'Ivoire"), http://www.instituteforlegalreform.com/resource/scotus-decides-not-to-review-9th-circuits-controversial-doe-v-nestle-decision. See also *Daimler AG v. Bauman*, 134 S. Ct. 746, 751 (2014) ("The complaint alleged that during Argentina's 1976–1983 'Dirty War,' Daimler's Argentinian subsidiary, Mercedes–Benz Argentina (MB Argentina) collaborated with state security forces to kidnap, detain, torture, and kill certain MB Argentina workers, among them, plaintiffs or persons closely related to plaintiffs"). Cf. Dia Kayyali, "EFF Files Amicus Brief in Case That Seeks to Hold IBM Responsible for Facilitating Apartheid in South Africa," Electronic Frontier Foundation, 5 February 2015, https://www.eff.org/deeplinks/2015/02/eff-files-amicus-brief-case-seeks-hold-ibm-responsible-facilitating-apartheid. "*In Re: South African Apartheid* ... seeks to hold IBM's headquarters in New York responsible for purposefully facilitating apartheid, by creating a computerized national ID system that the South African government used to strip the country's black population of its rights as citizens ... [W]e point out the disturbing parallels between IBM's actions vis-à-vis South Africa and Nazi Germany." *Id.*
10   See E.L. Gaston, *Mercenarism 2.0? The Rise of the Modern Private Security Industry and Its Implications for International Humanitarian Law Enforcement*, 49 *Harv. Int'l L.J.* 221, 229 (2008) ("Much of the controversy surrounding [private military and security companies (PMSCs)] has been due to frequent reports of unpunished criminal misconduct, human rights abuses, and potential war crimes by PMSC personnel"). Cf. P.W. Singer, *Corporate Warriors: The Rise of the Privatized Military Industry* (Ithaca:

One response to these concerns has been the 2011 Guiding Principles on Business and Human Rights: Implementing the United Nations "Protect, Respect and Remedy" Framework (hereafter GPs or Framework), issued by UN Special Representative John Ruggie:[11]

> The *Framework* rests on three pillars. The first is the State duty to protect against human rights abuses by third parties, including business enterprises, through appropriate policies, regulation, and adjudication. The second is the corporate responsibility to respect human rights, which means that business enterprises should act with due diligence to avoid infringing on the rights of others and to address adverse impacts with which they are involved. The third is the need for greater access by victims to effective remedy, both judicial and non-judicial.[12]

The GPs, however, are not without their critics. For example, one commentator has noted that many "view the Guiding Principles to be toothless, failing to directly impose obligations upon corporations, and call for binding international obligations on corporate entities."[13] More generally, Susana C. Mijares Peña has asserted that currently "there are no legal mechanisms available to ensure that ... corporations abide by international standards and voluntary codes."[14] This is in part a function of the "soft law" status of much of the relevant guidance:

> While the UN Human Rights Council unanimously endorsed the Guiding Principles, they are still considered soft law and have yet to translate into

---

Cornell University Press, 2003) (documenting private military deployments in the Balkans, Colombia, and Africa in addition to Iraq).

11 The final report on the *Guiding Principles* is available at http://www.business -humanrights.org/media/documents/ruggie/ruggie-guiding-principles-21 -mar-2011.pdf (hereafter *Guiding Principles*). See generally Virginia Harper Ho, *Of Enterprise Principles and Corporate Groups: Does Corporate Law Reach Human Rights?*, 52 *Colum. J. Transnat'l L.* 113 (2013) ("The *Framework* is noteworthy, in part, because it considers the potential intersections of corporate law and human rights").

12 *Guiding Principles*, at 4.

13 Cindy S. Woods, "'It Isn't a State Problem': The Minas Conga Mine Controversy and the Need for Binding International Obligations on Corporate Actors," 46 *Geo. J. Int'l L.* 629, 629 (2015); see also *id.* ("In June 2014, the Human Rights Council adopted a resolution to draft international legally binding human rights norms for business entities; however, key players in the international arena have already announced they will not cooperate with such efforts").

14 Susana C. Mijares Peña, *Human Rights Violations by Canadian Companies Abroad: Choc v Hudbay Minerals Inc*, 5 *Western Journal of Legal Studies* 1 (forthcoming), http:// ssrn.com/abstract=2617394. But cf. Manson Gwanyanya, "The South African Companies Act and the Realisation of Corporate Human Rights Responsibilities,"

mandatory regulation. Other existing voluntary standards (e.g., OECD Guidelines for Multinational Enterprises, ILO's Tripartite Declaration of Principles concerning Multinational Enterprises and Social Policy, and UN Global Compact) and self-regulation (e.g., codes of conduct) have been largely ineffective in shaping corporate behavior as they lack independent monitoring and enforcement mechanisms and are thus subject to critiques of greenwashing.[15]

Obstacles to accountability include the US Supreme Court's 2013 *Kiobel* decision.[16] As William Dodge explains:

> In the United States, litigation brought by private parties under the Alien Tort Statute (ATS) has been one of the principal tools for business and human rights accountability. But a series of decisions by the U.S. Supreme Court – including its 2013 ruling in *Kiobel v. Royal Dutch Petroleum Co.* – has placed substantial limits on such litigation and may well bring the era of business and human rights litigation in U.S. courts to an end.[17]

The obstacle that *Kiobel* placed in front of plaintiffs seeking to hold corporations accountable for human rights violations via the ATS was to require that "even where the claims touch and concern the territory of the United States, they must do so with sufficient force to displace the presumption against extraterritorial application."[18] In addition, holding

---

  Potchefstroom Electronic Law Journal 18, no. 1 (13 April 2015), (arguing that "if interpreted properly and in a manner that the *Constitution* envisages, the *Companies Act* has to a certain extent confirmed that there are human rights responsibilities for companies operating within South Africa"), http://ssrn.com/abstract=2621628.

15 Galit A. Sarfaty, *Shining Light on Global Supply Chains*, 56 *Harv. Int'l L.J.* 419, 426–7 (2015).

16 133 S. Ct. 1659. See also *Jesner*, 138 S. Ct. at 1407 ("the Court holds that foreign corporations may not be defendants in suits brought under the ATS").

17 William S. Dodge, "Business and Human Rights Litigation in U.S. Courts Before and after Kiobel," *Business and Human Rights: From Principals to Practice*, 1 April 2015 ("The first suits against corporations under the ATS were filed in 1996. The most famous was *Doe v. Unocal*, in which villagers ... alleged that an American oil company had aided and abetted the Myanmar military in subjecting them to forced labor, murder, rape, and torture while Unocal built a pipeline"), http://ssrn.com/abstract=2625691.

18 *Kiobel v. Royal Dutch Petroleum Co.*, 133 S. Ct. 1659, 1669 (2013). But cf. *In re S. African Apartheid Litig.*, 15 F. Supp. 3d 454, 460 (S.D.N.Y. 2014): "The standards laid out in *Kiobel* and *Daimler* for overcoming the presumption against territoriality and exercising personal jurisdiction under a long-arm statute are stringent. They may be difficult to meet in all but the most extraordinary cases. But the Supreme Court has now written two opinions contemplating that certain factors in combination with corporate presence could overcome the presumption against extraterritoriality or permit a court to exercise personal jurisdiction over a foreign corporation in an ATS case." *Id.*

corporations liable for aiding and abetting human rights violations under the ATS requires satisfying a plausibility standard at the pleading stage vis-à-vis intent, which can be extremely difficult given the lack of meaningful discovery.[19] At least some of this procedural morass has been provocatively explained by Phillip Blumberg as a consequence of a "dysfunctional" failure to account for the shift to holding companies:

> Concepts of the corporate juridical personality were developed in the Anglo-American legal system centuries ago to distinguish corporations from their stockholders. This is entity law. With the development in the last century of the holding company with its unlimited number of subsidiar[ies] and the formation of corporate groups, the law mistakenly failed to recognize that the older jurisprudence of entity law reinforced by the principle of limited liability no longer fairly served the newer economic society. Principles developed to shield investors from the debts of the corporation in which they were shareholders became largely dysfunctional when applied to multi-tiered corporate groups ... Entity law shapes the doctrines of procedure as well as the law of substantive liability ... [D]octrines grounded on entity law in the area of in personam jurisdiction, forum non conveniens, and perhaps joinder create procedural barriers of great magnitude to efforts to obtain a hearing in the United States of cases involving international human rights. This has the unhappy consequence that as far as the judicial system is concerned, American multinational corporations are not fully accountable for their conduct abroad.[20]

Meanwhile, improved disclosure of corporate social responsibility has been touted as a means of improving corporate conduct and performance, and "lawmakers in the United States, Canada, Europe, and California have passed human rights disclosure legislation."[21] In addition, "dozens of stock exchanges have imposed either mandatory or voluntary

---

19 Cf. Sophia Cope, "Unrealistic Pleading Standards: Another Injustice for Human Rights Victims," *Electronic Frontier Foundation*, 30 July 2015 ("the appellate court said in effect that, at least without smoking gun evidence, under *no circumstances* would the judges ever *believe* that IBM could have 'purposefully' aided and abetted the human rights abuses perpetrated by the apartheid government"), https://www.eff.org/deeplinks/2015/07/unrealistic-pleading-standards-another-injustice-human-rights-victims.

20 Phillip I. Blumberg, "Asserting Human Rights against Multinational Corporations under United States Law: Conceptual and Procedural Problems," 50 *Am. J. Comp. L.* 493, 528–9 (2002).

21 Marcia Narine, "Disclosing Disclosure's Defects: Addressing Corporate Irresponsibility for Human Rights Impacts," 47 *Columbia Human Rights Law Review* 1 (forthcoming), http://ssrn.com/abstract=2697672.

non-financial disclosure requirements, in sync with the UN Principles."[22] However, Marcia Narine, a law professor who has served as an executive in the supply chain industry and a member of the SEC Disclosure Reform Working Group of the US Chamber of Commerce, and who co-authored an amicus brief on the Dodd-Frank conflict minerals legislation, has concluded that "these efforts do not work."[23] Narine argues that the failure of these programs is rooted in a "flawed premise that, armed with specific information addressing human rights, consumers and investors will either reward 'ethical' corporate behavior, or punish firms with poor human rights records."[24] However, according to Narine, the evidence shows that "disclosures generally fail to change behavior."[25]

The frustrations surrounding a perceived lack of corporate accountability transcend the human rights arena. Many continue to wonder how so many banks and bank executives emerged from the financial crisis apparently unscathed and enriched while Main Street workers have had to fight ongoing battles against unemployment and wage stagnation.[26] Following the recent Volkswagen emissions scandal, set in motion by revelations that Volkswagen executives "admitted cheating on pollution emissions tests," one news outlet asked: "Do large corporations and their executives have a get-out-of-jail free card that protects them from prosecution for criminal wrongdoing?"[27] The elephant in the

---

22 *Id.*

23 *Id.*

24 *Id.*

25 *Id.* But cf. Reuven S. Avi-Yonah, "Corporations, Society, and the State: A Defense of the Corporate Tax," 90 *Va. L. Rev.* 1193, 1220 (2004) ("[T]he real entity view of the corporation as separate from both the state and the shareholders ... identifies corporate management as the source of 'abuse of power' and suggests that the imposition of the corporate tax will enable the government, the shareholders, and the public to obtain information that will serve as the basis for restricting such managerial abuses of power").

26 Cf. Frank Hong Liu, Lars Norden, and Fabrizio Spargoli, "Why Banks Want to Be Complex," *The CLS Blue Sky Blog*, 7 January 2016 ("The quasi collapse of the global financial system during the crisis of 2007–2009 has triggered an extensive debate about the role of large complex banks"), http://clsbluesky.law.columbia.edu/2016/01/07/why-banks-want-to-be-complex.

27 Robert Weissman and Gary Bass, "This is Obama's last chance to make big business pay," *Salon.com*, 25 October 2015 ("Volkswagen has been caught lying about emission standards, but will it pay? If past is prologue, probably not"), http://www.salon.com/2015/10/25/this_is_obamas_last_chance_to_make_big_business_pay. See also Jamie Lincoln Kitman, "Volkswagen Lied and Cheated 11 Million Times. Will Anyone Go to Jail for That?," *The Nation*, ("[I]n the current enforcement climate, fines of such bankrupting magnitude will never come to pass. There is no such thing as capital punishment for a capitalist enterprise gone fatally wrong."),

room here may be the concern that at least some MNCs have outgrown the ability of states to truly regulate them.[28] As one set of commentators noted, "[t]here is a point at which corporate influence can be viewed as an interference with a country's state sovereignty."[29]

Finally, in terms of setting the stage for more specific discussion of the corporate death penalty, corporate personality theory, and the intersection of these with human rights, it is worth noting the concomitant expansion of corporate rights. In other words, at the same time that awareness of a potential corporate accountability deficit is growing, corporate rights in areas such as political speech and religious freedom are being expanded. The two primary points of focus here are the US Supreme Court cases of *Citizens United*[30] and *Hobby Lobby*.[31] These cases will be discussed in more detail in the upcoming section on corporate personality theory, but for now it is worth noting that *Citizens United* held that "the First Amendment does not allow political speech restrictions based on a speaker's corporate identity,"[32] which unleashed a torrent of corporate financing of elections, according to many;[33] and that *Hobby*

---

http://www.thenation.com/article/what-will-vw-pay. But see Sonari Glinton and Rachel Gotbaum, "Former Volkswagen CEO Indicted over Emissions Testing Scandal," *NPR*, 4 May 2018 ("Martin Winterkorn, the former head of Volkswagen, was indicted on Thursday along with five other former VW executives on charges of conspiracy and fraud in connection with a years-long scheme by the automaker to cheat on auto emissions tests"), https://www.npr.org/sections/thetwo -way/2018/05/04/608374639/former-volkswagen-ceo-indicted-over-emission -testing-scandal.

28 Cf. Jolanta Olender, Georgina Fry, Sigrid Robinson, Sara Anicic, and Kath Hall, "Thinking Big: Student Led Research on the World's Largest Global Corporations," 17 December 2015, ("Globalisation has ... facilitated unprecedented economic growth and profitability for corporations. In 2012, 40 of the world's largest 100 economic entities were corporations"), http://ssrn.com/abstract=2705225.

29 *Id.* Cf. Sara L. Seck, "Transnational Judicial and Non-Judicial Remedies for Corporate Human Rights Harms: Challenges of and for Law, 31 *Windsor Y.B. Access to Just.* 177, 181 (2013) ("the line between 'state' and 'corporation' is not always an easy one to draw when account is given to the important role played by state-owned enterprises (SOEs) in the global economy, and the history of trading companies in the colonization process is remembered").

30 *Citizens United v. Fed. Election Comm'n*, 558 U.S. 310 (2010).

31 *Burwell v. Hobby Lobby Stores, Inc.*, 134 S. Ct. 2751 (2014). Cf. Masterpiece *Cakeshop*, 138 S. Ct. at 1731 (ruling in favour of incorporated baker who refused to bake a wedding cake for a gay couple because "the Commission's treatment of Phillips' case violated the State's duty under the First Amendment not to base laws or regulations on hostility to a religion or religious viewpoint").

32 *Citizens United*, 558 U.S. at 347.

33 Cf. Michael Hiltzik, "Five years after Citizens United ruling, big money reigns," *Los Angeles Times*, 24 January 2015 ("By taking the reins off big-money electoral

Lobby held that closely held corporations could assert a sincere religious objection to providing health care to employees – care that would otherwise have been required under a generally applicable mandate.[34]

III. The Corporate Death Penalty

Assuming there exists a corporate accountability deficit when it comes to human rights, one may reasonably question whether the full panoply of accountability tools is being marshalled to address the deficit.[35] One particular tool that critics identify as underused is the corporate death penalty.[36] By "corporate death penalty," I mean any sanction that either directly or indirectly threatens the ongoing viability of the corporation.[37]

---

donations by corporations and labor unions, *Citizens United* has unmistakably broadened the political influence of the wealthy and powerful"), http://fw.to/etLjmnG; *id.* ("Nor is it a virtue of *Citizens United* that it took contribution limits off corporations and labor unions alike; U.S. corporations are richer than ever, and labor unions in a long decline").

34 *Hobby Lobby*, 134 S. Ct. at 2775 (2014) ("we hold that a federal regulation's restriction on the activities of a for-profit closely held corporation must comply with [the Religious Freedom Restoration Act]"). Cf. Adam Winkler, "*Masterpiece Cakeshop*'s Surprising Breadth: The Supreme Court granted constitutional religious liberty to corporations – without explaining why," *Slate*, 6 June 2018 ("future courts, when confronted with corporate assertions of religious liberty, [may] say that *Masterpiece Cakeshop* leaves the issue open and sets no definitive precedent"), https://slate.com/news-and-politics/2018/06/masterpiece-cakeshop-grants-constitutional-religious-liberty-rights-to-corporations.html.

35 Cf. Alexandra Garcia, "Corporate Liability for International Crimes: A Matter of Legal Policy Since Nuremberg," 24 *Tul. J. Int'l. & Comp. L.* 97 (2015) ("This Article addresses the question whether, at this point, there exists sufficient basis to conclude that holding corporations liable for international crimes before a permanent international tribunal is not only legally sound, but also the most suitable response to an impunity gap that has not yet been fully addressed by civil liability mechanisms and domestic jurisdictions").

36 Diane Marie Amann, "Capital Punishment: Corporate Criminal Liability for Gross Violations of Human Rights," 24 *Hastings Int'l & Comp. L. Rev.* 327 (2001) ("There is, in U.S. law at least, the concept of the corporate death penalty, the termination of the license to do business. But, it is very rarely, if ever, used"); Kent Greenfield, "Ultra Vires Lives! A Stakeholder Analysis of Corporate Illegality (with Notes on How Corporate Law Could Reinforce International Law Norms)," 87 *Va. L. Rev.* 1279, 1360 (2001) ("the state has at its disposal the possibility of revoking the corporate charter").

37 Cf. Mary Kreiner Ramirez, "The Science Fiction of Corporate Criminal Liability: Containing the Machine through the Corporate Death Penalty," 47 *Ariz. L. Rev.* 933, 943–5 (2005) ("The Organizational Sentencing Guidelines ... provide for a corporate death penalty by imposing fines large enough to divest a corporation of all of its net assets, although the application of this provision is limited to instances where the organization is found to exist for a primarily 'criminal purpose'"); *id.* at 945–6

On the one hand, imposing the corporate death penalty risks killing the goose that lays the golden eggs in terms of wealth and job creation, as well as innovation.[38] On the other hand, so long as there exists an implicit understanding among market participants that regulators will avoid imposing the corporate death penalty at all costs, there will exist the likelihood of moral hazard (and market inefficiencies) as parties adjust risk calculations to account for what is in effect a state guarantee that the worst offences will not be met with the strongest sanction. As Shlomit Azgad-Tromer noted in a related context:

> The elevated probability of rescue in case of failure makes the socially important non-financial institution prone to unwarranted expansion, and distorts its corporate governance well before failure occurs. The resulting moral hazard creates both enhanced incentives for excessive leverage and risk-taking, and elevated incentives for empire building due to the weaker corporate governance mechanisms available.[39]

As alluded to above, the corporate death penalty can take the form of revoking the corporate charter, or imposing sanctions (including the revelation of certain facts) that effectively undermine the corporation's ability to keep operating profitably in a competitive market.[40] Perhaps the most iconic example of the latter in recent memory involves the infamous case of Arthur Andersen.

("For some businesses, the imprisonment of the owners can lead to its demise. Additionally, the financial injury of a large fine, the cost of a criminal defense, or the negative publicity from reaction to public reports of potential criminal acts or liability can [lead to] ... bankruptcy or even liquidation"); *id.* ("civil lawsuits based upon the underlying proven criminal conduct can be even more injurious").

38 *Id.* at 972–3 ("[C]oncern about the greater economic impact of imposing criminal sanctions on the organization has neutralized the State's will to fully prosecute criminal conduct"). Cf. Jonas Heese, "Government Preferences and SEC Enforcement," *Harvard Law School Forum on Corporate Governance and Financial Regulation*, 29 June 2015 ("large employers, as they contribute more to the government's policy of promoting employment, are subject to more lax SEC enforcement"), https:// corpgov.law.harvard.edu/2015/06/29/government-preferences-and-sec -enforcement.

39 Shlomit Azgad-Tromer, "Too Important to Fail: Bankruptcy Versus Bailout of Socially Important Non-Financial Institutions, 17 October 2015), http://ssrn.com /abstract=2551237.

40 Cf. Sara Sun Beale and Adam G. Safwat, "What Developments in Western Europe Tell Us about American Critiques of Corporate Criminal Liability," 8 *Buff. Crim. L. Rev.* 89, 159 (2004) ("A final type of sanction is the equivalent of a corporate death penalty: both the French statute and the Council of Europe's 1988 proposal provide for the dissolution of a corporation in extreme cases of criminal delinquency") .

In 2001, Enron Corporation collapsed under the weight of a massive accounting fraud.[41] Not long afterwards, Arthur Andersen, Enron's auditor, was indicted for obstruction of justice, accused of shredding documents related to Enron as news of Enron's problems became public.[42] The indictment effectively ended Andersen's viability as a for-profit corporation.[43] While the resulting conviction of Andersen was ultimately overturned by the US Supreme Court on the basis of a faulty jury instruction,[44] and while the Andersen name has actually been revived for business,[45] the demise of Andersen has created in the minds of many an "unquestioned dogma that a criminal indictment alone can easily destroy even a large, powerful corporation."[46] However, Gabriel Markoff has argued that "there is no evidence that the 'Andersen Effect' exists and thus ... the 'corporate death penalty' is no more than a bogeyman"; moreover, "an informed, data-driven debate [can reveal] when and how corporate criminal prosecutions should occur."[47]

---

41 Cf. Pierre Ciric, "Stuck between a Rock and a Hard Place: Are Public Accounting Firms Subject to Diverging Standards of Conduct between Federal Courts and the Pcaob in Securities Fraud Claims?," 9 *J. Bus. & Tech. L.* 229, 230 (2014) ("the Public Company Accounting Reform and Investor Protection Act of 2002 (the 'Sarbanes-Oxley Act') became law on July 30, 2002 following a wave of corporate scandals at large corporations like Enron, Worldcom, Cendant, or Bristol-Myers Squibb").

42 *Arthur Andersen LLP v. United States*, 544 U.S. 696, 702 (2005) ("In March 2002, petitioner was indicted in the Southern District of Texas ... The indictment alleged that, between October 10 and November 9, 2001, petitioner 'did knowingly, intentionally and corruptly persuade ... other persons ...' to withhold documents from ... 'official proceedings ...'").

43 See "The fall of Andersen," *Chicago Tribune*, 1 September 2002 ("On Saturday, a firm that once stood for trust and accountability ended 90 years as an auditor of publicly traded companies under a cloud of scandal and shame"), http://www.chicagotribune.com/news/chi-0209010315sep01-story.html.

44 *Arthur Andersen LLP v. United States*, 544 U.S. 696, 708 (2005) ("the jury instructions here were flawed in important respects").

45 Robert Schmidt, "Arthur Andersen Name Returns Decade after Firm's Collapse," *Bloomberg.com*, 1 September 2014 ("WTAS LLC, a San Francisco-based tax consultancy founded out of Andersen's ashes, will go by AndersenTax as of today").

46 Gabriel Markoff, "Arthur Andersen and the Myth of the Corporate Death Penalty: Corporate Criminal Convictions in the Twenty-First Century," 15 *U. Pa. J. Bus. L.* 797, 800 (2013).

47 Gabriel Markoff, "Arthur Andersen and the Myth of the Corporate Death Penalty: Corporate Criminal Convictions in the Twenty-First Century," 15 *U. Pa. J. Bus. L.* 797, 836 (2013). Cf. Andrew Baker, "Prosecuting in the Shadows: How Unsupported Fear of Collateral Consequences Impedes Corporate Prosecution," *Medium*, 12 June 2018 (noting "the DOJ's lack of subject matter expertise in determining corporate systemic importance," and recommending that "the DOJ should

Regardless of Markoff's claims, it can be argued that fear of the Andersen Effect has strongly encouraged prosecutors to avoid corporate criminal prosecutions at all costs. In fact, one commentator has described the Justice Department's handling of corporate criminal cases as a "protection racket": that is, corporate executives are protected from jail time and the corporation is protected from the "death penalty" in exchange for the payment of hefty fines that are ultimately paid for by "innocent" shareholders.[48]

In addition to the Andersen Effect, the recent financial crisis has left many worried that imposing the corporate death penalty can not only negatively impact the prosecuted corporation's stakeholders but also, if the corporation is systemically significant enough, send unwanted shockwaves through much larger segments of the economy. For example, Court Golumbic and Albert Lichy have noted that the Justice Department's "failure to bring criminal charges against any financial institutions for their perceived role in causing the 2008 financial crisis prompted members of Congress, the press, and the public to question whether the agency has maintained a *de facto* policy that certain corporations are 'too big jail' given their size and economic significance."[49] The combination of the Andersen Effect and "too big to jail" concerns then set the stage for underenforcement and recidivism. As Bill Black has noted, "The incentives created by treating the bank and the banksters as too big to be prosecuted ... are so perverse that they guarantee just what developed – recurrent, massive crimes by the largest banks."[50]

---

divest its undue collateral consequences determination to an agency with the requisite expertise"), https://medium.com/@Andrew___Baker/prosecuting-in-the-shadows-e2a7b27838fe.

48 Howard Darmstadter, "Corporations in the Dock," *Business Law Today*, February 2015, http://www.americanbar.org/publications/blt/2015/02/05_darmstadter.html. Cf. Baker, "Prosecuting in the Shadows" ("this notion of 'innocent shareholders' fundamentally misconstrues the role of shareholders in public companies ... shareholders generally profit from malfeasance on behalf of the company, and ... select the board of directors").

49 Court E. Golumbic and Albert D. Lichy, "The 'Too Big to Jail' Effect and the Impact on the Justice Department's Corporate Charging Policy," 65 *Hastings L.J.* 1293, 1295 (2014).

50 William K. Black, "Lanny Breuer's Defense of Not Prosecuting HSBC and Its Officers," *New Economic Perspectives*, 29 April 2015, http://neweconomicperspectives.org/2015/04/lanny-breuers-defense-of-not-prosecuting-hsbc-and-its-officers.html. Cf. Ben Protess and Michael Corkery, "5 Big Banks Expected to Plead Guilty to Felony Charges, but Punishments May Be Tempered," *New York Times*, 13 May 2015, ("[W]hen five of the world's biggest banks plead guilty to an array of antitrust and fraud charges as soon as next week, life will go on, probably without much of a hiccup"), http://nyti.ms/1Flw1dp.

A related piece of the puzzle here involves deferred and non-prosecution agreements.[51] Cindy Alexander and Mark Cohen describe the agreements as follows:

> Over the past decade, two novel approaches to corporate criminal prosecution have emerged, the Deferred Prosecution Agreement ("DPA") and Non Prosecution Agreement ("NPA"). DPAs and NPAs have been used in virtually all areas of corporate criminal wrongdoing including antitrust, fraud, domestic bribery, tax evasion, environmental violations as well as foreign corruption cases. These legal mechanisms bypass the traditional plea-bargaining process and instead involve a negotiated settlement whereby the organization may agree without pleading guilty (or nolo contendere) to a combination of restitution, forfeiture, monetary sanctions, and other legal and structural governance reforms. DPAs and NPAs did not arise from any change in the federal statutes but through an innovation in criminal enforcement practices and related coordination between criminal and civil enforcement authorities.[52]

Alexander and Cohen go on to note that "[i]t could very well be that the rise of these deferred and non-prosecution agreement deals represents a victory for the forces of big business who for decades have been seeking to weaken or eliminate corporate criminal liability."[53] However, in

---

51 See generally, *United States v. Saena Tech Corp.*, 140 F. Supp. 3d 11, 37 (D.D.C. 2015) ("the current use of deferred-prosecution agreements for corporations rather than individual defendants strays from Congress's intent when it created an exclusion from the speedy trial calculation for the use of such agreements"); Peter R. Reilly, "Corporate Deferred Prosecution As Discretionary Injustice," 2017 *Utah L. Rev.* 839, 841 (2017) ("employing DPAs to resolve allegations of corporate criminal misconduct goes far afield from the Congressionally-intended purpose of using the agreements to promote the social rehabilitation of a narrow category of disadvantaged individuals whose social and economic profiles contrast starkly with those of corporate entities and the white collar professionals who run them").

52 Cindy R. Alexander and Mark A. Cohen, "The Evolution of Corporate Criminal Settlements: An Empirical Perspective on Non-Prosecution, Deferred Prosecution, and Plea Agreements," 52 *Am. Crim. L. Rev.* 537, 537 (2015). But see David M. Uhlmann, "Reconsidering Corporate Criminal Prosecution," *The CLS Blue Sky Blog*, 19 August 2015, ("[W]ith public alarm increasing over the lack of criminal prosecutions for the financial crisis, the pendulum swung, and criminal prosecutions were back in vogue. In 2014, the Justice Department brought record-setting criminal prosecutions ... Similar prosecutions followed during 2015"), http://clsbluesky. law.columbia.edu/2015/08/19/reconsidering-corporate-criminal-prosecution.

53 *Id.* at 539. Cf. Uhlmann, "Reconsidering Corporate Criminal Prosecution" ("A cynical response would be that the revolving door between Criminal Division leadership and white collar law firms leads to a lack of resolve about the need to prosecute corporations").

September 2015 the DOJ "announced via the 'Yates Memorandum' that ... [c]ompanies will no longer get favourable deferred or nonprosecution agreements unless they cooperate at the beginning of the investigation and provide information about culpable individuals."[54] Only time will tell the extent to which these pronouncements change the landscape.[55]

Besides leading to underenforcement and increased recidivism, declining to prosecute corporations for fear of bankrupting them may significantly undermine the public's faith in free markets. David Uhlmann identifies three societal benefits that are associated with appropriate criminal prosecution of corporations, which he argues flow from the expressive function of criminal law:

> The expressive function of the criminal law plays an ... essential role in the corporate context. First, we confer significant benefits on corporations with the expectation – indeed, the mandate – that corporations exist for legal purposes alone. When a corporation exploits those benefits and violates the public trust by engaging in illegal conduct, we must make clear that its behavior is unacceptable and condemn its conduct as criminal. Second, corporations have outsized power and influence in our society. When a corporation abuses that power and influence by committing crimes, we must impose blame, require accountability, and insist upon acceptance of responsibility. Third, corporations can neither be jailed nor have their individual liberties restricted. The distinctive feature of corporate criminal prosecution is its ability to label corporate lawlessness as criminal, which is qualitatively different than labeling misconduct as a civil or administrative violation and critical to assuring society that corporate criminals are brought to justice.[56]

---

54   Marcia Narine, "Are Crooked Executives Finally Going to Jail? DOJ's New White Collar Criminal Guidelines and the Questions for Compliance Officers and In House Counsel," *Business Law Prof Blog*, 10 September 2015, http://lawprofessors. typepad.com/business_law/2015/09/are-crooked-executives-finally-going-to-jail -dojs-new-white-collar-criminal-guidelines-and-the-quest.html. Cf. Brandon L. Garrett, "It Takes a Plan (to End 'Too Big to Jail')," *The CLS Blue Sky Blog*, 14 October 2015, ("The [Hillary] Clinton plan would do, among its recommendations, four key things to tackle too big to jail"), http://clsbluesky.law.columbia .edu/2015/10/14/it-takes-a-plan-to-end-too-big-to-jail.

55   Cf. Jim Letten, *DOJ's Yates Memorandum 5 Years Down the Road: Alive but is it Kicking? FCPA Enforcement of Individuals Post-"Yates,"* JD Supra (27 March 2020) ("against some expectations, the articulated shift in DOJ charging policies which began with the previous administration have been retained, embraced, and continue somewhat modified"), https://www.jdsupra.com/legalnews/doj-s-yates -memorandum-5-years-down-the-41789.

56   David M. Uhlmann, "The Pendulum Swings: Reconsidering Corporate Criminal Prosecution," 49 *U.C. Davis L. Rev.* 1235, 1243 (2016).

Having hopefully covered some useful ground in terms of understanding the corporate death penalty, including various pros and cons, as well as the risk of moral hazard and public mistrust associated with underenforcement, we turn now to the issue of corporate personality theory.

IV. Theories of Corporate Personality

I have devoted a significant amount of my scholarship the past few years to examining the role of corporate personality theory in discussions about the role of corporations in society.[57] My interest in this topic was sparked in part by the US Supreme Court's 2010 *Citizens United* opinion.[58] As referenced above, *Citizens United* held that "the First Amendment does not allow political speech restrictions based on a speaker's corporate identity."[59]

Citizens United was decided by a 5–4 majority, and when I first read the opinion I was struck by how diametrically opposed the majority and the dissent were when it came to how they conceived of corporations. From the majority's perspective, corporations were to be viewed as nothing more than one of many types of associations of citizens.[60] The dissent of Justice Stevens, meanwhile, saw corporations as state-created entities that: (1) "differ from natural persons in fundamental ways"[61]; (2) "have no consciences, no beliefs, no feelings, no thoughts, no desires"[62]; and (3) "must engage the political process in instrumental terms if they are to maximize shareholder value."[63] Of particular note, the dissent asserted that "corporations

---

57   See Stefan J. Padfield, "Corporate Social Responsibility & Concession Theory," 6
 William & Mary Bus. L. Rev. 1 (2015); Padfield, "Rehabilitating Concession Theory,"
 66 *Okla. L. Rev.* 327 (2014); Padfield, "The Silent Role of Corporate Theory in the
 Supreme Court's Campaign Finance Cases," 15 *U. Pa. J. Const. L.* 831 (2013); Pad-
 field, "The Dodd-Frank Corporation: More Than a Nexus of Contracts," 114 *W. Va.
 L. Rev.* 209 (2011).

58   *Citizens United v. Fed. Election Comm'n*, 558 U.S. 310 (2010).

59   *Citizens United*, 558 U.S. at 347.

60   See, for example, *Citizens United*, 130 S. Ct. at 906–07 (asserting that the Court's
 prior ruling in *Austin* "permits the Government to ban the political speech
 of millions of associations of citizens"); *id.* at 908 (asserting that under the
 challenged statute "certain disfavored associations of citizens – those that
 have taken on the corporate form – are penalized for engaging in ... political
 speech").

61   *Id.* at 971–2n72 (Stevens, J., concurring in part and dissenting in part).

62   *Id.* at 972.

63   *Id.* at 965.

have been 'effectively delegated responsibility for ensuring society's economic welfare.'"[64]

From my readings of *Citizens United*, the conclusions of the majority and the dissent flow directly from these competing characterizations of corporations.[65] However, the majority was silent on the issue of corporate personality theory, and the dissent went so far as to expressly disavow any role for the topic.[66] Wrote Justice Stevens: "Nothing in this analysis turns on whether the corporation is conceptualized as a grantee of a state concession ... a nexus of explicit and implicit contracts ... a mediated hierarchy of stakeholders ... or any other recognized model."[67] Suffice it to say that I was not the only scholar to find this assertion incredible, as Stephen Bainbridge quickly called out Justice Stevens in a blog post for what Bainbridge described as Stevens advancing a "Pernicious Version of the Concession Theory."[68]

In this section, I set forth a basic outline of corporate personality theory. I explain some of the terms used in the preceding paragraphs that may have been unfamiliar to the reader, such as "concession theory." Once this framework is established, I will integrate it with the prior discussion of corporations and human rights, and the corporate death penalty, in order to advance the thesis that corporate personality theory

---

64 *Id.* at 971 (quoting Milton C. Regan, Jr., *Corporate Speech and Civic Virtue, in Debating Democracy's Discontent: Essays on American Politics, Law, and Public Philosophy* 289, 302 [Anita L. Allen and Milton C. Regan Jr. eds., 1998]).

65 But see Reuven S. Avi-Yonah, "Citizens United and the Corporate Form," *Wis. L. Rev.* 999, 1001 (2010) ("both the majority and the dissent in *Citizens United* adopt the real entity view").

66 It is worth noting that a failure to analyse corporate personality issues does not necessarily equate to a rejection of corporate personality theory. Viewing corporations as associations of citizens is at least as likely to represent a preference for the aggregate theory of corporate personhood as it is to represent a rejection of corporate personality theory. Cf. Adam Winkler, *We the Corporations: How American Businesses Won Their Civil Rights* 381 (New York: W.W. Norton, 2018) ("*Citizens United*, represented a rejection of corporate personhood").

67 *Id.* at 971n72 (Stevens, J., dissenting in part and concurring in part).

68 Stephen Bainbridge, "*Citizens United v. FEC*: Stevens' Pernicious Version of the Concession Theory," *ProfessorBainbridge.com*, 21 January 2010, 4:05 p.m., http://www.professorbainbridge.com/professorbainbridgecom/2010/01/citizens-united-v-fec-stevens-pernicious-version-of-the-concession-theory.html. I attempt to provide some possible explanations for the Court's avoidance of the corporate personhood issue in "The Dodd-Frank Corporation: More Than a Nexus-of-Contracts," 114 *W. Va. L. Rev.* 209, 226–7 (2011) ("there are a number of possible explanations ...: (1) federalism concerns; (2) a failure to appreciate the significance of corporate theory; and/or (3) a desire to avoid the appearance of imposing unconstitutional conditions on incorporation").

has a role to play in bridging the related accountability gaps when it comes to corporations and their impact on human rights.

A. Corporate Personhood Versus Corporate Personality Theory

There is an important distinction to be made between corporate personhood and corporate personality theory. Corporate personhood is the means by which we expressly extend rights to corporations that would otherwise be limited to natural persons. Two of the primary sources of corporate personhood are cases arising under the US Constitution and specific statutory grants. As to the former, the US Supreme Court's famous (or infamous) 1886 decision in *Santa Clara County v. Southern Pacific Railroad Co.*,[69] which involved a challenge to the taxation of railway companies, is often cited for the proposition that corporations can be persons under the US Constitution.[70] The syllabus for that opinion asserted without any discussion or analysis:

> The court does not wish to hear argument on the question whether the provision in the Fourteenth Amendment to the Constitution, which forbids a State to deny to any person within its jurisdiction the equal protection of the laws, applies to these corporations. We are all of opinion that it does.[71]

---

69 118 U.S. 394 (1886).

70 Cf. Adam Winkler, *We the Corporations: How American Businesses Won Their Civil Rights* (New York: W.W. Norton 2018), xiii–xiv (recounting an argument before the Supreme Court that laid the foundation for the corporate rights referenced in *Santa Clara*: "Conkling insisted the [14th] amendment's drafters intended to cover business corporations ... As a member of Congress during Reconstruction, Conkling had been on the very committee that wrote the amendment ... There was just one small problem with Conkling's account of the drafting of the Fourteenth Amendment: it was not true").

71 *Id.* at 396. See Frank D. Wagner, "How Not to Write A Syllabus," 15 *Scribes J. Legal Writing* 153, 155–7 (2013).

   The Reporter of Decisions who wrote the [*Santa Clara County*] syllabus was John Chandler Bancroft Davis (1822–1907) ... Davis was the scion of an influential Massachusetts political family ... Generations of commentators have considered the *Santa Clara County* syllabus to be evidence that Davis simply made up, out of whole cloth, the important rule that corporations enjoy the same rights to sue and be sued in court as natural persons ... But further delving into the historical record reveals that Davis may not have been totally out in left field when he wrote the *Santa Clara County* syllabus ... C. Peter Magrath, recounted that Davis had written the *Santa Clara County* syllabus after first asking the Chief Justice "whether I correctly caught your words." Chief Justice Waite replied to Davis: "I think your memo expresses with sufficient accuracy what was said before the argument began. I leave it with you to determine whether anything need be said about it in the report inasmuch as we avoided meeting the constitutional question in the decision." *Id.* Cf. *Connecticut*

As to the statutory basis for corporate personhood, the much more recent US Supreme Court case of *Hobby Lobby* provides an excellent example.[72] While many assume that case, which allowed closely held corporations that could assert a sincere religious objection to refuse to provide health care to employees that would otherwise be required under a generally applicable mandate, arose under the Free Exercise clause of the 1st Amendment,[73] it was actually a statutory case arising under the Religious Freedom Restoration Act of 1993 (RFRA),[74] and the Court relied on the Dictionary Act[75] to establish the requisite corporate personhood:

> RFRA applies to "a person's" exercise of religion, and RFRA itself does not define the term "person." We therefore look to the Dictionary Act, which we must consult "[i]n determining the meaning of any Act of Congress, unless the context indicates otherwise." Under the Dictionary Act, "the wor[d] 'person' ... include[s] corporations, companies, associations, firms, partnerships, societies, and joint stock companies, as well as individuals."[76]

Thus, corporate personhood grants standing to corporations to assert rights granted to natural persons in certain situations, but it does not tell us much else about the nature of this juridical person to help us determine when reasons might exist to limit these very same rights. For example, and as the majority acknowledged in *Citizens United*, the Court "has upheld a ... class of speech restrictions that operate to the disadvantage of certain persons ... based on an interest in allowing governmental entities to perform their functions."[77] These cases include limiting the rights of federal civil employees,[78] military personnel,[79] prisoners,[80] and

---

Gen. Life Ins. Co. v. Johnson, 303 U.S. 77, 89–90 (1938) (Black, J., dissenting) ("This amendment sought to prevent discrimination by the states against classes or races ... Yet, of the cases in this Court in which the Fourteenth Amendment was applied during the first fifty years after its adoption, less than one-half of 1 per cent invoked it in protection of the negro race, and more than 50 per cent asked that its benefits be extended to corporations").

72 *Burwell v. Hobby Lobby Stores, Inc.*, 134 S. Ct. 2751 (2014).

73 U.S. Const. amend. I ("Congress shall make no law respecting an establishment of religion, or prohibiting the free exercise thereof ...").

74 107 Stat. 1488, 42 U.S.C. § 2000bb et seq.

75 1 U.S.C. § 1.

76 *Burwell v. Hobby Lobby Stores, Inc.*, 134 S. Ct. 2751, 2768 (2014).

77 *Citizens United v. Fed. Election Comm'n*, 558 U.S. 310, 341 (2010).

78 *United States Civil Service Commission v. National Ass'n of Letter Carriers*, 413 U.S. 548 (1973).

79 *Parker v. Levy*, 417 U.S. 733, 759 (1974).

80 *Jones v. North Carolina Prisoners' Labor Union, Inc.*, 433 U.S. 119 (1977).

high school students.[81] However, in *Citizens United* the majority simply baldly asserted that "[t]he corporate independent expenditures at issue in this case ...would not interfere with governmental functions, so these cases are inapposite."[82] The dissent, meanwhile, retorted that "Congress and half the state legislatures have concluded, over many decades, that their core functions of administering elections and passing legislation cannot operate effectively without some narrow restrictions on corporate electioneering paid for by general treasury funds."[83]

In light of this line of cases limiting the Constitutional rights of natural persons on the basis of the type of person they are (e.g., federal employee, military service member, prisoner, or high school student), it seems incomplete at best to assess the applicability of these cases to corporations without delving into the nature of corporate personhood, which is what corporate personality theory is designed to do. Importantly, even if the movement to end corporate personhood succeeds,[84] it is likely that there will be little to prevent, for example, Congress from simply adding corporations expressly as beneficiaries of statutory rights as needed or desired. In other words, while we would not be able to rely on "person" including corporations in the text of a statute, we could simply draft the relevant provision to apply to "natural persons and corporations."[85] Then we would arguably be right back to asking

---

81 *Bethel School District No. 403 v. Fraser*, 478 U.S. 675 (1986).

82 *Citizens United v. Fed. Election Comm'n*, 558 U.S. 310, 341 (2010).

83 *Id.* at 421n46 (Stevens, J., dissenting); cf. *First Nat'l Bank of Bos. v. Bellotti*, 435 U.S. 765, 804 (1978) (White, J., dissenting) ("[A]n examination of the First Amendment values that corporate expression furthers and the threat to the functioning of a free society it is capable of posing reveals that it is not fungible with communications emanating from individuals and is subject to restrictions which individual expression is not.").

84 Susanna Kim Ripken, "Corporate First Amendment Rights after *Citizens United*: An Analysis of the Popular Movement to End the Constitutional Personhood of Corporations," 14 *U. Pa. J. Bus. L.* 209, 215 (2011) ("[T]he Corporate Abolitionists believe the abolition of corporate personhood is an issue of human rights, like the abolition of slavery. The whole institution is fundamentally wrong and must be eradicated if we are to have true democracy."); William Quigley, "Catholic Social Thought and the Amorality of Large Corporations: Time to Abolish Corporate Personhood," 5 *Loy. Pub. Int. L.* 109 (2004) ("This paper suggests that the modern large corporations are by size, power, and operation of law either amoral or immoral and so powerful that they cannot be made to act in accordance with Catholic social thought under current legal regulations. Since other arrangements are making little progress, legal corporation personhood should be abolished.").

85 I do not mean to minimize the implications of a constitutional amendment denying corporations personhood status under the law, I merely wish to point out that expressly denying personhood status under the US Constitution and/or other laws and regulations is likely to be both under- and over-inclusive.It is likely to be

the sorts of questions about whether corporations should be granted the relevant rights that corporate personality theory is uniquely designed to help answer.[86]

B. The Competing Theories of Corporate Personality

The three primary theories of corporate personality[87] are (1) concession / artificial entity theory, (2) aggregate theory, and (3) real entity theory.[88]

Concession theory is often associated with the following quote from the US Supreme Court's 1819 *Dartmouth College* opinion:

> A corporation is an artificial being, invisible, intangible, and existing only in contemplation of law. Being the mere creature of law, it possesses only

---

overinclusive to the extent we lose, at least initially, corporate rights that are generally agreed to be beneficial (such as the right to hold property and enter into contracts), but underinclusive to the extent legislative and/or judicial work-arounds such as expressly including "corporations" within the scope of relevant statutes (as opposed to merely including them in the relevant definition of "person") would ultimately make fewer inroads into corporate power than originally hoped for by the backers of such amendments. Of course, working around a constitutional amendment as opposed to a statutory fix would be far more difficult, if not practically impossible.

86 But cf. Susanna Kim Ripken, *Corporate First Amendment Rights After Citizens United*, 209, 242–43 (2011). ("What will happen if the Corporate Abolitionists are successful in abolishing corporate personhood? ... Corporations would once again be viewed as concessions of the government, subject to strict regulation and privileged to have only the limited rights the state chooses to bestow statutorily.").

87 While it is certainly possible to draw connections, one should be careful not to confuse theories of corporate personality with theories of corporate governance. Modern theories of corporate governance seek to explain what the ends of corporate governance should be/are (e.g., shareholder wealth maximization or corporate sustainability), as well as who should/does have primary responsibility for attaining that goal (e.g., shareholders or management). Modern corporate governance theories include director primacy, shareholder primacy, and team production theory. See generally, Stefan J. Padfield, "Corporate Social Responsibility and Concession Theory," 6 *Wm. & Mary Bus. L. Rev.* 1, 6 (2015) ("[A]s Stephen Bainbridge put it ...: 'Corporate law and economics scholarship initially relied mainly on agency cost and nexus of contracts models.' In recent years, however, 'various scholars have built on those foundations to construct three competing models of corporate governance: director primacy, shareholder primacy, and team production.'") (quoting letter from Stephen Bainbridge, 3 June 2013 [on file with author]).

88 But cf. Winkler, *We the Corporations*, 61–2 (describing "two contrasting ways of thinking about corporations ... personhood and piercing," with "personhood" largely equating to the artificial entity view of corporate personhood, and "piercing" largely equating to the aggregate or associational view of corporate personhood).

those properties which the charter of its creation confers upon it, either expressly, or as incidental to its very existence. These are such as are supposed best calculated to effect the object for which it was created ... The objects for which a corporation is created are universally such as the government wishes to promote.[89]

While the Court in *Dartmouth College* actually sided with the corporation that was resisting an attempt by the State of New Hampshire to unilaterally amend Dartmouth College's charter,[90] concession theory is typically associated with a pro-regulatory perspective, at least when contrasted with the other two dominant corporate personality theories.[91]

Aggregate theory arguably arose at least in part in response to calls from capitalists to free the corporate form from what were viewed by some as excessive regulations. The premise is that a corporation is a mere legal fiction that should essentially be ignored when it comes to determining its rights. Rather, one should look to the aggregation of natural persons – primarily, if not exclusively, the "owners"[92]/shareholders that make up the corporation – and not allow the government to "punish" those natural persons by limiting their freedom of action solely on the basis of their having chosen to act through the corporate form. The US Supreme Court's 1886 decision in *Santa Clara*,[93] discussed

---

89 *Trustees of Dartmouth Coll. v. Woodward*, 17 U.S. 518, 636–37 (1819). But cf. Winkler, *We the Corporations*, 66 (arguing that it is a mistake to interpret that language in *Dartmouth College* "to mean that Marshall embraced corporate personhood").

90 *Dartmouth Coll.*, 17 U.S. at 652 ("the act 'to amend the charter, and enlarge and improve the corporation of Dartmouth College,' increases the number of trustees to twenty-one, gives the appointment of the additional members to the executive of the state, and creates a board of overseers").

91 *Cf. Dartmouth Coll.*, 17 U.S. at 712 (1819) (Story, J., concurring) ("If the legislature mean to claim such an authority, it must be reserved in the grant. The charter of Dartmouth College contains no such reservation ..."); Eric W. Orts, "Beyond Shareholders: Interpreting Corporate Constituency Statutes," 61 *Geo. Wash. L. Rev.* 14, 69 (1992) ("Advocates of Contract Clause protection for shareholders are aware of the 'reserve' clauses resulting from *Dartmouth College*, but they appear to underestimate the full import of these powers. States have 'reserved' the freedom ... to 'impair' the rights of shareholders").

92 Cf. Martin Lipton and Paul K. Rowe, "The Inconvenient Truth about Corporate Governance: Some Thoughts on Vice-Chancellor Strine's Essay," 33 *J. Corp. L.* 63, 66 (2007) ("The whole point of the corporate form is to make clear that shareholders are not owners – that their share ownership gives them no right to claim or exercise control over their pro rata share of the corporation's assets or profits").

93 118 U.S. 394 (1886).

briefly above, is often cited as the case where the Court shifted from the artificial entity to the aggregate view.[94]

A problem with aggregate theory, however, is that in removing the legal fiction of the corporation one also removes a primary justification for providing limited liability to shareholders.[95] Thus, another theory was needed to address the concerns about overregulation associated with concession theory, and that theory was real entity theory. At the risk of oversimplifying, real entity theory continues to highlight the private nature of corporations by associating them with natural persons, but avoids the limited liability problem raised by aggregate theory by identifying the relevant natural persons either as some group arising in connection with the corporation that should be counted in our ontology,[96] or as the board of directors.[97] A number of commentators trace the arrival of real entity

---

94 *See* Stefan J. Padfield, *Rehabilitating Concession Theory*, 66 *Okla. L. Rev.* 327, 336 (2014) ("Morton Horwitz has convincingly argued that the Supreme Court's famous 1886 decision in *Santa Clara County v. Southern Pacific Railroad Co.* represented a shift to the aggregate view of the corporation") (citing Morton J. Horwitz, *The Transformation of American Law, 1870–1960: The Crisis of Legal Orthodoxy* 67 [Oxford: Oxford University Press, 1992]).Cf. *id.* ("While Horwitz acknowledges that many have characterized *Santa Clara* as a real entity case, he goes on to demonstrate that 'a "natural entity" or "real entity" theory of the corporation that the *Santa Clara* case is supposed to have adopted was nowhere to be found in American legal thought when the case was decided.'") (citing Horwitz, *Transformation*, at 67). But see Margaret M. Blair and Elizabeth Pollman, "The Derivative Nature of Corporate Constitutional Rights," 56 *Wm. & Mary L. Rev.* 1673, 1682 (2015) ("although the Court recognized that incorporating meant creating a separate artificial being, from its earliest case considering the treatment of corporations under the Constitution, the Court saw the corporation as representing the identifiable group of people who had chosen to associate through the corporate form").

95 See Thomas C. Folsom, "Evaluating Supernatural Law: An Inquiry into the Health of Nations (The Restatement of the Obvious, Part II)," 21 *Regent U. L. Rev.* 105, 148 (2008) ("Limited liability entities are based on the moral intuition of nonagency because there is separation of ownership from control").

96 *Cf.* Padfield, *Rehabilitating Concession Theory*, 66 *Okla. L. Rev.* at 338 ("According to Horwitz, the organic view traces its roots to German legal theorists, including Otto Gierke, who 'insist that the distinctiveness of the corporate personality is as real as the individuality of a physical person.'") (citing Horwitz, *Transformation*, at 102); David Sloan Wilson, "Updating Paul Krugman, 'Evolution Groupie,'" *Evonomics. com* ("the dogma that all human social group processes are to be explained by laws of individual behaviour – that groups and social organizations have no ontological reality ... might be theoretically justified in cases where selection takes place entirely within groups ... but not when groups are the unit of selection"), http:// evonomics.com/updating-paul-krugman-evolution-groupie-econ.

97 Cf. Stephen M. Bainbridge, "Director Primacy: The Means and Ends of Corporate Governance," 97 *Nw. U. L. Rev.* 547, 560 (2003) ("[T]o the limited extent to which the corporation is properly understood as a real entity, it is the board of directors that personifies the corporate entity").

theory to the US Supreme Court's 1906 case of *Hale v. Henkel*, in which the Court extended 4th Amendment protection to corporations.[98]

Thus, we have three primary theories of corporate personality, and two of them, aggregate theory and real entity theory, tend to locate corporations on the private side of the relevant private/public divide, equating corporations with natural persons and generally leaning toward granting corporations rights coextensive with natural persons. At least some commentators have aligned both *Citizens United* and *Hobby Lobby* with these theories.[99] Concession/artificial entity theory, on the other hand, locates corporations more on the public side of the relevant private/public divide, and tends to be more deferential to legislative conclusions that corporations need to be regulated. Perhaps not surprisingly, the dissents in *Citizens United* and *Hobby Lobby* have both been associated with artificial entity theory.[100]

---

98   201 U.S. 43, 76 (1906). *See* Ron Harris, "The Transplantation of the Legal Discourse on Corporate Personality Theories: From German Codification to British Political Pluralism and American Big Business," *Washington & Lee L. Rev.* 1421, 1472 (2006) ("*Hale v. Henkel* ... is considered the first U.S. Supreme Court case to apply real entity theory"). The Court, however, refused to extend the 5th Amendment privilege against self-incrimination to corporations. *Hale,* at 70 ("The amendment is limited to a person who shall be compelled in any criminal case to be a witness against himself; and if he cannot set up the privilege of a third person, he certainly cannot set up the privilege of a corporation"). Cf. Reuven S. Avi-Yonah, "Corporations, Society, and the State: A Defense of the Corporate Tax," 90 *Va. L. Rev.* 1193, 1226–7 (2004) ("[B]y 1920, the Court viewed the corporation as a real entity ... The same real entity view underlay most, although not all, of the arguments made when the corporate tax was adopted in 1909.").

99   Martin Petrin, "Reconceptualizing the Theory of the Firm – from Nature to Function," 118 *Penn. St. L. Rev.* 1, 17 (2013) ("[I]n *Citizens United v. Federal Election Commission,* the Court ... struck down statutory provisions limiting corporate election contributions based on the real entity and aggregate theories"); Thomas W. Joo, "Corporate Speech and the Rights of Others," 30 *Const. Comment.* 335, 339 (2015) ("in *Hobby Lobby,* the Court applied the aggregate theory to non-constitutional free exercise rights").

100   Stephen Bainbridge, "*Citizens United v. FEC*: Stevens' Pernicious Version of the Concession Theory," *ProfessorBainbridge.com,* 21 January 2010, http://www .professorbainbridge.com/professorbainbridgecom/2010/01/citizens-united-v -fec-stevens-pernicious-version-of-the-concession-theory.html; Stefan J. Padfield, "Hobby Lobby Redux: 7 Corporate Law/Theory Quotes," *Business Law Prof Blog,* 14 September 2014, http://lawprofessors.typepad.com/business_law/2014/09 /hobby-lobby-redux-7-corporate-lawtheory-quotes.html.

Until this litigation, no decision of this Court recognized a for-profit corporation's qualification for a religious exemption from a generally applicable law, whether under the Free Exercise Clause or RFRA. The absence of such precedent is just what one would expect, for the exercise of religion is characteristic of natural persons, not artificial legal entities. As Chief Justice Marshall observed nearly two centuries ago, a corporation is "an artificial being, invisible, intangible, and existing only in contemplation of law."

Id. (quoting *Hobby Lobby* dissent of Justice Ginsburg and Justice Sotomayor).

V. How Corporate Personality Theory, the Corporate Death Penalty, and Human Rights Intersect

The thesis of this chapter is that (1) assuming there exists some meaningful accountability deficit when it comes to corporations and their impact on human rights, and (2) assuming that part of this accountability deficit is related to an unwillingness to impose the corporate death penalty, then (3) corporate personality theory has some meaningful role to play in correcting these problems. One might fashion the underlying arguments as follows.

First, while corporate personality theory has been relied upon recently to expand corporate freedom from regulation in cases like *Citizens United* and *Hobby Lobby*, thereby arguably empowering and enriching corporations, making them more able to impact the lives of natural persons for better or worse (including by facilitating human rights violations), as well as increasing the ability of corporations to influence and control the very people we entrust with the authority to protect us from corporate abuses[101] – the lack of commitment to, or honesty regarding, the role of corporate personality theory allows reasonably expectable concomitant responsibilities to be avoided in cases like *Kiobel*.[102] For example, Beth Stephens, in discussing the opinion of the Second Circuit in *Kiobel* (which denied that the ATS could reach corporate defendants, an opinion ultimately upheld on other grounds by the US Supreme Court),[103] noted that "if we study carefully the logic and reasoning of *Citizens United* and compare it to the [Second Circuit's] *Kiobel* decision holding that corporations are not bound by international human rights norms, we find a fundamental difference

---

101   Cf. Dan Danielsen, *Corporate Power and Instrumental States: Towards a Critical Reassessment of the Role of Firms, States, and Regulation in Global Governance* in *International Law and Its Discontents: Confronting Crises* (B. Stark, ed., Cambridge University Press, 2015) ("the modern nation state might be better understood as a participant and enabler of the capitalist economy rather than its other or limit"), http://ssrn.com/abstract=2710870.

102   Cf. Roger M. Michalski, "Rights Come with Responsibilities: Personal Jurisdiction in the Age of Corporate Personhood," 50 *San Diego L. Rev.* 125, 127 (2013) ("Corporate personhood is a place where courts have split rights and obligations asunder to dangerous effect.").

103   Beth Stephens, "Are Corporations People? Corporate Personhood under the Constitution and International Law: An Essay in Honor of Professor Roger S. Clark," 44 *Rutgers L.J.* 1, 2 (2013) ("the Second Circuit in *Kiobel v. Royal Dutch Petroleum Co.* [621 F.3d 111 (2d Cir. 2010), *aff'd on other grounds*, 133 S. Ct. 1659 (2013)] found that international human rights norms, including the prohibition against genocide, do not apply to corporations").

in the way that the courts analyzed the nature of a corporation."[104] Specifically, "the [Second Circuit's] *Kiobel* majority, and commentators endorsing its views, ignored the robust corporate identity that many are quick to adopt when considering a corporation's constitutional rights."[105] While admittedly an oversimplification, in at least some of these cases it seems that corporations are deemed to be just like people when seeking rights, but different when avoiding responsibility. Justice Sotomayor made similar arguments in her *Jesner* dissent.[106]

Second, to the extent that corporate personality theory is being employed selectively and (arguably) without accountability to expand corporate power without a concomitant increase in corporate responsibility, opposition to imposing the corporate death penalty is enhanced because (1) corporate influence over the relevant decision-makers has increased,[107] and (2) the emphasis placed on shareholders as "innocent" victims when the corporate death penalty is imposed is supported by

---

104 *Id*, at 4.

105 *Id.*, at 5.

106 *Jesner*, 138 S. Ct. at 1425 (Sotomayor, J., dissenting) ("Instead of asking whether there exists a specific, universal, and obligatory norm of corporate liability under international law, the relevant inquiry in response to the question presented here is whether there is any reason – under either international law or our domestic law – to distinguish between a corporation and a natural person who is alleged to have violated the law of nations under the ATS. As explained above, international law provides no such reason."); *id*. at 1437 ("Immunizing corporations that violate human rights from liability under the ATS undermines the system of accountability for law-of-nations violations that the First Congress endeavored to impose. It allows these entities to take advantage of the significant benefits of the corporate form and enjoy fundamental rights, see, e.g., *Citizens United*; *Hobby Lobby*, without having to shoulder attendant fundamental responsibilities.") (internal citations omitted).

107 Cf. Jon D. Michaels, "An Enduring, Evolving Separation of Powers," 115 *Colum. Rev.* 515, 516 (2015) ("Increasingly the forces of privatization are consolidating state and commercial power in ways that compromise administrative separation of powers"); Leo E. Strine, Jr, and Nicholas Walter, "Conservative Collision Course?: The Tension between Conservative Corporate Law Theory and *Citizens United*," 100 *Cornell L. Rev.* 335 (2015) ("*Citizens United* ... undercuts conservative corporate theory's reliance upon regulation as an answer to corporate externality risk, and strengthens the argument of its rival theory that corporate managers must consider the best interests of employees, consumers, communities, the environment, and society – and not just stockholders – when making business decisions"); Stephen M. Bainbridge, "Corporate Social Responsibility in the Night-Watchman State," 115 *Colum. L. Rev. Sidebar* 39 (2015) (responding to Strine and Walter); David G. Yosifon, "The Citizens United Gambit in Corporate Theory: A Reply to Bainbridge on Strine and Walter" (Santa Clara Univ. Legal Studies, Research Paper no. 4–14, 2014), https://ssrn.com/abstract=2510967.

the selective application of aggregate-like theories of the corporation.[108] Compare, for example, the explanation William Bradford gives of how corporate legitimacy theory supports the corporate death penalty:

> [C]orporate legitimacy theorists contend that, because corporations, like states, are not natural creatures endowed with natural rights but in fact are artificial social constructions that owe their existence entirely to positive acts of legislation, society possesses the power to remake or even abolish them by the same legislative process if they cannot be justified morally ... [M]ore- over, implied in the theory of corporate legitimacy is that corporations that resist attempts to convert them from private to quasi-public entities would face sanctions up to and including a corporate "death penalty."[109]

There is more to say about how corporate accountability for human rights violations, the corporate death penalty, and corporate personality theory intersect, and I am going to use the following section, which addresses criticisms of the perspective I advance here, to further flesh out the pros and cons of the approach advocated for herein, which is to (1) increase acknowledgment of the role of corporate personality theory in cases involving the rights and duties of corporations, and (2) apply the relevant theory more consistently.

VI. Criticisms

A number of criticisms have been levelled against the proposition that corporate personality theory does or should have any role in deter- mining the rights and responsibilities of corporations. In this section, I set forth some of the most frequently cited critiques as well as some responses to them.

---

108 Cf. Andrew Baker, "Prosecuting in the Shadows: How Unsupported Fear of Collateral Consequences Impedes Corporate Prosecution," *Medium,* 12 June 2018) ("this notion of 'innocent shareholders' fundamentally misconstrues the role of shareholders in public companies ... shareholders generally profit from malfea- sance on behalf of the company, and ... select the board of directors"), https:// medium.com/@Andrew___Baker/prosecuting-in-the-shadows-e2a7b27838fe.

109 William Bradford, "Beyond Good and Evil: The Commensurability of Corporate Profits and Human Rights," 26 *Notre Dame J.L. Ethics & Pub. Pol'y* 141, 189–90 (2012). But see H. Lowell Brown, "The Corporate Director's Compliance Oversight Responsibility in the Post *Caremark* Era," 26 *Del. J. Corp. L.* 1, 72 (2001) ("Early English common law held that corporations were not subject to criminal indict- ment ... As a legal abstraction, the corporation lacked both physical capacity and a 'soul' and therefore could not be blameworthy.").

One commonly expressed concern is that focusing on corporate personality theory detracts from the more important task of determining the optimal allocation of corporate rights and responsibilities on a case-by-case (or issue-by-issue) basis via the assessment of the particular rights and responsibilities in question, in light of the particular underlying policies – what is often referred to as a functional approach. For example, Elizabeth Pollman has written: "[A] metaphor or philosophical conception of the corporation is not helpful for the type of functional analysis that the Court should conduct. The Court should consider the purpose of the constitutional right at issue, and whether it would promote the objectives of that right to provide it to the corporation – and thereby to the people underlying the corporation."[110]

There are a couple of responses to advocates of this functional approach. First, whatever may be optimal from a normative perspective, if the relevant decision-makers who track corporate personality theory are in fact relying on preconceived notions of what corporations are, then ignoring this aspect of the decision-making process leaves underanalysed an important component of the means by which we assign corporate rights and responsibilities. Second, even from a normative perspective one may question the utility of relying solely on a functional approach to the complete exclusion of any type of corporate personality theory analysis because to say we are going to ignore corporate personality theory and focus on "the people underlying the corporation" is at least in some sense to choose aggregate theory, and to make this choice without fully engaging the corporate personality theory literature risks excluding a perspective that could otherwise provide additional clarity.

Another criticism is that there is actually no problem that corporate personality theory needs to address. In other words, to the extent that advocates of corporate personality theory argue that our ambivalence toward corporate personality theory is problematic (i.e., that we rely on conceptions of the corporation to guide our decision-making, but then deny that fact and/or refuse to engage in any meaningful discussion of the strengths and weaknesses of these conceptions), the market or other legal doctrines are already in the process of providing solutions.[111] The

---

110 Elizabeth Pollman, "Reconceiving Corporate Personhood," 2011 *Utah L. Rev.* 1629, 1631 (2011).

111 Cf. Gwynne Skinner, *Rethinking Limited Liability of Parent Corporations for Foreign Subsidiaries' Violations of International Human Rights Law*, 72 *Wash. & Lee L. Rev.* 1769, 1769–70 (2015) ("three primary solutions various authors and practitioners have advocated thus far to address the problem [are] the enterprise liability approach, the due diligence approach, and the direct parental duty-of-care approach");

response here is simply that while it is certainly fair to point out that we are in some sense looking for the least worst system as opposed to some utopian ideal, and while it is also important to recognize the ability of markets, creative lawyers, and others to come up with solutions to various problems, the extent to which corporate personality theory can or should play a positive role in this area is in some meaningful sense yet to be determined, and the fact that it already is playing a role as a positive matter suggests we should at least try to clarify the role it does play. In other words, these are not mutually exclusive paths. We can pursue the optimal balance of corporate rights and responsibilities via various forms of market responses and private ordering, while at the same time unearthing and clarifying the role of corporate personality theory.

Yet another commonly cited criticism is that corporate personality theory is too malleable and indeterminate to serve any useful purpose. For example, Reuven Avi-Yonah has noted that

> in 1926, John Dewey published an article in the Yale Law Journal in which he dismisses as irrelevant the debate among the aggregate, artificial entity, and real entity views of the corporation. These views, he explains, could be deployed to suit any purpose; and he uses examples relying on the cyclical nature of these theories. His conclusion is that theory should be abandoned for an examination of reality.[112]

I have previously addressed this concern by noting Morton Horwitz's 1992 response to Dewey's criticism:

> I wish to dispute Dewey's conclusion that particular conceptions of corporate personality were used just as easily to limit as to enhance corporate

---

Alison Frankel, "In RJR case, Supreme Court to decide if RICO reaches abroad," *Reuters.com*, 1 October 2015 ("Just as human rights lawyers previously capitalized on a novel interpretation of the Alien Tort Statute from the 2nd Circuit [prior to *Kiobel*] ... they [may] seize [a] new opportunity to bring civil RICO suits unless the Supreme Court steps in"), http://blogs.reuters.com/alison-frankel/2015/10/01/in-rjr-case-supreme-court-to-decide-if-rico-reaches-abroad.

112 Reuven S. Avi-Yonah, "Citizens United and the Corporate Form," 2010 *Wis. L. Rev.* 999, 1022–3 (citing John Dewey, "The Historical Background of Corporate Legal Personality," 35 *Yale L.J.* 655, 673 (1926)). Cf. Eric W. Orts, "Theorizing the Firm: Organizational Ontology in the Supreme Court," 65 *DePaul L. Rev.* 559 (2016) ("Writing during the legal realist period in American jurisprudence, Dewey believed that questions of legal personality should turn not on any inquiry 'regarding the nature of things' (such as corporations) but rather on an examination 'in terms of consequences' (such as determining what it would mean practically to recognize corporations as having rights or duties in particular circumstances)").

power. I hope to show that, for example, the rise of a natural entity theory of the corporation was a major factor in legitimating big business and that none of the other theoretical alternatives could provide as much sustenance to newly organized, concentrated enterprise.[113]

Furthermore, "[t]o the extent Horwitz achieved his goal, it may well be the better view that while corporate theory may not be able to precisely predict outcomes in all cases, it is nonetheless meaningful in terms of eliminating certain conclusions and allocating burdens."[114]

Finally, at least for purposes of this section, there is the more narrowly focused criticism that concession / artificial entity theory is no longer viable, and thus corporate personality theory has little to offer as currently constituted because the aggregate and real entity theories both rest on the private side of the relevant private/public divide. In a previous article, "Rehabilitating Concession Theory," I expose a number of the myths underlying this argument, including the argument that "the unconstitutional conditions doctrine trumps concession theory," so I will leave the interested reader to follow up there if interested.[115]

VII. Conclusion

I conclude this chapter by summarizing what I see as its three main points. Note, however, that I view all these points as essentially calls for further research, and I encourage the reader to think critically about which propositions may reasonably be empirically tested. Furthermore, I admit that I have to at least some extent blurred the line between

---

113   Stefan J. Padfield, "Rehabilitating Concession Theory," 66 *Okla. L. Rev.* 327, 343 (2014) (quoting Morton J. Horwitz, *The Transformation of American Law, 1870–1960: The Crisis of Legal Orthodoxy* 68 (1992)).

114   *Id.*

115   *Id.* ("This Part addresses four arguments frequently advanced to undermine concession theory: (1) that corporate theory is excessively malleable; (2) that concession theory died along with special charters; (3) that listeners' rights trump corporate theory; and (4) that the unconstitutional conditions doctrine trumps concession theory"); *id.* at 354 ("Were the Court to directly confront the issue, there are at least five good reasons to conclude that the unconstitutional conditions doctrine would not constitute an insurmountable obstacle to the viability of concession theory"). Cf. Adam Winkler, *We the Corporations: How American Businesses Won Their Civil Rights* 75 (New York: W.W. Norton, 2018) ("[F]or those today who wish to see the Supreme Court restrict the constitutional rights of corporations, looking back to Webster's era reveals a potential model. By embracing corporate personhood, rather than piercing the corporate veil, the Taney court imposed boundaries on the rights of corporations.").

corporate personality theory generally and artificial entity (concession) theory in particular. This, too, is an area that warrants further research, and reasonable minds may differ regarding the extent to which advocates of human rights and corporate accountability can rely on corporate personality theory in general, as opposed to artificial entity theory in particular, to advance their goals as suggested here. Having said that, I believe the points made in this chapter and summarized below are worthy of our consideration even in light of the foregoing qualifications.

First, corporate personality theory has played a role in the apparent recent expansion of corporate rights and powers. In *Citizens United*, for example, the five justices in the majority who granted corporations expanded political speech rights did not expressly address corporate personality theory, while the four justices in the dissent expressly disavowed any role for it. In both the majority opinion and the dissenting opinion, however, the impact of the diverging perspectives on the nature of corporations was made clear in the substance of the discussion. Had the dissent been more aggressive in terms of embracing artificial entity theory and forcing the majority to respond thereto, one might envision a different outcome, as one or more of the justices in the majority might well have struggled to defend, and become uncomfortable committing to, a vision of the corporation that so starkly contradicts public sentiment or undermines corporate limited liability.[116] And even if the outcome did not change, the precedential and analytical value of the discussion would have been an improvement over the backhanded way in which the issue was actually handled.

Second, corporate personality theory has a role to play in the apparent accountability gap surrounding corporate conduct vis-à-vis human rights. To begin with, legal issues like campaign finance and human rights are not siloed. For example, the Second Circuit referenced *Citizens United* in its *Kiobel* decision.[117] While that particular reference was

---

116 Cf. Brooke Jarvis, "Citizens United? The need to get money out of politics may be the one thing Americans agree on," *YES! Magazine*, 21 January 2011) ("The Hart survey found broad, bipartisan support for the notion of amending the U.S. Constitution to affirm that corporations don't have the same rights as people"); Erik Voeten, "How the Supreme Court Responds to Public Opinion," *Washington Monthly*, 28 June 2013) ("political scientists have amassed an impressive array of evidence in favor of the hypothesis that the Court follows changes in public opinion").

117 *Kiobel v. Royal Dutch Petroleum Co.*, 621 F.3d 111, 118 n.11 (2d Cir. 2010), *aff'd*, 133 S. Ct. 1659 (2013) ("The idea that corporations are 'persons' with duties, liabilities, and rights has a long history in American domestic law. It is an idea that continues to evolve in complex and unexpected ways. *See, e.g., Citizens United v. Fed. Election Comm'n*, 558 U.S. 50, 130 S.Ct. 876, 175L.Ed.2d 753 (2010).") (internal citations omitted).

made in the context of brushing away concerns about balancing corporate power and responsibility,[118] it is at least possible that it would have been more difficult for the Second Circuit to brush aside those concerns had *Citizens United* made a stronger statement about the extent to which corporations are subject to government regulation by their very nature. For example, Beth Stephens has argued that a greater emphasis on corporate personhood could have led to a different result in the Second Circuit's *Kiobel* decision regardless of which particular theory of corporate personality was endorsed:

> The well-established understanding of the nature of a corporation that is central to *Citizens United* highlights a key problem with the Second Circuit opinion in *Kiobel*: Judge Cabranes essentially ruled that the corporation is unknown to international law ... But all of the Supreme Court justices in *Citizens United* recognized that a corporation is a well-known legal entity with discernible characteristics and that it exists as a legally recognizable actor. They did not require that particular norms explicitly refer to corporations because they know what a corporation is, and can apply neutral rules to it based on the role it plays in law, economics, and society at large.[119]

In addition, the ability of corporations to resist being held accountable for their participation in human rights violations turns in large part on corporate power generally. Thus, to the extent that corporate personality theory has played a role in the apparent upsurge in corporate power, it has thereby at least an indirect link to this accountability deficit.

Finally, corporate personality theory has a role to play in the hesitancy with which the corporate death penalty is imposed. William Bradford (see above) has noted that corporate legitimacy theory, which I believe we may fairly align with artificial entity / concession theory, supports imposition of the corporate death penalty because under that theory, "corporations ... are not natural creatures endowed with natural rights but in fact are artificial social constructions that owe their existence entirely to positive acts of legislation,"[120] and thus, "society possesses the power to remake or even abolish them by the same legislative process if they cannot be justified morally."[121] In addition, Bradford's

---

118 *Id.* ("The history of corporate rights and obligations under domestic law is, however, entirely irrelevant to the issue before us – namely, the treatment of corporations as a matter of *customary international law*").

119 Beth Stephens, *Are Corporations People? Corporate Personhood under the Constitution and International Law: An Essay in Honor of Professor Roger S. Clark*, 44 *Rutgers L.J.* 1, 36 (2013).

120 *See supra*, text accompanying n98.

121 *Id.*

account arguably supports the notion that while the aggregate and real entity theories of the corporation support focusing on the "innocent" (my quotation marks, not his) shareholders as a rationale for avoiding the corporate death penalty, the artificial entity theory would arguably cut the other way.[122] When decisions like *Citizens United* and *Kiobel* marginalize corporate personality theory generally (and artificial entity theory in particular), it arguably becomes easier to do so in the context of the corporate death penalty, leading to excessive avoidance of imposition of the corporate death penalty. This effectively subsidizes corporate power, which can then be reallocated to advancing the corporate agenda in cases like *Citizens United* and *Kiobel*.[123]

Thus, failure to critically examine the use and avoidance of corporate personality theory in judicial (and other) decision-making supports the current regime of increasing corporate power while limiting corporate accountability. Of course, as has been alluded to already, the current state of affairs may in fact be the least worst regime available. However, so long as serious discussion of the role of corporate personality theory is avoided or affirmatively rejected, the extent to which the aggregate and real entity theories are accepted uncritically while artificial entity theory is disdainfully ignored should be cause for concern.[124]

---

122 Cf. William Bradford, *Beyond Good and Evil: The Commensurability of Corporate Profits and Human Rights*, 26 *Notre Dame J.L. Ethics & Pub. Pol'y* 141, 191 (2012) (noting that critics of corporate legitimacy theory argue "corporations are simply larger and wealthier ... than most natural persons, and thus no more responsible for the protection of human rights").

123 Cf. Nicole Flatow, "The Chamber Of Commerce Won More Than Two-Thirds of Its Supreme Court Cases This Term," *ThinkProgress*, 2 July 2014) ("the Chamber's influence remains unique because the lobbying shop that claims 3 million member businesses has been venturing into increasingly radical territory in arguments that call for rolling back years of established precedent that disfavor its business interests"); Winkler, *We the Corporations*, 346 ("'Business can pay for the best counsel money can buy,' explained Justice Ruth Bader Ginsburg, unlike many ordinary citizens").

124 Compare Bainbridge, "*Citizens United v. FEC*: Stevens' Pernicious Version of the Concession Theory," *ProfessorBainbridge.com*, 21 January 2010 ("It has been over half-a-century since corporate legal theory, of any political or economic stripe, took the concession theory seriously"), http://www.professorbainbridge.com /professorbainbridgecom/2010/01/citizens-united-v-fec-stevens-pernicious -version-of-the-concession-theory.html, with Padfield, "Rehabilitating Concession Theory," 66 *Okla. L. Rev.* 327, 330 (2014) (demonstrating "why concession theory remains viable by rebutting some of the primary arguments against its relevance").

7 Already Artificial: Legal Personality and Animal Rights

ANGELA FERNANDEZ[1]

Many of the chapters in this volume deal with the inappropriate extension of legal personhood to that most controversial artificial legal person, the corporation, which has been extended rights that (arguably) should be confined to natural persons – for example, free speech in the (in)famous 2010 United States Supreme Court case *Citizens United v. Federal Election Commission*.[2] The criticism is essentially that the granting of personhood to corporations comes at the expense of natural persons. So, for example, Richard Hardack, whose chapter appears in Part II of this volume, argues that "personhood is a zero-sum game, and that the more 'personhood' and human rights corporations attain, the less of those traits and rights people retain."[3] This inverse relationship, if true, is deeply disturbing and suggests we should be restricting the spread of the attribution of legal personhood in order to safeguard values and

1 Associate Professor, Faculty of Law, University of Toronto (angela.fernandez@utoronto.ca). This chapter benefited from presentation at the 2014 Inter-Law School Works-in-Progress Summer Workshop, Faculty of Law, University of Toronto (co-organized with Kim Brooks), a Faculty Workshop at the Faculty of Law, University of Toronto, and a session with the University of Toronto, Jackman Humanities Institute Working Group "Animals in the Law and Humanities," both in the fall of 2016. Lesli Bisgould provided especially valuable comments. Feedback from the editors and reviewers has also been very helpful. Many thanks to Camille Labchuk of Animal Justice Canada, who facilitated access to a copy of *Unlocking the Cage*, and to Stephanie Damgaard of Films We Like for providing me with a link to the film I used for early drafts. Michael Boyuk of Films We Like pulled the three stills from the film *Unlocking the Cage* reproduced below, and Frazer Pennebaker of Pennebaker and Hegedus Films graciously gave permission to use them here.
2 *Citizens United v. Federal Election Commission*, 558 U.S. 310 (2010).
3 Richard Hardack, "Exceptionally Gifted: Corporate Exceptionalism and the Expropriation of Human Rights." See also Hardack, "New *and* Improved: The Zero Sum Game of Corporate Personhood," *Biography* 37, no. 1 (2014): 36–68 at 46–7.

rights we hold dear for human beings. Some of the most promising work in the area of animal rights – notably the work of Steven Wise and the Nonhuman Rights Project – pulls in precisely the opposite direction, arguing for an (at least partial) *extension* of the attributes of personhood to (at least some) other animals.

This chapter examines the 2016 documentary film *Unlocking the Cage* as a means to unpack the argument for non-human animal legal personhood. That film focuses on the litigation efforts made by the Nonhuman Rights Project in 2013–14 on behalf of a number of chimpanzees held in a variety of inappropriate situations in New York State.[4] I use segments of it as well as Wise's own writings to situate, explain, and respond to three important criticisms his approach faces: (1) the danger of singling out higher cognitively functioning non-human animals for legal protection; (2) the wisdom of drawing connections between non-human animals and other groups facing social and legal discrimination; and (3) the challenges inherent in treating corporate personhood as analogous to non-human animal legal personhood.

As a caveat, Chris Hegedus and D.A. Pennebaker, who made *Unlocking the Cage*, are deeply sympathetic to Wise's project, as am I, though I share the concerns raised in the criticisms I explore in this chapter. Indeed, I believe it is important to discuss key reservations to this approach so that if non-human animal legal personhood (or some version of it) does come to pass, we do it with open eyes as to its limitations and problems in order to think about how they might be best addressed. A second caveat: I also discuss the decisions in 2017 and 2018 that were made after the film appeared and how they interact with the arguments made in the film and in Wise's writings, specifically *Rattling the Cage*, first published in 2000.[5]

There have been steps forward and backward since the film was made. The legal decision from the First Department in 2017 is generally a step back, and appeal to the state's highest court, the New York Court of Appeals, was denied in early 2018.[6] However, May 2018 saw

---

4   *Unlocking the Cage*, dir. Chris Hegedus and D.A. Pennebaker (2016).

5   *Matter of Nonhuman Rights Project, Inc. v. Lavery*, 2017 NY Slip Op 04574 (Appellate Division, First Department), 8 June 2017), http://www.nycourts.gov/reporter/3d-series/2017/2017_04574.htm [hereafter *Lavery* and Kiko, First Department]; Steven M. Wise, *Rattling the Cage: Toward Legal Rights for Animals* (Boston: De Capo Press, [2000]2014).

6   See *In re Nonhuman Rights Project Inc. v. Patrick C. Lavery*, 2018 NY Slip Op 61538 (Appellate Division, First Department), 18 January 2018, http://www.nycourts.gov/reporter/motions/2018/2018_61538.htm.

an encouraging concurrence from one of the judges of the New York Court of Appeals.[7]

The decision to deny leave to appeal was unanimous. However, Justice Eugene Fahey wrote a concurrence "to underscore that denial of leave to appeal is not a decision on the merits of petitioner's claim. The question will have to be addressed eventually [by the highest level of court in the state, as opposed to the individual Judicial Departments]. Can a nonhuman animal be entitled to release from confinement through the writ of habeas corpus? Should such a being be treated as a person or as property, in essence a thing?"[8] He identified the question of whether "an intelligent nonhuman animal ... thinks and plans and appreciates life as human beings do" and whether they "have the right to the protection of the law against arbitrary cruelties and enforced detentions visited on him or her [...] a deep dilemma of ethics and policy that demands our attention."[9] He noted his own "struggle" and second thoughts about whether he should have voted to deny the motion for leave to appeal in 2015 given the "profound and far-reaching" nature of the question.[10] Relying on the "simple either/or proposition" of whether a party is a "person" or a "thing," he wrote, "amounts to a refusal to confront a manifest injustice."[11]

Other steps forward include a declaration in 2014 that the Ganga (the Ganges under British rule) and Yamuna Rivers in India are legal persons.[12] In Argentina, an orangutan named Sandra was declared a non-human person in a *habeas corpus* argument in 2015 and moved from a zoo to a sanctuary for great apes in Florida.[13] In 2016, the breeding of

---

7 See *In the Matter of Nonhuman Rights Projects, Inc., on Behalf of Tommy, Appellant, v. Patrick C. Lavery, &c, et al., Respondents; In the Matter of Nonhuman Rights Project, Inc., on Behalf of Kiko, Appellant, v. Carmen Presti et al., Respondents*, Motion no. 2018-268 (State of New York, Court of Appeals), 8 May 2018, http://www.ny-courts.gov/ctapps/Decisions/2018/May18/M2018-268opn18-Decision.pdf.

8 Ibid., 2.

9 Ibid., 5.

10 Ibid., 6–7.

11 Ibid., 6.

12 A PDF of this decision is available at https://www.nonhumanrights.org/content/uploads/WPPIL-126-14.pdf.

13 See Emiliano Giménez, "Argentine orangutan granted unprecedented legal rights," *CNN*, 4 January 2015, http://edition.cnn.com/2014/12/23/world/americas/feat-orangutan-rights-ruling; Alaa Elassar, "Sandra the orangutan, freed from a zoo after being granted 'personhood,' settles into her new home," *CNN*, 9 November 2019, https://www.cnn.com/2019/11/09/world/sandra-orangutan-florida-home-trnd/index.html.

captive killer whales at Sea World was ended.[14] In the United States in May 2017, the Ringling Brothers and Barnum and Bailey Circus closed down after 146 years.[15] A bipartisan bill that would prohibit the use of non-human animals in travelling circuses maintains its place on the legislative agenda in the United States.[16] The highest court in the Indian state of Uttarakhand declared in 2018 that all non-human animals (including birds and aquatic life) have rights "similar to" those of human beings and that all citizens of the state stand *in loco parentis* to these animals.[17] In 2019, Canada passed a bill prohibiting any further importation of cetaceans as well as any captive breeding of them.[18] I have no doubt that steps like these will continue around issues related to animal welfare and the legal personhood of non-human animals and other entities. What I offer here is an overview framed around *Unlocking the Cage*.

Documentary films have played an important role in the very recent histories of both legal personhood and animal rights. During the 2004 US presidential campaign, advertisements promoting Michael Moore's movie *Fahrenheit 9/11*, which criticized the Bush government and its "war on terror," prompted Citizens United, a conservative not-for-profit group, to file a complaint with the Federal Election Commission (FEC) that a ban on election advertising too close to election day was being violated.[19] When the FEC denied the complaint, Citizens United produced a DirecTv political documentary, later found to be essentially a long negative advertisement,

---

14   See "SeaWorld Agrees to End Captive Breeding of Killer Whales," *NPR*, 17 March 2016, http://www.npr.org/sections/thetwo-way/2016/03/17/470720804/seaworld-agrees-to-end-captive-breeding-of-killer-whales.

15   See "Ringling Bros. and Barnum & Bailey Circus Just Officially Closed Down," *The Mind Unleashed*, 24 May 2017, http://themindunleashed.com/2017/05/ringling-bros-barnum-bailey-circus-just-officially-closed.html.

16   The bill is called the Travelling Exotic Animal and Public Safety Protection Act (TEAPSPA), reintroduced in Congress on 21 May 2019, https://www.congress.gov/bill/116th-congress/house-bill/2863/text?format=txt.

17   See Vineet Upadhyay, "Animals Have Equal Rights as Humans, says Uttarakhand High Court," *India Times*, 5 July 2018, https://timesofindia.indiatimes.com/city/dehradun/members-of-animal-kingdom-to-be-treated-as-legal-entities-ukhand-hc/articleshow/64860996.cms.

18   See Laura Howells, "'A more humane country': Canada to ban keeping whales, dolphins in captivity, " *CBC* News, 10 June 2019, https://www.cbc.ca/news/canada/hamilton/whales-1.5169138.

19   *Fahrenheit 9/11*, dir. by Michael Moore (2004).

called *Hillary: The Movie*, which was extremely critical of Hillary Clinton and which it intended to release during the 2008 campaign. Citizens United argued that if *Fahrenheit 9/11* did not violate the ban on close pre-election advertising, then neither would *Hillary: The Movie*. When the FEC disagreed, Citizens United sued, claiming that the FEC definition of "electioneering communications" violated its free speech rights.[20] The majority of US Supreme Court justices agreed, in one of their most controversial decisions in recent decades, one that unleashed the funding of political parties by independent (and often untraceable) moneyed interests and watered down the definition of corruption in American democratic and political life.[21]

In my reading of historical work focused on non-human animals, I am impressed by how important a role visibility has played in mobilizing mainstream initiatives to improve conditions for non-human sentient creatures. So, for instance, in her fine book on the genesis of animal protection societies in nineteenth-century England, Hilda Kean documents how the abuse of horses and donkeys in the streets of London generated public outrage and support for parliamentary responses, such as providing drinking troughs for horses. Ordinary upper- and middle-class Londoners grew tired of stepping out of their houses and seeing horses that desperately needed water and donkeys often brutally beaten by their owners whose carts they were pulling. Kean emphasizes the day-to-day neglect and violence inflicted on these animals and the important role that the high visibility of this abuse played in the founding of animal protection societies and the passing of laws to protect animals.[22]

Food companies today understand the mobilizing power of the visual. That is why they keep slaughterhouses out of sight and more recently have been pressuring states to pass "Ag Gag" laws that criminalize the recording of working conditions and animal abuse and neglect

---

20 See "Background" to *Citizens United v. FEC*: https://en.wikipedia.org/wiki/Citizens_United_v._FEC.

21 See Heather K. Gerken and Erica J. Newland, "The *Citizens United* Trilogy: The Myth, the True Tale, and the Story Still to Come," in *Election Law Stories*, ed. Joshua A. Douglas and Eugene D. Mazo (New York: Foundation Press, 2016), 359–404 (explaining how pretty much any influence peddling is permissible with only *quid pro quo* cash for votes counting as corruption).

22 Hilda Kean, *Animal Rights: Political and Social Change in Britain since 1800* (London: Reaktion Books, 1998).

in feedlots, slaughterhouses, and meat-packing plants.[23] Some states have even passed laws that prohibit speaking in a "disparaging" way about powerful economic entities like the cattle industry, the famous case being the Texas cattlemen who sued Oprah Winfrey for saying she would not eat another hamburger after hearing from a guest that cattle are routinely fed other cattle.[24] In a post-Covid-19 world, it seems hard to believe that the public will accept less transparency rather than more around the conditions in which non-human food animals are kept, given the connections that we know exist between diseases that can arise in factory farm conditions, as well as wild-life markets, and jump between species, including to humans.[25]

There is no more powerful example of the potential of the documentary film to shape social and political consciousness around the question of animal rights than SeaWorld's decision in 2016 to terminate its captive breeding program for killer whales in the wake of *Blackfish*, a documentary about the death of SeaWorld trainer Dawn Brancheau in 2010.[26] In the 1990s, it would have been unthinkable for an iconic institution like SeaWorld to be forced into such a concession by those concerned about the living conditions of these animals.[27]

Tilikum, the killer whale at the centre of the *Blackfish* story, came to the United States from Sealand of the Pacific in Victoria, British Columbia, and there is extremely moving footage in the movie of whales like him being captured in the wild and then footage of their living conditions in

---

23 See Justin F. Marceau and Alan K. Chen, "Free Speech and Democracy in a Video Age," 116 *Columbia Law Review* (2016): 991–1062. These statutes have also come to Canada. See Alberta's Bill 27, *The Trespass Statutes (Protecting Law-Abiding Property Owners) Amendment Act* (providing for fines of $10,000 for individuals and $20,000 for organizations trespassing on farms) and the proposed Bill 156, *Security from Trespass and Protecting Food Safety Act* (providing for up to $15,000 fines and $25,000 for subsequent offences and making it illegal to enter a property under false pretenses to document conditions). See Jessica Scott-Reid, "New Ag gag law prevents exposing animal abuse on farms," *The Star*, 3 December 2019, https://www.the-star.com/opinion/contributors/2019/12/03/new-gag-law-prevents-exposing-animal-abuse-on-farms.html.

24 Oprah's guest on this famous show in 1996 was Howard Lyman, otherwise known as the "Mad Cowboy," was also sued under the food disparagement statute. It took six years for them to obtain their acquittal. See Howard F. Lyman, *Mad Cowboy: Plain Truth from the Cattle Rancher Who Won't Eat Meat* (New York: Simon and Shuster, 2011).

25 See Aysha Akhtar, Corona Healers Education and Solutions Summit: Day 15, "How Can We Prevent Future Pandemics," climatehealers.org.

26 *Blackfish*, dir. Gabriela Cowperthwaite (2013).

27 See, for example, Susan G. Davis, *Spectacular Nature: Corporate Culture and the Sea World Experience* (Berkeley: University of California Press, 1997).

concrete pools like those at the now defunct Victoria aquarium. Tilikum died in 2017.[28]

YouTube videos and documentaries on Netflix and other streaming services are today's equivalent of nineteenth-century street visibility when it comes to the abuse and mistreatment of non-human animals. The thoughtful and extended treatment of a topic in a documentary film has an incredible power to mobilize, change hearts and minds, and inspire the Gestalt switch often associated with eating less meat, or more humane meat, or cutting out meat altogether and moving to a plant-based diet (whether for reasons of health, the environment, violence toward non-human animals, or some combination of these). Steven Wise's legal team was smart to harness this power of the visual as a means to generate sympathy and identification with their cause. Adopting the legal personhood argument first and foremost requires people wanting to do it, and that desire must come from somewhere. An important means for fostering that desire is consciousness-raising for the purpose of altering social and cultural norms.

Wise, the Nonhuman Rights Project, *Unlocking the Cage,* and the Animal Legal Personhood Cases

Attorney and teacher of animal law Steven Wise founded the Nonhuman Rights Project in 2007. The organization describes itself as an advocacy group working to change "the common law status of great apes, elephants, dolphins, and whales from mere 'things,' which lack the capacity to possess any legal right, to 'legal persons,' who possess such fundamental rights as bodily liberty and bodily integrity."[29] Wise wrote a number of American law review articles in the mid- to late 1990s arguing that the legal view of non-human animals as property is deeply flawed.[30] He calls the distinction between property and persons rooted in Roman law

---

28 Ray Sanchez, "Killer whale at center of 'Blackfish' dies," *CNN*, 6 January 2017, http://www.cnn.com/2017/01/06/us/sea-world-orca-tilikum-dies/index.html.

29 https://www.nonhumanrights.org/who-we-are.

30 See, for example, Steven M. Wise, "How Nonhuman Animals Were Trapped in a Nonexistent Universe," 1 *Animal Law* (1995): 15–45 (exploring how Greek, Roman, and Hebrew cosmology viewed the universe as created for the benefit of human beings, what Wise termed "teleological anthropocentrism," that is, non-human animals exist for the sake of humans); see also Wise, "The Legal Thinghood of Nonhuman Animals," 23 *Boston College Environmental Affairs Law Review* (1995–96): 471–546 (exploring the idea that all law was established for humans and in that law all non-human animals were property); Wise, "Hardly a Revolution – the

the "Great Legal Wall," with every human a legal person possessing legal rights on one side and every other non-human thing with no rights on the other.[31] Wise points out that "[t]hose beings who were believed to lack free will – women, children, slaves, the insane, and nonhuman animals were all at some time classified as property, [yet] [n]onhuman animals never shed their property status, never had rights, and were never subject to duties. They were always classified as *res* and not as *personae*."[32]

In a 1999 law review article, Wise wrote that "the flexibility and responsiveness of the common law" made it the "ideal battering ram" for obtaining legal rights for non-human animals.[33] His idea was that the right judge, in the right case, at the right time, might recognize the legal personhood of non-human animals – by, say, recognizing a chimp as a legal person and granting a *habeas corpus* application – and that this would create a favourable precedent for releasing chimps on a case-by-case basis if there was a more appropriate place for them to go (such as Save the Chimps, a Florida island sanctuary for chimps, featured in *Unlocking the Cage*).[34] So in 2013 the Nonhuman Rights Project started litigating cases on behalf of chimps held in a variety of inappropriate situations in New York State. The film crew followed the legal team on their journey to locate a litigant (three prospects they found died before a petition could be brought);[35] visited the island sanctuary

---

Eligibility of Non-Human Animals for Dignity-Rights in a Liberal Democracy," 22 *Vermont Law Review* (1997–98): 793–915 (arguing that the overarching values and principles of traditional Western law demand that dignity rights be extended to all qualified to receive them, irrespective of species).

31 Steven Wise, "Animal Thing to Animal Person – Thoughts on Time, Place, and Theories," 5 *Animal Law* (1999): 61–8 at 61. See also Wise, *Rattling the Cage*, 4 ("a thick and impenetrable legal wall has separated all human from all nonhuman animals"), 270 ("the ancient Great Wall that has for so long divided humans from every other animal is biased, irrational, unfair, and unjust. It is time to knock it down").

32 Wise, "Legal Thinghood," 493.

33 Wise, "Animal Thing to Animal Person," 62. See also Wise, *Drawing the Line: Science and the Case for Animal Rights* (Cambridge, MA: Perseus Books, 2002), 26 (describing the common law as "ideal for peg-rounding," the round hole being the legal system and the square peg being recognition of legal rights for non-human animals).

34 See http://www.savethechimps.org.

35 Reba and Merlin were being kept at a roadside zoo, the Bailiwick Ranch Discovery Zoo. We do not meet Reba in the film, as she died a few days prior to Wise's visit there. There is a very sad scene in which then executive director of the Nonhuman Rights Project, Natalie Prosin, returns to find that Merlin now also died just the night before. See *Unlocking the Cage*, 28:10–30:00. The third death was Charlie, owned by the same person who owned Kiko, who was raised like a human child and trained to do karate by his owner. Kiko's case is described more below.

and other sanctuaries, talking to people who know chimps and can explain their social and emotional lives and cognitive capacities; and captured the legal proceedings and the team's reactions to the rulings, negative and positive.

Unlocking the Cage is surprisingly compelling for a movie that centres on a set of legal issues and cases. I attended the screening at Hot Docs in Toronto in May 2016 with friends and students working in legal fields, some of whom are supporters of animal rights. I expected them to be gripped by the ins and outs of the legal arguments, but it surprised me that the rest of the audience – which must have included some non-lawyers – was equally riveted. The filmmakers were not lawyers, and they were careful to explain legal concepts like *habeas corpus* and to present the legal issues in a style that was neither overly didactic nor pedantic or technical. The courtroom scenes in *Unlocking the Cage* are not flashy and dramatic. The movie features footage of actual judges listening to the Nonhuman Rights Project arguments, reacting to and asking questions about the arguments offered. The viewer sees the faces of the judges, generally a sober and serious bunch, variously registering disbelief or impatience or scepticism or sympathy. The black robes and the sterile surroundings communicate an air of formality. Yet it is perfectly evident that some of the judges are politely listening and not very open to persuasion, while others are more engaged and attentive. This element of selective judicial detachment or even incredulity or hostility is probably a hallmark of cases involving the legal personhood of animals, although in many cases judges make a visible effort to hide their lack of interest in or hostility toward what may well be a predetermined position on the central issues at stake in such cases.

The contrast between what judges really think or feel and what they believe it is appropriate to express in the field of animal law is nowhere more clearly on display than in the case of a Japanese macaque named Darwin in what has come to be known as the Ikea Monkey case. In 2012, Darwin was found at the entrance to a Toronto-area Ikea store wearing a diaper and a shearling coat. Probably, it was the coat that was largely responsible for the international attention the case received: celebrity journalists like CNN's Anderson Cooper looped and relooped the video of Darwin dressed up like a little upper-class toddler. Darwin's owner, a Toronto lawyer named Yasmin Nakhuda, had left him in her locked car while she visited the Ikea store. Darwin unlocked his crate and the car and went into the store. Animal Control Services was called, and they seized Darwin. Nakhuda went to retrieve him from their offices, where she signed a transfer of ownership, worried, she later said, about being in violation of a prohibition on keeping exotic animals within city limits and hoping that if she signed the form she would not be charged. She later regretted signing the form, claiming she had done so under duress and that she did not know it was an ownership transfer. When Animal Services sent Darwin to a sanctuary that kept other Japanese macaques, Nakhuda sued the sanctuary for his return.

The judge ruled against Nakhuda, rejecting her argument that she did not know what she was doing when she signed Darwin over, because among other things this was inconsistent with comments she had made during the extensive media coverage of the incident.[36] The reasoning in the case – that Darwin was a wild animal and ownership of him was established by the old Roman law rule of possession or capture – was weak.[37] Surely Darwin was not wild in the sense of being native to the North York parking lot or the Ikea store. He was a pet, who had the ability to unlock a car and go into the store. He was not trying to escape back into the wild, his wild, five thousand miles away, assuming he was born in Japan (he could have been, and likely was, born in captivity, which could have been anywhere given the way the legal and illegal wild animal trade operates). He certainly was not dressed like a wild animal.

One of the ways of extending the qualified property entitlement in a wild animal is to ask if they are in the habit of, or have the intention of, returning (*animus revertendi*). An animal like a trained hawk or pigeon, although out of immediate possession, is still owned by the trainer to whom it has an intention of returning.[38] The judge found it was unclear whether Darwin had such an intention and that Nakuda did not pursue him immediately enough to retain possession of him.[39] Darwin did not run off into the wilderness of North York where he would be subject to new ownership by capture. The stronger reasoning is that Nakhuda had ownership of Darwin as a domestic animal (i.e., a pet), that she

---

36 *Nakhuda v. Story Book Farm Primate Sanctuary*, 2013 ONSC 5761, paras. 34–50.

37 See ibid., paras. 16–22. The common law interpretation of a wild animal should probably not include non-indigenous animals. See Mary J. Shariff, "A Monkey in the Middle: Reflections on Darwin the Macaque and the (R)evolution of Wild Animals in Canadian Common Law," in *Canadian Perspectives on Animals and the Law*, ed. Peter Sankoff, Vaughan Black, and Katie Sykes (Toronto: Irwin Law, 2015), 83–104.

38 See William Blackstone, *Commentaries on the Laws of England* (Oxford: Clarendon Press, 1765–69), vol. 2, *The Rights of Things* (1766): 392, https://avalon.law.yale.edu/18th_century/blackstone_bk2ch25.asp

39 *Nakuda v. Storybook Farm Sanctuary*, para. 22; paras. 25–6.

transferred it by signing the form, and that as a lawyer she would be expected to understand the nature of the form she signed.[40]

The Ontario judge wrote: "[T]he monkey is not a child. Callous as it may seem, the monkey is a chattel, that is a piece of property. The court may apply only property principles when considering the issues in this case."[41] The parties agreed not to argue the case on the basis of what was in the best interests of Darwin, the test usually used for human children in custody disputes.

The judge's comment that the monkey was not a child was probably prompted by references to Nakhuda in the media as the "monkey mom" and her repeated statements that Darwin was her child and she was his mom.[42] Yet in rejecting the application and allowing Darwin to live at a sanctuary with other members of his own species rather than continuing to live with his former owner in her condo, dressed up in human clothes, with other pets of the family (e.g., dogs and exotic birds), the judge almost certainly acted in Darwin's best interests.[43] The decision then reads like a classic instance of ends-oriented reasoning, with the decision actually motivated by what would be in the best interests of Darwin: the judge was determined to get there but was unwilling to state that this was the basis for the decision.

---

40 The judgment inconsistently holds that Nakhuda lost ownership of the monkey when she lost possession of him (when, as the court saw it, Darwin ran away into the wild) and that Nakhuda transferred ownership when she signed the Toronto Animal Services Form. See ibid., para. 53. Is it difficult to see how Nakhuda could have transferred ownership she lost if she lost it when Darwin escaped from the car. The decision was not appealed. Nakhuda was ordered to pay $83,000 in costs to the sanctuary, so appealing would have been an extremely expensive proposition. She subsequently moved to a part of the province where it is not illegal to keep these monkeys and obtained two other Japanese macaques. See "Ikea monkey Darwin's former owner has 2 new monkies," *CBC*, 20 January 2015, http://www.cbc.ca/news/canada/toronto/ikea-monkey-darwin-s-former-owner-has-2-new-monkeys-1.2920000.

41 *Nakhuda v. Story Book Farm Sanctuary*, para. 4.

42 The judge refers to an online chat Nakhuda held through the *Toronto Sun* newspaper on 19 December 2012 in which, in response to the question whether her efforts might be better spent on a needy child, she wrote that Darwin is her "needy 'child' [...] he needs his mother."

43 There is controversy that it was in Darwin's best interests, as many comments on the Internet indicate, essentially saying it would be great to be the monkey-child of this lady, who would buy you such nice clothes. I would think though that deference should be given to what a primatologist would say looking at the situation as best as one can from the non-human animal's perspective and choosing for them the life closest to what the non-human animal would have in its natural environment or habitat of origin.

"Are all legal decisions like this?," non-legal members of an animal Working Group I belong to asked when we read the case together. It seemed obvious to them that the judge was motivated to make the findings on both the wild animal question and the validity of the ownership transfer based on doing what was best for Darwin. The ends-oriented aspect of judicial decisions such as the one in the Ikea monkey decision – implicitly at least rejecting the best interests argument yet appearing actually to be motivated by it – is difficult to explain to some non-lawyers, many of whom expect to encounter in a legal decision a purity of thought detached from strategy and consequences. Yet legal reasoning, for better or worse, is often a much more mixed affair. This judge at any rate was not prepared to blast through the "Great Legal Wall" between property and persons and adopt a best interests of the animal legal test, which might implicitly at least equate human and non-human animals by acknowledging that the test for human children is the same test that should be used for higher-order non-human animals like Darwin. Yet she probably wanted to do the right thing for Darwin.

Unlocking the Cage depicts the stop and start, twist here, turn there, nature of legal reasoning in the Nonhuman Rights Project litigation decisions. It also depicts the centrality of the crucial role played by individual judges in cases related to the legal personhood of animals as they are tried under the common law. Wise wrote at the end of *Rattling the Cage* (2000):

> The decision to extend common law personhood to chimpanzees and bonobos will arise from a great common law case. Great common law cases are produced when great common law judges radically restructure existing precedent in ways that reaffirm bedrock principles and policies. All the tools for deciding such a case exist. They await a great common law judge, a Mansfield, a Cardozo, a Holmes to take them up.[44]

This search for "a great common law judge" willing to grant a limited form of legal personhood on chimpanzees is what the Nonhuman Rights Project went looking for in the litigation followed and captured by the documentary filmmakers.

We see in the film how Justice Barbara Jaffe almost became that judge, first by ruling that a *habeas corpus* hearing would be given to two chimps, Hercules and Leo, and second by giving the Nonhuman

---

44 Wise, *Rattling the Cage*, 270.

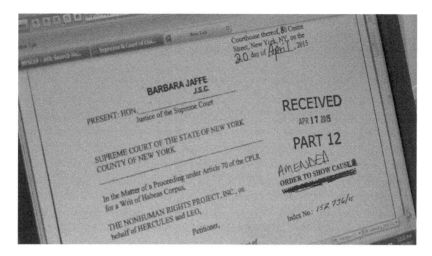

Figure 7.1. Justice Jaffe's Order from *Unlocking the Cage*

Rights Project a serious and evidently sympathetic hearing, excerpts of which are shown in the film.[45] These two young chimps were being held at the State University of New York (SUNY) at Stony Brook, leased from a Louisiana chimp research company, New Iberia Chimps, where they were used for locomotion research in the department of anatomy. The Nonhuman Rights Project initially claimed that granting the hearing was itself a recognition of the legal personhood of Hercules and Leo. However, the judge amended the order the next day, striking out the words "& WRIT OF HABEAS CORPUS" (see Figure 7.1). The drama surrounding the judge's correction of what she took to be a misunderstanding of her order is dramatically depicted in the film, complete with telephone conversations, back and forth with the court clerk, emails, press releases, and an image of the document with the words struck out.[46]

Ultimately Justice Jaffe felt constrained to reject the application based on the appellate court ruling in an earlier Nonhuman Rights

---

45 For the full transcript of the Hercules and Leo hearing, see http://www.nonhumanrightsproject.org/wp-content/uploads/2015/06/Transcript-of-5.27.15-Hearing-Hercules-and-Leo.pdf.

46 *Unlocking the Cage*, private video on Vimeo, 1:15:30. A PDF of the amended document is available at https://www.nonhumanrights.org/content/uploads/Order-to-Show-Cause-Amended-4-21-15.pdf. Image here provided by Films We Like and reproduced with the permission of Pennebaker and Hegedus Films.

Project case, *Lavery*.[47] Patrick C. Lavery was the owner of Tommy, then a twenty-six-year-old chimpanzee living in Gloversville, New York, a former film actor being kept in a dark room in a warehouse on a used trailer lot with only a television set for company.[48] In that case, the judges held that it would be inappropriate to extend rights to a non-human animal who was not capable of executing correlative or corresponding duties.[49] As Wise expresses it in the film, it is a "philosophically conservative way of saying because animals cannot enter into contracts, essentially you can make them slaves for their whole lives."[50] Wise finds the duty-based notion of personhood particularly problematic for chimps, given the explicit analogy between chimps and young children, who are not treated by the law as duty bearers although they are rights bearers. They are not rights bearers in all respects. So, for instance, they cannot make contracts. They also do not have a right to vote. But they are, as Wise puts it, "not to be reduced to legal things, enslaved, or vivisected."[51]

The other adverse precedent by the time the Hercules and Leo application was heard was the case of Kiko. Kiko was also twenty-six years old at the time of filing, and like Tommy was a survivor of the entertainment industry.[52] The *habeas corpus* application was rejected in Kiko's case because he was not going to be completely liberated by being moved to Save the Chimps.[53] Wise argued that *habeas corpus* has been

---

47 *People ex rel. Nonhuman Rights Project, Inc. v. Lavery* 2014 NY Slip Op 08531 [124 AD3d 148] (Appellate Division, Third Department), 4 December 2014 (hereafter *Lavery*, Third Department), http://www.nycourts.gov/reporter/3dseries/2014/2014_08531.htm.

48 Tommy had a role playing one of the laboratory mates to the star chimp Virgil in the film with the human star Matthew Broderick, *Project X*, directed by Jonathan Kaplan (1987).

49 See *Lavery*, Third Department, 3 ("the ascription of rights has historically been connected with the imposition of societal obligations and duties. Reciprocity between rights and responsibilities stems from principles of social contract, which inspired the ideals of freedom and democracy at the core of our system of government ... legal personhood has consistently been defined in terms of both rights *and duties* ... chimpanzees cannot bear any legal duties, submit to societal responsibilities or be held legally accountable for their actions").

50 *Unlocking the Cage*, 1:06:58–1:07:05.

51 Wise, *Rattling the Cage*, 256–7.

52 Kiko starred in the movie *Tarzan in Manhattan*, directed by Michael Schultz (1989). His owner explains in the film that he bit someone, was hit, and as a result lost about 90 per cent of his hearing.

53 *In the Matter of the Nonhuman Rights Project, Inc., on behalf of Kiko, Petitioner-Appellant v. Carmen Presti, individually and an officer and director of the Primate Sanctuary, Inc.,*

used to move someone into a different (and better) form of protective custody (e.g., cases involving enslaved children, apprentices, and those today with mental disorders). The standard is not complete liberation. Given how much better the island sanctuary would have been for Kiko, insistence on the standard of complete liberation seemed like a convenient reason to reject the application.

As Wise puts it in the film, the judges in the Kiko and Tommy cases

> were either consciously or unconsciously thinking, "if they're not human they're not going to have rights," and so what they've done is they try and find some other reason for us to lose. That's a frightening thing for an advocate to feel – that you're up against someone who either consciously or unconsciously believes that there is nothing I can tell them that's ever going to cause them to rule in my favour.[54]

It is also an indictment of the idea that judges hear cases with a fair and open mind and render decisions that track their actual reasons for judgment. The evidence from both these animal personhood cases suggests that in legal cases involving non-human animals as litigants, something else is afoot – most likely speciesism.

I would be remiss here not to mention the other famous legal case involving a Japanese macaque, this one named Naruto, who took a flattering and captivating selfie and became known to the world as the selfie monkey. The photograph became the subject of protracted dispute between the man who owned the camera with which the photograph was taken, David Slater, and Wikipedia, which claimed that the now-famous photograph was in the public domain, as it had not been taken by a human animal. A lawsuit brought by People for the Ethical Treatment of Animals against Slater for copyright violations of the photograph they say was taken by and therefore owned by Naruto was dismissed by a San Francisco judge in 2016.[55] That dismissal was upheld in 2018.[56]

Christie E. Presti, individually and as an officer and director of the Primate Sanctuary, Inc. and the Primate Sanctuary, Inc., Respondents-Respondents 1300 CA 14-00357 (Appellate Division, Fourth Judicial Department) (January 2, 2015), http://www.nycourts.gov/courts/ad4/Clerk/Decisions/2015/01-02-15/PDF/1300.pdf.

54 *Unlocking the Cage*, 1:09:44–1:10:08.

55 See *Naruto v. Slater*, 2016 WL 362231 (United States District Court, N.D. California).

56 See *Naruto v. Slater*, No. 16-15469 D.C. No. 3:15-cv-04324-WHO (Appeal from the United States District Court, N.D. California), 23 April 2018), https://cdn.ca9.us-courts.gov/datastore/opinions/2018/04/23/16-15469.pdf.

Since the film was released, the 8 June 2017 decision by the First Department has affirmed the decisions respecting Tommy and Kiko. On
the point about complete liberation raised in Kiko's case, this court said
that merely transferring the animal to a different facility made it an inappropriate situation in which to grant *habeas* relief.[57] It also affirmed the
point about duty raised in Tommy's case *Lavery* from the Third Department, stating that chimpanzees cannot be held legally accountable for
their actions.[58] Infants or the comatose would be in the same situation,
but they have legal rights because they "are still human beings, members
of the human community."[59] Historical evidence of animal trials where
non-human animals (e.g., pigs) were tried, convicted, and punished as if
they were humans and could be held criminally responsible was rejected
as support for the claim that those animals could be duty bearers.[60] The
idea that chimps could be persons from the perspective of bringing a
habeas corpus claim was firmly rejected.[61] So too was the idea that because
habeas corpus is "the Great Writ" it could be brought again and again.
This court, at any rate, was looking for new evidence and changed circumstances in Tommy and Kiko's case.[62] Legal personhood for a river
in New Zealand and Indian sacred entities were singled out as "not relevant to the definition of 'person'" in the United States or New York.[63]

Criticisms

This part of the chapter canvases three problems with Wise's approach.
There are others.[64] However, I focus on the three that were brought out

---

57 *Lavery* and Kiko, 7.
58 Ibid., 5.
59 Ibid., 6.
60 Ibid., 5 ("[N]one of the cases cited [of animals being tried for offences such as
    attacking human beings and eating crops] took place in modern times or in New
    York").
61 Ibid., 4 ("This position is without legal support or legal precedent").
62 Ibid., 3–4.
63 Ibid., 6.
64 So, for instance, Maneesha Deckha has criticized focus on the concept of person-
    hood as anthropocentric, a point she explores in "Beingness: A New Legal Sub-
    jectivity for Animals," in *Animals as Legal Beings: Gender, Culture, Race, Species, and
    a Post-Anthropocentric Legal Order* (under review). Jesse Donahue has pointed out
    that moving animals to sanctuaries is not a panacea when there are good and bad
    sanctuaries just as there are good and bad (or worse) zoos; also, there are pros and
    cons to sanctuaries. See Jesse Donahue, "Introduction: The Legal Landscape and
    Possibilities for Change," and Ron Kagan, "Sanctuaries: Zoos of the Future?," in
    Increasing Legal Rights for Zoo Animals: Justice on the Ark, ed. Jesse Donahue (Lan-
    ham: Lexington Books, 2017), xiii–xxv and 131–45.

by my own experience watching *Unlocking the Cage* and reflecting on it in light of my subsequent reading of Wise's work.

First, animal rights activists want to know why Wise is not seeking to protect *all* non-human animals, when in their view sentience or the ability to feel pain, as this was articulated by Peter Singer in the 1970s, is the relevant criterion for legal protection.[65] Using cognitive capacity and the similarity of non-human animals to humans reinforces the idea at the heart of speciesism that humans are superior to all other animals and that legal rights are only for them and those who are most like them.

Second, those who challenge the existence of animal rights (or the wisdom of recognizing them) often express outrage at the comparisons that are drawn between the current situation of non-human animals and that of groups who have been historically discriminated against, who at different times have been thought of as lacking full legal personhood – for example, married women and slaves, and today children and those with mental deficiencies, and, perhaps most controversially, Jews killed in the Holocaust.

Third, other critics allege that the personhood approach involves a misunderstanding of law, namely, that it is there to further convenient human interests and uses rather than to facilitate justice and provide blocks against inhumane and unacceptable treatment. We live in the era of human rights. This collection is about hostility to human rights. Wise sees animal rights as an extension of the logic of human rights. Those who police the species boundary want to keep and preserve rights on the other side of the human–non-human divide.

Each of the three critical reactions to Wise's work brings out the tensions or compromises involved in the legal personhood approach to animal rights. Together they serve to illustrate just how difficult it is to move from an unjust world in which non-human animals are violently pressed into service to satisfy the needs and desires of one species toward a more just world shared more equally between sentient creatures.

The legal approach to non-human animals has always been to treat them as property even when they are obviously not like inanimate property. Wise's project pushes us to try a thought experiment. What would reversing this legal presumption look like? What if we treated non-human animals as persons even when they were obviously not exactly like human persons? We would be making some of

---

65 Peter Singer, *Animal Liberation: A New Ethics for our Treatment of Animals* (New York: Random House, 1975).

the compromises this chapter canvasses. However, we would also be committing far fewer injustices against those animals and perhaps in the long run (if there is a long run) against the planet. Rather than seeing compromise as inconsistency resulting in self-defeat, we would accept that purity is impossible and refuse to accept this as an excuse for non-action.

Why Not Pigs (or Other Non-Human Animals)?

At the Toronto screening of *Unlocking the Cage* I attended, two audience members asked the filmmakers a question that comes up often in discussions of non-human animal personhood: why the exclusive focus on higher-intelligence animals – for the Nonhuman Rights Project, chimps and now elephants?[66] Is it not problematic to recognize limited legal rights for only these animals, the ones that are most like us, the "brainier" species?[67] Moreover, even within this limitation, why are primates, elephants, and orcas accorded special status over other intelligent non-human animals such as pigs?

One questioner at my screening, Anita Krajnc, founder of Toronto Pig Save, had been arrested in the summer of 2015 and charged with mischief (interference with private property) for giving water to pigs in distress on a particularly hot day as they were being transported to a slaughterhouse near Burlington, Ontario. She was acquitted in May 2017.[68]

Krajnc wanted to know: If chimps should be given some of the rights of personhood, then why not pigs? And indeed, one expert witness at her trial testified that pigs were persons in terms of their emotional and

---

66 The elephant clients are Beulah, Karen, and Minnie, who are owned by the Commerford Zoo in Goshen, Connecticut. Visit https://www.nonhumanrights.org/clients-beulah-karen-minnie. Happy, an elephant at the Brooklyn Zoo, is the most recent client.

67 Wise, "*Rattling the Cage* Defended," 649 (quoting review of *Rattling the Cage* by Robert M. Verchick, "A New Species of Rights," 89 *California Law Review* (2001): 207–29 at 220).

68 See Samantha Craggs, "'Pig Trial': Anita Krajnc found not guilty of mischief charge for giving water to pigs," *CBC News*, 3 May 2017, http://www.cbc.ca/news/canada/hamilton/pig-trial-verdict-1.4098046. For an analysis of the case, see Maneesha Deckha, "The 'Pig Trial' Decision: The Save Movement, Legal Mischief, and the Legal Invisibilization of Farmed Animal Suffering," 50 *Ottawa Law Review* (2019): 65–98. On the Save Movement more generally, see Maneesha Deckha, "The Save Movement and Farmed Animal Suffering: The Advocacy Benefits of Bearing Witness as a Template for Law," 5:1 *Canadian Journal of Contemporary and Comparative Law* (2019): 78-110.

psychological functioning.[69] The problem with pigs is that many people love to eat them, and the agricultural industry has an enormous interest in maintaining their property status. The sheer number of agricultural or farmed animals like pigs killed is staggering: nearly ten billion farm animals a year in the United States.[70] *Every Twelve Seconds* documents the slaughter of 2,500 cattle a day at one slaughterhouse in the United States, all the while hiding from ordinary view what that involves in (gruesome) practical terms.[71]

Wise first wrote about the treatment of farm animals in the 1980s.[72] Since that time, health awareness has led some people to reduce the amount of meat they eat. The ultimate issue for many vegetarians and vegans is violence: for ethical reasons, they do not support violence against animals, nor do they literally want to ingest it. Overt violence is part of the fear animals experience when they are being slaughtered, see it happening to others, and hear their cries or smell their blood.[73] Horrific practices encountered in the food industry include the sorting of male from female chicks (kept for meat and egg production), with the male chicks thrown out while still alive in garbage bags, where they are left to suffocate (footage of which appears in the documentary *Food, Inc.*), or are later ground up alive (both practices can be seen in the twelve-minute documentary *Farm to Fridge*).[74] There is also indirect

---

69   The judge took exception to this expert testimony. See *R. v. Krajnc*, Court File no.: Halton 15–2464, Ontario Court of Justice, 4 May 2017 (D.A. Harris J.), paras. 29–36. The legal personhood argument was not however expressly argued by the defendants' lawyers (contrary to the statement in para. 28).

70   Wise, "*Rattling the Cage* Defended," 667 (citing a summary on livestock slaughter from the USDA in 2000).

71   Timothy Pachirat, *Every Twelve Seconds: Industrialized Slaughter and the Politics of Sight* (New Haven: Yale University Press, 2011).

72   Steven M. Wise, "Of Farm Animals and Justice," 3 *Pace Environmental Law Review* (1985–86): 191–227.

73   Hence the need for what has been termed "humane slaughter," a system for slaughtering large factory-farmed animals such as cows and sheep made famous by Dr. Temple Grandin. See *The Ghosts in Our Machine*, directed by Liz Marshall (2015), for footage of Grandin's system and of animals being fed through a machine up "the Stairway to Heaven" and electrocuted quietly in the head, which stuns them before their throats are cut. See also Erika Ritter, *The Dog by the Cradle, the Serpent Beneath: Some Paradoxes of Human–Animal Relationships* (Toronto: Key Porter Books, 2009), 16–21, 25–31, 52–5, describing her interview with Grandin and an exploration of the paradox of "killing with kindness." Research on the stress inflicted on animals when they must watch others being slaughtered describes this as "witnessing the slaughter of conspecifics." See Charlotte Montgomery, *Blood Relations: Animals, Humans, and Politics* (Toronto: Between the Lines), 137–8.

74   *Food, Inc.*, dir. Robert Kenner (2008); *Farm to Fridge*, made by Mercy for Animals (2011), https://www.youtube.com/watch?v=THIODWTqx5E This video is very graphic.

violence in terms of keeping chickens in dark pens where they cannot scratch the ground or engage in natural behaviours and as a consequence engage in self-mutilating pecking or exhibit aggression (including cannibalism) toward other chickens, causing ethicists to seriously ask whether it would in fact be more humane to raise blind chickens, who would engage less in these behaviours.[75] Another current practice, debeaking, causes pain and exists on a continuum of other painful procedures performed on factory-farmed animals such as branding, cow castration, and the removing of tails from pigs and cows without anaesthetic, grisly footage of which can be seen in *Farm to Fridge*. Selective breeding has resulted in birds (chickens and turkeys) that are too big (designed to be meat-heavy) to stand or move more than a few steps. Some of these chickens can be seen in *Food, Inc.*

The arc of the challenge Krajnc put to the filmmakers illustrates the supposed slippery slope argument that invariably arises in all discussions of animal rights. First, the chimps, then the pigs, then the chickens, until eventually you end up unable even to kill a mosquito in good conscience. It turns out that fish feel pain.[76] Perhaps we will discover that plants have something analogous to sentient feeling or consciousness.[77] All of us must navigate the moral and ethical imperatives arising from such developing awareness. Practically speaking, there are differences in degree and quality between the choices we expect to be able to make as individual consumers and those we can expect the law to make. A common first choice is to protect the "brainier" species.

Most of Wise's writing since the mid-1990s has focused on higher-intelligence animals such as chimpanzees, and the personhood argument he articulates is intimately tied to the recognition that a "practical" autonomy is enough to engage blocks against rights violations (such a bodily interference).[78] What Wise calls "full Kantian autonomy,"

---

75 See Peter Sandøe, Paul M. Hocking, Bjorn Förkman, Kristy Haldane, Helle H. Kristensen, and Clare Palmer, "The Blind Hens' Challenge: Does It Undermine the View That Only Welfare Matters in Our Dealings with Animals," *Environmental Values* 23 (2014): 727–42 (explaining problems with feather-pecking and cannibalism).

76 See Victoria Braithwaite, *Do Fish Feel Pain?* (Oxford: Oxford University Press, 2010); Jonathan Balcombe, *What a Fish Knows: The Inner Lives of Our Underwater Cousins* (New York: Scientific American / Farrar, Straus and Groux, 2016).

77 Michael Pollan, "The Intelligent Plant," *The New Yorker*, 23 and 30 December 2013, http://www.newyorker.com/magazine/2013/12/23/the-intelligent-plant.

78 See Wise, "*Rattling the Cage* Defended," 655 (he called this "realistic autonomy" in *Rattling the Cage*).

which many human beings such as young children, the mentally handicapped, and those in persistent vegetative states do not possess, is not required in order to establish that there is a dignity right (in addition to negative liberties of bodily non-interference).[79] The point is not to say that those human individuals do not deserve a dignity right or that it should be taken away from them; rather, it is to see that we use a legal fiction to protect them and that we should think about whether there are other groups that ought to be protected in the same way by extending legal personhood to them.

As Wise's farm piece from the mid-1980s shows, he does not fear the slippery slope or think it would be problematic to move beyond the higher-thinking animals used for entertainment and research to the higher-thinking animals commonly eaten by humans, such as pigs and other factory-farmed animals. Wise is quite upfront in the movie that he takes the pragmatic view – you have to start somewhere.[80] The higher-intelligence animals used for entertainment and research are the easiest place to start, because there are so many fewer of them and they engage much less significant corporate economic interests. The SeaWorld and Ringling Brothers examples demonstrate what Rob Laidlaw of Zoocheck Canada predicted in the late 1990s, namely, that circuses and other venues for performing animals would soon be pushed out by protests and by competition from exciting non-animal shows.[81]

Critics think that the failure to provide guidelines as to a stopping point will be there in the minds of judges, even if they do not say it.[82] They are probably right about that. However, the difficulty of the line-drawing exercise is not an excuse not to engage in it to the best of our abilities if we think it is appropriate to do so. And indeed, Wise does just this in a subsequent book, *Drawing the Line: Science and the Case for Animal Rights* (2002), assigning an "autonomy value" to each of a variety of species.[83]

The animals Wise examines in *Drawing the Line* are the gorilla, orangutan, dolphin, elephant, African Grey parrot, dogs, and honeybees. Of these, dogs and honeybees do not make the basic liberty cut. In other

---

79 See Wise, "Hardly a Revolution," 870–5.
80 See, for example, *Unlocking the Cage*, 10:34.
81 See Montgomery, *Blood Relations*, 204. Laidlaw predicted it would be ten years. It is taking more like twenty.
82 See Wise, "*Rattling the Cage* Defended," 640–1 (providing examples of those who make that criticism).
83 See Wise, *Drawing the Line*, 35–8 (explaining how the category and point ranking system works).

words, the mosquito and the ant do not make it in.[84] Wise has then, in a meaningful way, helped to push the debate past the slippery slope argument on which it so often sticks even if such ranking systems (in terms of both design and outcome) are sure to be controversial and create discomfort. Even those who think that making such distinctions between species is fundamentally misguided might be prepared to do so for the short term. Hence, here we have the first compromise.

Controversial Comparisons

The argument that legal personhood should be extended to non-human animals – and that we will recognize it was wrong for the law to treat them as property, just as we now recognize that it was wrong to treat married women or slaves or children as property – is a powerful one. Wise wants to detach dignity from a select species (human beings) and reassign it to non-human animals on the basis of capacities (to include some of the higher-intelligence non-human animals). He thinks this is the right argument because dignity, especially since the end of the Second World War, has become the primary feature of Western political culture and has so pervaded Western law that it can be said that "it is because humans have dignity that they have human rights."[85] If some non-human animals have the same kind of dignity, then they should have something like a human right, a non-human right that would involve at least certain minimal guarantees in terms of liberty, equality, and fair treatment.[86]

The analogy between the way we treat non-human animals and how human societies have long treated slaves is central to Wise's work and has been there from the earliest days. So, for instance, the farm animal piece in the mid-1980s quoted from the influential work of Winthrop Jordan, *White over Black: American Attitudes towards the Negro* (1969), on "the strangeness and seeming savagery of the Africans," which led to "the sense of *difference* which provided the mental margin absolutely

---

84 Hercules and Leo Hearing Transcript, 53 (addressing the slippery slope argument: "If you do this then it's going to do this, and then all of a sudden ants are going to be having writs of *habeas corpus*, but that's not it. We have made it really clear that the line that we're drawing is based upon ... autonomy").

85 Wise, "Hardly a Revolution," 869.

86 Ibid., 907 ("The legal thinghood of qualified nonhuman animals subverts the core idea of traditional Western law that fairness, equality, liberty, and reasoned judicial decision-making are hierarchically superior values. It calls their very legitimacy into question for human being. In this sense, the rights of qualified nonhuman animals are human rights").

prerequisite for placing the European on the deck of the slave ship and the Negro in the hold."[87] It also quoted from a source on animal law that "the legal position of animals is not unlike that of human slaves at the beginning of the nineteenth century in the United States."[88] And it noted that the word "dominion" is used to describe human dominance over the non-human animal as well as that of the master over the slave.[89]

The *habeas corpus* litigation strategy used in the New York cases documented in *Unlocking the Cage* comes from the use of that writ in the famous Lord Mansfield decision *Somerset v. Stewart* (1772) to free an enslaved "negro," James Somerset, a case about which Wise wrote yet another book in 2005.[90] Given the issues that animal rights advocates had overcoming standing barriers in terms of non-human animals suing in their own name, the *habeas corpus* route used to free the slave in *Somerset* recommended itself because any person has the power to seek a writ of *habeas corpus* if she believes that another is being held unlawfully.[91] And the command to produce the body (or show cause as to why the body is imprisoned) may be brought again and again. As Wise put it at the Hercules and Leo hearing, "you can indeed keep filing writs of habeas corpus again and again and again and again." Why? "Because of the fact that we are dealing with the most important writ involving the most important characteristic of a person, the fact that they are imprisoned." "It's not called the Great Writ, capital G capital W, for nothing."[92]

Wise has often compared the situation of non-human animals to that of slaves in Greek and Roman societies. For example, he quotes the following observation about the unthinking use of slaves: "No one ever gave a thought to slaves ... Everywhere the way of life depended on them. One cannot say they were accepted as such, for there was no acceptance. Everyone used them; no one paid attention to them."[93]

---

87 Wise, "Farm Animals and Justice," 197. Also quoted in *Drawing the Line*, 15.

88 Ibid., 198.

89 Ibid., 208n60.

90 Steven M. Wise, *Though the Heavens May Fall: The Landmark Trial That Led to the End of Human Slavery* (Boston: De Capo Press, 2005). For an exploration of the influence of this case on Wise's work, see Angela Fernandez, "Legal History and Rights for Nonhuman Animals: An Interview with Steven M. Wise," 41.1 *Dalhousie Law Journal* (Spring 2019): 197–218 at 198–9.

91 See Wise, "Hardly a Revolution," 813. See also 815, 820, 865, 894–5. See also Wise, *Rattling the Cage*, 49–50 (summarizing the *Somerset* case), and 52–3 (about the Kama dolphin case from 1991).

92 Quotes taken from Hercules and Leo Hearing Transcript, 14–15.

93 Wise, "Legal Thinghood," 489. Also quoted in Wise, *Rattling the Cage*, 31; *Drawing the Line*, 14.

This is a powerful point, given the high level of unconscious use of non-human animals – eating them without thinking about what animal the meat came from and how it was turned into meat, or not thinking about how leather or fur used for trim on winter jackets was once attached to an animal.[94] There is a negative and a positive message in the point. The negative message is that meat-eaters will look like the slave owners of yore to future generations, participating in something they ought to know is morally problematic; convenience and self-interest dissuaded them from doing anything about it individually or collectively. The positive is the end part of the quote, which Wise sometimes provides: "To think about it [slavery] was to condemn it."[95]

"A broad 'animals are property' rule," Wise writes, "is as anachronistic as human slavery. It can be overturned."[96] Similarly, Wise argues that "just as the domestication of nonhuman animals may have served as the model for the enslavement of human beings, so can the destruction of human slavery model for the destruction of the legal thinghood of nonhuman animals."[97] He discusses infamous slavery cases like *Dred Scott* (1857) and *Plessy v. Ferguson* (1896), cases that form part of an anti-canon of American constitutional law cases, the inference being, who wants to be today's Chief Justice Taney of *Dred Scott*, denying constitutional rights for African Americans?[98]

In *Unlocking the Cage*, Wise is firmly told by one panel of judges, in effect, "Do not go there – don't talk to us about human slavery and seeing non-human animals as being like formerly enslaved African Americans." This moment happens in oral argument before an intermediate Court of Appeal in Tommy's case, *Lavery*. Presiding Justice Karen K. Peters tells Wise: "I have to tell you. I keep having a difficult time with your using slavery as an analogy to this situation. I just

---

94 See criticism by Animal Justice Canada of the ubiquitous Canada Goose winter coat with fur trim, which was claimed to be humane, though it was obtained using inhumane leg-hold traps on coyotes. Visit https://www.youtube.com/watch?v=1Tgd58900jA.

95 Dr. Jane Goodall and Steven M. Wise, "Are Chimpanzees Entitled to Fundamental Legal Rights," 3 *Animal Law* (1997): 61-73, 70; Wise, "Hardly a Revolution," 914; Wise, *Drawing the Line*, 15. The quotation is from Edith Hamilton, *The Echo of Greece* (New York: W.W. Norton, 1957), 23–4.

96 Wise, "Animal Thing to Animal Person," 62.

97 Wise, "Hardly a Revolution," 906.

98 See, for example, Wise, "Hardly a Revolution," 907. See also Wise, *Rattling the Cage*, 50–1 (discussing *Dred Scott*).

Figure 7.2. Justice Peters from *Unlocking the Cage*

have to tell you."[99] And when Wise persists, she tells him, "My sug-
gestion is you move in a different direction" (see Figure 7.2).[100]

Justice Peters does not say more, and one is left to assume that she
is objecting to Wise drawing a comparison between not just any human and any non-human animal but between African Americans and
chimpanzees in particular. This is probably due to the persistence of a
stereotype associating those of African descent with the jungle and the
apes who live there, which along with other stereotypes about African
Americans continues to have pernicious racist material effects.

White Europeans and those descended from them have long thought
of Africans and other racialized non-Europeans as being closer to
non-human animals such as apes due to their supposedly more primitive stage of development. This prejudice, common among late nineteenth and early twentieth-century anthropologists and other scientists,
was especially evident at the human zoos that were organized at huge
events such as the Paris world fairs of 1878 and 1889.[101] Those zoos were

---

99 *Unlocking the Cage*, 1:01:25–35.
100 Ibid., 1:01:46. Image here provided by Films We Like and reproduced with the per-
    mission of Pennebaker and Hegedus Films.
101 The *Exposition Universelle* held in Paris in 1878 displayed a Negro village, and the one
    in 1889 put four hundred indigenous people on display. See Irus Braverman, *Zool-
    and: The Institution of Captivity* (Stanford, Calif.: Stanford University Press, 2013), 73.

massive affairs, designed to demonstrate to the public what had been held as a foregone conclusion among the white scientists who designed the exhibits and recruited the "specimens" – that the white man was on the top rung of human development and superior to darker-skinned and more primitive people. The pygmy especially was singled out as "the missing link" between apes and larger, lighter-skinned human animals.[102]

In the United States, a Congolese man named Ota Benga, a pygmy refugee from just such an exhibit at the Louisiana Purchase Exposition held in Saint Louis, Missouri, in 1904, ended up on display in the monkey house of the Bronx Zoo in 1906, where he was encouraged to perform as if he were one of the apes and was routinely taunted and jeered at by zoo visitors. A famous photograph of Benga shows him posing with a chimpanzee (Figure 7.3).[103] Benga committed suicide in 1916, and in reporting the news of the suicide the *Zoological Society Bulletin* callously characterized his life and death as the story of "a savage who vainly tried to leap from savagery to civilization over the intermediate stage of barbarism."[104]

These pseudo-scientific ideas about stages of civilization and racial hierarchies were popularized by world fairs and zoos attended by millions of visitors, who were entertained by the human exhibits and "educated," directly and indirectly, as to the superiority of those of European decent, the world's colonizers. A widespread popular belief associating Africans with primitivism persisted in such things as 1950s pop culture references to African American music as "jungle music." There was also the 1990s term "jungle fever" to describe interracial dating between black men and white women, which Spike Lee used to explore the "colorism" of Black men preferring lighter-skinned black women.[105] White art photographer Jean-Paul Goude used the term for the title of a collection of photographs published in 1982, mostly taken

---

102 See *The Human Zoo: Science's Dirty Secret*, dir. Srik Narayanan (2009), at https://www.youtube.com/watch?v=7Abi8MEz7zU&feature=youtu.be.

103 Ota Benga [photograph], ca. 1915, Bain News Service, in US Library of Congress, https://www.loc.gov/item/2014702691/

104 "Suicide of Ota Benga the African Pygmy," *Zoological Society Bulletin* 19, no. 3 (May 1916), 1356. The literature on Ota Benga includes Phillips Verner Bradford and Harvey Blume, *Ota: The Pygmy in the Zoo* (New York: St. Martin's Press, 1992) (co-written by the grandson of the man who brought Ota Benga to America, Samuel Verner); and Pamela Newkirk, *Spectacle: The Astonishing Life of Ota Benga* (New York, NY: Amistad, 2015).

105 *Jungle Fever*, dir. Spike Lee (1991).

Figure 7.3. Otto Benga with unidentified chimpanzee

in the 1970s, which featured on its cover a provocative photograph of model Grace Jones naked and snarling in a cage.[106]

Marjorie Spiegal has called the striking historical parallels between human and animal slavery "the dreaded comparison."[107] Why is it dreaded? Because people will have the reaction that the judge in *Lavery* did, namely, think it is a bad idea to compare chimpanzees to human slaves, who also came from Africa. Yet it is *because* the parallels between human and non-human animal slavery are so dreadful that they should

106 Jean-Paul Goude, *Jungle Fever* (London: Quartet Books, 1982). Goude denied permission to reproduce the image here because it is controversial and cannot, in his opinion, be understood when taken out of the context of the disco clubs of the 1970s. Email to the author from Virginie Laguens, 27 July 2019). The image may be seen at: https://www.amazon.com/Jungle-Fever-Jean-Paul-Goude/dp/0937950017.
107 Marjorie Spiegel, *The Dreaded Comparison: Human and Animal Slavery* (New York: Mirror Books, 1996).

not be passed over in silence. The point is not to say that slaves were non-human animals but rather that non-human animals are now being treated the way human slaves were in the past. Like non-human animals today, it was the legal powerlessness of human slaves that made them ripe for economic exploitation and abuse. It is a chilling moment in *Unlocking the Cage* to hear the presiding judge, literally the voice of the law in those proceedings, declare that this obvious, evident, and powerful comparison is not something that should be spoken about.[108]

Some women too, might be expected to balk at being compared to non-human animals. Yet those writing about the connections between misogyny and the treatment of non-human animals also insist on pointing out the parallels that (sadly) so evidently exist, not just historically but in our present-day culture.[109] There is the (in)famous case of Sara Baartman, known as "the Hottentot Venus," whose genitalia, along with a cast of her body, were put on display in England and Paris in the early nineteenth century, and exhibited at the Museum of Man in Paris until 1982. Like the story of Ota Benga, this has become a notorious example of racist European science.[110]

The purported closeness of women – especially women of colour – to non-human animals would give some people reason to pause over restating that particular comparison.[111] Making that comparison risks reinforcing it – what Martha Minnow called "the dilemma of difference." Yet by not naming the difference (or in this case, the historically similar treatment), one risks not attending to that difference (or historical comparison that can shed light on the present).[112]

---

108   Wise deals with the tension/disapproval regarding the comparison at two other moments in the film. See *Unlocking the Cage*, 51:20–33 (a sceptical African American talk show host interviewing Wise); and 1:02:47-1:03:09 (a media scrum in which Wise is asked after Tommy's hearing if he compared Tommy's condition to slavery).

109   See, for example, Carol J. Adams, *The Sexual Politics of Meat: A Feminist-Vegetarian Critical Theory* (New York: Continuum, [1990]2010).

110   See Z.S. Strother, "Display of the Body Hottentot," in *Africans on Stage: Studies in Ethnological Show Business*, ed. B. Lindfors (Bloomington: Indiana University Press, 1999), 1–61. Stephen Jay Gould made her case famous in his book *The Mismeasure of Man* (New York: Norton, 1981). Her remains were returned to South Africa for burial in 2002. Visit https://en.wikipedia.org/wiki/Saartjie_Baartman.

111   But see Maneesha Deckha, "Salience of Species Difference for Feminist Theory," 17 *Hastings Women's Law Journal* (2006): 1–38 (arguing that feminists should advocate for animal rights and scrutinize species difference in the same way they examine other differences such as race and gender).

112   See Martha Minnow, *Making All the Difference: Inclusion, Exclusion, and American Law* (Ithaca: Cornell University Press, 1990).

Children provide the most analogous case to chimpanzees, which, as *Unlocking the Cage* points out, generally have the emotional and intellectual intelligence of a five-year-old human child.[113] We would not think it was acceptable to lock up a five-year-old child in a cage.[114] Young children cannot be on the bench to take offence at these comparisons, as women and/or African Americans are. However, one can easily see that some of the arguments Wise has made about the very young and the severely disabled – that they are given dignity rights even when they lack key capacities for autonomy, whereas non-human animals who do have capacities are denied them – could offend and attract disdain from those who are disabled, or who advocate for disabled rights, or who are worried about losing dignity rights for humans who somehow "do not make the cut."[115] Even if the point of that argument is not to detract from the dignity rights of the weak and powerless but to say that dignity rights should be extended to the weakest and most powerless.

The truth of it is, it is not usually a complement to be compared to a non-human animal, given the low regard in which they are generally held and the terrible ways in which they are treated. And people who belong to groups that have been discriminated against over the centuries, legally and socially, might well resent the comparison.

Instructive regarding the pragmatic way in which legal reasoning works in practice is Wise's willingness when he is before the *Lavery* judges to move quickly off the slavery point (despite how fundamental

---

113 Most of the cognitive capacity evidence in the book puts the chimpanzee at the level of a two or three-year old human. See Wise, *Rattling the Cage*, 163–237. However, it has been sixteen years since the book was published, and I am assuming that the comment in the film is based on more recent scientific evidence. Wise notes in his argument in the case of Hercules and Leo in 2015 that half of the scientific articles cited by the Nonhuman Rights Project scientists were published after 2000 and six of them after 2010. See Hercules and Leo Hearing Transcript, 37. Opposing counsel points out in that hearing the chimpanzee was compared to a five-year-old. See ibid., 51.

114 See *Snowpiercer*, dir. Bong Joon-ho (2013) for a fictional apocalyptic depiction of human existence on a train perpetually circling a frozen Earth. The train is segregated sharply into classes living in different sections of the train. The train's continued running depends on the slave labour of two five-year-old boys, stolen from the parents of those who live at the back of the train. The children are kept under the floorboards of the engine room, a space in which only a child can fit so as to manipulate the machinery.

115 See Wise, "*Rattling the Cage* Defended," 653; Wise, *Drawing the Line*, 31. Singer's comments on the suffering of the disabled have drawn criticism from disability advocates. See, for example, Katie Booth, "What I Learned about Disability and Infanticide from Peter Singer, *Aeon*, 10 January 2018, https://aeon.co/ideas/what-i-learned-about-disability-and-infanticide-from-peter-singer.

his writings clearly take the analogy to be) once it is clear that they are not interested in hearing this argument and that he is probably alienating them by making it. This is the advocate in action. And, indeed, the group has been filing cases since 2017 on behalf of zoo elephants in response to the charge that the comparison between chimpanzees and slaves is racist.[116] "No one has compared African Americans to elephants," said Wise in an interview I conducted with him in the summer of 2018.[117]

As historical and philosophical as Wise is in his extensive writings, he, like the judge in the Ikea Monkey case, is ultimately less interested in the purity of the ideas than in results, ends, and consequences. This advocacy orientation opened *Rattling the Cage* up to criticism by prominent legal academics at the University of Chicago, Martha Nussbaum and Richard Posner, both of whom wrote lengthy reviews of the book when it appeared more than fifteen years ago.[118]

Nussbaum criticized Wise's philosophical and historical understanding of how the ancient Greeks viewed non-human animals, alleging essentially that it was not sufficiently nuanced, in other words, that it was only as nuanced as an advocate would make it. Wise's defence, quite rightly I think, was to say that he was providing sketches or summaries of long sweeps of history in the book with a very specific question in mind – animals and their legal thinghood status – canvassing this in the works of many philosophers and jurists from Gaius to Justinian and on.[119] This was probably bound to appear inadequate to an expert in ancient Greek philosophy and history. I can say that reading it as a (primarily nineteenth-century) historian and a legal historian (with a philosophical background), I found Wise's account to be perfectly acceptable and did not expect the discussion to be highly nuanced and differentiated in the way that the history of a particular period or individual thinker would be.[120] It was just not that kind of thing.

---

116 See Fernandez, "Legal History and Rights for Nonhuman Animals," 204.
117 Ibid., 206.
118 See Martha C. Nussbaum, "Animal Rights: The Need for a Theoretical Basis," 114 *Harvard Law Review* (2001): 1506–49; Richard A. Posner, "Animal Rights," 110 *Yale Law Journal* (2000): 527–41. Wise responds to these and other book reviews (both critical and positive) of *Rattling the Cage* in "*Rattling the Cage* Defended," 43 *Boston College Law Review* (2002): 623–96.
119 Wise, "*Rattling the Cage* Defended," 626 ("*Rattling the Cage*, limited to about 250 pages, could not provide a thick, rich, unbroken history of how the West has viewed nonhuman animals from ancient times").
120 See Nussbaum, "Animal Rights," 1513 ("[T]he historical part of the book is written carelessly ... employing little scholarship and a haphazardly chosen set of historical

Posner was bothered by the advocacy orientation of *Rattling the Cage*: "Wise's practitioner's perspective is ... both the strength and the weakness of the book."[121] He added, less charitably, that it "is not an intellectually exciting book" – a puzzling statement given that he was obviously engaged by the innovative arguments it set forth.[122] Clearly, he disagreed with those arguments, calling for continuing categorization of animals as property (their "commodification") in order to protect them (noting the "'liberating' potential" of private property).[123] This claim is difficult to square with the long history and continued treatment of non-human animals; it is also an odd argument to advance given that the premise of *Rattling the Cage* is that non-human animals' status as property/commodities is what opens them up to abuse in the first place. Wise wrote in response to Posner's argument about the supposed liberty of commodification:

> A major lesson of our long experience with human slavery is that, at the level of basic rights, there is no more liberating potential in commodification whatsoever and that humans are more likely to exploit what they own than they are to protect it, especially if they can obtain more of the commodity once they have used it up. We continue to learn this hard lesson in the area of the environment.[124]

The environmental analogy Wise raises here is apt. Thus, for instance, we have the capture rule in an (in)famous American property law case, *Pierson v. Post*, which holds that as between an initial pursuer and an interloper, the one who successfully captures the hunted fox is the owner. This principle has been applied to other fugitive resources like oil and gas, with anti-social and anti-environmental consequences.[125] The idea that commodifying everything one possibly can because humans are more likely to protect than to waste or abuse what they own feels more like an article of faith than a rational assessment of what would be best for any particular natural resource, including non-human animals, especially given what we know about how they are bred and then treated in human institutions.

---

reference points), 1514 ("Wise's conception of Greek history tends to be overly simple, failing to describe the complexity of ancient philosophical thinking").
121 Posner, "Animal Rights," 527.
122 Ibid.
123 Ibid., 539 ("One way to protect animals is to make them property, because people tend to protect what they own").
124 Wise, "*Rattling the Cage* Defended," 667.
125 See Angela Fernandez, *Pierson v. Post, The Hunt for the Fox: Law and Professionalization in American Legal Culture* (New York: Cambridge University Press, 2018).

Wise's approach is the litigator's approach. When writing a defence to his critics, he makes no apology for this. And even if the case is lost and even if offence has been taken, something has been won, because "reflection upon an injustice opens the possibility that it will end."[126] Before that there is only unthinking use and what Robert Nozick described many years ago in *Anarchy, State, and Utopia* (1974) as Kantianism for humans and utilitarianism for non-human animals.[127] When we stick to that route, Wise points out, then we live with the same paradox as the ancient Greeks, building a society premised on both liberty and slavery.[128] That is a powerful indictment and one that many people are uncomfortable continuing to perpetuate. This is perhaps especially so for those who identify with groups that have been historically discriminated against, for whom speciesism looks very much like another form of discrimination, asserted by those who have the power to be at the top of the food chain and in whose self-interest it operates and who view it as natural and sanctioned by a belief in their God-given superiority (e.g., their superior brains). It sounds very much indeed like Victorian racialized science all over again.

A word about the Holocaust. Comparisons of factory farming to an "eternal Treblinka" give offence to many in the postwar West.[129] The point of this "dreaded comparison" is not that Jews were non-human animals but that they were treated, wrongly, in the Holocaust as if they *were* – shipped in cattle cars through communities that continued to go about their daily lives, largely turning a blind eye to what was going on. Critics like Posner point out that the Nazis believed passionately in animal rights, a point that he concedes is neither here nor there.[130] *Unlocking the Cage* does not weigh in on this particular comparison.

---

126   Wise, "Hardly a Revolution," 914.
127   Wise, "*Rattling the Cage* Defended," 658. See also Man Ha Tse, "The Unity of Being: Groundwork for a Theory of Obligations to Other Animals," LL.M. Thesis, Faculty of Law, University of Toronto (2015) (engaging with the work of Christine Korsgaard, who argues for a version of Kantian autonomy for non-human animals).
128   Wise, "Legal Thinghood," 546; *Rattling the Cage*, 48.
129   The quote is by Isaac Bashevis Singer and reads "What do they know – all these scholars, all these philosophers, all the leaders of the world – about such as you? They have convinced themselves that man, the worst transgressor of the species, is the crown of creation. All other creatures were created merely to provide him with food, pelts, to be tormented, exterminated. In relation to them, all people are Nazis; for the animals it is an eternal Treblinka."
130   Posner, "Animal Rights," 535 ("The Nazis were constantly blurring the line between the human and animal kingdoms, as when they described Jews as vermin. The other side of this coin was the glorification of animals that had good

Writing about what he perceives as the dangers posed by the animal rights movement, Richard Epstein has pointed out that slaves were not treated as "mere things": "From the earliest time they [slaves] were governed by a set of rules that treated them as legal hybrids, part property and part human beings."[131] Yet this hybridity hardly recommends that legal status. A key question would seem to be: Would you put yourself there? Would you agree to be private property? None of us would.

These critics see animal rights as a threat to human specialness. They contend that recognition of these rights will result in a levelling down of the human rather than a raising up of the non-human. Posner warns that "if we fail to maintain a bright line between animals and human beings, we may end up treating human beings as badly as we treat animals, rather than treating animals as well as we treat (or aspire to treat) human beings."[132] Martha Nussbaum similarly writes: "We might treat chimpanzees better, or we might treat humans worse."[133] The Assistant State Attorney General representing SUNY in the Hercules and Leo hearing, Christopher Coulston, expressed a similar thought when he said, "I worry about the diminishment of these rights in some way if we expand them beyond human beings."[134] Here we have a version of the zero-sum charge that Hardock and others make about the expansion of legal personhood to corporations.

This line of criticism seems to presuppose that dignity and respect exist as a fixed pie and that there is only so much of them to go around. Proponents of animal rights tend to think the opposite – that empathy fosters empathy. As David Favre, the editor of the inaugural issue of the journal *Animal Law*, put it in 1995, the idea is that an awareness of the needs and interests of the non-human animal will make us more

---

Nazi virtues, predatory animals like the eagle ... the tiger, and the panther ... These are examples of how animal-rights thinking can assimilate people to animals and animals to people"); 536 ("I do not mean to suggest that the animal rights movement is tainted by Hitler's support for animal rights, any more that Hitler's enthusiasm for four-lane limited-access highways should be an embarrassment to highway builders. I mean only to suggest that animal rights have no intrinsic political valence. They are as compatible with right-wing as with left-wing views").

131 Richard A. Epstein, "The Dangerous Claims of the Animal Rights Movement," *The Responsive Community* 10, no. 2 (2000): 28–37, 30.
132 Posner, "Animal Rights," 535.
133 Nussbaum, "Animal Rights," 1522.
134 Hearing Transcript, 51; *Unlocking the Cage*, 1:23:03.

aware of the needs and interests of the human animal.[135] Wise writes that "the extension of dignity-rights to every being qualified to receive them is not a zero sum game. Instead, it strengthens the dignity-rights of all."[136] And he asks: "If we open our moral umbrella a bit to shelter apes or primates or mammals or vertebrates, and believe every one of them inviolable and equal in dignity, why would we no longer believe the same of all humans, who would be a subset of those whom we believe to be inviolable and of equal dignity?"[137] Wise then points out that "there is no reason specifically linked to the rights of nonhuman animals to believe that we may ever treat humans as badly as we do nonhuman animals."[138]

Nussbaum writes that she wants to be able to say that humans are "special."[139] The question then seems to be whether there is a real danger that when push came to shove we human animals will never let go of that. It seems unlikely.[140] However, most of what we are talking about is not a matter of push comes to shove; it is more about not eating animal meat when non-meat alternatives are readily available, choosing not to wear fur even if it is fashionable, not going to the zoo or aquarium when there are other things to do with your kids, and saying no as an individual researcher or country to primate and other non-human

---

135 David Favre, "Time for a Sharper Legal Focus," 1 *Animal Law* (1995): 1–4 at 2 ("To focus on animal issues is not to suggest that human issues have been solved or are not important. But it is time to widen the scope of our societal vision and concern. Perhaps by reaching out beyond humankind, we will be more aware of the need for universal human rights at the same time. To argue for the recognition of the interests of animals can only be done in a context that presumes and promotes the recognition of the interests of the human animal"). This journal is housed at the Northwestern School of Law of Lewis and Clark College and was organized by students there with initial financial support from the Animal Legal Defense Fund. This is also the school that published the first environmental law journal.

136 Wise, "Hardly a Revolution," 795–6.

137 Wise, "*Rattling the Cage* Defended," 647–8.

138 Ibid., 648.

139 Nussbaum, "Animal Rights," 1521.

140 Even Gary Francione, a very loud voice in the argument against treating non-human animals as property, concedes that when a human and a non-human life conflict in a true emergency, it is right to save the human. See Gary L. Francione, "Animals – Property or Persons?," in *Animal Rights: Current Debates and New Directions*, ed. Cass R. Sunstein and Martha C. Nussbaum (New York: Oxford University Press, 2004) 108, 133–4. Think of the tragic case of Harambe at the Cincinnati zoo in May 2016. Visit https://en.wikipedia.org/wiki/Killing_of_Harambe. See also Gary L. Francione, *Introduction to Animal Rights: Your Child or the Dog* (Philadelphia: Temple University Press, 2000).

animal experimentation, which is generally used to confirm scientific findings otherwise independently arrived at, and, worse, can actively mislead researchers, with negative impacts on human health.[141]

Is there really a danger that we would ever fail to safeguard our own specialness? The propertied are in no great threat of being treated as property. Where is the evidence that those in the world who have little or no property would be treated worse as a result of the better treatment of animals? Perhaps the worry is that when resource conflicts arise, non-human animals will be preferred by the state. Posner seems to have something like this is mind when he refers to sheep ranchers and the protection given to wolves.[142] Epstein in this regard refers to farmers who "have been unfairly forced to stand aside while protected animals decimate their sheep and cattle herds."[143] Similar conflicts exist in places liked Brazil, where environmentalists oppose the clearing of ecologically precious land for cattle grazing. These resource conflicts are political conflicts. They are of high importance, as the documentary film *Cowspiracy* signals.[144] Yet such conflicts can hardly be said to result in human animals such as Brazilian ranchers being treated as if they are non-human animals. Indeed, in Brazil it is the activists who oppose big ranching and logging interests who are being silenced and often gunned down.[145]

---

141 See, for example, http://animalresearch.thehastingscenter.org/report/the-case-for-phasing-out-experiments-on-primates. On how the non-human animal testing requirement in the United States actually misleads, telling us that certain drugs are safe when they are not, leading us to be able to cure cancer in mice but not humans, and resulting in missed opportunities for drugs that might not work on rats but do on human beings, see Lisa Kramer and Ray Greek, "Human Stakeholders and the Use of Animals in Drug Development," *Business and Society Review* 123, no. 1 (2018): 3–58.

142 Posner, "Animal Rights," 533.

143 Epstein, "The Dangerous Claims of the Animal Rights Movement," 31.

144 *Cowspiracy: The Sustainability Secret*, dir. Kip Anderson and Keegan Kuhn (2014), offers an extended and powerful argument that clearing land and trying to grow all the feed for livestock animals to eat and then the earth having to absorb their waste in the air and the oceans is the number one threat to the environment, greater than the carbon emissions that have been the focus of social and political conversation since Al Gore's *An Inconvenient Truth*. Not eating meat, then – especially beef – is one of the most immediate and effective things a person can do to reduce their environmental footprint, far surpassing the sort of messages we ordinarily hear about recycling, short showers, low-flow shower heads, and even driving a car.

145 See *They Killed Sister Dorothy*, dir. Daniel Junge (2009), which documents the brutal shooting of American-born Brazilian nun Dorothy Stang. See also https://www.washingtonpost.com/news/morning-mix/wp/2015/08/27/why-are-brazils-environmentalists-being-murdered.

When Epstein wrote that "there would be nothing left of human society if we treated animals not as property but as independent holders of rights," Wise responded: "Epstein exaggerates: plenty would be left to human society. But the massive industries that have developed around the exploitation of nonhuman animals would be damaged, perhaps destroyed. Certainly industries that depend upon inflicting bodily harm upon nonhuman animals, such as meat or biomedical research industries, would be severely affected if the animals upon which they depend were given a legal right to bodily integrity."[146] Is it then the interference with private property that is the concern? Is *that* the right critics are worried about diminishing? It is an important political consideration certainly, just as it was when activists called for the abolition of slavery in the United States. Slaves were the property of their slave owners, and abolition would divest those owners of their property. But again, this comparison hardly calls for us, in the name of human rights or human specialness, to deny legal rights to other animals that demonstrate the requisite autonomy (or some other characteristic). Wise's point is that this ultimately undermines human rights because it is "arbitrary, biased and therefore unjust."[147] It also belies what we should be doing in law at this point in history, namely, extending rights to those who need them most. Our refusal to do so, even while we create and zealously guard constitutional and free speech rights for corporations, is ironic indeed.

Rivers and Corporations as Legal Persons Yes, but Not Non-Human Animals

Two scenes in *Unlocking the Cage* make the striking point that we are used to extending artificial legal personhood to non-natural entities as a means to heighten (not hinder) their usefulness to humans. This is different from extending legal personhood for non-human animals, which would require us to refrain from treating them in convenient and useful ways, that is, from doing certain things to them because they are rights bearers.

The first of these scenes is the moment when the Assistant State Attorney General in the Hercules and Leo application argues that, yes, legal personhood is given to corporations but that is because it is in humans' interest to do so. Corporate personhood was adopted in order to allow the humans involved in their operations to do some very useful things that were deemed necessary (or at least convenient) for economic

---

146   Wise, *Drawing the Line*, 11.
147   Ibid., 8.

growth and expansion.[148] That is why, for instance, it is widely viewed as acceptable for the directors of a corporation to shield themselves from personal liability for the company's actions.[149] Legal personhood allows an entity to sue and be sued, hold property, make contracts, and so on. From this it is a short, though not inevitably disastrous, step to say it has constitutional legal rights such as the right to free speech.[150]

I think Coulston was correct to point out that it is useful to explain the legal fiction and the imaginative leap. Historically, husbands had the same kind of self-interest in maintaining the legal fiction that husband and wife were one person in law, when they clearly were not literally one person and there were many legal exceptions to this generalization.[151] This is a positivist view of law as something human beings create to further their interests. It is, however, a very narrow way of understanding what law is. This more narrow conception does not invariably depart in significant and problematic ways from what

---

148 The US Supreme Court has held that in addition to freedom of speech (see *Citizen's United*), corporations enjoy freedom of religion (under a federal statute, not the Constitution). In *Hobby Lobby*, the Court held that the employer corporation, Hobby Lobby Stores, did not have to follow the Affordable Care Act, which required them to cover contraception for their female employees. See *Burwell v. Hobby Lobby Stores, Inc.*, 573 U.S. (2014).

149 See Richard Danzig, "*Hadley v. Baxendale*: A Study in the Industrialization of the Law," 4:2 *The Journal of Legal Studies* (1975): 249–84.

150 I say not inevitably disastrous, for other jurisdictions such as Canada grant free speech rights to corporations without extending that to removing limits on campaign spending. See, for example, *RJR-MacDonald Inc. v. Canada (A.G.)*, 3 S.C.R. 199 (1999), http://scc-csc.lexum.com/scc-csc/scc-csc/en/item/1290/index.do. The problem in *Citizen's United* was that the free speech right was interpreted as so absolute that the FEC's attempts to cap campaign financing were considered to be an interference with the ability to exercise that right. In Canada, a court would ask in the face of similar legislation whether there had been a violation of the right and if there had been, whether it was justified in a free and democratic society. Limits on campaign spending by third-party interest groups have been found by the Supreme Court of Canada to be justified given that the point of such limits is to produce a level playing field for democracy to operate. See *Harper v. Canada (AG)*, 1 S.C.R. 827 (2004) available at http://scc-csc.lexum.com/scc-csc/scc-csc/en/item/2146/index.do (upholding a $3,000 spending limit by third parties).

151 See Angela Fernandez, "Tapping Reeve, Coverture, and America's First Leal Treatise," in *Law Books in Action: Essays on the Anglo-American Legal Treatise*, ed. Angela Fernandez and Markus D. Dubber (Oxford: Hart), 63–81; Fernandez, "Tapping Reeve, Nathan Dane, and James Kent: Three Fading Federalists on Marital Unity," in *Married Women and the Law: Coverture in England and the Common Law World*, ed. Tim Stretton and Krista J. Kesselring (Montreal and Kingston: McGill-Queen's University Press, 2013), 192–216.

would be just, but it can certainly do so, and to the extent it does, it should be resisted.

Wise argues that at least since the Second World War, there has been an equal if not more important understanding of law as embodying and furthering core beliefs relating to human dignity, liberty, and equality – beliefs that we decide are not subject to compromise. This conception of law is more like natural law; it issues from international norms about human beings and what is and is not acceptable to do to them, taking a moral view of human rights as general rights.[152] Wise argues that it is speciesism – a new kind of discrimination – to say that other animals that have the capacity for limited autonomy are not entitled to it.[153] Species-specificity is important for sexual reproduction, Wise often points out.[154] But like the idea that husband and wife literally became one through the sex act, it is outdated in the extreme to make this biological/religious point central to a legal framework dealing with dignity-recognizing entitlements.

The second striking moment in the film relating to legal personhood occurs when Wise is waiting to go on a television talk show program and encounters another guest backstage, a civil rights lawyer and TV commentator Ron Kirby, who says he is more interested in Wise's topic than in his own and asks for further explanation.[155] When Wise tells him that a New Zealand court has recently granted personhood to a river and that there are examples of Hindu idols being declared legal persons, Kirby responds with scepticism – yes, that is all well and good, but that is not going to convince anyone to make chimpanzees legal persons. He states: "I guess I would look at the Supreme Court's basis for declaring corporate personhood since that strikes me as much more precedential for American purposes than Hindu idols or New Zealand rivers frankly."[156]

The Assistant Attorney General captured both these points at the hearing for Hercules and Leo:

---

152 See Patrick Macklem, *The Sovereignty of Human Rights* (New York: Oxford University Press, 2015), 7 ("Moral accounts treat human rights as general rights. They arise from the fact of humanity, they can be claimed by all, and they impose obligations on all. Human rights are not special rights. They do not reflect special bonds that exist among members of particular communities, they do not vest in some people and not others.").

153 See Wise, *Drawing the Line*, 24 (on "speciesism").

154 See, for example, Wise, "Hardly a Revolution," 884 (species membership is "merely a taxonomic classification of a population of genetically similar individuals able naturally to interbreed").

155 *Unlocking the Cage*, 50:15.

156 Ibid., 50:39–52.

The exceptions that do exist to legal personhood being assigned to some-body who's not human ... it[']s something that in some way relates to hu-man interest. Whether [it] [i]s a corporation, whether a ship is treated as a legal person. They have gone far afield to New Zealand to actually find a river, where not by matter of common-law but by agreement between the government and indigenous people there, I believe a right was assigned to the river of ownership of the riverbank. That is based on the religious significance of that river to the people in the area. It[']s still serving the interest of those people. There is nothing about the river itself that enti-tled it to rights.[157]

Those who are developing ideas of Earth Justice, Wild Law, or Green Legal Theory would disagree with Kirby.[158] *Should Trees Have Legal Standing* can be understood narrowly as a way to eliminate standing issues when groups come forward to protect the interests of a natural resource or a religiously significant artefact.[159] But that end might be accomplished more directly as a matter of civil procedure by granting wider public interest standing, or under an idea of guardianship. There is also a wider approach to such decisions that would bring them closer to the same kind of imaginative leap required for non-human animals. Non-human animals cannot speak for themselves; similarly, the river is legally voiceless unless or until it is granted legal personhood or, as this movement would probably put it, unless or until its pre-existing rights to personhood are recognized by the legal system.

A living, breathing animal is closer to a natural person than either rivers or corporations (or ships or trusts or municipalities or unions or churches or any of the other examples of artificial legal persons). Indeed, the cognitive capacity approach Wise takes is much more about show-ing how *close* chimps and bonobos are to humans in ways that neither corporations nor rivers can be. All animals that feel pain and share sen-tience would seem to have a superior claim, although it may be that this claim to superiority suffers from the same bias of human-centricity – and

---

157 See Hearing Transcript, 47..

158 Ibid. See, for example, Cormac Cullinan, *Wild Law: A Manifesto for Earth Justice*, 2nd ed. (White River Junction: Chelsea Green, 2011).

159 Wise often cites the earlier famous article version of this book: Christopher D. Stone, "Should Trees Have Standing? Towards Legal Rights for Natural Objects," 45 *Southern California Law Review* (1972): 450–501. Also available as Christopher D. Stone, *Should Trees Have Standing? Law, Morality, and the Environment* (Los Altos: W. Kaufmann, 1974). See also Matthew Hall, *Plants as Persons: A Philosophical Botany* (Albany: SUNY Press, 2011).

from variances in terms of how similar or dissimilar non-human animals are to human animals – that is a weak spot in Wise's approach. The key point is that just as with non-living entities like corporations, legal rights for non-human animals will require individual humans (since law is a human institution) to decide "yes, that is useful," or "yes, that is right." Once that decision is made by enough people with an ability to access and effect political change (be they common law judges or politicians in the legislature), then, as with corporations, it will no longer matter how counter-intuitive the ascription of personhood or rights might seem. The counter-intuitive will fall away in the face of usefulness or justice – that is, what *we* want when there is a consensus about what that is. This is likely to be different from what animal-use industries want.

Conclusion

Legal persons are (and have always been) already artificial, so there is no end of things this specific legal fiction might be used to do, the corporation probably being our most creative (and, to some, controversial) example. This argument is appealing to lawyers and law professors, who are used to legal fictions and how they operate. If we give legal personhood to corporations, then why not also to at least some other non-human animals?

But we are unlikely (at least immediately) to convince the public at large that it is wrong to treat non-human animals as if they were made for us (after all, most of us were born into the biblical world view and, thus, eat meat, go to zoos, and use non-human animals as entertainment) or that human laws are not for furthering the interests of human animals (utilitarianism is fine for non-human animals because, after all, their happiness does not count for much). Peter Singer's work, with its emphasis on cruelty and the wrongness of using non-human animals as we please based on their sentience, is probably more immediately compelling than Wise's arguments about legal personhood and autonomy.

The influence of Singer's work cannot be overstated. There is a scene in *Unlocking the Cage* where Wise shows us his beaten-up copy of *Animal Liberation*, explaining how that book was the starting point of his library, which grew up around it. He, like many others in the animal rights world, have taken tremendous inspiration from it (see Figure 7.4).[160]

---

160 *Unlocking the Cage*, 4:01. Image here provided by Films We Like and reproduced with the permission of Pennebaker and Hegedus Films.

Figure 7.4. Peter Singer's *Animal Liberation* from *Unlocking the Cage*

However, Singer's work has been circulating since the 1970s, and while it has had an enormous impact on probably all animal rights advocates (because of the sordid details he revealed and the ethical questions that accompanied them), much of what it criticized still happens and indeed has gotten worse. As the global population grows, the demand for non-human meat and for land to grow the crops to fatten livestock has increased, and factory farming has intensified, not just in terms of numbers of animals but also in terms of the concentration of corporate control over methods of production – methods that for sectors like chicken and egg production are terrible but are considered perfectly acceptable by the industry.[161] Free-range eggs seem like a better option, but feeding cattle on grass (a healthier and some feel more ethical production method) requires even more land for grazing than it takes to raise crops for factory-farmed animals. Temple Grandin's (in)famous system of humane slaughter for cattle is now used by half the large producers in the United States, Canada, and Australia, but what about the other half in those countries, and what about the rest of the world?[162] The ethical choices for meeting the protein needs of humans will have to include plant-based options, and the sooner people make

---

161 See *Farm to Fridge.*
162 See footage in ibid. to see what at least some of the other 50 per cent of the cows face.

this switch the better the outcomes will be for human health and the environment.[163]

Wise does not comment in the film on the compatibilities and incompatibilities of his approach with Singer's. In the original edition of *Animal Liberation* in 1975, Singer wrote that "the language of rights is a convenient political shorthand ... It is in no way necessary."[164] However, in 1993 Singer co-founded with Paola Cavalieri "the Great Ape Project," which advocates for a United Nations Declaration that would give chimpanzees, bonobos, gorillas, and orangutans basic legal rights (right to life, liberty, and freedom from torture), an approach that is certainly compatible with what Wise is doing (i.e., trying to use *habeas corpus* in the US state court system). Philosophically, though, sentience throws a much wider net than the cognitive sophistication of the great apes, which Singer seems to agree is where things should begin. In his view, the language of rights is not inappropriate as a means to make certain concrete gains.

Hilda Kean is sceptical of the language of rights, pointing out that Britain's two-hundred-year history of efforts to end cruelty to animals does not capture "the historical practice of people campaigning to protect animals."[165] If those people were driven mostly by humanitarian concerns, then it seems that a history of animal rights as we know them started only in the 1970s.[166] Present-day advocates go for rights because only rights can create a block, a legal wall, against deciding this or that human use is more important than the terrible treatment of a non-human animal when it is seen as necessary to further some human end, which can be serious (some forms of medical research) or trivial

---

163 June 2018 saw the release of an important study in the journal *Science* by two Oxford University researchers, who reported that meat and dairy provide just 18 per cent of calories and 37 per cent of protein consumed by humans but use the vast majority of agricultural land – 83 per cent, while producing 60 per cent of agricultural greenhouse gas emissions. Thus, avoiding meat and dairy products is by far the most effective way for people to reduce their environmental impact. See Damian Carrington, "Avoiding meat and dairy is 'single biggest way' to reduce your impact on Earth," *The Guardian*, 31 May 2018, https://www.theguardian.com/environment/2018/may/31/avoiding-meat-and-dairy-is-single-biggest-way-to-reduce-your-impact-on-earth. The study was by J. Poore and T. Nemecek, "Reducing Food's Environmental Impacts through Producers and Consumers," 360 *Science*, 1 June 2018, 987–92, http://science.sciencemag.org/content/sci/360/6392/987.full.pdf?ijkey=ffyeW1F0oSl6k&keytype=ref&siteid=sci.

164 Singer, *Animal Liberation*, 8.

165 Kean, *Animal Rights*, 11.

166 See Samuel Moyn, *The Last Utopia: Human Rights in History* (Cambridge, MA: Belknap Press of Harvard University Press, 2010).

(it tastes good). And humanitarian efforts have proven to be woefully inadequate.

Hardly anyone (at least publicly) defends the human right to treat animals in gratuitously cruel and sadistic ways, and anti-cruelty and animal welfare statutes have at least purported to protect against this for a long time. Those laws, however, are notoriously underenforced, and they suffer from a general problem, which is that, as animal rights lawyer and academic Lesli Bisould puts it, they may protect against "unnecessary suffering" or require "humane treatment" but they do not protect "the interests animals have in living their own lives and in not being made to suffer for human purposes."[167] The standard of cruelty, Bisgould explains, only prohibits the *extra*ordinarily bad treatment of non-human animals in a world where the terrible treatment of those animals is utterly ordinary.[168] "If many people find it convenient, enjoyable, or profitable to do things that hurt animals, those things are not legally cruel," Bisgould writes. "So long as causing suffering is not the only object of the act, the fact that they suffer as a result becomes irrelevant."[169] Hence by "prohibiting 'unnecessary' pain and suffering, we create a corollary and thereby permit the causing of pain and suffering that is 'necessary.'"[170] This effectively gives human animals the permission to hurt non-human animals as they see fit and means that "there is no act, however violent or harmful, that is categorically illegal."[171]

However, Katie Sykes argues that "unnecessary" need not be interpreted like this.[172] It is understood that way given the costs and inconvenience of doing factory farming in a more humane way (e.g., pain is not necessary if it can be prevented by using anaesthesia in a castration or tail docking or debeaking, or animals can be given more space).[173]

---

167 Lesli Bisgould, *Animals and the Law* (Toronto: Irwin law, 2011), 280.
168 Ibid., 279.
169 Ibid.
170 Ibid., 3.
171 Ibid.
172 Katie Sykes, "Rethinking the Application of Canadian Criminal Law to Factory Farming," in *Canadian Perspectives on Animals and the Law*, ed. Peter Sankoff, Vaughan Black, and Katie Sykes (Toronto: Irwin Press, 2015), 33–56 at 33 (explaining how there is an "implicit farming exemption" in the Criminal Code provision that makes it an offence to wilfully cause unnecessary pain, suffering, or injury to an animal or bird, s. 445.1(a). It permits "almost anything done to animals as part of the business of producing animal food.").
173 Ibid., 35 ("Many standard practices in factory farming, including tail docking, castration, beak cutting, and confinement in extremely small spaces, involve severe suffering for animals. Conventional wisdom has it that these practices are justified

What is needed is a social consensus that humane treatment must be required even if it is costly and inconvenient.

Wise wants to build a new legal wall that we all will then have to respect – that is, a buffer around those non-human animals whose similarity to human animals ironically makes them more susceptible to invasive exploitation (the chimp is dressed up at a birthday party because she resembles a human being in those clothes, then is later infected with different strains of HIV because of her nearly identical genetic similarity to us).[174] "Rights demand respect," Wise writes in response to critics like Posner who ask why we don't focus on animal welfare and on extending legislative protection and increasing enforcement.[175] Legal persons, the only entity that can have legal rights, are "the unit of the legal order."[176] Legal personhood is a vessel in which to pour legal rights.[177]

Unlocking the Cage is a way to make the argument for a new legal wall more palatable and understandable to a popular audience. It also shows the challenges involved in getting judges, even postwar human rights–oriented judges, to accept the argument. The difficulty is there in the looks on their faces, which the film expertly captures. It then appears in what they write in decisions such as *Lavery*, which are essentially

---

because their purpose is to produce food ... cheaply and efficiently ... The logic of the implicit farming exemption is that if these things are done for the a socially accepted purpose, then they are not *unnecessary* – no matter how extreme the suffering involved and even if other options that involve less suffering are available ... this is simply a misinterpretation of the [*Criminal*] *Code*, and in particular of the word 'unnecessary'").

174 Photographer Jo-Anne McArthur tells the story of a chimpanzee named Ron, who lived in a five-foot by five-foot by seven-foot cage suspended above the ground for the twenty-nine years he was a research laboratory chimp. When he was moved to Save the Chimps and given access to space to roam, he nonetheless usually chose to stay indoors, where he would carefully arrange his blankets in a circle to create a nest, a habit he had acquired at the research laboratories in which he was held for so long. See Jo-Anne McArthur, *We Animals* (New York: Lantern Books, 2013), 186. There is a moving photograph of Ron surrounded by his blankets on the cover. I read about this picture in then University of Toronto master's student Man Ha Tse's thesis and happened to have a friend's copy of the book on hand at the time. Reading more about Ron, I realized that he and I shared a birthday, year and day, and I felt very strongly that I ought to write something that would connect to him. The new legal wall Wise calls for reminds me of Ron's wall of blankets, which ought to offer better comfort and protection than it did for Ron, who died a premature death in 2011.

175 See Wise, "*Rattling the Cage* Defended," 679, 677–8.

176 Quoting Roscoe Pound, in Wise, *Drawing the Line*, 21.

177 See Wise, preface to 2014 edition of *Rattling the Cage*, xviii (referring to legal personhood "as a 'rights container' into which legal rights can be poured").

variations on "no way!" As in the Ikea Monkey case, the point about the need for tightly corresponding rights and duties – the chimp needs to be able to enter into a contract (at least a social contract) – reads like an excuse, a rejection of the more radical or revolutionary request to recognize this non-human animal as a legal person (rather than property) and to make a decision that is expressly in the animal's best interests. This, despite the fact that there are grounds and some legal precedent for taking that approach.[178]

During the question-and-answer session with the filmmakers at the Hot Docs screening in Toronto I attended, an announcement was made that the New Iberia Research Center at the University of Louisiana, which own Hercules and Leo, had agreed to send them along with 218 other chimpanzees to a sanctuary called Project Chimps![179] Hercules and Leo finally arrived on 21 March 2018.[180] The Nonhuman Rights Project litigation certainly made that happen, and impending publicity from the documentary no doubt also helped. These are victories for the individual animals, 220 of them, and for those involved with these initiatives. It is also then another example, like *Blackfish*, of the power of the documentary film. However, like the Ikea Monkey case, the New York cases have left "the Great Wall" intact. Indeed, both cases arguably strengthened that wall by affirming the "thinghood" of non-human animals and rejecting the claim for personhood in cases that, ironically for the common law approach adopted by the Nonhuman Rights Project, have set unfavourable precedents. As Wise wrote in 1999, "if these early cases are brought at the wrong time, in the wrong place, or before the wrong judges, they may strengthen the Great Legal Wall."[181] This is probably true of the 2017 First Department decision, which along with many of the other damaging points discussed above punts dealing with captive chimps to the state legislatures.[182]

---

178 See Bisgould, *Animals and the Law*, 154–7 (exploring Canadian cases where the idea of best interests has arisen in custody disputes over non-human animals).
179 This news was released the day I attended the Hot Docs screening, 3 May 2016. Visit http://www.nonhumanrightsproject.org/2016/05/03/nonhuman-rights-project-chimpanzee-clients-hercules-and-leo-to-be-sent-to-sanctuary.
180 See David Grimm, "U.S. chimp retirement gains momentum, as famed pair enters sanctuary," *Science*, 21 March 2018), http://www.sciencemag.org/news/2018/03/us-chimp-retirement-gains-momentum-famed-pair-enters-sanctuary.
181 Wise, "Animal Thing to Animal Person," 68.
182 *Lavery* and Kiko, First Department, 7. There is even a legislative intent argument in relation to the New York statute, that there was no evidence that "the Legislature intended the term 'person' ... to expand the availability of *habeas* protection beyond humans" (5).

There is further irony in Wise's work in his reliance on the very kind of scientific experiments on non-human animals done to determine their cognitive capacities that one might expect him to object to because of the way in which they treat non-human animals. So, for instance, Wise tells us that Lucy, the encultured ape, famous for her vacuum-cleaner masturbation in the house of her human family, featured in *Rattling the Cage*, ended up shot and skinned in Gambia by poachers, her hands and feet to be sold as trophies, when she could no longer be kept by her American family.[183] Documentary film watchers might be familiar with *Project Nim: The Human Chimp*, a project Wise is critical of, as are the filmmakers who show Nim being passed from graduate student to graduate student and cycled through endless teachers with very little knowledge of the American Sign Language (ASL) they were trying to teach him.[184] Both experiments are of a moment in the 1960s and '70s when the human experimenters did not think it was problematic to enculturate chimps by teaching them ASL without regard to the fact that this would make it impossible for those chimps to lead ordinary chimp lives and dangerous for them to expect to be able to do so, as was demonstrated in the case of Lucy, who used those hands that ended up cut off by the poachers to make tea in the family kitchen every morning for her ASL tutor.[185] Or the sad case of Booee, a signing chimp who was eventually sent for medical experiments and who, despite the fact that he had been there for five years, when visited by one of his former teacher's students, signed to him "Key out."[186]

If Wise is correct that awakening to the plight of non-human animals happens in something like a Gestalt shift, then the film showing the courage and perseverance of the lawyers involved in fighting for this issue will help people make that shift.[187] The other documentaries I have referred to in this chapter try to move their viewers to action using the power of the visual, whether that is through providing shocking

---

183 See Wise, *Rattling the Cage*, 194, 239. See also 210–11 (relying on an example of Lucy attempting to cover up the fact that she had defecated on the carpet, intentional deception being a hallmark of high cognition and very similar to how a young human child might behave).

184 *Project Nim: The Human Chimp*, dir. James Marsh (2011). See also Wise, ibid., 172–74 (criticizing the Nim Project).

185 See Wise, *Rattling the Cage*, 166, describing "breakfast with Lucy" from the book by Maurice K. Temerlin, *Lucy: Growing Up Human* (Science and Behavior Books, 1975).

186 Wise, *Rattling the Cage*, 240. Wise does say that once the cognitive capacity of an animal has been shown, there is no need to keep repeating it. If one animal can do it, the case has been proven. See *Drawing the Line*, 25.

187 See, for example, "Hardly a Revolution," 829.

footage as in *Farm to Fridge*, which concludes with the message "move to a plant-based diet," or the nuanced and moving coverage of the complexities of non-human animals living in human animal environments in *Ghosts in Our Machine*, where we see beagle rescue dogs finding happy homes and lucky farm sanctuary animals saved from industry use and death (along with the awful mink farms and pigs being trucked to slaughter). Like our nineteenth-century ancestors, this visual information is likely striking an empathetic or humanitarian chord, and indeed, the filmmaking is designed to do precisely that.

John Berger wrote influentially about the marginality of zoo animals in his famous essay "Why Look at Animals?"[188] These documentaries use the power of the visual to fight against that marginalization. In the photographs of *We Animals*, many of which were taken during the filming of *Ghosts in Our Machine*, we find a gaze we can return, or imagine we return.[189]

Yet one is very aware that progress, if it is happening, marches, as Wise likes to put it, "funeral by funeral."[190] And it happens with the heightened awareness among those committed to doing something about the legal powerlessness of non-human animals that they must be prepared to acknowledge and accept that we think and argue about these topics with a high level of inconsistency, expediency, and compromise.

So, first, no pigs for now (at least for Wise), along with lots of other sentient non-human animals, even though dividing animals based on their cognitive capacities and generally attaching protection based on their similarity to the human animal problematically reaffirms the idea that humans are the centre of the universe. Second, the "dreaded comparison" and others are necessary even as they risk giving offence and repeating old racist and sexist stereotypes. And, third, legal personhood for non-human animals is a strategic choice, one that acknowledges how problematic that concept has been when it comes to corporations and how fraught its exclusions continue to be, as many authors in this volume explore – whether it relates to the stateless who are not given human rights protection (Joshua Barkan), the poor who are not the unborn (Angela Mitropoulos), or, generally, the way in which human

---

188   See John Berger, "Why Look at Animals?" in *About Looking* (Random House, 1990), 3–28.

189   See also Jo-Anne McArthur, *Captive* (New York: Lantern Books, 2017).

190   See Wise, "Hardly a Revolution," 829n191. A remark by economist Paul Samuelson quoted by E.O. Wilson in "From Ants to Ethics: A Biologist Dreams About a Unity of Knowledge," *New York Times*, 12 May 1998), C6.

personhood is devalued even while corporate personhood is enhanced (Hardack). Those exclusions and devaluations are not justified. Extending legal personhood to non-human animals is very different from extending it to corporations (and withdrawing it from actual humans). It is less artificial and more real (the heartbeat, sentience or the ability to feel pleasure and/or pain, giving live birth to and nursing young, having vertebrae or a central nervous system). And it will produce more justice, not less.

These are all strategic choices that those who think about these topics do realize. However, the alternative, doing nothing while the situation of non-human animals gets worse and worse, is not a viable alternative. The distinctions and the comparisons, along with the compromises, seem, at least for now, as if they must be made.

PART FOUR

Corporate Personification

Any interrogation of corporate personhood inevitably raises the question of rights. Juridical personhood is essential to the Western vocabulary of equality. In natural law, personhood grounds one's capacity to participate in the legal order. As Hegel puts it, "personality essentially involves the capacity for rights ... Hence the imperative of right is: 'Be a person and respect others as persons.'"[1] This imperative to be a person and to respect personhood is the premise of most justifications of legal rights and obligations, such as a right to bodily integrity, to own property, to transact contractually, to be liable for (and subject to) civil wrong, and to be held responsible under a criminal justice system. The defining act of personality for Hegel is the exercise of will. Imaginably, there are ways of construing will as emanating from collectives, animals, artificial intelligences, trees, and so forth; however, for all intents and purposes natural law discusses personality as belonging to a singular, individual, mentally competent, will-wielding, property-in-the-self-owning human being.

Jensen and Meckling's nexus of contracts theory of the corporation treats the corporation as the outcome of free and equal exchange between free and equal beings. Their theory of the corporation attempts to resolve an agency problem that Edmund Burke faced during the prehistory of the corporation, as described by our contributor Scott MacKenzie. MacKenzie asks us to treat literary genres as mediating between the individual and the collective. Pastoral poems, for instance, "construct an authorizing subject (or a subject authorized to speak) who is neither a private person nor a set of localizable interests, but rather a fictional voice of generalized orthodoxy that speaks for all without speaking as any." According to MacKenzie, Edmund Burke's

---

1 36. (I) *Hegel's Philosophy of Right*, 37.

Reflections on the Revolution in France (1791) resorted to the pastoral genre to establish a voice that is not any one particular voice, but is the voice of the nation. He locates a prehistory of corporate personhood and corporate legal theory in James Hogg's "Marion Jock," an 1822 short story in which the peaceable sheep find themselves in "radical disharmony," with their interests at odds with the proprietorship and management of Scottish landowners. Hogg's conflictual pastoral contrasts with Burke's peaceable world of voluntary associations in much the same way that Berle and Means's nihilist corporate theory bubbles underneath Jensen and Meckling's world of contractual harmony – a world that promises a plenitude of voluntarism.

That underlying strife bubbles to the surface in Peter Jaros's contribution. Jaros writes of the prehistory of corporate personhood doctrine in the United States, using popular prints and satires to demonstrate that, from the start, charges of an obscenely abstract, unnatural, practically monstrous essence to the corporation were on display for all to see and confront. By analysing the tropology of the corporation in Jacksonian America, Jaros argues that the struggle to figure the corporation was a conflict over how to imagine the rights and obligations of political subjects in relation to the corporation. The corporation seemed like a monstrous outgrowth of the state, either a sub-state or a supra-state depending on where you stood. And where you stood in relation to the corporation helped – as it still helps – to define Americanness. Banking corporations, argued satirists, twisted equality such that the new juridical person represented by the corporation would be – by its collective, excessive nature – more equal than all others. Jaros's historical inquiry names the outrage felt today at the corporation as a result of this monstrous in/equality, whereby an entity granted personhood on the grounds that it is an economic caretaker of the people becomes a usurper.

8 The Livestock That Therefore We Are: Two Episodes from the Prehistory of Corporate Personhood

SCOTT R. MACKENZIE

Animal is a word that men have given themselves the right to give.... in order to corral a large number of living beings within a single concept: "the Animal" ... reserving for them, for humans ... the very thing that the others in question would be deprived of, those that are corralled within the grand territory of the beasts.
                                                                              – Jacques Derrida,
                              "The Animal That Therefore I Am (More to Follow)"[1]

This chapter examines a pair of works whose preoccupations and whose relation to each other can be understood as influential or otherwise relevant to the nineteenth-century socio-political forces that have coalesced in capitalist corporatism. The works are Edmund Burke's *Reflections on the Revolution in France* (1791) and James Hogg's story "Marion's Jock" (first published as an inset tale in the 1822 novel *The Three Perils of Man*; republished 1832 as a stand-alone story in *Altrive Tales*). A comparative analysis of these two texts may appear incongruous, but I will rely on a small set of parallel features to ground my discussion: Burke's critique is structured by a mode of enunciation adapted from the literary pastoral, which is to say he puts on a "rustic" voice to explicate a conservative model of Whig political orthodoxy; Hogg's tale by comparison can be read as a satirical lament for the breakdown of pastoral social relations informed by the author's Tory advocacy of mutual interests that landowners and labourers ought to share. My claim is that some (if not most) late eighteenth- and early nineteenth-century uses of the literary pastoral to organize paradigms of political legitimacy generate a kind of *avant la lettre* corporate personhood because they construct an authorizing subject (or a subject authorized to speak) who is neither a private person

---

1 Trans. David Willis, *Critical Inquiry* 28, no. 2 (Winter 2002): 369–418 at 400.

nor a set of localizable interests, but rather a fictional voice of generalized orthodoxy that speaks *for* all (or many) without speaking *as* any.

By the end of the eighteenth century, a number of scholars have argued, the corporation had already acquired many of the political and legal attributes that it has possessed ever since. These attributes include collectivity: corporations are, like states, "composed of individuals united in a single body."[2] They sustain themselves "through time and across space," without dependence on particular individual constituents: a corporation "persist[s] beyond single human life spans," "a Body Politick that indureth in perpetual succession."[3] The corporation is, at least nominally, a contractual entity whose contractuality "erases potential conflicts between the range of individual interests," allowing it to "direct the actions of people within it."[4] It is also a fiction and/or a figuration in its etymologically signalled embodiment, which has been traced to medieval church doctrine and the logic of the king's two bodies.[5] "A Corporation," William Sheppard wrote in 1659, "or an Incorporation (which is all one) is a Body, in fiction of law."[6] A second and related fiction of the corporation is the feature of modern corporate law and practice on which this volume focuses, personhood. Corporations are "artificial persons whose corporate personas are 'distinct from the individual shareholders who comprise them,'" which are "immortal for the good of their members."[7] The fiction/figure of personhood has been traced to Thomas Hobbes and his figuration of sovereign power in *Leviathan* (1651), but whose modern legal and juridical inception comes at least nineteen years after Burke's text and well beyond the socio-political sphere in which James Hogg wrote.[8]

---

2   Joshua Barkan, *Corporate Sovereignty: Law and Government under Capitalism* (Minneapolis: University of Minnesota Press, 2013), 5.

3   Ibid., 23; John O'Brien, *Literature Incorporated: The Cultural Unconscious of the Business Corporation, 1650–1850* (Chicago: University of Chicago Press, 2016), 3; William Sheppard, *Of Corporations* (1659), quoted in O'Brien, *Literature Incorporated*, 3.

4   Barkan, *Corporate Sovereignty*, 21; Joel Barkan, *The Corporation: The Pathological Pursuit of Profit and Power* (New York: Free Press, 2005), 1.

5   See Ernst Kantorowicz, *The King's Two Bodies: A Study in Medieval Political Theology* (Princeton: Princeton University Press, 1957); and O'Brien, *Literature Incorporated*, 3.

6   Quoted in O'Brien, *Literature Incorporated*, 3.

7   Purnima Bose and Laura E. Lyons, "Life Writing and Corporate Personhood," *Biography* 37, no. 1 (Winter 2014): v–xxii, x; Edmund Burke, *Reflections on the Revolution in France*, ed. L.G. Mitchell, Oxford World's Classics (Oxford: Oxford University Press, 1993), 141.

8   The first juridical recognition of corporate personhood is sometimes identified in *Santa Clara Co. v. Southern Pacific Railroad* (1886), but Morton J. Horwitz argues influentially that *Dartmouth College v. Woodward* (1819) is the watershed: "*Santa Clara* Revisited: The Development of Corporate Theory," *West Virginia Law Review* 88 (1985): 173–224 at 174.

Rather than corporate personhood as such, I will focus on sovereignty, the legal/political (not to say philosophical) problem at the centre of Hobbes's *opus*, which Joshua Barkan has sought to bring to the forefront of discussions about modern relations between private corporations and the state. "Corporate power," Barkan argues, "should be rethought as a mode of political sovereignty," because its relationship to state power binds the two powers "together through a principle of legally sanctioned immunity from law."[9] Corporations, prior to the eighteenth century, operated under charter as autonomous or semi-autonomous institutions carrying out the will of the sovereign, and later "to benefit public welfare," a distinction that allowed increasingly broad interpretations of public welfare and, in the first era of Smithian laissez faire, the development of a kind of corporate self-interest.[10] It seems to me that Burke and Hogg participate as sceptical critics in this genealogy of corporate personhood. O'Brien and Barkan both contend that Hobbes foresaw how corporations "could become rivals to the state, attaining a kind of sovereignty of their own," and Burke in the *Reflections* is profoundly anxious about exactly that possibility, particularly where corporate sovereignty is self-proclaimed without authorization by law or state.[11] Hogg also frets over proliferating and fragmenting sovereignties, though he understands them as generated by the intrusive effects of state-sanctioned corporate structures. Burke, nonetheless, also adopts a pastoral-corporate position in order to authorize his defence of the British constitution, while Hogg's pastoral registers mostly in its fragmentation and failure, reflecting what he sees as the displacement of the old land-labour corporations by alienating managerial systems.

In a 2015 article I made a pair of related claims on which this chapter will elaborate.[12] The first is that, in the second half of the British eighteenth century, despite its generally accepted position of subordination to georgic (as a master discourse for enlightenment, improvement, and national prosperity), the pastoral mode remained in at least one sense a hegemonic system: its double-voicedness enabled expression of ruling-class theme and sentiment in the speech and melody of rusticity, "to imply a beautiful relation between rich and poor, [by making]

---

9 Barkan, *Corporate Sovereignty*, 4.
10 Ibid., 16; on corporate self-interest, see Daniel M. Stout, *Corporate Romanticism: Liberalism, Justice, and the Novel*, Lit Z Series (New York: Fordham University Press, 2017), 28–9.
11 O'Brien, *Literature Incorporated*, 4.
12 Scott R. MacKenzie, "Pastoral against Pastoral Modernity: Voices of Shepherds and Sheep in James Hogg's Scotland," *European Romantic Review* 26, no. 5 (October 2015): 527–49.

simple people express strong feeling (felt as the most universal subject, something fundamentally true about everybody) in learned and
fashionable language."[13] Pastoral functioned, in this sense, as a means
of mediating collectivities including national unity, common prosperity, and relations of production. The best-known instance of pastoral's
constitutive mediation is that outlined by Raymond Williams: the
eighteenth-century socio-economic transformation that makes the city
the destination of rural production even as rural life becomes ever more
thoroughly the form that national collectivity imagines for itself.[14]

My second claim is that James Hogg's works in the pastoral mode
critique and resist what I have called pastoral modernity. The voices he
simulates tend to be inarticulate, incomprehensible, or inchoate, and
often explicitly fail to "represent subaltern Scottish experience" or to
"gain a hearing for the subaltern voice."[15] I argue that Hogg's pastoral
does not contain

> a secret kernel that might displace, or expose as fake, the moral and
> political "truth" of imperialism ... The shepherd's voice and song are not
> exhaustible, not explicable by critical analysis or economies of meaning.
> Like the voices of sheep, the songs of the Ettrick shepherd include tones
> that are polymorphic, vertiginous, and not necessarily distinguishable
> from silence. (MacKenzie 543)

Ambiguity and unintelligibility in Hogg imply what Ian Duncan calls
"a condition outside literature – a position from which literature becomes visible as a political economy, a set of stratifying codes and practices, a material product and 'remains.'"[16] Inarticulate pastoral operates
precisely to short-circuit the Enlightenment mandate that any particular element of "primitive" culture must be translated to the registers of
"universal" stadial history (or quantifying political economy) before it
can come to signification, be comprehended, so to speak.

---

13 William Empson, *Some Versions of Pastoral* (New York: New Directions Press), 11.
14 See Williams, *The Country and the City* (Oxford: Oxford University Press, 1973);
    see also Karen O'Brien, "Imperial Georgic, 1660–1789," in *The Country and the City
    Revisited: England and the Politics of Culture, 1550 – 1850*, ed. Gerald MacLean, Donna
    Landry, and Joseph P. Ward (Cambridge: Cambridge University Press, 1999): 160–79.
15 Suzanne Gilbert, "James Hogg and the Authority of Tradition," in *James Hogg and the
    Literary Marketplace: Scottish Romanticism and the Working-Class Author*, ed. Sharon Alker
    and Holly Faith Nelson (Farnham: Ashgate, 2009): 93–109 at 94; Douglas S. Mack, *Scot-
    tish Fiction and the British Empire* (Edinburgh: Edinburgh University Press, 2006), 2.
16 Ian Duncan, *Scott's Shadow: The Novel in Romantic Edinburgh* (Princeton: Princeton
    University Press, 2007), 286.

I will use these premises to examine a version of pastoral modernity that constructs a version of corporate sovereignty: Edmund Burke's characterization, in his *Reflections*, of the British public as "thousands of great cattle, reposed beneath the shadow of the British oak," who "chew the cud and are silent."[17] Paradoxically, I will argue, Burke's explicit disavowal of the possibility that the *Reflections* "might appear as the act of persons in some sort of corporate capacity" (6) becomes the means by which he imposes a pastoral corporation upon the silent cattle of Britain. He does not speak *as* or *for* the state (or as a statesman) but rather *for* the population that does not speak but that *is* the nation. His disavowal of corporate speech also conditions his critique of the "congratulatory address" of the Constitution Society to the French National Assembly, which he condemns as masquerading not only a voice of public collectivity but also a self-appointed sovereign right. If such autonomous sovereignties are allowed to flourish, Burke asserts, they will endanger the constitution's permanent sovereign legitimacy, whose essence is its indivisibility and continuity. The British cattle compose a permanent body of transient bodies, as I will explain further below.

Against Burke's livestock model I will counterpose Hogg's story "Marion's Jock," which exemplifies the failure of pastoral mutuality in rural Scotland, manifested in radical disharmony between labourer and master. Jock's status as labourer is muddled by his clearly implied animality, but he cannot be reconciled to the condition of livestock and his resistance to the managerial structures in which he gets entangled causes havoc, disrupting the diegetic order of Jock's world as well as the story's generic affiliations. Hogg's critique (implied in this story but explicit in other writings) blames the alienation that afflicts Jock at least partly on the disaggregation of proprietorship from management in Scottish agriculture that has separated the interests of landowners from those of labourers. For Hogg the corporation as a mechanism of sovereign self-interest cannot be effectively implemented, much less sustained, in rural Scotland. The fictive/figurative body of the capitalist farm corporation disintegrates because its debauching of sociocultural norms and its corruption of land proprietorship and territorial organization upset the meaning systems within which fictionality and figurality should function. Humans, animals, and institutions occupy incommensurable varieties of personhood, for which the fictive and the figural cannot provide coherent categorizations, so collectivity and continuity are dispersed rather than sustained by the biopolitical processes they play out (supervision, provision, guidance, consumption, and so forth).

---

17 Burke, *Reflections*, 85.

Further, I will suggest that the figure of cattle employed by Burke and the various animals that appear in Hogg's story can be understood as more densely imbricated in the ideological schemas with which each author engages than simply as literary metaphor or metonymy. The livestock system, a network of discourse and social relations for representing, controlling, and evaluating organic life, death, exchange, and consumption, has always been part of larger networks that extend to include both inorganic matter and human life. Conceptions of stock that underpin eighteenth-century developments in livestock management include not just the commodity exchanges and capitalizations of market stocks, but also parish stocks — repositories of goods, money, animals, and human labour power – which had helped sustain British social orders for centuries prior to the ascendency of capitalism.

Burke's cattle metaphor for the population of Britain becomes something more than metaphor where it meets his description of the British political system, "wherein, by the disposition of a stupendous wisdom, moulding together the great mysterious incorporation of the human race, the whole, at one time, is never old or middle-aged or young, but, in a condition of unchangeable constancy, moves on through the varied tenor of perpetual decay, fall, renovation, and progression" (*Reflections* 34). Within this system the human is already dissolved into indifferentiation. The matter of human bodies has the same basic fluidity as what is now termed biomass: life, death, growth, and reproduction are homogenized by the logics and functions of the body politic. The "great mysterious incorporation" is functionally immortal because its constituents continually renew themselves in a biological cycle, "a Body Politick that indureth in perpetual succession." Hogg's tale, with its lurid scenes of unappeasable appetite at war with scarcity, parsimony, and petty tyranny, seems to contest Burke's vision of rustic contentment and being-toward-death. The organic matter in the tale, living or edible, whirls in a maelstrom of libidinal and bestial violence that leaves hardly any element wholly intact.

"Neither for nor from any description of men"

The opening pages of Burke's *Reflections* are a catalogue of disavowals: his insistence upon retaining the "form of address" of a private letter, which the author has found "difficult to change," though "a different plan ... might be more favourable"; the "too little consequence" that has rendered his sentiments unworthy "to be very anxiously either communicated or withheld"; his insistence that "I shall speak of nothing as of a certainty, but what is public"; his "individual and private capacity" as no more than a "plain man" (*Reflections* 3–7). "I should think it improper and irregular," he protests, "for me to open a formal public correspondence with the actual government of a foreign nation without the express authority of the government under which I live" (6), and his letter is written "neither for nor from any description of men" (4). The insolent voice masquerading "some sort of corporate capacity" (6), to which Burke contrasts his own voice, is that of the Rev. Richard Price in his address to the Revolution Society, "A Discourse on the Love of Our Country" – the textual template that the *Reflections* is formally and thematically designed to counter.[18]

The mode of address is key: Burke will not write as a member of (or the voice of) any collective, nor will he assume any sovereign right or chartered authority. "I should be," he continues, "unwilling to enter into that correspondence under anything like an equivocal description, which to many, unacquainted with our usages, might make the address, in which I joined, appear as the act of persons in some sort of corporate capacity acknowledged by the laws of this kingdom and authorized to speak the sense of some part of it" (6–7). To guard against such abuse of correspondence, Burke promises that by "indulging [him]self in the freedom of epistolary intercourse," he will "throw out [his] thoughts, and express [his] feelings, just as they arise in [his] mind, with very little attention to formal method" (10). The private letter is a genre whose rule is informality: a law that the law need not take an interest here.

The freedom of epistolary intercourse, however, has its perils: "the effect of liberty to individuals is, that they may do what they please" (8), a kind of sovereign exemption. "We ought to see what it will please them to do, before we risque congratulations ... Prudence would dictate this in the case of separate insulated private men" (8–9). Particularly unnerving is the possibility that separate, insulated, private men may please themselves by abandoning their separate insulation: "liberty, when men act in bodies, is *power*" (9). This assertion of power is exactly what the Constitutional and Revolution societies have done by "giving an authoritative sanction" to the National Assembly with their congratulatory addresses (6). They are "acting as a committee in England

---

18 Price's address was delivered at the Old Jewry in London on the 101st anniversary of the Glorious Revolution (4 November 1789). *Reflections* works to negate parallels between the Glorious Revolution and the French Revolution, displacing Price's parallel instead to the English Civil War, and in particular the execution of Charles I. Burke pairs Price himself with the Rev. Hugh Peters, a dissenting minister who had preached a sermon widely viewed as endorsing the regicide. The other corresponding society, to which Burke refers less directly, was the Constitution Society.

for extending the principles of the National Assembly" (5). "Hencefor-ward," Burke scoffs, "we must consider them as a kind of privileged persons; as no inconsiderable members in the diplomatic body" (5). From the perspective of corporate studies, Burke might be said to cri-tique what he sees as the societies' attempts to grant themselves rights that belong to the chartered corporation. Specifically, these "privileged persons" imagine a right to address another sovereign corporate body / person collectively and on behalf of the British national collective.

Not long before writing the *Reflections*, Burke had opened the impeachment of Warren Hastings with a similar attack on unearned sovereignty. Hastings, Burke claims,

> has declared his opinion that he is a despotic prince; that he is to use arbi-trary power; and, of course, all his acts are covered with that shield ... Will your lordships submit to hear the corrupt practises of mankind made the principles of government? *He* have arbitrary power! – my lords, the East India Company have not arbitrary power to give him, the king has no arbitrary power to give him; your lordships have not; nor the Commons; nor the whole Legislature.[19]

Sovereign exemption from the law is something that cannot be self-asserted, nor can it be conferred by a chartered corporation such as the East India Company or granted by any mechanism of state or the law. "No man can lawfully govern himself according to his own will," Burke argues, "much less can one person be governed by the will of another. We are all born in subjection – all born equally, high and low, governors and governed, in subjection to one great, immutable, preex-istent law," which "does not arise from our conventions or compacts; on the contrary, it gives to our conventions and compacts all the force and sanction they can have." Contracts, charters, and other kinds of incor-poration can only operate within the confines of this notional transcen-dental law; if anyone "were mad enough to make an express compact, that should release their magistrate from his duty, and should declare their lives, liberties and properties, dependent upon, not rules and laws, but his mere capricious will, that covenant would be void" (3:327). Such is, of course, what Burke sees happening in France and what the Revolution societies are trying to enact for themselves in Britain.

Burke has no doubt that "if things were ripe to give effect to their claim," the revolution societies "would soon erect themselves into an electoral

---

college," putting into effect the "right" that these insurgent bodies have already construed for themselves on behalf of the people of England: "1. To choose our own governors. / 2. To cashier them for misconduct. / 3. To frame a government for ourselves" (*Reflections*, 15–16). In the teeth of his own disavowals, then, Burke has implied that the atomization, separation, and insulation of addressors in which he locates his own enunciation is an anterior condition for the Revolution Society's masquerade of authoritative speech. The private isolation by which Burke legitimates his own modest, unauthorized sentiments ("I speak from observation, not from authority" [85]) is also a breeding ground for the corresponding societies, "the little, shrivelled, meager, hopping, though loud and troublesome, insects of the hour" (85) who threaten to disturb Britain's pastoral repose. Price has followed this formula, atomizing first and a sham-corporatizing after: his ecclesiastical doctrine encourages congregants who "should find nothing to satisfy their pious fancies in the old staple of the national church" to "improve upon non-conformity; and to set up, each of them, a separate meeting house upon his own particular principles" (12). Burke argues that Price promotes no doctrine beyond plain dissent; he wants only to distribute corporations and their sovereign exemptions as widely and as loosely as possible.[20]

Price's place of enunciation, the pulpit from which he delivers his sermon, is also key to the extra-constitutional circuit of authorizations that Burke condemns. Burke mistrusts the preacher's capacity to speak under licence from a higher power, whether that power be spiritual or temporal ("[t]his pulpit style ... had to me the air of novelty, and of a novelty not wholly without danger" [12]). In the theatre, an audience "would not bear" Price's antics; "the first intuitive glance, without any elaborate process of reasoning, would shew, that this method of political computation, would justify every extent of crime" (81). Poets, "who must apply themselves to the moral constitution of the heart, would not dare to produce such a triumph [as the attack on the king and queen of 6 October 1789] as a matter of exultation" (81), but in his mock church, Price insulates himself from such judgment.[21] Burkean political legitimacy requires aesthetic coherence, whether it be the sublimity of tragedy or of massed indignation in defence of distressed beauty ("I thought ten thousand swords must have leaped from their scabbards to avenge even a look that threatened her with insult" [76]) or the beauty that

---

20 "[Price's] zeal ... is not for the propagation of his own opinions, but of any opinions ... Let the noble teachers dissent, it is no matter from whom or from what" (12).

21 Hence Burke's well-cited claim that "the theatre is a better school of moral sentiments than churches" (81).

inspires such vengeance: "[t]o make us love our country, our country ought to be lovely" (78).[22] At the same time, whatever aesthetic arousal occurs, the audience must remain audience, and the breakdown of that division is key to the failure of French governance: "The assembly, their organ, acts before them ... like the comedians of a fair before a riotous audience ... who .... sometimes mix and take their seats amongst them ... As they have inverted order in all things, the gallery is in the place of the house" (69). In France, addressor and addressee have merged, upsetting that crucial relation that Burke insists must organize political authority and other varieties of corporation.

Even in spite of all Burke's distinctions, divisions, and disavowals, there is still a danger that the self-appointed and non-conformist Price may not be so easy to tell apart from the self-appointed and non-conformist Burke. The singularity or ipseity of their utterances and the solitude and insulation out of which each speaker enunciates imply a foundational identity between the two. Just as Burke's sentiments are of "too little consequence" (4), Price's declamations echo among those "who attempt to hide their total want of consequence in bustle and noise" (85). Both are inconsequential. They both exceed the office from which they speak: in Price's case "politics and the pulpit are terms that have little agreement" (11); in Burke's the "form of address" has become inadequate because his "sentiments had grown to a greater extent, and had received another direction" (3) from those that prompted the initial resort to private correspondence. Indeed, in the often-cited view of Mary Wollstonecraft, had Burke "been a Frenchman, [he] would have been, in spite of [his] respect for rank and antiquity, a violent revolutionist."[23]

Burke finally distinguishes himself from Price, and exposes Price as dangerously consequential, not on account of the latter's separated insulated private purposes or opinions, but because of Price's unwitting participation in a kind of perverted pastoral: he "naturally *philipizes*, and chaunts his prophetic song in exact unison with [the] designs" of

---

22 For further discussion of the instabilities of Burke's theatrical analogies, see Tom Furniss, *Edmund Burke's Aesthetic Ideology*, Cambridge Studies in Romanticism 4. (Cambridge: Cambridge University Press, 1993), 161–3.

23 Qtd in ibid., 121. The slender distinction between Burke's constructions of himself and of Price in the *Reflections* is noted by Anne Mallory with regard to the way each figure responds to the tedium of statecraft: "Price differs from Burke not so much in being bored as in daring to express his boredom in such an unguarded and public fashion": "Burke, Boredom, and the Theater of Counterrevolution," *PMLA* 118 (2003): 224–38 at 228. The difference is located in the addressor/addressee relation. Burke represents himself as "[l]ess an anti-Price than a better Price" (229).

"literary caballers, and intriguing philosophers; with political theologi-
ans, and theological politicians, both at home and abroad ... [who] set
him up as a sort of oracle" (*Reflections* 11). Price's is a rustic voice that
expresses complex, indeed insurrectionary, meaning beyond his ken.
He is a simpleton whose voice mediates the "fusing ... [of] a simple and
a sophisticated awareness."[24] "[I]t is very probable" that the machinat-
ing politicians have made Price their mouthpiece through the agency
of his own audience, the Revolution Society: "for some purpose, new
members may have entered among them; and ... some truly Christian
politicians, who love to dispense benefits, but are careful to conceal
the hand which distributes the dole, may have made [the society] the
instruments of their pious designs" (*Reflections* 6). This mode of pastoral and this variety of collectivity are constituted by the addressees,
who contrive simultaneously to make themselves the addressors, the
caballers who determine what their dummy will speak back to them.

Against this histrionic pastoral of Jacobin insurgency Burke proposes
a counter-pastoral: the silence of the "thousands of great cattle, reposed
beneath the shadow of the British oak" (85). The collectivity of these
livestock is organized by their refusal either to speak or to be spoken
for.[25] Burke assertively corrects the French misapprehension that "our
contemptuous neglect" of the "petty cabals" is "a mark of general
acquiescence in their opinions" (85). Rather, the British cattle are a stubborn herd of resistors and non-participants: "[w]e are not the converts
of Rousseau; we are not the disciples of Voltaire; Helvetius has made no
progress amongst us. Atheists are not our preachers; madmen are not
our lawgivers" (86). Indeed the British public is defined significantly
by negation: "[w]e know that *we* have made no discoveries; and we
think that no discoveries are to be made, in morality; nor many in the
great principles of government, nor in the ideas of liberty, which were
understood long before we were born" (86).

The "we," among whom Burke has emplaced himself in a kind of
free indirect discourse, look forward to the moment when "the silent
tomb shall have imposed its law upon our pert loquacity" (86). Burke's
national pastoral is something akin to that of Gray's elegy, though "sullen

---

24 Paul Alpers, *What Is Pastoral?* (Chicago: University of Chicago Press, 1996), 21.
25 The step from *cattle* to *livestock* is, I think, justified by the relative etymologies
    of each word. The former from Old French and the latter from Old English both
    emerge from root forms meaning property or goods and come to mean living prop-
    erty (including enslaved persons) in general by the eighteenth century. See "cattle,
    n.," *Oxford English Dictionary*, 3rd ed., http://www.oed.com. I will discuss the ety-
    mology of *livestock* in more detail below.

resistance" (86) and "cold sluggishness" (86) rather than chill penury tie the tongues of these mute inglorious Miltons. The French public might have been equally "[h]appy if they had all continued to know their indissoluble union, and their proper place!" (79), but the atomization of a legitimate sovereign collectivity produces new and destructive collectivities: "do you seriously think that the territory of France, upon the republican system of eighty-three independent municipalities (to say nothing of the parts that compose them), can ever be governed as one body or can ever be set in motion by the impulse of one mind?" (52). Without homogeneity there can be no incorporated body politic: "when they framed democratic government, they had virtually dismembered their country" (53). Proliferating sovereignties fragment the body of state. As a result, "learning will be cast into the mire, and trodden down under the hoofs of a swinish multitude" (79). The French national livestock have been transformed from easily herded cattle (cows) into unruly pigs.

The implication of Burke's pastoral vision is the dissolution of his own text/voice, a fading into insignificance and a consuming silence that drowns out the voices of Price and his caballers. Consider the first full publication title of the book: *Reflections on The Revolution in France and on the Proceedings in Certain Societies in London Relative to that Event in a Letter Intended to have been sent to a Gentleman in Paris*. The negative conditional of "intended to have been sent" suggests something like the same fading away: the letter never reaches its addressee; it anticipates its own erasure. In fading this way, Burke's voice joins with those for whom he speaks: "The very idea of the fabrication of a new government is enough to fill us with disgust and horror. We wished at the period of the Revolution, and do now wish, to derive all we possess as an inheritance from our forefathers" (31); "we" will not undermine ideas "understood long before we were born, altogether as well as they will be after the grave has heaped its mould upon our presumption" (86). By joining with this body, Burke inverts the carnival of the National Assembly, where the "riotous audience ... sometimes mix and take their seats amongst" the delegates (69). Instead Burke mixes himself with the silent, unmoved audience, whose disapproval is sufficient to restrain any kind of revolutionary performance.

Through these roundabout means of disavowal and negation, then, Burke finds himself able to speak on behalf of the great British public: "This new and hitherto unheard-of bill of rights, though made in the name of the whole people, belongs to [the Revolution Society] and their faction only. The body of the people of England have no share in it. They utterly disclaim it." (16). Crucially, those lives are defined by their proximity to death. The *we* with whom Burke mixes comprehends not only those who gather beneath the British oak today, but also those upon whom the grave has heaped its mould, stretching at least as far back as 1688 ("We wished at the period of the Revolution, and do now wish ... " [31]) and those not yet born ("the English nation did at [the Revolution] most solemnly renounce and abdicate [any right to elect kings], for themselves and for all their posterity forever" [20]).

Here is where I register my claim that Burke speaks through a kind of corporate personhood. He erases his own participation as a private person by short-circuiting the addressor–addressee relationship (he does not speak to us, nor to Depont, nor in fact does he really speak at all except to renounce the power of authorized speech). He does not speak on behalf of anyone in particular. His text, and the subject position from which it is enunciated, is a fiction because it speaks what no private person is licensed to say and what those who would collectively speak will never say because they also do not speak. This position is a focalization without a focus (or locus). In a parallel sense, the voice without place or person figures as a key legitimating feature of corporate collectivity: it is not simply a grouping in which members surrender their personal claims; it erases all constituent persons in favour of a corporate body that "is unified *through time* and *across space*."[26] It persists regardless of who its constituent persons are and where, and when they depart, die, change, or join.

The disembodied voice also provides Burke a means to resolve the problem of where his body politic reposes (so to speak) its rights: "If the sovereignty of the state emerges through agreements and contracts, what prevents the proliferation of sovereigns or the diffusion of sovereignty to smaller groups? What distinguishes the corporate body of the state from other corporate bodies in society?" (Barkan, *Corporate Sovereignty*, 23). One of the most significant blunders by the revolutionaries, according to Burke, is their commitment to natural rights, whose "abstract perfection is their practical defect" (60). While Burke does not reject a discourse of rights out of hand, he argues against *a priori* "metaphysic" rights (61), which "in proportion as they are metaphysically true, ... are morally and politically false" (62). Human rights are "incapable of definition, but not impossible to be discerned" (62), and they demand both a concentration on distributive justice and restraint of passions and inclinations "in the mass and body [of society] as well as in the individuals" (60). This restraint is, indeed, the founding and governing right instituted by civil society.[27] The rights of personal

---

26   Barkan, *Corporate Sovereignty*, 23.
27   "[E]ach person has at once divested himself of the first fundamental right of unconvenanted man, that is, to judge for himself, and to assert his own cause. He abdicates all right to be his own governor ... That he may secure some liberty, he makes a surrender in trust of the whole of it": *Reflections* 59–60.

sovereignty were renounced when the social contract was established and must remain so.

Hence Burke reads the 1689 Declaration of Right, which was enacted by Parliament to settle the succession after James II's abdication, not as an assertion of positive rights, but as a renunciation of any right "to elect our kings ... for themselves and for all their posterity forever" (20).[28] Sovereign rights in Burkean civil society are definitionally corporate, and as such not instrumentally available to individual actors except through the mediation of the state and social institutions that the state has granted the sanction of law. Burke's system, it is not hard to see, is susceptible to the charge of generalizing the interests of propertied and ruling-class actors as the national interest. In the final section of this chapter I will argue that Hogg implicitly levels such a critique, not directly at Burke, but at similar political/institutional structures that he sees emerging in Scotland.

"Moulding together the great mysterious incorporation of the human race"

As I remarked in my introduction, the metaphoric cattle by which Burke defines his British public should be considered in light of at least one other structuring figuration in the *Reflections*:

> Our political system is placed in a just correspondence and symmetry with the order of the world, and with the mode of existence of a permanent body composed of transitory parts; wherein, by the disposition of a stupendous wisdom, moulding together the great mysterious incorporation of the human race, the whole, at one time, is never old or middle-aged or young, but, in a condition of unchangeable constancy, moves on through the varied tenor of perpetual decay, fall, renovation, and progression. (33–4)

Like the public, in ecstatic anticipation of the silent tomb, and like livestock, the Burkean political system consists of organic matter that is always already becoming dead. Indeed, the public and the system are not merely *like* livestock, they essentially *are* livestock because "decay, fall, renovation, and progression" absorb them so thoroughly. The crucial difference between livestock and the dead or unborn is life, but that difference is contingent (the difference between cattle and humans is also

---

28 Price had read the Declaration in the opposite manner, as conferring rights: "1. 'To choose our own governors.' / 2. 'To cashier them for misconduct.' / 3. 'To frame a government for ourselves'": *Reflections* 16.

contingent, as I will explain below). They are all obdurate matter, in various states of becoming, that has renounced individuation and seems to lack all motion except in the homeostatic circuits of decay and renovation.

This kind of collectivity is corporate insofar as it is indivisible, indissociable. The living, dead, not-yet-born Burkean British public, *in its embodiment as public*, pays no heed to qualitative interdistinctions – "everyone counts, which is to say everyone is folded into quantity indifferent to difference in kind."[29] The public body remains itself perpetually, regardless of which members are living, which are dead, and which have not yet been born, immortal for the good of the whole. Within that social body, one constituent member is not so much *like* all others as simply *of* the body as a whole, immanent in the same manner as Bataille's animal, "like water in water."[30] An animal, in other words, lacks a discernable "ability to transcend itself" (24). Thus animality – especially animality instrumentalized as livestock — defines a model of collectivity in which the participant individual is only itself insofar as it is continuous with and not clearly divisible from the mass to which it belongs – a collectivity readily comparable to Burke's body politic and indeed adjacent to if not continuous with it.

Recognizing the logic outlined by Jacques Derrida in "The Animal That Therefore I Am," we might speculate that animality is an essential mediating category for Burke's undifferentiated yet atomized body politic: "there is an immense multiplicity of other living things that cannot in any way be homogenized, except by means of violence and willful ignorance, within the category of what is called the animal" (416). The violent aetiology of this kind of homogeneous collectivity is, of course, obfuscated in the *Reflections*, but pointedly literalized in the Hogg narrative that I will discuss below. Derrida has also argued that animality comprehends a variety of sovereignty: beast and sovereign "both share that very singular position of being outlaws, above or at a distance from the law, the beast ignorant of right and the sovereign having the right to suspend right, to place himself above the law that he is, that he makes, that he institutes, as to which he decides, sovereignly."[31] For Burke's

---

29 Ron Broglio, *Beasts of Burden: Biopolitics, Labor, and Animal Life in British Romanticism*, Studies in the Long Nineteenth Century series (Albany: SUNY Press, 2017), 26.

30 Georges Bataille, *Theory of Religion*, trans. Robert Hurley (New York: Zone Books, 1990), 24: "[T]he animal world is that of immanence and immediacy, for that world, which is closed to us, is so to the extent that we cannot discern in it an ability to transcend itself ... The animal is in the world like water in water" (23–4).

31 Jacques Derrida, *The Beast and the Sovereign*, ed. Michel Lisse, Marie-Louise Mallet, and Ginette Michaud, trans. Geoffrey Bennington, 2 vols. (Chicago: University of Chicago Press, 2009), 32.

purposes, the "legally sanctioned immunity from law" (Barkan, 4) of unrestrained sovereignty and of the swinish multitude is restrained under the British constitution by renunciation. The state has renounced any embodiment or transferability of arbitrary authority and the public preserves its own ignorance of power ("liberty, when men act in bodies, is *power*"). The sovereign exemption is practised only in its own negation.

There are many bodies in the *Reflections*, which intersect with and differ from the body politic in a variety of ways. They include the National Assembly (69); the "diplomatic body" (5); "the bodies of our ancient sovereigns" (23); "that great body of our statute law" (23); the body of the Princess Sophia, "stock and root of inheritance to our kings" (24); writers "when they act in a body" (112); "the great body of [French] landed men" (135); "the body of [French] clergy" (144); "the whole body of the monied and commercial interest" (153); "the body of all true religion [which] consists ... in obedience to the will of the Sovereign of the world" (159); "a great body of landed property" (226).[32] Some of these bodies are consistent with Burke's conceptions of legitimacy. Others are not. "[I]t is the substance and mass of the body," he asserts, "which constitutes its character and must finally determine its direction. In all bodies, those who will lead must also, in a considerable degree, follow" (41).

Some of Burke's bodies are constitutively material. Others have more distant relations to matter as such. As I have noted, matter as such tends to operate as the homogenizing principle, acting as "substance and mass" to ensure that in its becoming dead, the body has political and economic immortality. Hence I think it is plausible to identify in Burkean politics (not to say aesthetics) a more-than-emergent variety of biopolitics, both in the sense developed by Michel Foucault, and in that attributed to Rudolf Kjellén, who describes nation-states, for instance, as "super-individual creatures ... which are just as real as individuals, only disproportionately bigger and more powerful."[33] In its incorporation of the dead and the not-yet-born, the Burkean "mass and body" also seems to anticipate the necessary compounding of modern corporate personhood with (or out of) structures and accumulations of capital. Nicole Shukin, for example, argues that "the reproduction of capital's conditions of production and the very biophysical conditions of '*life*

---

32 "The Electress Sophia of Hanover (1630–1714), granddaughter of James I and mother of the future George I, was, at the time of drafting the Act of Settlement, the (Protestant) person with the strongest claim to the throne": Burke, *Reflections*, 296n.

33 See Michel Foucault, *The History of Sexuality*, vol. 1, trans. Robert Hurley (New York: Vintage, [1978]1990), 140ff. Kjellén quoted in Thomas Lemke, *Biopolitics: An Advanced Introduction*, trans. Eric Frederick Trump (New York: NYU Press, 2011), 9–10.

itself have become one and the same thing."[34] Thus, though it is difficult to imagine Burke assenting to this claim, his social bodies include, and are in total, non-human as well as non-living beings. This political mass can be seen as a variety of biomass.[35] The "great cattle" who "chew the cud and are silent" in an important sense actually are livestock.

That Burke's social-body figurations have as much to do with livestock as they do with human organic life in particular is at least partly because livestock as an instrumental concept was always already an agglomeration of human and non-human, living and non-living, organic and non-organic constituents. The term *livestock* came into regular use in English during the eighteenth century and referred promiscuously to both animal and human (primarily enslaved) property as tradable commodity or as capital resource.[36] The latter sense: herd/population size as a measure of capital resource is the governing assumption of *populationniste* economic theory, which held sway through much of the eighteenth century.[37] The herd figure also helps naturalize emerging population sciences, helping ensure that "any differentiation [within population] is subordinated to or falls 'below' the categories determined by the matrix of quantification" (Broglio, *Beasts of Burden*, 29). Scepticism about populationism informs the complaint of Henry Fielding's Lady Booby that Fanny will "stock the Parish with Beauties," and Josiah Childe's sixteenth century warning that children born in beggary

---

34 Nicole Shukin, *Animal Capital* (Minneapolis: University of Minnesota Press, 2009), 17. The italicized phrase *"life itself"* is quoted from James O'Connor, *Natural Causes: Essays in Ecological Marxism* (New York: Guilford, 1998), 12.

35 The term "biomass" is used in more than one sense. Both are implicated in its usage here. In ecological terms, biomass refers to "[t]he total mass (or weight) of plants and animals in a particular area; can be a particular group of plants or animals or a single species. This measurement can be used instead of counting individuals to help determine abundances in an area." "Ecological Risk Assessment Glossary of Terms," US Environmental Protection Agency, http://iaspub.epa.gov/sor_internet/registry /termreg/searchandretrieve/glossariesandkeywordlists/search.do?details= &vocabName=Eco%20Risk%20Assessment%20Glossary, accessed 15 February 2016. The term is also used in a more explicitly production-oriented sense to mean "biological material derived from living, or recently living organisms. In the context of biomass for energy this is often used to mean plant based material, but biomass can equally apply to both animal and vegetable derived material." "What is Biomass" Biomass Energy Centre UK, http://www.biomassenergycentre.org.uk/portal/page? _pageid=76,15049&_dad=portal&_schema=PORTAL, accessed 15 February 2016.

36 See, for example, "livestock, n." *Oxford English Dictionary* 3rd ed., http://www.oed.com.

37 The Reverend John Acland, a Devonshire magistrate, wrote in 1786 of population as "the greatest and truest riches of a state." *A Plan for Rendering the Poor Independent on Public Contribution Founded on the Basis of the Friendly Societies Commonly Called Clubs* (Exeter: R. Thorn, 1786), 59.

"grow up with habits of idleness; become vicious, and stock the country at last with beggars."[38]

Further, the term *stock* by itself is effectively capable of carrying the full meaning and implication that *livestock* naturalizes and obfuscates – Nicole Shukin coins the phrase "animal deadstock" to undo that obfuscation (86). Burke's example of the Electress Sophia ("stock and root of inheritance to our kings") acknowledges the horticultural genealogy of the word *stock*: "Upon that body and stock of inheritance," (24) he later adds, "we have taken care not to inoculate any scion alien to the nature of the original plant" (31). Further still, the etymology of *stock*, which the *OED* concludes is primarily botanical, also accommodates the unliving, "the type of what is lifeless, motionless, or void of sensation" in that the oldest usage of *stok* means a tree stump.[39] The earliest *OED* example of its sense as living "trunk or stem of a (living) tree" post-dates the metaphoric sense as lifeless or motionless.[40]

From these etymologies can be traced the semantic logic of another kind of stock that informs the concepts of stock and livestock available to Burke: the primordial English social institution of the parish stock. Called *Instaurum* in Latin and codified by statute in 1287, it consisted of a "small stock of communally held goods: animals, domestic utensils, charitable bequests, and small parcels of land," which were managed by stock wardens and used to assist parishioners or "lent for a fee."[41] For example, "[t]he church stock of St. Oswald's, Durham in 1580 included three tenements which each yielded 4s. ... The stock of a number of West Country Parishes included farm animals which were either managed directly or leased to parishioners ... Pall and bier were hired out for funerals, and the stock of dishes and platters for private celebrations" (Pounds 240).

My contention is not that Burke crowds all of these implications into his image of cattle beneath the oak, but rather that the image provides

---

38 "[S]o this Wench is to stock the Parish with Beauties, but Sir, our Poor is numerous enough already." Henry Fielding, *Joseph Andrews and Shamela*, ed. Douglas Brooks-Davies and Martin C. Battestin, Oxford World's Classics (Oxford: Oxford University Press, 1980), 246. Quoted in George Rose, *Observations on the Poor Laws*, 2nd ed. (London: J. Hatchard, 1805), 5.

39 *OED* "stock, n.[1] and adj." A n[1]. I. 1. c. "As the type of what is lifeless" and a. "A tree-trunk deprived of its branches."

40 *OED* "stock, n.[1] and adj." A n[1]. I. 2. a. "The trunk or stem of a living tree."

41 N.J.G. Pounds, *A History of the English Parish: The Culture of Religion from Augustine to Victoria* (Cambridge: Cambridge University Press, 2000), 5, 186. *Instaurum* is also a term of law found in "old English deeds. A stock or store of cattle, and other things; the whole stock upon a farm, including cattle, wagons, plows and all other implements of husbandry." Henry Campbell Black, *A Law Dictionary Containing Definitions of the Terms and Phrases of American and English Jurisprudence, Ancient and Modern*, 2nd ed. (Saint Paul: West, 1910), 639.

a focal point for his project in the *Reflections* of shoring up the modern, contractual, and market-governed features of Whig policy with sturdy, ancient, and material foundations, of which the long genealogies of stock and livestock in England are one category. This goal is attested by his regular use of buildings as metaphors for state, government, and constitution – "it is with infinite caution that any man ought to venture upon pulling down an edifice which has answered in any tolerable degree for ages the common purposes of society" (61) – and by his insistence upon the airy abstraction of France's revolutionary institutions – "they load the edifice of society by setting up in the air what the solidity of the structure requires to be on the ground" (49). Perhaps the best example of his hybrid ancient–modern politics is his treatment of the Declaration of Right, which "is the cornerstone of our constitution as reinforced, explained, improved, and in its fundamental principles for ever settled" (16–17).

I take particular note of the term *improved* in the previous quotation. The prominence of improvement in the "scientific farming" and capitalizing rural management policies advocated by Burke's acquaintance Arthur Young could hardly have eluded Burke, who owned and ran a farm at Beaconsfield in Buckinghamshire, which Young visited in 1769 and mentioned with approval in his *Farmer's Tour through the East of England*.[42] "I have too great a desire of improving in agriculture not to profit by your obliging invitation, and will do myself the honour of visiting your farm," Burke wrote to Young in 1771.[43] Here, as in the *Reflections*, Burke is intent on reconciling old orders with new. He seeks to reaffirm the old king's-two-bodies metaphor for political legitimacy by reframing it as continually embodied in the impersonal institutions that mediate modern social relations (markets, contract, home):

> By adhering in this manner and on those principles to our forefathers, we are guided not by the superstition of antiquarians, but by the spirit of philosophic analogy. In this choice of inheritance we have given to our frame of polity the image of a relation in blood, binding up the constitution of our

---

42 "Mr. Burke has been an arable farmer but a short time; he has however made as good a use of it, as to have formed several experiments, which will speak sufficiently for themselves." Young, qtd in Elizabeth R. Lambert, *Edmund Burke of Beaconsfield* (Newark: University of Delaware Press, 2003), 58. In 1795 Burke began, but did not finish, composing a letter to Young "on the Projects talked of in Parliament for an Encrease of Wages to Day Labourers, and other topics of Rustic Oeconomy." Cited in F.P. Lock, *Edmund Burke*, vol. 2: *1784–1797* (Oxford: Clarendon Press, 2006), 514n24.

43 *Correspondence of the Right Honourable Edmund Burke; between the Year 1744, and the Period of His Decease, in 1797*, 4 vols., ed. Charles William and Richard Bourke, vol. 1 (London: Francis and John Rivington, 1844), 251.

country with our dearest domestic ties, adopting our fundamental laws into the bosom of our family affections, keeping inseparable and cherishing with the warmth of all their combined and mutually reflected charities our state, our hearths, our sepulchres, and our altars. (*Reflections* 34)

The circuits of "perpetual decay, fall, renovation, and progression" that maintain the life of the Burkean polity return always to the mould that the grave will heap "upon our presumption" and that is also, literally, the soil from which English prosperity springs, a substance that Burke knew well, as when he wrote to Young about the "objection of farmers against ploughing up the dead earth, or going beyond what is called the staple; that is, that body of dark-coloured mould, which seems to be in part formed of rotten vegetables and animal substances" (*Correspondence* 265).

"The mildew of all profit or success"

Finally, I turn to James Hogg's tale "Marion's Jock," not because I see in it any direct response to Burke, but because it presents a case of what might be called agrarian alienation that seems to address some of the conditions of collectivity and sovereignty that I have identified in Burke's work, and because Hogg's Tory perspective on agricultural modernity stands in critical opposition to the kinds of transformation that Burke's Whiggism has helped produce in the English landscape. The story, which appears in Hogg's 1832 *Altrive Tales* volume, and which was originally published as an inset tale told by the "laird of Peatstacknowe" in *The Three Perils of Man* (1822), exemplifies the failure of pastoral mutuality, depicting radical disharmony between labourer and master.[44] What produces this disharmony is, at least in part, the imposition of modern, corporate structures on agrarian life, so as to install managerial functions distinct from and able to thwart both landowning and labouring interests. The effects that Hogg exemplifies in "Marion's Jock" include both alienating homogenization under rules of austerity and, paradoxically, an irrepressible proliferation of sovereign exceptions.

Jock, a "gilliegaupy of a callant," is the only child of Marion, who cannot provide for the gigantic "craving appetite within him," which

---

44 James Hogg, *Altrive Tales*, ed. Gillian Hughes, The Stirling/South Carolina Research Edition of the Collected Works of James Hogg, vol. 13 (Edinburgh: Edinburgh University Press, 2003); Hogg, *The Three Perils of Man: A Border Romance*, ed. Judy King and Graham Tulloch, The Stirling/South Carolina Research Edition of the Collected Works of James Hogg, vol. 27 (Edinburgh: Edinburgh University Press, 2012).

keeps them at constant battle over the inadequate supply of food in the house (172). To resolve the problem Marion sends Jock to work as a sheep and cattle herd for Goodman Niddery, promising Jock free access to "the fat beef, the huge kebbucks, and the parridge sae thick that a horn spoon wadna delve into them, till he grew impatient for the term-day" (172). But Niddery offers Jock no such provisions, though he possesses them: he keeps hung "above the fire ... two sides of bacon, more than three inches deep of fat ... with ... rich drops of juice standing on the skin" (173), to which Jock is denied any rights. "Would they but give me orders to do it," he laments, "would they even give me the least hint, how slashingly I would obey!" (173). But all Jock gets for his first dinner at his new establishment is "broad bannocks, as hard as horn, a pail of thin sour milk, called whig, and a portion of a large kebbuck positively as dry as wood" (174). The bannocks and kebbuck (cheese) are transformed by similitude into inedible organic substances, and the sour milk, whose name, "whig," is an etymological variant of whey, implies the baleful influence of the party for which *The Edinburgh Review* served as the Scottish mouthpiece (Hogg wrote for the Tory *Blackwood's Magazine*) as well as the austere radical Protestantism of the seventeenth-century Scottish church, whose depredations are a staple of Hogg's historical fiction. The story is laden from the beginning with distortions of category that hint at conditions of scarcity exacerbated (but not caused) by Jock's rapacity, which has a kind of monstrous animality about it: "[w]hen he had gained the possession [of something edible], by whatever means, he feasted with the greatest satisfaction, licking his large ruddy lips, and looking all about him with eyes of the utmost benevolence" (172).

Before departing, Marion asks the goodwife of the house whether Jock "will see enough" (174). The response is an equivocation prefaced by a disavowal: "[t]here are some misleared servants wha think they never get enough" (174). But the terse disclaimer ("I shall answer for that part o't") is "a capital hint" to Jock, who decides "I shall verify my mother's good cautionary" and takes a slice of the bacon, sets it in the coals to cook, and "turning his back to it, and his face to the company, he stood with his drawn dirk, quite determined to defend his prey" (174). Again Jock is coded as animal and is set immediately at odds with his employer. Soon after, he has a second knife-drawn standoff with Niddery, is sent to bed without supper, and the next morning is fed a "scanty breakfast" in full sight of the fat bacon (175–6). When inevitably Jock makes another attack on his prey, Niddery rushes "from his concealment, and, by one blow of his staff, laid him flat on the floor" (176).

This warfare between tenant and labourer is symptomatic of conditions that Hogg has elsewhere argued are severely harming Scottish farming. In an 1817 article, for example, he declares,

> It is well known, that no gentleman ever makes any profit by farming his own land. I therefore judge the mutual jealousy that subsists between the landlord and tenant to be an unnatural feeling, and one that is prejudicial to the interests of both ... Now, it is not only natural that generosity should be extended from the higher to the lower class, but in the present instance, it is necessary.[45]

That proprietors cannot succeed in sheep farming, he speculates, "is haply owing ... to the circumstance of his not being able to oversee his affairs himself: – he has, in consequence, far too many people to employ, every one of whom imposes on him in a less or greater degree" ("On the Present State," 148). As a consequence, a managerial class has emerged, ostensibly to mediate but effectively to obfuscate the intermutual interests of landowner and labourer. In another article published the year before *Altrive Tales*, Hogg blames "those changes which have gradually taken place in the habits, amusements, and conditions of our peasantry" in part on "the gradual advancement of the *aristocracy* of farming ... district after district being thrown into large farm, which has placed such a distance between servants and masters, that in fact they have no communication whatever, and very little interest in common."[46]

Niddery is the kind of representative manager whose existence has come about because of the capitalization of farming. He embodies a corporate interest that actively thwarts the interests of owner and labourer but at the same time also a corrupted personal despotism that exploits both owner and labourer. Hogg too identifies and laments the disaggregation of proprietorial interest from managerial oversight that Berle and Means see as foundational to the modern corporation: "Under the corporate system, the second function, that of having power over an enterprise, has become separated from the first [ownership]. The position of the owner has been reduced to that of having a set of legal and factual interests in the enterprise while the group which we have called control,

---

45 James Hogg, "On the Present State of Sheep-Farming in Scotland," *The Farmer's Magazine*, LXX (5 May, 1817): 144–9 at 147.

46 James Hogg, "On the Changes in the Habits, Amusements, and Condition of the Scottish Peasantry," in *A Shepherd's Delight*, ed. Judy Steel (Edinburgh: Canongate, 1985): 40–51 at 40. Reprinted from *The Quarterly Journal of Agriculture*, vol. III (February 1831–September 1832), 40, 50.

are in the position of having legal and factual powers over it."[47] The Niddery household demonstrates on a small scale how modern corporatism is able to "exercise prerogatives of sovereign power in the name of governing life," and simultaneously reveals "the politics of abandonment that results from such a formulation" (Barkan, *Corporate Sovereignty*, 8).

The 1817 article also decries the failure of mutuality between landowner and tenant: "[f]ew of that [tenant] class think of publishing their difficulties, or any statement of facts, further than laying them before their lairds; who seem, of all men, the least disposed to give publicity to such statements, or even to admit of their reality," even though "[t]heir interests are not merely connected, they are literally and invariably the same" ("On the Present State," 144–5). These sentiments help explain why, as I have argued elsewhere, Hogg often uses disruptions of the literary pastoral to exemplify the crisis he sees in Scottish pastoral agriculture, and in social relations generally ("Pastoral against Pastoral Modernity," 532–3). Shepherd and master can no longer join their voices in a harmony of reciprocally honoured obligations. Berle and Means argue, "[i]f we are to assume that the desire for *personal profit* is the prime force motivating control, we must conclude that the interests of control are different from and often radically opposed to those of ownership; that the owners most emphatically will not be served by a profit-seeking controlling group" (114). They do not attend particularly to labouring interests in this portion of their analysis, but it seems reasonable to extrapolate for Hogg's purposes an equal, if not greater, divergence between the interests of management and those of labourers that produces no compensatory solidarity between proprietor and labourer.

"Formerly," Hogg writes, "every master sat at the head of his kitchen table, and shared the meal with his servants. The mistress ... did not sit down at all, but stood at the dresser behind, and assigned each his portion, or otherwise overlooked the board, and saw that every one got justice" ("On the Changes," 43–4). Jock's first dinner in the Niddery household has exactly this arrangement, except that the master and mistress are managers rather than landowners and they tyrannize their charges under the taunting gaze of bacon "so juicy, that even the brown skin on the outside of it was all standing thick o' eebright beaming drops like morning dew" ("Marion's Jock," 173). "The menial," Hogg argues in the 1832 article, "of course feels that he is no more a member of a community, but a slave; a servant of servants, a mere tool of labour in the hand of a man whom he knows or deems inferior to himself, and

---

47 Adolf A. Berle, Jr. and Gardiner C. Means, *The Modern Corporation and Private Property* (New Brunswick: Transaction, [1932]2009), 113.

the joy of his spirit is mildewed" ("On the Changes," 44–5). The odd possessive of the story's title, which suggests Jock's profound entwinement with the maternal, might be explained in this sense as an indicator of Jock's unsuitability for the impersonal institutionality that seems to be upsetting familial relations in the Niddery household.

Jock, despite his alienation in the midst of the Niddery household, is "determined to take good care of" the "six cows, some mischievous calves, and ten sheep" in his charge (177). But among the sheep is "one fat lamb-ewe, the flower of the flock, which the goodwife and the goodman both loved and valued above all the rest" (178) – including, it seems clear, above the human labour. This animal-person has a greater claim to sovereign right than the human labourer who "cares" for her. Jock's voracity overcomes him, and the hierarchy of personhood, and in a grotesque sequence that confuses slaughter, murder, sacrifice, and rape he kills the ewe, "as beautiful and playful as innocence itself, and, withal, as fat as she could lie in her skin" (178). His feasts on the carcass in the succeeding days, combined with terror of discovery, finally assuage his monstrous appetite – at dinner he does not even look at the hanging bacon (179).

Of course he is found out, and the mergings and confusions of category that have multiplied throughout the tale multiply still further. Niddery assaults Jock and drags him to the "place of sacrifice," where the lamb's remains have been discovered (185). The (attempted) killing of Jock is framed as sacrifice, as revenge, as punishment, as murder, as slaughter for agricultural production ("would you choose to have your throat cut, or to have your feet tied to be skinned alive?"), and as "a battle between an inveterate terrier and a bull-dog" (184–5). The master also appears demonic, "crying out, with the voice of a demon" and catching Jock by the "cuff of the neck" (184) in a gesture that the editors point out has much in common with other scenes of demonic assault in Hogg's fiction (285n184[a]). That sense is reinforced when Jock succeeds in wresting his knife free and killing Niddery, who "sprang up as if he had been going to fly into the air, uttered a loud roar, and fell back" (184). The proliferating confusions of genre and figuration register multiplying incompatibilities (religious versus legal versus commercial versus moral versus aesthetic) in the systems of authority, selfhood, and sovereignty competing for priority over the pastoral modernity of Hogg's Scotland. Varieties of corporate personhood have become confused with and are undermining conventional personhood.

Jock himself passes into the supernatural as he flees, faster and faster until his "swiftness ... actually became beyond the speed of mortal man" (186). His flight carries him into a sort of inverted transcendence:

"flying with the speed of a fox from all the world, and yet still flying into the world. He had no home, no kindred to whom he durst now retreat, no hold of anything in nature, save of his own life and his good whittle" (186).[48] Thrown into a kind of absolute and unwanted sovereign autonomy, he becomes at once more than human and less than animal; in the world, but not of the world, beast and sovereign, like Sandy Tod, the titular character of Hogg's 1807 "pastoral":

Man, the lord o' the creation,
Lightened wi' a ray divine,
Lost to feelin', truth, an' caution
Lags the brutal tribes behind![49]

The havoc occasioned by Jock's brief appointment at the Niddery farm makes a mockery of Burke's political system and its "just correspondence and symmetry with the order of the world" (*Reflections*, 34). Not in Hogg's Scotland is there any "moulding together the great mysterious incorporation of the human race ... in a condition of unchangeable constancy," nor is there a particularly consistent cycle "of perpetual decay, fall, renovation, and progression" (*Reflections*, 34).

Where for Burke the biomassification of human political life sustains institutional boundaries (between the sacred, legal, sexual, economic, and other divisions of human sociality), for Hogg it disturbs them, but also dissolves any clear distinction between human and other conditions of animal life, which include not simply the status of livestock, but also the perverse partial humanity of the pet, the demonic (in a Deleuzean sense) wild animal, the recursive status of meat that has been prepared for consumption, and even the abjected matter of inedible remains.[50] "People," Hogg writes in the 1817 article, "may be an

---

48 Ron Broglio argues that "Hogg finds ways of resisting the homeostasis that benefits the nation but is detrimental to traditions in Scottish rural life. Wonder produced in Hogg's tales signals a way of dwelling that is incompatible with national progress" (50).

49 James Hogg, "Sandy Tod: A Scottish Pastoral," in *The Mountain Bard*, ed. Suzanne Gilbert, The Stirling/South Carolina Research Edition of the Collected Works of James Hogg, vol. 20 (Edinburgh: Edinburgh University Press, 2007): 95–100, 99. I discuss this poem in "Pastoral against Pastoral Modernity," 542.

50 For Gilles Deleuze and Felix Guattari's discussion of demonic animals, see *A Thousand Plateaus: Capitalism and Schizophrenia*, trans. Brian Massumi (Minneapolis: University of Minnesota Press, 1987), 240–1. They name "individuated" pet animals "Oedipal animals" (ibid., 240). It is unclear whether livestock, for Deleuze and Guattari, fall into the category of "State animals" (ibid., 240–1) or demonic animals. It may be that they would consider the category of livestock something other than, or only partly, animal.

advantageous stock upon land, when all of them maintain themselves; but a large number of domestics is the mildew of all profit or success" ("On the Present State of Sheep Farming," 148). The stable system of autonomous but intermutual interests that Hogg associates with a Tory model of governance fragments and collapses. Personal and collective interests disarticulate, producing irreconcilable sovereignties, which for Hogg are a putrefying combination of corrupting personal depravity and dissimulating impersonal officiousness. For Hogg, the corporate person is a monstrous amalgamation of those attributes: despotic hedonism and equivocating superintendence, not so much "moulding together the great mysterious incorporation" as reducing all to a rancid filth.

The tenuous boundaries between life and death, organic and inorganic, natural and unnatural in "Marion's Jock" map Hogg's (in the phrasing of Hardt and Negri) topography of exploitation.[51] Hardt and Negri coin a phrase that seems readily applicable to the biomass figuration: "social flesh," the "common productive flesh of the multitude" (159), which "has been formed into the global political body of capital, divided geographically by hierarchies of labor and wealth, and ruled by a multilevel structure of economic, legal, and political powers" (189). Here we can see the ground in which corporate personhood takes root and flourishes. Organic bodies dissolve into mould that fertilizes cycles of production and growth. In Hogg the shadow of the corporate person looms over the master's free assertion of his rights as proprietor, sacrificial priest, butcher, and executioner – none of these "personages" are actually his. It is only by allying himself with impersonal/supra-personal institutionality that Niddery can grant himself these sovereign forms of authority. This self-mediation is, as I have argued above, an abuse that can be understood as enabled by the model of rights that Burke constructs for his version of civil society.

The odd generic slippages, in "Marion's Jock," between realist fiction and oral folk tale register the irreconcilable distance between labour, management, and ownership that Hogg laments throughout his career. The narrative voice's shambling passage through incongruous genre categories also enunciates (as do Hogg's fragmentary pastorals), in its cacophony, the critique of Burkean social relations – they organize social collectivity under the rule of a livestock model that harmonizes voices in stubborn silence, rather than fostering harmonies of intermutual

---

51 Michael Hardt and Antonio Negri, *Multitude: War and Democracy in the Age of Empire* (New York: Penguin Press, 2004), 159.

song. Along with the division of proprietorship from management, Hogg blames the "changes ... in the conditions of our peasantry" on "the great falling off ... in SONG" (41), "arising in a great degree" from ballad collecting and publication (50).

Social flesh, biomass, livestock, and the body politic are hyperobjects, fitting the definitional criteria established by Timothy Morton: they are "massively distributed in time and space relative to humans"; they "are nonlocal ... any 'local manifestation' of a hyperobject is not directly the hyperobject. They involve profoundly different temporalities than the human-scale ones we are used to"; and "they exhibit their effects interobjectively; that is, they can be detected in a space that consists of interrelationships between aesthetic properties of objects."[52] They also "outlast us all."[53] Morton's examples of hyperobjects do not typically include specifically human components, but Burke's body politic expressly dissolves its individuated human elements – Nicole Shukin's use of *rendering* is applicable — and displaces their distributed personhoods in favour of a mass-in-process that is simultaneously alive, dead, and not-yet-born.[54] Burke, in imagining the impossible utterance of this hyperobject, generates a kind of spectral hypersubject: human and not human, alive and not alive, organic and inorganic. The omniscient narrator of Burke's "great volume" of history, "drawing the materials of future wisdom from the past errors and infirmities of mankind" (*Reflections* 141), would be a version of this hypersubject, a primordial corporate person. So too are the great British cattle, whose silence is the collective expression of the sovereignty in which they participate, but whose instrumentality they have renounced.

---

52 Timothy Morton, *Hyperobjects: Philosophy and Ecology after the End of the World*, Post-humanities Series (Minneapolis: University of Minnesota Press, 2013), 1.

53 Idem, *The Ecological Thought* (Cambridge, MA: Harvard University Press, 2010), 130.

54 "Rendering signifies both the mimetic act of making a copy, that is, reproducing or interpreting an object in linguistic, painterly, musical, filmic, or other media ... *and* the industrial boiling down and recycling of animal remains." Shukin, *Animal Capital*, 20.

9 Immortal and Intangible? Corporate Metaphysics in Jacksonian America

PETER JAROS[1]

Artificial Souls

In the closing note to her recent book of poems on the corporate form, Jena Osman writes that the "separation of the corporation from the individuals that make it up reanimates age-old ideas of a mind-body split."[2] As the collection's final poem, "Industrial Palace," suggests, there's something inevitably clunky about this Cartesian separation of material body and immaterial mind:

> a suited one reads alone in the office of sensation
> three argue around a table in the office of reason
> a lab-coated one checks the dials in the gland center
> two work the switchboard of the muscle center
> three suited ones discuss the will[3]

With its juxtaposition of early modern faculty psychology and retro-futuristic industrial bureaucracy, Osman's image of "an army of homunculi" demystifies the mind by playfully turning the notion of organizational psychology inside out.[4] Conversely, the poem's final line announces the mystery of the body, whether human or corporate: "look at the body: it moves."[5] The problem of the corporation, Osman suggests, is the problem of animation: the relation between – or mutual constitution of – bodies and souls.

---

1 I gratefully acknowledge research support from the National Endowment for the Humanities and the Library Company of Philadelphia.
2 Jena Osman, *Corporate Relations* (Providence: Burning Deck/Aynart, 2014), 73.
3 Osman, "Industrial Palace," in ibid., 71–2, ll. 3–7.
4 Ibid., l. 52.
5 Ibid., l. 55.

In fact, the *locus classicus* for the question of bodies and souls as it pertains to corporations predates even Descartes's *cogito*. The case of *Tipling v. Plexall* (1613) reports Chief Baron Manwood's concise and surprisingly durable theory:

> The opinion of Manwood Chief Baron was this, as touching corporations, that they were invisible, immortall, and that they had no soule; and therefore no subpoena lieth against them, because they have no conscience nor soule; a corporation, is a body aggregate, none can create soules but God, but the King creates them, and therefore they have no soules: they cannot speak, nor appear in person, but by attorney, and this was the opinion of Manwood Chief Baron, touching corporations.[6]

The metaphysical status of the corporation, by this often invoked standard, derives from the analogy between the divine creation of (soulful) natural persons and the royal creation of (soulless) artificial persons. This doctrine of artificial persons would be reiterated in various forms by Coke, Blackstone, Stewart Kyd, and the United States Supreme Court. In Chief Justice Marshall's words, "[a] corporation is an artificial being, invisible, intangible, and existing only in contemplation of law. Being the mere creature of law, it possesses only those properties, which the charter of its creation confers upon it, either expressly, or as incidental to its very existence."[7] Marshall's language articulates the concession theory of the corporation – that a corporation derives its existence from a specific governmental grant of powers. While concession theory minimizes the ontological footprint of the corporation, Marshall's account nonetheless stresses the corporation's metaphysical properties: its artificiality, invisibility, and intangibility.

Despite such apparently settled doctrine, the American lawyer Amasa Mason Eaton observed in 1903 that Manwood's "curious scholastic reasoning" might be applied to bodies as well as souls, leading the way to a *reductio ad absurdum*:

> It would be equally correct (and equally childish) to reason that none can create bodies but God, but the King creates corporations, therefore they

---

6 *Tipling v. Plexall*, 2 Bulstrode 233. *The English Reports, Vol. LXXX: King's Bench Division, IX* (Edinburgh: William Green, 1907), 1085.

7 *Trustees of Dartmouth College v. Woodward*, 17 US (4 Wheat.) 518 (1819), 636. The afterlife of the doctrine of corporate soullessness includes Poe's lament in "The Business Men" that corporations lack bodies to be kicked or souls to be damned. See Peter Jaros, "A Double Life: Personifying the Corporation from *Dartmouth College* to Poe," *Poe Studies* 47 (2014): 4–35.

have no bodies. Therefore a corporation has no soul nor body. Having no soul nor mind, it can do nothing requiring the exercise of mental powers; having no body it can have no members and can do nothing requiring the exercise of physical powers. It has no arms, no hands, etc. It cannot sign a deed nor affix the corporate seal; nor can it express intention to have these things done for it. It cannot do anything.[8]

Eaton rejects this "childish" vision of the incapacitated corporation in favour of a reversal of Manwood's logic that anticipates Osman's play with bodies and souls: "If any force is to be given to such reasoning as that in Bulstrode ... instead of coming to the conclusion that a corporation has no soul, it would be more correct to conclude that a corporation is nothing but a soul, it being an immaterial entity, a persona ficta."[9] A corporation is an artificial soul.[10]

This chapter investigates the prehistory of contemporary debates over corporate personhood through the lens of an earlier conflict over corporations: the so-called Bank War of the 1830s. It contends that Eaton's apparently fanciful notion of the animate corporation had crucial if unlikely precursors in critics of the antebellum American banking system, who summoned and attacked the *persona ficta* of the corporation through polemical prose and satirical prints. With attention to legal articulations, architectural embodiments, and satirical representations of corporate personhood, it examines how these seemingly topical debates engage with and bear on the legal, philosophical, and theological genealogies of the corporation and the person. By confronting artificial souls in idioms borrowed from mythology and theology, Jacksonian writers and printmakers not only attended to the recognizably material structures and networks that undergirded the banks but also speculated on the immaterial entities or forces that animated them. Both advocates and critics of antebellum banking and business corporations recurrently considered questions of corporate metaphysics in oratory and print, architectural paper and stone, and lithographic stone and paper.[11] The questions raised by such an archive – What is the essence of the

---

8 Amasa Mason Eaton, *The First Book in English on the Law of Incorporation* ([s.l.]: [s.n.], 1903) (reprinted from the *Yale Law Journal*, March–April 1903), 10.

9 Ibid., 11.

10 John Dewey also identifies the *persona ficta* as one of the two threads central to the genealogy of the corporation. Dewey, "Corporate Personality" (1926), in *The Later Works, 1925–1953*, ed. Jo Ann Boydston (Carbondale: Southern Illinois University Press, 1984).

11 My phrasing and my research are both indebted to Erika Piola, ed., *Philadelphia on Stone: Commercial Lithography in Philadelphia, 1828–1878* (University Park: Pennsylvania State University Press, 2012), and the associated exhibition at the Library Company of Philadelphia.

corporation? Is it fundamentally a material or immaterial entity? – take the same paradoxical shape that Osman and Eaton trace: when corporations are involved, it can become maddeningly difficult to discern what counts as originary or derivative, material or immaterial, body or soul. As I have argued elsewhere, the rapid rise of business and banking corporations in the early nineteenth-century United States spurred legal and literary investigations into the ontology of the corporate form. To grapple with the corporation was to confront the wide-ranging material effects to which nominally immaterial entities could give rise, and to consider the ways in which notionally invisible and immortal beings could prove visible and mortal.[12] In unsystematic but expansive and compelling ways, antebellum discourse of the corporation challenges us to attend to the effects of immaterial entities.[13] Neither a rote repetition of Christian or Cartesian categories nor an idealizing erasure of the messy realities of embodiment and economic life, its rich visual and rhetorical vocabulary offers an illuminating context to recent confrontations, both popular and scholarly, with corporate personhood.

Nineteenth-century discourse of the corporation asks us to take the immaterial registers of law and theology seriously; in doing so, it productively disrupts our commonsense notions of the priority of the natural, the material, and the human. As Morton Horwitz has shown, subsequent debates over corporate rights often hinged on contrasting notions of what a corporation "really" was: Was it a grant of privilege from the state to pursue particular ends (concession theory), a business reducible to the private agreements of its proprietors (partnership or contract theory), or an entity existing prior to the law, for which incorporation was a mere technicality (real entity theory)? Notwithstanding the significant differences between these theories, they share a prosaic set of ontological building blocks: the state, the individual, and sometimes the association.[14] The polemical writers and printmakers

---

12 Jaros, "A Double Life"; "The Faculties of Law: Robert Montgomery Bird's *Sheppard Lee* as Legal Fiction," *J19: The Journal of Nineteenth-Century Americanists* 3, no. 2 (2015): 307–35.

13 Anthropologists including Daniel Miller have given particular attention to "the plurality of forms of materiality" and the plurality of ways that the material is understood to relate to the (also plural) immaterial. Miller's edited collection *Materiality* avoids the ontological traps into which materialist cultural study has sometimes stepped. Many of the studies Miller gathers converge on the spheres of finance and religion. Both of these areas rely on mechanisms for materializing the immaterial (the Eucharist, for instance, or securitization, which turns mathematical abstractions into tradable assets); both religion and finance, moreover, accord special status to the mediating experts for whom "immateriality is power." Daniel Miller, ed., *Materiality* (Durham: Duke University Press, 2005), 3, 28.

14 Morton J. Horwitz, "*Santa Clara* Revisited: The Development of Corporate Theory," *West Virginia Law Review* 88 (1986): 173–224.

I examine below sometimes present, *in nuce*, theories of the corporation that Horwitz describes as emerging decades later. In contrast to later theorists, of course, they do not formulate legal doctrine; rather, they generate metaphorical or catachrestic depictions of corporations in terms of the varied arrangements of bodies and souls. In contrast to the law's orientation toward practical results and systematic accounts, they speculate more freely, even wildly, about what corporations are and what they are like. The theological and mythological registers they tap exceed the boundaries of the practical and the natural, yet offer powerful means for representing and critiquing corporations.[15]

The outrage that greeted the US Supreme Court's ruling in *Citizens United v. Federal Elections Commission* (2010) centred on its endorsement of the doctrine that corporations are persons entitled to constitutional rights; it has often taken the form of reasserting the priority of the natural over the fictional. One anti–*Citizens United* group, for instance, describes the court as having ruled "that corporations are persons, entitled by the U.S. Constitution to buy elections and run our government," and declares, in contrast, that "human beings are people; corporations are legal fictions."[16] The history of corporate personhood, however, suggests that the self-evidence of human personhood is a tenuous basis for critiquing the increasing political power of corporations. In the rallying cry "Corporations are not people!," it isn't hard to hear the continuing reverberation of post–Second World War human rights discourse – and the problems it entails.[17] In contrast, the debates of the 1830s offer a critique of corporate rights that isn't grounded in the opposition between human personhood and corporate non-personhood. Rather, they sometimes imagine corporations as monstrous, godlike, or diabolical persons, and sometimes as impersonal but coherent entities like machines or networks. They suggest that the dangers corporations pose to human rights might be better understood not by depersonalizing corporations but by hyper-personalizing them. What if the very fissures inherent in legal and

---

15   In doing so, they undercut later theorists' appeals to methodological individualism – the premise that the fundamental entity of law and politics is the individual. On the challenge posed by the corporation to individualist theory see ibid., 181.

16   movetoamend.org, accessed 4 May 2016.

17   For an analysis of the widespread repetition and appeal of "corporations are not people" and its limitations, see Kent Greenfield, "If Corporations are People, They Should Act Like It," *TheAtlantic.com*, 1 February 2015, accessed 17 May 2016. It's worth noting that Chief Justice Morrison Waite, in *Santa Clara County v. Southern Pacific Railroad* (1886), found the personhood of corporations for 14th Amendment purposes equally self-evident.

philosophical articulations of the person constituted chinks in the corporate armour?

As the philosopher Roberto Esposito has recently pointed out, the 1948 Universal Declaration of Human Rights – perhaps the most canonical of all formulations of human rights discourse – is both founded on the figure of the person and compromised by it. Critics since Hannah Arendt have pointed out that asserting the personhood of human beings risks futility insofar as it fails to protect those human beings who, lacking state recognition, are defined only in terms of their humanity.[18] Esposito goes beyond Arendt in contending that this failure of human rights "occurs *because* of the conceptual lexicon of the person, not in spite of it."[19] He situates Arendt's critique as one moment in a genealogy of what he calls the *dispositif* of the person: an apparatus, spanning discourses including theology, law, anthropology, and biopolitics, that has both theorized and put into force a model of personhood constructed around a central fissure. Esposito's account of this apparatus reveals the commonalities of theories and institutions ranging from Roman slavery to nineteenth-century race science to twentieth-century human rights discourse. As he writes, the *dispositif* of the person functions as "an entire mechanism of social discipline, which works specifically by continuously shifting the categorical thresholds that define, or create, the status of all living beings" and produces a "perpetual oscillatory movement between the extremes of person and thing that makes each of them at the same time the opposite and the horizon of the other."[20] This mechanism, he argues, arises from "the assumed, continuously recurring separation between person as an artificial entity and the human as a natural being, whom the status of person may or may not befit."[21] By illuminating various conceptions of personhood, particularly those in which the natural human being is not accorded personhood, Esposito stresses the way the person separates the realms of nature and rights rather than grounding one in the other. This "profound gap between rights and life" is formulated most strikingly in Roman law, for which "no human being was a person by nature – not as such."[22] Thus, while Jacques Maritain's notion of the "human person," which anchors the 1948 Declaration, appears to close the division between the mere *homo*

---

18 Roberto Esposito, *Third Person: Politics of Life and Philosophy of the Impersonal*, trans. Zakiya Hanafi (Cambridge: Polity, 2012), 69. See also Hannah Arendt, *The Origins of Totalitarianism* (New York: Harcourt, 1968).
19 Esposito, *Third Person*, 74.
20 Ibid., 9–10.
21 Ibid., 9.
22 Ibid., 74, 79.

and the legally recognized *persona*, it actually, perhaps ironically, enforces that division insofar as it inherits and recapitulates a notion of the person grounded in "a distinction, in the human being, between an individual dimension with a moral, rational character and an impersonal dimension with an animal nature."[23] Esposito's account of this dilemma underscores the insufficiency, in our own moment, of asserting human beings' personhood and corporations' lack thereof. To do so is not only to confuse cause and effect, but also to ignore the fact that personhood, conceived as "an extracorporeal core [in the human] defined in terms of will and reason," ultimately "ends up thrusting the body ... in direct contact with the sphere of things."[24]

As his engagement with human rights discourse suggests, Esposito's account deals primarily with human persons – natural persons, in the language of the common law. Yet the *dispositif* of the person opens a fissure in the natural: it "divide[s] a living being into two natures made up of different qualities – the one subjugated to the mastery of the other – and thus to create subjectivity through a process of subjection and objectivization."[25] This structure, for Esposito, reveals an affinity between apparently divergent models of the person:

> No matter how inextricably personhood is linked to a living body, the two are not wholly coextensive; and indeed what is most intrinsic to the person, that which allows it to pass into the afterlife, is precisely the fact that it is not coextensive with the body. This defining trait is so fundamental that it recurs, secularized of course, in the Cartesian dualism between *res extensa* and *res cogitans* and, through it, in modern culture as a whole.[26]

Traversing theological, philosophical, legal, and scientific discourses, the *dispositif* of the person identifies, separates, and subjugates the natural in human nature. Like Osman's image of the human body

---

23 Ibid., 75. As Esposito argues, for the Christian, Cartesian, and Lockean models of personhood on which Maritain draws, "'person' qualifies that which, in a human being, is other than and beyond body... the irreducible difference that separates the living being from itself" (76). In tracing how this difference is instantiated in various theological, philosophical, and political vocabularies, Esposito's formulation goes beyond Agamben's famous distinction between *bios* and *zoe*. See Giorgio Agamben, *Homo Sacer: Sovereign Power and Bare Life*, trans. Daniel A. Heller-Roazen (Stanford: Stanford University Press, 1998).

24 Ibid., 91.

25 Esposito, "The *Dispositif* of the Person," *Law, Culture, and the Humanities* 8, no. 1 (2012): 21.

26 Esposito, *Third Person*, 8–9. See also Esposito's discussion of Christian, Cartesian, and Lockean formulations, 75–6.

as corporation, this apparatus draws a line that separates sovereign subjectivity (or executive function) from the mere material under its control. Asserting the personhood of natural persons, in this light, is inextricably linked to subordinating the part of the person – whether an individual body or a racialized population – deemed natural.[27] If, as Esposito argues, human personhood is grounded in a gap between law and the body that subordinates the latter, the hope of protecting human rights from corporations in the name of the "natural person" would appear to be self-defeating. We need means to contend with corporations beyond the figure – tautological at best and counterproductive at worst – of the natural person. What might a critique of the corporation look like that doesn't proceed from the premises of human personhood and corporate non-personhood? It might begin by investigating the kind of persons or impersonal entities corporations are and the legal mechanisms that structure them.

As geographer Joshua Barkan points out, Esposito's analysis of the person has important consequences beyond "the convergence of law, personhood, and biology" on which *Third Person* centres.[28] Given the genealogy of regimes Esposito treats – from Roman law to Christian doctrine to the Hobbesian theory of sovereignty to Enlightenment liberalism – there is little reason to consider this separation simply as "one between reason and biology."[29] In particular, Barkan argues for the value of extending Esposito's account to consider corporations, long understood as persons in law. As he shows, the constitutive separation Esposito identifies at the heart of the concept of the person also operates in the corporation, which is considered a person in law and is enmeshed in questions of "sovereignty, property, and right."[30] Yet while he departs from Esposito's insistence on biology, Barkan still centres his analysis on corporations' exercise of biopolitical power.[31] Drawing on Foucault's paradigm of governmentality, Barkan attends to the ways in which corporations have historically functioned as "police

---

27 In this respect Esposito's debt to Arendt's critique of "human rights" in favour of the "right to have rights" is particularly clear. Arendt, *Origins*, 296–7.

28 Joshua Barkan, "Roberto Esposito's Political Biology and Corporate Forms of Life," *Law, Culture, and the Humanities* 8, no. 1 (2012): 85.

29 Ibid., 87.

30 Ibid.

31 As he shows, any genealogy of biopolitics is incomplete without a consideration of the modern corporation as a biopolitical institution, "commoditizing life, economizing existence, and valuing individuals in relation to the total processes of production, circulation, and consumption of commodities." Barkan, "Corporate Forms of Life," 99.

institutions," instruments through which state power was "delegated and dissipated" even as it was affirmed through the sovereign's prerogative of granting charters.[32]

More glancingly, Barkan notes the corporeal and biological tropes that have long served as metaphors for corporate bodies. Hobbes, for instance, ambivalently figures corporations both as muscles – integral parts of the body politic – and as "lesser Common-wealths in the bowels of a greater" – parasites that threaten its integrity.[33] Nineteenth-century critics of corporate monopolies employed a similar trope, "literally figur[ing] the corporation as diseases within the body politic."[34] The metaphor of disease, along with the related figures of the symbiosis or competition among bodies politic, corporate bodies, and the lives of populations and individuals, constituted a crucial register for early theorists and critics of corporations. But it is hardly the only one. As Barkan himself notes, "we can chart the changes in the corporation by looking at its representations."[35] Examining these representations beyond the biopolitical – whether in terms of the governance and subjection of living bodies or as a metaphorical register that naturalizes corporations – reveals understudied facets of the apparatus of corporate personhood.[36] By drawing on metaphorical registers including the supernatural, the polemical writers and printmakers to whom I now turn offer revealing ways to think about corporate agency.

The Bank War, which pitted President Andrew Jackson against the Second Bank of the United States (BUS) and its president, Nicholas Biddle, offers a crucial if oblique window into the constitution of corporate personhood. In 1832, four years before the expiration of the bank's twenty-year charter, Congress voted to recharter the bank. Jackson vetoed this new charter and further weakened the bank in 1833 by removing the federal government's deposits and redistributing them to smaller banks. The seemingly moribund BUS, however, was revived by a new charter from the state legislature of Pennsylvania. The ensuing controversy made the status of corporations, and of banks in particular, a central point of contention at Pennsylvania's 1837–38 constitutional

---

32 Ibid., 96. See also Barkan, *Corporate Sovereignty: Law and Government under Capitalism* (Minneapolis: University of Minnesota Press, 2013).

33 Ibid., 95.

34 Ibid., 97.

35 Ibid., 45.

36 For a related account of the literary imaginary of the corporation as it pertains to the law and metaphysics of the will, see Lisa Siraganian, "Theorizing Corporate Intentionality in Contemporary American Fiction," *Law and Literature* 27, no. 1 (2015): 99–123.

convention.[37] While dispute over the bank did not centre on corporate personhood per se, both the status of incorporation and the trope of personification were central to the debate. Arguments over the practical role of corporations, and over the bank in particular, frequently took extravagant rhetorical, architectural, and iconographic form. Rather than simply reiterate the common law distinction between natural and artificial persons, the bank's critics and defenders depicted corporations variously as natural, unnatural, or supernatural; material or immaterial; mechanical or spiritual. Such depictions indicate that we ought not limit to our analysis of the corporation to what Barkan calls "corporate forms of life" at the expense of registers of corporate ontology and tropology that include but also exceed life: the monumental and the mythological, the godlike and ghostlike. These figures capture dynamics we miss when we reduce the person to the human and politics to biopolitics.

Arguments in the 1830s over the naturalness, unnaturalness, or supernaturalness of corporations, their materiality or immateriality, reveal the persistence of theology – and sometimes demonology, phantasmology, or pneumatology – in the constitution of personhood. These debates thus address many of the central issues raised by Esposito's analysis of the person – its theological and legal genealogy, its constitution around a cleavage, and the ways it might be reimagined from the perspective of the impersonal. At the same time, they reveal an aspect of the corporation that is less biopolitical than metaphysical. We ought to take their vocabulary of gods, devils, idols, and monsters seriously as a way of grappling with corporations' ways of being rather than simply as a mystification of biopolitics. Playful yet pragmatic, these early accounts of corporate metaphysics can inform our own confrontations with corporate power by opening perspectives beyond the ineffectual and circular assertion of human personhood and corporate non-personhood. They extend a typology of forms of corporate personality and impersonality that pushes us beyond the binaries of natural and artificial, life and law.

Natural and Supernatural Growth

Debates about corporations during the 1830s – their essence, their growth, and their legal status – regularly invoked the language of nature and its others. The doctrine of the corporation as artificial person promulgated in *Trustees of Dartmouth College v. Woodward* (1819) came

---

37 See Roy H. Akagi, "The Pennsylvania Constitution of 1838," *The Pennsylvania Magazine of History and Biography* 48 (1924): 301–33.

into conflict with intuitions about the life and growth of natural entities and the ways artificial beings might inhabit, infect, or infiltrate their world. Whereas the law contrasts artificial corporate persons with natural human persons, Jacksonian critics of corporations availed themselves of the broader resonance of "natural" and its varied antonyms: artificial, unnatural, supernatural, divine. In one sense, their arguments anticipated the valorization of the natural person as moral centre that today characterizes both human rights discourse and recent anti-corporate activism. But perhaps unwittingly, 1830s critics of corporations developed an ontology of non-human persons that remains surprisingly relevant for considering corporate entities not as failed humans or parasitic states but as entities in their own right.

Marshall's landmark ruling in *Dartmouth College* outlines a doctrine of the corporation at once bold and ambiguous: the corporation is at once artificial, invisible, and intangible; it is possessed of "immortality, and, if the expression may be allowed, individuality; properties, by which a perpetual succession of many persons are considered as the same, and may act as a single individual."[38] Despite its axiomatic form, this doctrine carried with it its own resistance, as when Kyd, in his 1793 treatise on corporations, insisted that despite its putative invisibility, "a corporation is as visible a body as an army."[39] Critics of burgeoning nineteenth-century corporations often echoed Kyd as they strove rhetorically to reconceive the notionally artificial, invisible, and intangible corporation as a natural, visible, and tangible entity.

Post–*Dartmouth College* accounts of American corporations often frame them in the language of natural growth, health, and reproduction. An 1832 review of the first major American treatise on corporate law notes that corporations had "multiplied" over the previous thirty years "to an extent without parallel in any other country."[40] The numbers gathered by twentieth-century historians like Joseph S. Davis and James Willard Hurst support his observation. From 1781 to 1800, 317 charters were issued the United States; in the first three decades of the nineteenth century, almost 1,900 corporations received charters in New England alone.[41] Of course, the language of multiplication is not only

---

38 *Trustees of Dartmouth College v. Woodward*, 17 US (4 Wheat.) 518 (1819), 636.
39 Stewart Kyd, *A Treatise on the Law of Corporations* (London: printed for J. Butterworth, 1793), 1:15–16.
40 "Angell and Ames on Corporations," *American Jurist* 8 (1832), 105.
41 Joseph S. Davis, *Essays in the Earlier History of American Corporations* (Cambridge, MA: Harvard University Press, 1917), 2:27; James Willard Hurst, *The Legitimacy of the Business Corporation in the Law of the United States, 1780–1970* (Charlottesville: University of Virginia Press, 1970), 14.

mathematical but also biopolitical, figuring artificial persons as capable, like natural persons, of reproduction. Given the uncanny position of corporations in the rhetorical and juridical borderlands of personification and anthropomorphism, it should come as no surprise that the prosaic matter of counting them triggered questions of what corporations are and what figures might best capture that growth.

Rather than stress corporations' artificiality, anti-bank pamphleteers frequently utilize the rhetoric of the unnatural, in the sense of natural processes that yield abnormal or deviant results. In doing so, they open a fissure within the category of nature, one that can be construed narrowly with the healthy and desirable, or more broadly to embrace the "unnatural" as well. As noted above, anti-corporate writers regularly figure corporations as parasites or diseases. In particular, they use this figure to distinguish between healthy and unhealthy growth. By depicting society as a natural body threatened by parasitic growths, they recast the legal distinction between natural and artificial persons as a normative biopolitical distinction between desirable and undesirable forms of reproduction. Thus the Bostonian businessman and politician David Henshaw contrasts desirable "business corporations," the "natural offspring" of a republican body politic, to banks "placed beyond legislative control" and allowed to "become monopolies and perpetuities": what he calls "alarming excrescences."[42] The Philadelphia lawyer and legislator Charles Jared Ingersoll similarly decries this rising corporate aristocracy as "a vast fungus grown upon government, upon property, upon liberty and equality."[43]

This conceit of natural growth and its malevolent or parasitic aberrations is particularly pervasive in *What Is a Monopoly?*, an 1835 pamphlet by the New York lawyer and anti-monopolist writer Theodore Sedgwick III. Like many Jacksonians, Sedgwick opposed the BUS's monopoly status and urged the liberal bestowal of charters. He describes the "increase" and "multiplication of corporations in the United States" and identifies banks as the "most mischievous offspring of our vicious legislation."[44] He thus suggests that managing

42 David Henshaw, *Remarks upon the Rights and Powers of Corporations, and the Rights, Powers, and Duties of the Legislature toward Them. Embracing a Review of the Opinion of the Supreme Court of the United States, in the Case of Dartmouth College, in New Hampshire, Given in 1819* (Boston: Beals and Greene, 1837), 9–10.

43 Charles Jared Ingersoll, "Speech of Charles J. Ingersoll, Esq., in the Convention of Pennsylvania, on Legislative and Judicial Control over Charters of Incorporation," *Democratic Review* 5, no. 13 (1839): 97–144, 111.

44 Theodore Sedgwick, *What Is a Monopoly? or Some Considerations upon the Topic of Corporations and Currency* (New York: Printed by George P. Scott & Co., 1835), 4, 12, 37.

individual health, managing the national population, and managing corporate growth are isomorphic problems amenable to the same sorts of medical or biopolitical solutions. Like Henshaw and Ingersoll, he weaves the figure of "mischievous offspring" with the common-place of the body politic, decrying as aristocratic and un-republican the common law heritage of special acts of incorporation, which "[give] to one set of men the exercise of privileges which the main body can never enjoy." The health of that "main body" becomes his central standard for judging corporations: "but though the sore [of corporate grants] has been deeply probed, enough of the gangrene yet remains to taint the body politic."[45] Having built up the conceits of chartered banks as reproducing organisms or spreading gangrene, he concludes: "The whole system itself must be done away. Let the same axe which strikes at corporate grants, be laid deep into the root of privileged banking; let this lucrative business be thrown open to universal competition."[46] Opposed to special charters rather than banking or incorporation per se, Sedgwick asserts that a deep root can be identified and an evil tree felled so that a thousand charters might bloom in its place – a vision that can be hard to imagine on the other side of the era of free (or wildcat) banking that Jackson disastrously inaugurated.

Both Sedgwick's argument and his figures reveal a departure from the concession theory of the corporation that prevailed in *Dartmouth College*. Although general incorporation was increasingly available under state law in the early 1800s, corporators regularly sought special charters, which granted particular privileges – including monopoly provisions – but narrowly defined the arenas in which corporations could operate.[47] The contrast Sedgwick draws between "one set of men" and "the main body" indicates a different view of corporations: that without special privilege they would be no different from partnerships

---

Sedgwick came from a prominent literary and political family: his mother Susan Anne Ridley Sedgwick and aunt Catherine Maria Sedgwick were noted writers; his father Theodore Sedgwick II and grandfather Theodore Sedgwick had played important roles in Massachusetts and national politics.

45 Ibid., 13.
46 Ibid., 30.
47 A corollary of the concession theory, as Horwitz explains, is the notion that corporations can only operate within their explicitly granted powers (*intra vires*); nonetheless, the doctrine of *ultra vires* would not be clearly established until 1846. Horwitz, "*Santa Clara* Revisited," 177–8; see also Harold J. Laski, "The Personality of Associations," *Harvard Law Review* 29 (1916): 404–26 at 409.

(so-called contract or partnership theory). Thus, even as it critiques the aristocratic tendencies of special privilege, his account ends up minimizing the footprint of the corporate form.

Sedgwick's mixed metaphors reveal the tension in his position: the image of a singular root belies his earlier figures of unchecked multiplication and gangrenous taint. While these figures, like Ingersoll's and Henshaw's tropes of fungus and excrescence, present incorporated banks as parasites dangerously imbricated in a singular body politic, his arboreal metaphor imagines an established growth that prevents the flourishing of a field of individuals. One image calls for a physician, the other for a lumberjack. Which metaphor is more apposite depends, of course, on one's understanding of the corporation – whether it exists as a grant from the state or as the creation of private corporators. Despite this difference, all of these depictions of "unnatural" corporate growth threatening to outpace the "natural" growth of the body politic remain within the metaphorics of life. Even as they acknowledge the difficulties of extricating parasitic growths, these figures suggest the possibility of a tangible cure for an intangible corporate infestation.

Late in his essay, however, Sedgwick describes the notes of dubious banks supported by "two cabalistic words, 'safety fund,' inscribed on them by the State" (31). A departure from his earlier figures of infestation and vegetation, this trope suggests that banks' contamination of the body politic is less medical than magical, perhaps even Jewish. In doing so, it recasts the concession theory of the corporation – that corporations are performatively constituted by the state – in supernatural or metaphysical terms.

The Metaphysics of the Bank

Associating the legal intangibility of the corporation with theological or metaphysical notions of the supernatural could lead in opposite directions, sometimes emphasizing the respectability of corporations and sometimes their evanescence; sometimes their worldliness and sometimes their ghostliness. Little attention, however, has been given to this facet of debates over corporations. Scholars including David Anthony, Kevin McLaughlin, and Mary Poovey have mapped the metaphysical scepticism and discomfort that paper money and credit met as apparently immaterial representations or falsifications of real – metallic – monetary value, yet work has attended principally to economic ontologies of credit rather than the legal metaphysics of the corporation itself.[48] Because prominent cases like *Dartmouth College* articulated the doctrine of the corporation as an artificial person, immortal and intangible, contemporaneously with widespread controversies over banking and currency, proponents and opponents of banking alike had access to a rich store of ways to understand the entities they debated. By the late nineteenth and early twentieth centuries – particularly with the ascendancy of the real entity theory – legal writers often referred dismissively to the "metaphysics" of corporate law.[49] But in the 1830s, corporate metaphysics constituted an important field of debate.

Second Bank president Nicholas Biddle, who condemned Ingersoll's anti-bank position as demagoguery, nonetheless would likely have embraced Ingersoll's emphasis on the bank's might. No one had done more than Biddle to establish the bank's brand of benign, classically balanced stability, embodied in the imposing architectural presence of William Strickland's Greek Revival Second Bank building (1818–24). Strickland's building was one of the most recognizable buildings in Philadelphia and arguably the most central, architecturally speaking, to Philadelphians' aspirations to make their city the Athens of America. In its design, the bank continues the Greek Revival idiom that Strickland's mentor Benjamin Latrobe had introduced to the United States. As Jeffrey Sklansky has pointed out, the Greek Revival in America owed its close association with banking largely to Biddle, a poet and a Hellenophile as well as a banker. As editor of the *Port Folio* Biddle published Latrobe's call to make Philadelphia "the Athens of the Western World," and "as chair of the bank's building committee and then as president, he saw to it that branches of the bank across the country – and scores of state banks as well – came to be modeled on Greek temples."[50] The textbook for this project – as for the Greek Revival more broadly – was James Stuart

---

48 David Anthony, *Paper Money Men: Commerce, Manhood, and the Sensational Public Sphere in Antebellum America* (Columbus: Ohio State University Press, 2009); Kevin McLaughlin, *Paperwork: Fiction and Mass Mediacy in the Paper Age* (Philadelphia: University of Pennsylvania Press, 2005); Mary Poovey, *Genres of the Credit Economy: Mediating Value in Eighteenth- and Nineteenth-Century Britain* (Chicago: University of Chicago Press, 2008).

49 F.W. Maitland, for instance, dismisses the "cloud of rhetoric or mysticism" surrounding the "group person" in favour of realist examination. "Translator's Introduction" to Otto von Gierke, *Political Theories of the Middle Age*, trans. Frederic Maitland (Cambridge: Cambridge University Press, 1900), xli. Harold J. Laski, discusses English lawyers' mistrust of "excursions ... into the world of legal metaphysics: "The Personality of Associations," 423. Horwitz describes critiques of legal metaphysics from the perspectives of both contract and real entity theory. "*Santa Clara* Revisited," 178.

50 Jeffrey Sklansky, "A Bank on Parnassus." *Common-Place* 6, no. 3 (2006).

and Nicholas Revett's four-volume *Antiquities of Athens* (1762–1816), a monumental work based on painstaking research at Athenian sites, in which Stuart and Revett reconstructed dilapidated and ruined buildings from the height of Periclean Athens as ideal forms. Strickland's design, with its eight Doric columns on an elevated platform or stylobate (Figure 9.1), reveals its debt to Stuart and Revett's measured drawings of the Parthenon – and especially to their recognition of the Parthenon as a paragon of classical architecture (Figure 9.2).[51] Disseminated early and often in prints, featured prominently in genres ranging from city views to banknotes, and sufficiently central to Strickland's identity that it is featured in the background of his 1829 portrait by John Neagle, the image of the Second Bank anchored both the city and the institution.

The spare and powerful Second Bank building thus served both as an idealizing homage to republican Athens and as a sign of Biddle's faith in banking as central to the American republic. It lent a reassuringly concrete form to a complex of abstractions: republican virtue, monetary value, and the law of corporations. Of course, the conjuncture of banking and republicanism had a vexed history. The long-standing debate in the early republic over banking corporations hinged partly on the question of whether they were mere legal abstractions, as defenders like Alexander Hamilton had alleged, or substantial entities, as their critics insisted. Urging support for a federal charter for the First Bank of the United States, Hamilton stressed the ontological lightness of the corporate form: "An incorporation seems to have been regarded as some great, independent, substantive thing – as a political end of peculiar magnitude and moment; whereas it is truly to be considered as a quality, capacity, or means to an end." Yet to incorporate a business, he insisted, "would only be to add a new quality to that association; to give it an artificial capacity by which it would be enabled to prosecute the business with more safety and convenience" – a position that anticipates the contract theory of the corporation.[52] In contrast, Thomas

---

51 Strickland "studied the volumes on Greek monuments in Latrobe's library, including *Antiquities of Athens.*" David Watkin, "Epilogue: The Impact of Stuart over Two Centuries," in *James "Athenian" Stuart, 1713–1788: The Rediscovery of Antiquity*, ed. Susan Weber Soros (New Haven: Yale University Press), 515–48 at 537–8. As Watkin points out, moreover, Stuart and Revett are largely responsible for the "myth" of "placing Greek architecture, and the Parthenon in particular, on a near-divine pinnacle of perfection." "The Myth of Greece and Its Afterlife," in *James "Athenian" Stuart,"* 19–57 at 35.

52 Alexander Hamilton, "Opinion on the Constitutionality of the Bank," 23 February 1791, *Papers* 8:97–106, http://press-pubs.uchicago.edu/founders/documents/a1 _8_18s11.html.

Figure 9.1. William Strickland (architect) and Samuel H. Kneass (delineator), Front Elevation of the Bank of the United States (1824). Library Company of Philadelphia.

Figure 9.2. Measured drawing of the Parthenon, from Stuart and Revett, *Antiquities of Athens* (1762–1816), vol. 2.

Jefferson, late in his life, predicted "government of an aristocracy, founded on banking institutions, and moneyed incorporations under the guise and cloak of their favored branches of manufactures, commerce, and navigation, riding and ruling over the plundered ploughman and beggared yeomanry."[53] Years later, Charles Jared Ingersoll would situate himself as Jefferson's anti-aristocratic heir in a speech arguing for the legislature's ability to revoke bank charters. Ingersoll quotes Hamilton against himself:

> We have lived to feel corporations – all that [Hamilton] treated as absurd creations of imagination – great independent substantive things, political engines of peculiar magnitude and moment. And it is as curious as it is instructive, that what Jefferson foretold and Hamilton treated as preposterous, is the reality of our present government by corporate supremacy.[54]

By the time Ingersoll made these remarks, however, bank proponents like Biddle had themselves emphasized the BUS's "magnitude and moment" – its status as a real entity. Ironically, then, the notion that corporations were substantive things and great "engines" ultimately did better service for the bank's proponents than for its critics. The bank's monumental architecture not only stressed the republican respectability of central banking but also lent satisfying heft to the sometimes frustratingly immaterial entities of law and finance – and anticipated by several decades the real entity theory of the corporation.[55]

The Maryland Whig and novelist John Pendleton Kennedy, in a pamphlet replying directly to Ingersoll, pooh-poohs the Jacksonian "hope that Pennsylvania will yet succeed in strangling 'the monster'" (6) while reconceiving that monster as a work of engineering:

> A corporation is a machine invented to do that, more expeditiously and effectually, which the individuals composing the machine might do, if I may so express it, by manual labour. It is like a steam engine; – it has its apparatus, and it performs its function according to the law of its nature: and you may with the same propriety call the peculiar mode by which the steam engine produces its result, the "privilege" of the engine, as to give that name to the correlative function of a corporation. (26)

---

53 Thomas Jefferson, letter to William B. Giles, 26 December 1825, in *The Writings of Thomas Jefferson*, ed. Paul Leicester Ford (New York: Putnam, 1892–99), 10:356.

54 Ingersoll, "Speech," 111.

55 The real entity theory, which "can truly be said to personify the corporation and treat it 'just like individuals,'" would not emerge in jurisprudence until the final years of the nineteenth century. Horwitz, "*Santa Clara* Revisited," 178.

Kennedy's explanation reduces the corporation from monstrous *lusus naturae* to an apparatus operating "according to the laws of its nature." Artificially created but natural in operation, substantive but inanimate, Kennedy's tidy corporation rationalizes the labour of its constituent individuals without monstrous magic or cabalistic words. Kennedy contests Ingersoll's emphasis on charters as concessions with a proto-real entity theory of the corporation as machine. (Given that exclusivity was such a major component of special charters like that of the BUS, this dismissal of "privilege" is surprising.) His rhetoric reduces the "unnatural growth" of corporations to natural laws and dismisses the supernatural beings described by his opponents, whom he characterizes as religious enthusiasts. Their opinions, he writes,

> were, before you announced them, already set down as the principles of a party, the tenets of a sect; and they are likely henceforth to be professed by an obsequious troop of disciples. I do not know to what apostle the honour of this new creed is to be ascribed, in what name it is to be glorified, – whether of Matthias or Mormon, of Joanna Southcote or the prophet of unknown tongues, – but I do know that it has its sectaries, its koran and its priests in Maryland. (4)

Kennedy's scornful tone frames his apology for incorporated banking as an enlightened secularist's refutation of the sectarianism of a "new creed." But it hardly closes the book on corporate theology. Whereas the pro-bank Kennedy describes corporations as reducible to their institutional, architectural, or mechanical bodies, his anti-corporate opponents see them as animated by government charters. As in Esposito's account, it's precisely what exceeds the mechanism of an apparatus operating "according to the laws of its nature" that marks the corporation as a person. With its imposing edifice and its much-debated federal charter, the BUS thus presented an image of a corporate person, body and soul: the conjunction, *avant la lèttre*, of the real entity and concession theories of the corporation.

Satirical depictions of the bank and the Philadelphia Merchants' Exchange regularly portray banking and stock-trading as religious – or diabolical – in their own right. Because the Parthenon itself had served both as a temple and as Athens's treasury, Biddle's Hellenic architectural program and Strickland's bank-as-temple offered, from a certain perspective, truth in advertising. Yet while critics of the Bank of the United States might have seized on this equivalence to reduce the idealized Greece of American banking to grubby material reality, they did not do so. Instead, they emphasized the image of the bank

Figure 9.3. "A Confederacy Against the Constitution and the Rights of the People, with an Historical View of the Component Parts of this Diabolical Transaction" (1833). Library Company of Philadelphia.

building as a temple, using its recognizable architecture to summon gods and monsters from pagan antiquity as well as Christian theology and demonology. In contrast to the uninhabited edifice of official bank iconography, their prints are populated with figures like devils and monsters that illustrate the bank's agency. These supernatural beings were more than just iconographic tropes that enlivened satirical images; they also served as explanatory figures for the ontology of banking and the corporation when materialist explanations reached their limits. Lithographic stone, caricaturists wagered, could reveal the mysterious animating forces that architectural stone obscured.

The anti-bank print "A Confederacy Against the Constitution and the Rights of the People, with an Historical View of the Component Parts of this Diabolical Transaction," probably published by the radical labour advocate Seth Luther, presents a crude version of the bank (with six Ionic rather than eight Doric columns) as the "Temple of Mammon" (Figure 9.3). Pro-bank figures, including Biddle, Henry Clay, Daniel

Figure 9.4. "Banks & Bribery vs. Balls & Bumbs, or the Destruction of Aristocracy Monopoly and Oppression" (1834). Library Company of Philadelphia.

Webster, and newspaper editors favourable to their interests, preside over a sinister scene of worship attended by well-dressed suppli-cants. The Devil, monkeys, a serpent, and a golden calf accompany a flag reading "No veto! The Bank! Down with the Democracy!" This supernatural iconography recasts the bank and its spokespeople as not simply venal but idolatrous, their transactions not merely corrupt but satanic. In "Banks & Bribery vs. Balls & Bumbs, or the Destruction of Aristocracy Monopoly and Oppression," published by Ezra Bisbee, Jackson and his fictional ally Major Jack Downing demolish the bank with the aid of weapons like the "veto mortar" – they've already hit the collapsing "deposits pillar" – while bankers, supported by their diabol-ical pressmen, bolster it with bags of money; a dismayed monster peers out from behind a column (Figure 9.4). Taken together, these prints sug-gest that crisis unleashes the supernatural powers otherwise obscured by the bank's architectural façade and reveals a political struggle as a battle against unholy agencies.

Figure 9.5. Edward Williams Clay, "The Downfall of Mother Bank" (1833). Library Company of Philadelphia.

Edward W. Clay's lithograph "The Downfall of Mother Bank" depicts the Bank's Doric architecture more precisely – albeit in pieces (Figure 9.5). Jackson's order for the removal of public deposits from the bank shoots out lightning bolts that cause the edifice to crumble. The confident figures of President Jackson and Jack Downing recall the familiar iconography of Jesus cleansing the Temple – or Titus destroying it – as the bank's denizens take flight. Biddle, in the guise of the devil himself, is surrounded by pro-bank newspapers and notes for exorbitant payments. He flees the wreckage, remarking, "It is time for me to resign my presidency." (Nearby, a bank director calls out, "No more fees to be obtained here! I move, we adjourn *sine die!*") The two latter images suggest that Strickland's apparently impervious edifice is in fact vulnerable to the forces – be they military or prophetic – of Jackson and the veto. At the same time, the supernatural beings that populate these images suggest that destroying a material edifice may be insufficient in itself, that from the temple façade may emerge diabolical forces beyond the reach of legislative or presidential action. The prints' supernatural iconography thus suggests that taking aim at

Figure 9.6. "Political Quixotism. Shewing the Consequences of Sleeping in Patent Magic Spectacles" (1833). Library Company of Philadelphia.

the bank's form – whether its Doric columns or its federal charter – is efficacious yet potentially insufficient.

The best-known mythological version of the bank – the many-headed hydra – departs from the bank building's architectural form but preserves its classical allusiveness. Two prints depict Jackson as Hercules attacking the monster – once (as published by Bisbee) as a hybrid but inhuman creature (Figure 9.6) and once (as published by Henry R. Robinson) with the heads of Biddle and the directors of the bank's branches (Figure 9.7). In the transposition from Greek Revival architecture to revived Greek mythology, the problem of destroying a single edifice has given way to the challenge – one that more accurately reflects the theory of the corporation – of confronting an immortal persona that can outlive the natural persons that make it up. In "General Jackson Slaying the Many Headed Hydra," Jackson issues a challenge to the bank's president and the directors of its branches: "Biddle thou Monster Avaunt!! avaunt I say! or by the Great Eternal I'll cleave thee to the earth, aye thou and thy Four and twenty hideous satellites."

Figure 9.7. "General Jackson Slaying the Many Headed Monster" (1836). Library of Congress.

He calls on the aid of Martin Van Buren and encourages Major Jack Downing: "at him again, and let us surround them!"

This confusion between the singular and plural (thee/you, him/them) suggests how aptly the mythological iconography of the hydra, at once singular and plural, characterizes both the managerial structure of the BUS and the legal doctrine of the corporation as an artificial, aggregate person. Downing offers a folksy echo of the doctrine of corporate immortality – "How now you nasty varmint, be you imperishable?" – and in doing so raises the question of whether Jackson's more elevated invocation of the "Great Eternal" is a vain appeal in the face of the bank's practical imperishability. "Political Quixotism" more explicitly invites the language of Christian demonology back in alongside that of mythology: "Monster!!! Crush it!!! Nick Biddle!!! Hell and the Devil!!! Bribery and Corruption!!!" On the one hand, then, the iconography of supernatural beings glosses the abstraction's legal doctrine in vivid images, rendering immaterial entities figuratively susceptible to physical attacks; on the other hand, it gives rise to an ontological jumble in which figures from Christianity and Greek polytheism rub shoulders with the political mythology of the larger-than-life Jackson and the fictional Downing, obscuring the prosaic if convoluted mechanisms of the bank's chartering, operation, and decline behind the image of a heroic contest.

Nick Biddle's associations with "Hell and the Devil" are amplified in a number of prints that repeat "Downfall"'s trope of the bank president as Old Nick himself. "Old Nick in Wall Street" layers its titular reference to Biddle as "the Monster ... Old Nick to be sure" with a parody of Shakespeare's *Richard III*, in which the devilish Biddle, flanked by portico columns, courts New York bankers' adulation (Figure 9.8). Both the Shakespearean allusion and the image's composition present Biddle as a stage villain, yet the superimposed figures – devil, monster, or corrupt sovereign – suggest a confused uncertainty as to the nature of Biddle's power. In "Old Nick's New Patent Plan ...", Biddle directs the efforts of pro-bank editors who turn screw presses, suggesting, in a complex visual pun, both printing presses and tightening access to credit. Even as they "put the screws on those poor workies" crowded beneath them, some refuse to "bow down to a golden calf" (Figure 9.9). Thus, even as temple architecture and religious iconography give way to this mechanized version of hell, the earlier prints' language of demonology and idolatry persists. What these images – particularly those that reject Strickland's bank façade – have in common is their insistence that dramatic scenes populated by supernatural beings can do more to explain the BUS, its inner workings, and its widespread and potentially disastrous effects, than either the official language of law or the material opacity and solidity of a marble edifice.

Despite Jackson's threat, of course, the BUS survived the veto when Pennsylvania's legislature granted it a new charter in 1836. Subsequent images mythologize this new life. In Edward W. Clay's "On the Way to Araby!," Biddle stands before a fluted column on a platform labelled "Old United States Bank" and holds up a Janus-faced devil mask before Jackson, with a legend reading "Charter of the Bank of the United States for Thirty years by the Legislature of the State of Pennsylvania" (Figure 9.10). In this ingratiating posture, he says, "General allow me to introduce an old friend with a new face." If Biddle and the Devil – or Biddle as the Devil – have taken turns as the face of the bank in earlier images, this one posits the clearest representation yet of the relationship between natural and artificial persons. Bank president, bank architecture, and charter scroll work in tandem to sustain the bank's mask – its artificial persona. The "old friend" appears to be nothing but a face – or succession of faces – even as the image underscores the conjuncture of architecture,

Figure 9.8. "Old Nick in Wall Street" (1832). Library Company of Philadelphia.

Figure 9.9. "Old Nick's New Patent Plan to Make Nova Scotia Tories, Federals, Coodies, Hartford Conventioners, Nullifiers, National Republican Bankites" (1834). Library Company of Philadelphia.

Figure 9.10. Edward W. Clay, "On the Way to Araby!" (1836). Library of Congress.

legal charter, and executive in the constitution of the bank's "new face." From the more diffuse hints of temple architecture, pagan polytheism, and devil worship that appear in the earlier Bank War images, Clay has constructed a picture theory of the corporation that emphasizes at once its legal personality and its devilish perseverance. On the one hand, the corporation's persona is more than its charter; on the other, insofar as it is animated by the charter, it is irreducible to a "real entity."

Images of William Strickland's Philadelphia Merchants' Exchange reveal a similar negotiation with Greek Revival architecture and iconography of the supernatural. Like the bank, the exchange quickly became a celebrated and widely reproduced image of Athenian Philadelphia. Commissioned in 1831 as the city's first dedicated stock exchange and constructed between 1832 and 1834, Strickland's building, like his BUS, showcased his fluency in the idiom of Stuart and Revett's *Antiquities*. The exchange's most prominent features are its rounded portico enclosed by Corinthian columns and its cupola, copied from Stuart and Revett's drawings of the Choragic Monument of Lysicrates (Figure 9.11). Strickland's rendering of the building, reproduced in John Sartain's mezzotint (Figure 9.12), tops it with a Triton, possibly

Figure 9.11. "Measured Drawing of the Choragic Monument of Lysicrates," from Stuart and Revett, *Antiquities of Athens* (1762–1816), vol. 1.

borrowed from Stuart and Revett's images of the Tower of the Winds. The figure looks towards the nearby docks along the Delaware River, apparently indicating the maritime trade that fuels the exchange.

The cupola is where things start to get interesting. Strickland's evocative triton ornament was never built; rather, images of the exchange after its construction feature a non-figurative spire, with a weathervane sometimes in the shape of a caduceus (an icon associated with commerce as well as medicine), which is clearly visible in an 1832 lithograph by Charles Fenderich (Figure 9.13). Fenderich's preparatory drawing for this lithograph, however, features neither the spire nor the triton (Figure 9.14). Rather, it depicts an ambiguous figure tentatively

Figure 9.12. William Strickland and John Sartain, Merchants' Exchange, Philadelphia (ca. 1835).

Figure 9.13. Charles Fenderich, "Philadelphia Exchange," lithograph (ca. 1833). Library of Congress.

Figure 9.14. Charles Fenderich, "Philadelphia Exchange," pencil and wash drawing (ca. 1833). Library of Congress.

identified by Library of Congress cataloguers as Hades. Holding a bident, one of Hades's iconic attributes, the figure evokes not the winds or the seas, but rather the god of the underworld and hoarded wealth – and the plutocrats who commissioned the building. In this remarkable, uncirculated drawing, the site of exchange of company stock – the materialized body of corporate abstraction – is governed by the supernatural figure occupying the intersection of Greek Revival classicism and anti-bank satire's devil iconography. This very intersection of pagan and Christian metaphysics would receive surprising elaboration in a contemporaneous piece of anti-bank oratory.

From Idolatry to Bank-ometry

Seth Luther, the Rhode Island labour advocate and probable publisher of "A Confederacy against the Constitution," was perhaps best-known in the 1830s for his stirring addresses delivered to working-class audiences in various northeastern cities. Framing labour struggles in the language of Christian morality, Luther's oratory both echoes anti-bank prints' iconography and further develops their theological implications. In his *Address to the Working Men of New England* (1833), Luther presents avarice in diabolical terms as "the father of *all crime* from the days of Adam until the present time. This *fiend* induced Judas to betray his master, and Benedict Arnold to make an attempt to sell his country. It induced a certain rich man to throw a poor sick slave into the sea from a slave ship, and *Avarice* afterwards placed *that man* in high office in his own country."[56] (As his broad-ranging, religiously-infused critique suggests, Luther is as good a candidate as any for the "apostle ... of this new creed" described by Kennedy.)

He expands this theme in his *Address on the Origin and Progress of Avarice* (1834), which not only repeats the examples of Judas and Arnold but also links them to the language of idolatry and devil worship. As in "A Confederacy Against the Constitution," Luther weaves together the figures of biblical idolatry (of both Babylonian and Israelite varieties) and Greek polytheism with the commonplaces of bank as temple, banker as priest, and money – particularly paper money – as idol:

> [W]e have been required to bow our necks to the image these modern Nebuchadnezzars have set up, or the calf, that some of their Aarons or Biddles have made, with the fruits of our labor. We are *worse* than the Israelites; they fell down and worshipped a golden calf, made of materials furnished by themselves; we are called upon to worship a paper calf. These **modern shrine makers** are worse than those who made silver images for Diana, the goddess of the Ephesians. For they have taken away the golden calf, and put a paper calf in its room, gilded with gold leaf, ten thousand times thiner [*sic*] than that used for looking glasses. We are made to believe, that it is the real Simon Pure, the veritable golden calf. While we are thus worshipping, we ought to have an inscription on the altars of Mammon, – the banks – "To THE UNKNOWN GOD," and may it well be said of us, "Ye know not what ye worship."[57]

---

56   Seth Luther, *An Address to the Working Men of New England, on the State of Education, and on the Condition of the Producing Classes in Europe and America. With Particular Reference to the Effect of Manufacturing (as Now Conducted) on the Health and Happiness of the Poor, and on the Safety of Our Republic. Delivered in Boston, Charlestown, Cambridgeport, Waltham, Dorchester, Mass., Portland, Saco, Me., and Dover, N.H.* (New York: blished at the Office of the Working Man's Advocate, by George H. Evans, 1833), 6.

57   Seth Luther, *An Address on the Origin and Progress of Avarice, and Its Deleterious Effects on Human Happiness, with a Proposed Remedy for the Countless Evils Resulting from an Inordinate Desire for Wealth. Delivered before the Union Association of Working Men, in the Town Hall, Charlestown, Mass., January 30, 1834* (Boston: published by the author, 1834), 14.

Luther's treatment of idolatry is ambiguous: his allusion to the story of the golden calf and his description, by analogy, of the "paper calf" of paper money together suggest an understanding of idolatry as error – the mistaken worship of an empty thing. Yet his references to Mammon and the Unknown God invoke an understanding of idolatry as disloyalty: the worship of a competing but real god.[58] Luther's final flourish deserves particular attention. It parodies Acts 17:23, in which the Apostle Paul preaches on the Areopagus that those who revere its altar to the Unknown God unknowingly worship Christ: "Whom therefore ye ignorantly worship, him declare I unto you." Fashioning himself as a new Paul, Luther reveals American banks as the inverted image of the altar of the Unknown God. He thus routes his central conceit of avarice as idolatry from Babylonian and Hebraic Old Testament sources to New Testament Greece. Playing on the architectural and ideological tropes whereby Biddle and Strickland cast Philadelphia as Athens and his bank as a temple, Luther invokes the Athens of Paul rather than Pericles to reveal banks as temples of Mammon, whom Luther accuses his audience of worshiping in dangerous and idolatrous ignorance.

A few pages later, Luther casts imprecations on legislators who "charter counterfeit Rag Money Mills" even as they "assemble ... with the oath of God upon them."[59] Here, the playful and figurative theological language of banking as idolatry clearly gives way to an earnest invocation of theology as a moral standard for public life. Luther's pursuit of the origins of Avarice leads him to "the conclusion that Avarice is *not* implanted in the human breast by the Great God of heaven and earth," but by an infernal agency: "Urged on by this accursed principle, men stake every thing for gold: health, life, reputation, *all – all* are sacrificed on the bloody altar of Mammon, this demon of hell."[60]

His subsequent language suggests a source at once diabolical, internal to individuals, and capable of permeating society:

> If any being should make his appearance in our world in a tangible shape, and cause all this misery, should we not start with horror at his approach? ... but this venomous reptile is in our hearts; the serpent Avarice grows and

---

58 Moshe Halbertal and Avishai Margalit identify four different conceptions of idolatry: as disloyalty, as error, as the worship of an intermediary, as foreignness or strangeness of worship. See their *Idolatry* (Cambridge, MA: Harvard University Press, 1992), esp. 237. See also Josh Ellenbogen and Aaron Tugendhaft, eds., *Idol Anxiety* (Stanford: Stanford University Press, 2011), esp. Marc Fumaroli, "The Christian Critique of Idolatry," trans. Benjamin Storey, 32–40.

59 Luther, *An Address on the Origin and Progress of Avarice*, 17.

60 Ibid., 19, 20–1.

thrives in our bosoms; its influence is felt more or less in all parts, and classes, and degrees of society. The bar, the bench, the pulpit, and the throne, are more or less impregnated with its deadly venom. Society, in its present state of organization, is accountable for all the evils produced by this hateful monster, with the sting of a scorpion, and the fangs of a viper. But let us inquire how we came possessed of the demon of darkness.[61]

With the extravagant figures of monsters and demons, Luther gestures at once toward a literal account of supernatural beings and to allegories of "our hearts" and institutions like "the bar, the bench, the pulpit, and the throne." He goes on to depict avarice at various scales, from the seemingly innocent cheating of children to the fully fledged greed of a bank director: "His heart is dead: soul, he has none; or if he has, it is the soul of a devil incarnate" – the soul, perhaps, of a corporation, embodied in its fiduciary officer.[62] Concluding that avarice, as a form of diabolical possession, is more easily prevented than cured, he closely paraphrases Matthew 6:20 and 24:

for it would be as impossible to cure a man who had this disorder in his heart, as it would be to wash the Ethiopian white ... It would seem – I speak with reverence – it would seem *almost* beyond the power of Almighty GOD; for we even see many who profess to have their treasure in heaven, grasping with intense desire the world, the world, the world; and it seems that the nearer they get to the earth, the closer they hug it. Such persons give no evidence whatever of being what they profess to be, followers of him who has said, "YE CANNOT SERVE GOD AND MAMMON."[63]

By weaving together various scriptural sources – Exodus, Daniel, and Matthew – Luther condemns avarice as diabolical idolatry even as he wavers between various understandings of idolatry – disloyalty or error, theological category or political allegory. In doing so, he lends a tone of moral urgency to the seemingly playful demonology of satirical anti-bank prints. Demonic possession and idolatry, it would seem, require cures more vigorous than laughter. By framing banking as avarice, defining avarice as idolatry, and routing idolatry through biblical sources, particularly Paul's early Christian confrontation with Greek polytheism, Luther brings us full circle to the problem of incarnation and incorporation, the relation of the material to the immaterial. Greed

---

61   Ibid., 21.
62   Ibid., 23.
63   Ibid., 34.

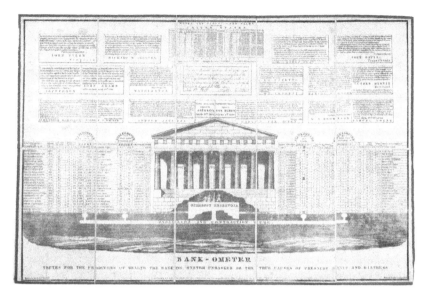

Figure 9.15. Seth Luther and Stephen Lawton, "Bank-ometer" (1840). Library Company of Philadelphia.

is a flawed conception of the relationship between body and spirit; incorporated banking is at once the expression of greed, the construction of idolatrous altars, and the conjuring of demons of hell. Bank charters, by this reckoning, are a terrifyingly efficacious form of diabolical magic. The perils they pose are irreducible to empty fiction or mere matter.

It is thus remarkable that Luther also designed the "Bank-ometer" (1840), produced together with the lithographer Stephen Lawton (Figure 9.15). Striking in its contrast with Luther's highly elaborated theological and supernatural tropes, this print promises "TRUTHS FOR THE PRODUCERS OF WEALTH THE BANKING SYSTEM UNMASKED OR THE TRUE CAUSES OF PANIC PRESSURE AND DISTRESS." Centred on a precise rendering of the BUS building, the print is plastered with quotations on the dangers of banking and paper money (from figures including Washington and Jefferson and even bank proponents like Hamilton and Clay), data on the rapid growth of American banking, and a streetscape-like grouping of charts: a Paperometer and Stockometer tracking the quantities of various assets in circulation, and a Flourometer and a Wageometer tracking workers' buying power. The image presents these charts as nodes in an interconnected system of tubes centred on the Currency Reservoir. Apparently located in the bank's foundation, this reservoir is linked to various conduits that control the money supply: the State Bank Tube, the Bank of England Tube, and, largest of all, the Expansion and Contraction Tube. In stark contrast to other critical images of the bank, particularly Luther's own, the subterranean expanses beneath the bank are free of devils or other supernatural agents. Instead of conjuring metaphysical figures of corporate personhood and financial abstractions, this image offers a vision of a material – apparently pneumatic – system situated in a physical underworld conveniently situated beneath the bank's edifice. The only figures in this complex image are the ones, in the attitude of labourers and the elegant dress of bankers, who turn the screw press that pressurizes the Currency Reservoir. (They echo the gentlemen operators squeezing the workies in "Old Nick's New Patent Plan.") At the same time, however, the "Bank-ometer"'s system of tubes links ontologically diverse entities – from the quotidian materiality of flour and wages to complex banking institutions and the financial abstractions of expansion and contraction – and situates the whole amid the discursive surround of quotations theorizing and critiquing banking. Thus, while it undoubtedly offers a materialist explanation of sorts, it does not insist on the ontological priority of any particular kind of material; rather, its heterogeneous association or assemblage anticipates the ontologically heterogeneous networks of actor–network theory.[64]

Despite their contrasting idioms, then, we might understand the networked ontology of "Bank-ometer" and the religious imagery of Luther's *Confederacy* and *Address* as sketching out different facets of a coherent world view: the "Bank-ometer" anatomizes the artificial god against which the address on idolatry makes its prophetic case. For Luther, the worship of idols, whether paper calves or marble banks, is not the veneration of empty representations; rather, the artificial gods to which they refer are all too real. The unknown god of the banks, whether considered in terms of diabolical influence, human machination, or the expansion and contraction of tubes, is hardly a nonentity. Luther's simultaneous materialist and theological projects approach from different angles the mysteries of the growth of greed and the money supply, as well as the mysteries, at once theological and legal, of animation and incorporation. In depicting the pressurized system of the Currency Reservoir and its network, the prophetic Luther does not simply disenchant the bank. Rather, in the context of his Christian anti-bank polemics, we might

---

64 On the descriptive value of such networks, see Bruno Latour, *Reassembling the Social: An Introduction to Actor-Network Theory* (Oxford: Oxford University Press, 2005).

read the "Bank-ometer" as figuring the interconnections between measurable quantities and the mysterious spirit of the bank, manifest in the gaseous expansions and contractions of the money supply. It materializes and quantifies the spirit of capitalism – or the evil spirits Luther had described in his earlier formulations. In the "Bank-ometer," that is, pneumatology manifests itself as pneumatics.

If Luther's "Bank-ometer" is still grounded in theology, it's a theology that departs from allegorizing the bank in favour of tracing its constitution. It neither hypostasizes a diabolical persona nor disenchants its material basis; instead, it depicts in detail the impersonal network that animates the bank. In doing so, it anticipates Esposito's notion of the impersonal. Drawing on Simone Weil and Gilles Deleuze, and particularly on the latter's notion of an impersonal "third person" that "does not represent a subject but rather makes a diagram of an assemblage," Esposito suggests that the impersonal might provide a basis for ethics and politics where the person has fallen short.[65] He builds on Deleuze's notion of becoming-animal, which "brings into relationship completely heterogeneous terms – like a human being, an animal, and a microorganism; but even a tree, a season, and an atmosphere," in hopes of illuminating "the association between impersonal and singular that can only be grasped through a radical rethinking of the category of person" (150). In this light, we might view Luther's diagram as portraying, if not becoming-animal, something like becoming-animate: it depicts a network constituting an artificial unity that does not correspond to any theological or biological – or for that matter, legal – unit. If Esposito's goal is a new conception of the human person that eludes the familiar cleavage into subject and subjected, Luther's "Bank-ometer" offers something complementary but related: not the legal personality of the bank but a vision of what we might call, following Deleuze and Esposito, its impersonal haecceity or singularity.[66] Attending to the singular form of the impersonal corporation, Luther offers neither an allegorized enemy nor a body rendered powerless by depersonalization, but rather a diagram of the bank's imbrication in its viewers' daily lives, a humble ontology of disindividuated entities: wages, flour, and savings. We're close, in one sense, to the medical register of some

---

65 Qtd. in Esposito, *Third Person*, 149.

66 "A season or a time of day, for example, are haecceities that are just as determinate as individuals as such; but they are not coextensive with them ... What these connote ... is a capacity to be composed with other forces, due to which they undergo an effect (or an affect), thereby being transformed, and transforming the others into more complex individualities, themselves subject to the possibility of further metamorphoses." Ibid., 148–9.

anti-bank pamphlets. But rather than figure an ailing body politic, Luther's figure of financial interconnectedness exposes the innards of the United States' most powerful artificial person, rendering "an artificial being, invisible, intangible, and existing only in contemplation of law" in visible, tangible terms that subject it to the laws of physics and physiology, pneumatics and pneumatology. Rather than an inert body awaiting direction from a sovereign soul, the "Bank-ometer" depicts the corporation's artificial soul as an assemblage in its own right. This artificial person, in any case, would prove mortal after all. The Second Bank, under its Pennsylvania charter, folded in 1841. If the ensuing rise of the corporate person would prove well-nigh unstoppable, its paradigmatic example was dead on the table.

By presenting the corporation as body and spirit – and by problematizing the junction between them, images and texts like Luther's anticipate Esposito's attention to the "continuously recurring separation between person as an artificial entity and the human as a natural being." They suggest a picture of corporate personhood that recognizes both the internal coherence of the corporation *and* its animation by the state – a creature of law whose existence could exceed the eye of the law to make it a being so powerful that Luther warned against its veneration.

Operating outside of the technicalities and rhetorical conventions of jurisprudence, polemicists and satirists like Luther developed understandings of the corporation that anticipated later theories yet also went beyond them. The figure of the supernatural corporation superimposes, *avant la lèttre*, concession and real entity theories: the bank is reducible neither to its visible "body" of employees, edifices, and transactions nor to the animating "soul" of its federal charter. Rather than treat bodies and souls as *a priori* facets of personhood, images of the BUS identify them with specific, contingent entities and events, such as Jackson's veto of the bank's charter, his removal of federal deposits, and the bank's rechartering. Beyond simply asserting corporeality or incorporeality, personhood or impersonality, these works strategically analyse the interplay and interdependence of the corporation's faces as entity and charter. Bank critics' idioms of the natural and unnatural, the supernatural and the artificial, thus offer eerily prescient, even prophetic views of the ascendancy of the corporate form and its subsequent legal landmarks from *Santa Clara* to *Citizens United*. As we continue to grapple with the corporate form, they suggest that rather than asking *Are corporations persons?* we ought to ask *How are we woven into their bodies, and how do we animate their spirits?*

Contributors

Joshua Barkan is an associate professor of Geography at the University of Georgia where he studies the intersection of legal geography, capitalism, and social and political thought. His writing focuses on corporations and modern regimes of power. His first book, *Corporate Sovereignty: Law and Government under Capitalism*, was published in 2013 by the University of Minnesota Press.

Angela Fernandez is a professor at the Faculty of Law and Department of History at the University of Toronto (angela.fernandez@utoronto.ca). She is an associate editor (Book Reviews) for *Law and History Review* and a fellow with the Oxford Centre for Animal Ethics, a member of the Board of Advisors for Animal Justice Canada, and a member of the Brooks Animal Studies Academic Network (BASAN) with the Brooks Institute for Animal Law and Policy. Her publications include a book on the famous first-possession foxhunting case from early nineteenth-century New York, *Pierson v. Post, the Hunt for the Fox: Law and Professionalization in American Legal Culture* (Cambridge University Press, 2018). Her new book project is a co-authored work on a late nineteenth-century overfishing case from the Supreme Court of Canada, *The Frederick Gerring*, which will appear in the University of British Columbia Landmark Cases in Canadian Law Series.

David Golumbia teaches Digital Studies in the Department of English at Virginia Commonwealth University. He is the author of *The Cultural Logic of Computation* (2009) and *The Politics of Bitcoin: Software as Right-Wing Extremism* (2016).

Jody Greene is Associate Vice Provost for Teaching and Learning and Professor of Literature at the University of California, Santa Cruz.

She is also the founding director of UCSC's Center for Innovations in Teaching and Learning. In addition to educational and organizational development in Higher Education, Greene's research interests include intellectual property, human rights, and the history of the institution of literature. In 2005, she published, *The Trouble with Ownership: Intellectual Property and Authorial Liability in England, 1660–1730* (University of Pennsylvania Press). Greene has edited special issues of *GLQ* and *Eighteenth-Century Studies*, and has published articles in journals such as *PMLA*, *Critical Inquiry*, and *The Eighteenth Century*. Her most recent writing has appeared in *Inside Higher Ed* and *The Chronicle of Higher Education.*

Richard Hardack received his doctorate in English and J.D. from UC Berkeley. A visiting assistant professor for four years at Bryn Mawr and Haverford Colleges, he has published more than fifty articles in American Studies and Literatures, including essays in *ELH*, *Callaloo*, *Contemporary Literature*, and *Textual Practice*. His first book, *Not Altogether Human: Pantheism and the Dark Nature of the American Renaissance*, was published in 2012 by the University of Massachusetts Press, and he is completing two more books, *Coming Between Africa and America: Transcendentalism and the Transcendence of Race, from Emerson to Morrison*, and *New and Improved: The Zero-Sum Game of Corporate Personhood*. He is also project editor for the history of NASA's Juno Mission to Jupiter.

Peter Jaros is Associate Professor of English at Franklin & Marshall College, where he teaches eighteenth- and nineteenth-century American and transatlantic literature and culture. His work has appeared in journals including *Early American Literature*, *American Literary History*, *J19*, *Poe Studies*, and *The Eighteenth Century: Theory and Interpretation*. He is completing a book that examines the literary genealogy of the corporate form in the antebellum United States.

Scott R. MacKenzie is Associate Professor of English at the University of Mississippi. He is author of *Be It Ever So Humble: Poverty, Fiction, and the Invention of the Middle-Class Home* (U of Virginia, 2013). His current project is provisionally titled *A Plague o' Both Your Households: Eighteenth-Century and Romantic Scarcity.*

Angela Mitropoulos is a Sydney-based academic and theorist who has written extensively on the histories and philosophies of infrastructure, contagion, law, finance, borders, and capitalism. She is the author of *Contract and Contagion: From Biopolitics to Oikonimia* (2012) and, forthcoming, *Pandemonium: The Proliferating Borders of Capital and the Pandemic* Swerve (2020).

Stefan Padfield is a professor of law at the University of Akron School of Law. He has published over a dozen law review articles addressing various business law topics, in addition to co-authoring a two-volume "concise treatise" on the history of economic thought. Prior to joining the Akron Law faculty, Professor Padfield clerked for The Hon. John R. Gibson of the U.S. Court of Appeals for the Eighth Circuit, and The Hon. William E. Smith of the U.S. District Court in Providence, Rhode Island. Professor Padfield also worked as a corporate attorney for Cravath, Swaine & Moore, LLP, in New York City. Professor Padfield received his BA from Brown University, and J.D. from the University of Kansas School of Law. While in law school, he was a member of the moot court team and the symposium editor for the Kansas Law Review.

Frank Pasquale is Professor of Law at Brooklyn Law School. He has also served as the Piper & Marbury Professor of Law at the University of Maryland and Professor of Law at Seton Hall University. He is an expert on the law of artificial intelligence, algorithms, and machine learning. His widely cited book, *The Black Box Society* (Harvard University Press, 2015), develops a social theory of reputation, search, and finance, and promotes pragmatic reforms to improve the information economy, including more vigorous enforcement of competition and consumer protection law. *The Black Box Society* has been reviewed in *Science* and *Nature,* published in Chinese, French, Korean, and Serbian translations, and its fifth anniversary of publication will be marked by an international symposium in *Big Data & Society.* He has testified before or advised groups ranging from the Department of Health and Human Services, the House Judiciary Committee, the House Energy and Commerce Committee, the Senate Banking, Housing, and Urban Affairs Committee, the Federal Trade Commission, and directorates-general of the European Commission.

Matthew Titolo is Professor of Law at West Virginia University where he teaches American Legal History, Contracts, Commercial Law, and Remedies. He received his law degree from the University of California, Berkeley and a PhD in English literature at the University of California, Los Angeles. His current book is *Privatization and Its Discontents: Infrastructure, Law and American Democracy* (Cambridge UP).

Sharif Youssef is Assistant Professor of English and Legal Studies at Ashoka University. He received his law degree from the University of

Toronto and a PhD in English literature from the University of Chicago. His writing has appeared in *Humanity*, *Law & Literature*, and *Criticism*, and in 2015 he co-edited a special issue of *Modern Language Quarterly* entitled "Inevitability." His book project, "The Actuarial Form: Moral Hazard in the Early Novel," is about how risk, and associate notions such as information, incentive, and influence, grew out of a confluence of new eighteenth-century genres such as the novel, political economy, scientific empiricism, and rational theology.

Index

Page numbers in italics refer to figures.

www.ingramcontent.com/pod-product-compliance
Ingram Content Group UK Ltd.
Pitfield, Milton Keynes, MK11 3LW, UK
UKHW041649020225
454515UK00003B/124/J